Computer Concepts
FOURTH EDITION – ILLUSTRATED

INTRODUCTORY ENHANCED

June Jamrich Parsons / Dan Oja

THOMSON
COURSE TECHNOLOGY™

Australia • Canada • Mexico • Singapore • Spain • United Kingdom • United States

THOMSON

COURSE TECHNOLOGY ™

Computer Concepts, Fourth Edition—Illustrated Introductory, Enhanced
is published by Course Technology.

Contributing Author:
Rachel Biheller Bunin

Developmental Editor:
Pamela Conrad

Managing Editor:
Nicole Jones Pinard

Product Manager:
Jeanne Herring

Production Editor:
Debbie Masi

Associate Product Manager:
Christina Kling Garrett

Editorial Assistant:
Elizabeth M. Harris

Interior Designer:
Betsy Young

Photo and Video Researcher:
Abby Reip

Composition:
GEX Publishing Services

Animations:
Planet Interactive

Media Developers:
Donna Schuch, Fatima Nicholls,
Keefe Crowley, Tensi Parsons

Photographers:
Greg Manning, Joe Bush

Illustrator:
Eric Murphy

CD Development:
MediaTechnics Corporation

Credits

Author Acknowledgements

I would like to offer my sincerest thanks to Dan Oja and June Parsons for entrusting me and the Illustrated team to adapt their groundbreaking, best-selling New Perspectives Concepts book into the Illustrated format. Special thanks to Nicole Pinard, for having the vision three editions ago to let me create the first Concepts Illustrated book. My most heartfelt thanks and admiration go to Pamela Conrad, the Developmental Editor, who has worked with me on this project through all four editions. Her ability to see the big picture and keep all the details in check, while sharing new ideas, is awesome. Emily Heberlein contributed extraordinary leadership as the Project Manager. Thanks to Debbie Masi; she is an unparalleled Production Editor. Thanks to Kendra Neville and GEX for all their work and all those timely .pdf files. Thanks also to Abby Reip for finding those great photographs to bring this book to life. Thanks to our manuscript reviewers, Catherine Murphy, Barbara Cress, Nancy Bogage, Mario Perez, Laurie MacDonald, and Jiin Wang for their insights and comments. On behalf of the entire Illustrated team, we hope you find this book a valuable resource for your students.

- Rachel Biheller Bunin, Adapting Author

We offer heartfelt thanks to all of the members of the Illustrated team for contributing their vision, talent, and skills to make this book a reality. Special thanks to Rachel Bunin for her fast and efficient work as the adapting author; Pamela Conrad for her insights as the developmental editor; Debbie Masi for her solid work as the Production Editor; Betsy Young for her beautiful new design; and Emily Heberlein for tracking all the bits and pieces of this project. Whether you are a student or instructor, we thank you for using our book and hope that you find it to be a valuable guide to computers and software.

- June Parsons, Dan Oja, and MediaTechnics for the New Perspectives Series

FIGURE No.

Unit A

Figure A-6: Courtesy of IBM Corporation

Figure A-9: Courtesy of Chris Conrad

Figure A-12: Courtesy of Microsoft Corporation

Unit C

Figure C-21: Courtesy of NASA

Figure C-25: Courtesy of Chris Conrad

Unit F

Figure F-4: AP/ World Wide Photos

Figure F-10: Photo courtesy of Gemplus

Figure F-11: Courtesy of DigitalPersona, Inc.

Figure F-12: Courtesy of Iridian Technologies, Inc.

Unit G

Figure G-1: Theodor Holm Nelson, Project Xanadu

Trends in Technology Unit

Figure T-1: Courtesy of Universal Display Corporation

Figure T-2: Courtesy of Fingerworks Inc.

Figure T-3: Courtesy of Advanced Micro Devices, Inc.

Figure T-4: Courtesy of Transmeta Corporation

Figure T-5: Courtesy of IBM Corporation

Figure T-6: Courtesy of My Docs Online, Inc.

Figure T-7: Courtesy of Apple Computer, Inc.

Figure T-8: Courtesy of the Institute of Electrical and Electronics Engineers, Inc.

Figure T-9: Courtesy of Reed Business Information and Texas Instruments Inc.

Figure T-11: ICQ screenshot © 1998-2002 ICQ, Inc. Used with permission.

Figure T-12: Courtesy of Macromedia, Inc.

Figure T-13: Courtesy of the American Telemedicine Association, www.americantelemed.org

Figures T-14 and T-17: Courtesy of Microsoft Corporation

Figure T-15: Courtesy of Zinio Systems, Inc.

Figure T-16: Courtesy of Carol A. Kunze

Bonus Issues and Up-to-Dates Unit

Figure 2: Courtesy of Einstein Group plc, organisers of the Brains in Bahrain contest.

Figure 3: Courtesy of AT&T Corporation

Figure 4: Courtesy of Intel Corporation

Figure 5: Courtesy of Internet2

Figures 6 and 7: Courtesy of Microsoft Corporation

Figure 8: Courtesy of Eastman Kodak Company, Inc.

Contents

= CD   = Info Web   = Lab

UNIT F Data Security   161

UNIT G The Web and E-commerce   193

UNIT H — Digital Media — 225

TRENDS — Trends in Technology — Enhanced 1

BONUS

Bonus Issues and Up-To-Dates   Enhanced 25

Preface

Welcome to Computer Concepts, Fourth Edition–Illustrated Introductory **Enhanced**. This Enhanced Edition contains the same page-for-page content and the same Interactive CD as the Fourth Edition, but includes two bonus units at the end:

- **Trends in Technology unit:** Provides students with 8 lessons of new material covering the most recent developments in computer technology. All new end-of-unit exercises add to your course, while the organization of the unit makes it easy to incorporate into an already existing curriculum.
- **Bonus Issues and Up-to-Dates unit:** Includes 8 additional Issues and Up-to-Date exercises that provide additional options for reinforcement and correspond in topic area to each of Units A–H. The exercises challenge students to expand their knowledge, and can be assigned at the end of each unit or at the end of the course.

As additional enhancements, the Online Buyer's Guide has been updated and the Instructor's Resource CD contains all-new material for the two new units.

The Enhanced Edition is closely integrated with the Interactive CD and the InfoWebLinks Web site to provide extensive opportunities for student exploration. Icons throughout the book indicate when a student can go to the Interactive CD or Web site for more. The resulting package is a fast-paced, engaging, technology and Web-enriched introduction to today's most cutting-edge computer concepts. Make sure you take a look at the Instructor's Resource CD and About the Technology sections in the Preface to learn more.

Reinforce essential computer concepts with Course Technology's interactive games available online at our Student Center. Our computer concepts games will engage students to learn important concepts such as Computer Basics, Information Systems, Storage, The Web & E-commerce, and much more! Students will have fun learning with 7 different games such as Flash Card, Hangman, Rags to Riche$, and Jumbled Words. What's even better, students can quiz themselves right on the site or they can take quizzes with them anywhere they go by downloading our QuizApp software to their PDA.

For more information and to view this dynamic Web site, go to http://www.course.com/studentcenter.

A single concept is presented in a two-page "information display" to help students absorb information quickly and easily

Easy-to-follow introductions to every lesson focus on a single concept to help students get the point quickly

Details provide additional key information on the main concept

UNIT B

Exploring CD/DVD technology

A CD-ROM drive is an optical storage device that is usually installed in one of the system unit's drive bays. **CD-ROM (compact disc read-only memory)** is based on the same technology as the audio CDs that contain your favorite music. Your computer can read data from a CD-ROM, but you can't store or record any of your own data on a CD-ROM disk. Two CD-writer technologies called CD-R and CD-RW allow you to create your own CDs. **DVD** ("digital video disc" or "digital versatile disk") is a variation of CD technology that was originally designed as an alternative to VCRs, but was quickly adopted by the computer industry to store data.

DETAILS

- A computer **CD-ROM disk**, like its audio counterpart, contains data that was stamped on the disk surface when it was manufactured. Today, when you purchase software from a computer store, the box typically contains CDs. Therefore, unless you plan to download all of your new software from the Internet, your computer should have a CD drive so that you can install new software. Figure B-11 shows how to place a CD in the drive. Figure B-12 illustrates how a CD-ROM drive uses laser technology to read data.

- CD-ROM technology provides a far larger storage capacity than floppy disks, Zip disks, or SuperDisks. A single CD-ROM disk holds up to 680 MB, equivalent to more than 300,000 pages of text. The surface of the disk is coated with a clear plastic, making the disk quite durable. Unlike magnetic media, the data on a CD-ROM is not susceptible to permanent damage by humidity, fingerprints, dust, or magnets.

- The original CD-ROM drives were able to access 150 KB of data per second. The next generation of drives doubled the data transfer rate and was consequently dubbed "2X"; and transfer rates are continually increasing. A 24X CD-ROM drive, for example, would transfer data at a rate of 24 × 150 KB, or 3,600 KB per second.

- A **CD-R (compact disc recordable)** drive records data on a special CD-R disk. The drive mechanism includes a laser that changes the reflectivity of a dye layer on a blank CD-R disk. As a result, the data on the disk is not actually stored in pits. Dark spots in the dye layer, however, play the same role as pits to represent data and allow the disks that you create to be read by not only a CD-R drive, but also by a standard CD-ROM or DVD

drive. The data on a CD-R cannot be erased or modified once recorded, but most CD-R drives allow you to record your data in multiple sessions.

- **CD-RW (compact disc rewritable)** technology allows you to write data on a CD and change that data at a later time. The process requires special CD-RW disks and a CD-RW drive, which uses phase change technology to alter the crystal structure on the disk surface. Altering the crystal structure creates patterns of light and dark spots similar to the pits and lands on a CD-ROM disk. The crystal structure can be changed from light to dark and back again many times, making it possible to record and modify data much like you can with a hard disk or a floppy disk. However, accessing, saving, and modifying data on a CD-RW disk is slower than on a hard disk.

- Both CD-R and CD-RW technologies are quite useful for archiving data and distributing large files. **Archiving** refers to the process of removing infrequently used data from a primary storage device to another storage medium, such as a CD-R.

- A computer's DVD drive can read disks that contain computer data (often called **DVD-ROM** disks) and disks that contain DVD movies (sometimes called DVD-Video disks). A DVD holds about 4.7 GB (4,700 MB), compared with 680 MB on a CD-ROM. Like a CD-ROM disk, a DVD-ROM disk is permanently stamped with data at the time of manufacture, so you cannot add or change data. The speed of a DVD drive is measured on a different scale than a CD drive. A 1X DVD drive is about the same speed as a 9X CD drive. Table B-1 provides additional speed equivalents.

Using DVD technologies

A computer DVD drive is not exactly the same as one that's connected to a television set. Even with the large storage capacity of a DVD, movie files are much too large to fit on a disk unless they are compressed, using a special type of data coding called **MPEG-2**. The DVD player that you connect to your television includes MPEG decoding circuitry, which is not included on your computer's DVD drive. When you play DVD movies on your computer, it uses the CPU as an MPEG decoder. The necessary decoder software is included with Windows, or can be located on the DVD itself. You cannot play DVDs on your CD-ROM drive, but you can play CD-ROM, most CD-R, and most CD-RW disks on your DVD drive.

44 COMPUTER CONCEPTS

Icons in the margins indicate that an interactive lab or InfoWeb is featured for that lesson

News to Use boxes relate the lesson material to real-world situations to provide students with additional practical information

Icons to the left of the figure captions direct students to the CD for a Video or ScreenTour, bringing the book to life

Large photos and screenshots illustrate the lesson concepts

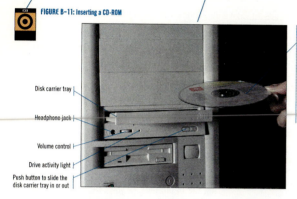

FIGURE B-11: Inserting a CD-ROM

Disk carrier tray

Headphone jack

Volume control

Drive activity light

Push button to slide the disk carrier tray in or out

Data is stored on the bottom of a CD-ROM disk in one continuous track that spirals out from the center of the disk; the track is divided into equal-length sectors; the printed side of the disk does not contain data; it should be face up when you insert the disk because the lasers read the bottom of the disk

FIGURE B-12: How a CD-ROM drive works

Laser lens directs a beam of light to the underside of the CD-ROM disk

Tracking mechanism positions a disk track over the laser lens

Drive spindle spins disk

Laser pickup assembly senses the reflectivity of pits and lands

TABLE B-1: Comparing DVD and CD speeds

DVD DRIVE SPEED	DATA TRANSFER RATE	CD SPEED
1X	11.08 Mbps	9X
2X	22.16 Mbps	18X
4X	44.32 Mbps	36X
5X	55.40 Mbps	46X

UNIT B: COMPUTER HARDWARE 45

The callouts point out key elements on each illustration

Tables provide quick reference information

Unit Features

Each unit contains the following features, providing a flexible teaching and learning package.

- **InfoWebs** The computer industry changes rapidly. Students can get up-to-date information by exploring the concept on the InfoWebLinks Web site, when indicated by an InfoWeb icon.

- **Tech Talk** Each of Units A–H ends with a Tech Talk lesson. These lessons go into greater depth on a technical topic related to the unit. Instructors have the option of assigning this section or skipping it, depending on the expertise of the students and the course goals.

- **Issue** It is important to keep abreast of issues that relate to technology. Each unit contains an interesting Issue article, followed by two types of questions to encourage students to form and express their own opinions. Interactive Questions can be collected electronically, and Expand the Ideas are open-ended, essay questions.

- **Key Terms** Students can use this handy list to review bold terms which represent key concepts from the unit. Definitions are provided in the glossary.

- **Unit Review** After completing the Unit Review, students will have synthesized the unit content in their own words.

- **Fill in the Best Answer** Students can complete this in the book or on the Interactive CD and get immediate feedback on how well they have learned the unit content.

- **Independent Challenges** These exercises enable students to explore on their own and develop critical thinking skills. Challenges with an E-Quest icon point students to the Web to complete the exercise.

- **Lab Assignments** Assignments let students work further with the interactive labs featured on the CD.

- **Visual Workshop** Based on a screenshot or illustration, Visual Workshops encourage independent thinking.

About the Illustrated Approach

What makes the information in this book so easy to access and digest? It's quite simple. As shown in this sample lesson, each concept is presented on two facing pages, with the main points discussed on the left page and large, dramatic illustrations presented on the right. Students can learn all they need to know about a particular topic without having to turn the page! This unique design makes information extremely accessible and easy to absorb, and makes a great reference for after the course is over. The modular structure of the book also allows for great flexibility; you can cover the units in any order you choose, and you can skip lessons if you like.

Instructor's Resources

The Instructor's Resources CD is Course Technology's way of putting the resources and information needed to teach and learn effectively into your hands. With an integrated array of teaching and learning tools that offers you and your students a broad range of technology-based instructional options, we believe this CD represents the highest quality and most cutting edge resources available to instructors today. Many of these resources are available at www.course.com. The resources available with this book are:

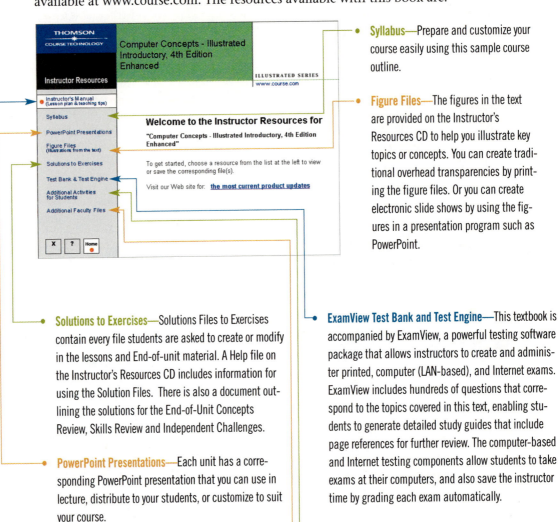

Syllabus—Prepare and customize your course easily using this sample course outline.

Figure Files—The figures in the text are provided on the Instructor's Resources CD to help you illustrate key topics or concepts. You can create traditional overhead transparencies by printing the figure files. Or you can create electronic slide shows by using the figures in a presentation program such as PowerPoint.

Solutions to Exercises—Solutions Files to Exercises contain every file students are asked to create or modify in the lessons and End-of-unit material. A Help file on the Instructor's Resources CD includes information for using the Solution Files. There is also a document outlining the solutions for the End-of-Unit Concepts Review, Skills Review and Independent Challenges.

PowerPoint Presentations—Each unit has a corresponding PowerPoint presentation that you can use in lecture, distribute to your students, or customize to suit your course.

Instructor's Manual—Available as an electronic file, the Instructor's Manual is quality-assurance tested and includes unit overviews, file listings and detailed lecture topics with teaching tips for each unit. The Instructor's Manual is available on the Instructor's Resources CD-ROM or you can download it from **www.course.com**.

ExamView Test Bank and Test Engine—This textbook is accompanied by ExamView, a powerful testing software package that allows instructors to create and administer printed, computer (LAN-based), and Internet exams. ExamView includes hundreds of questions that correspond to the topics covered in this text, enabling students to generate detailed study guides that include page references for further review. The computer-based and Internet testing components allow students to take exams at their computers, and also save the instructor time by grading each exam automatically.

Additional Activities for Students

Additional Faculty Files

About the Technology

These indicators in the book tell you when to use the Interactive CD and InfoWebLinks Web site.

CD Videos and ScreenTours

Videos and ScreenTours enhance learning and retention of key concepts. A CD icon next to a figure or text indicates you can view an interactive concept on the CD.

InfoWebs

InfoWebs connect you to Web links, film, video, TV, print, and electronic resources, keeping the book and URL's up-to-date. An InfoWeb icon indicates you can link to further information on the topic by accessing the InfoWeb site, using your browser and an Internet connection.

Interactive Exercises

A CD icon next to an exercise indicates that you can also complete this activity on the Interactive CD. Interactive exercises include the Issues, Fill in the Best Answers, Practice Tests, and Labs.

Labs

Concepts come to life with the Labs—highly interactive tutorials that combine illustrations, animations, digital images, and simulations. Labs guide you step-by-step through a topic, and present you with QuickCheck questions to test your comprehension. You can track your QuickCheck results using a Tracking Disk. (See the Before You Begin section for more information.) Lab assignments are included at the end of each relevant unit. A Lab icon on the left page of a lesson indicates a Lab is featured for the lesson concept. The following Labs are available with the Interactive CD.

Unit A
Making a Dial-Up Connection
Browsing and Searching
Using E-Mail

Unit B
Working with Binary Numbers
Operating a Personal Computer

Unit C
Using the Windows Interface
Installing and Uninstalling Software

Unit D
Benchmarking
Working with Windows Explorer

Unit E
Tracking Packets
Securing Your Connection

Unit F
Backing Up Your Computer

Unit G
Working with Cookies

Unit H
Working with Bitmap Graphics
Video Editing

Before You Begin

It's a snap to start the Interactive CD and use it on your computer. The answers to the FAQs (frequently asked questions) in this section will help you begin.

Will the Interactive CD work on my computer? The Interactive CD works on most computers that run Windows. The easiest way to find out if the Interactive CD works on your computer is to try it! Just follow the steps below to start the CD. If it works, you're all set. If you have trouble, check with your instructor or technical support person. You can also click the link on the Main Menu screen (see below) for Get Technical Support. This will provide you with Frequently Asked Questions as well as contact information for technical support if you have further questions. This information is available at www.mediatechnics.net/np5cd/support.htm

How do I start the CD? Follow these simple steps to get started:

1. Make sure your computer is turned on.

2. Press the button on your computer's CD-ROM drive to open the drawer-like "tray."

3. Place the Interactive CD into the tray with the label facing up.

4. Press the button on the CD-ROM drive to close the tray.

5. Wait about 15 seconds. During this time, the light on your CD-ROM drive should flicker. Soon you should see a screen that displays the Computer Concepts menu. The first time you use the Interactive CD, your computer will check for several necessary Windows components. Any missing components will be automatically installed. When this process is complete, you might be prompted to reboot your computer, and then you can continue to use any of the options on the Computer Concepts menu.

6. *Manual Start*: Complete these steps only if the menu did not appear after completing Step 5:

   a. Use the mouse to position the arrow-shaped pointer on Start, then click the left button on your mouse.

   b. When the Start menu appears, click Run.

   c. Type d:\start.exe, then click the OK button. If your CD-ROM drive is not "d" you should substitute the letter of your drive—for example, q:\start.exe.

FIGURE 1: Main Menu

▶ The Computer Concepts menu should appear on your computer screen after you insert the CD.

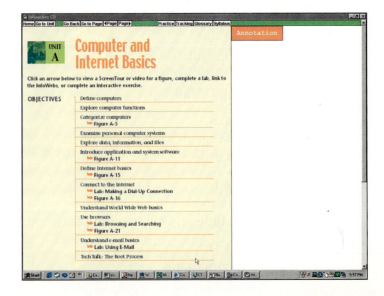

How do I use the Interactive CD? A menu bar, which stretches across each page, provides the options you'll need to navigate through the CD. See Figure 2. To read down to the text at the bottom of a page, drag the scroll box, or click the scroll bar at the side of the screen.

FIGURE 2: CD navigation from Unit A home page

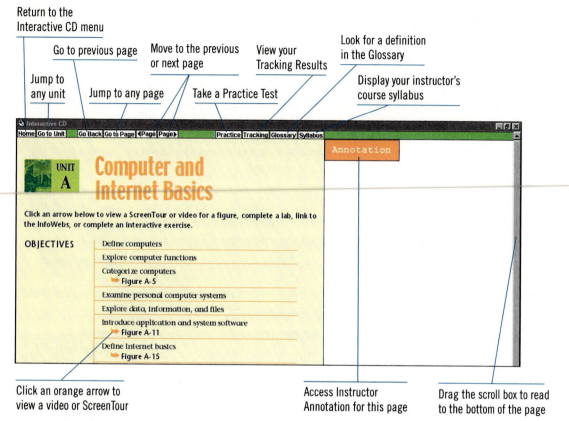

Return to the Interactive CD menu

Go to previous page

Move to the previous or next page

View your Tracking Results

Look for a definition in the Glossary

Jump to any unit

Jump to any page

Take a Practice Test

Display your instructor's course syllabus

Click an orange arrow to view a video or ScreenTour

Access Instructor Annotation for this page

Drag the scroll box to read to the bottom of the page

What if I don't see any Annotation or Syllabus buttons? These buttons only appear if your instructor has provided a link to the syllabus, or a note for a page, and you are using a Tracking Disk. When you send Tracking Disk data to your instructor, the Annotation links are downloaded to your Tracking Disk. If you do not see any Annotations, first use your Tracking Disk to send any results—the results from a QuickCheck, for example—to your instructor. If you still do not see any Annotations, check with your instructor.

How do I view videos, and ScreenTours? Each unit has a unit home page (See Figure 2), which lists all the objectives for the unit and provides links to all the CD and Web elements associated with that unit. To view a video or ScreenTour for a figure, simply click the arrow next to that figure.

How do I access the InfoWebs? You can either link directly to the Illustrated Computer Concepts Fourth Edition InfoWeb home page from the CD menu, or click the link from the unit home page on the Interactive CD. Or, type www.course.com/downloads/illustrated/concepts4 in the Address bar of your browser.

The InfoWebs work only if you have a browser and an Internet connection. If you can send e-mail and access the Web with your computer, you probably have such a connection. When you link to the InfoWebs from the CD menu or the unit home page, the Interactive CD will automatically start your Web browser software. When you complete your exploration of the InfoWebs, you can return to the CD by closing your browser. Click File on your browser's menu bar, then click Close or Exit.

How do I access the Interactive Exercises? The interactive exercises include a variety of activities you can use to review the unit material. You can link directly to the exercise on the CD you want to complete from the unit home page, or navigate through all the interactive exercises for the unit by clicking the Page navigation buttons on the menu bar. Additionally, you can take a Practice Test by clicking the Practice link on the menu bar.

Before You Begin

How do I access the Labs? You can link to a Lab in three ways. From the menu screen, you can click the Open a Lab link, and then click the name of the Lab. Or, you can link to the Lab from the unit home page in the Objectives list. You also can link to the lab from the Lab Assignments in the Interactive Exercises list.

How do I complete the Interactive Exercises and Labs with a Tracking Disk? To complete an activity, simply follow the instructions for these activities to enter your answers. When you complete the Interactive Questions for the Issue, you'll see a message that asks you if you want to save your answers. If you click the OK button, you will be prompted to insert your Tracking Disk, then your score will be saved on it.

When you complete a Lab, the Fill in the Best Answer activity, or a Practice Test, your responses are automatically checked and you are provided with a score. Then, you'll see a message that asks you if you want to save your score. If you click the OK button, you will be prompted to insert your Tracking Disk, then your score will be saved on it. For Practice Tests, you will also receive a study guide to help you find the answers to questions that you answered incorrectly. You can print the study guide by following the instructions on the screen.

The first time you save a score, you must follow the directions on the screen to create a Tracking Disk. To do so, click the Create button and insert a blank, formatted floppy disk. You only need to create a Tracking Disk one time. Once you create the Tracking Disk, just insert it into the floppy disk drive or your computer when you start the Interactive CD, or when prompted to do so.

You can view or print a summary report of all your scores by clicking the Tracking button on the menu bar. Your Issue responses are not listed here, but are submitted with your Tracking, Data. If your instructor wants you to submit your Tracking Data to track your progress, simply click the "Send your Student Tracking Data to your Instructor" link on the CD menu.

Can I make the type appear larger on my screen? If the type in the Interactive CD appears small, your monitor is probably set at a high resolution. The type will appear larger if you reduce the resolution by using the Start menu to select Settings and open the Control Panel. Double-click the Display icon, then select the Settings tab. Move the Screen Area slider to 800×600. This setting is optional. You can view the Interactive CD at most standard resolutions.

If your Interactive CD text looks jumbled, your computer might be set to use Windows large fonts, instead of standard fonts. The standard fonts setting is located on the Scheme list, which you can access by double-clicking the Control Panel's Display icon, and then selecting the Appearance tab.

How do I end a session? You must leave the Interactive CD in the CD-ROM drive while you use it. Before you remove it, exit the program by clicking the Exit button from the CD menu.

What if I have additional questions about how to use the Interactive CD or Web site? For answers to technical questions, click the Technical Support link on the Interactive CD menu. Additional technical information is provided in the Readme.doc file on your Interactive CD.

SYSTEM REQUIREMENTS

- A computer running Windows 98, ME, 2000, or XP is recommended. (This product can be used on older Windows 95 and Windows NT 4.x systems, but they might require updates for Microsoft Internet Explorer and Windows Media Player. The Interactive CD will not run on Windows 3.x)
- Microsoft Internet Explorer 4 (or higher)
- A current version of the Windows Media Player (version 6.4 or higher)
- High-color or True Color graphics with a resolution of at least 640×480 pixels, 800×600 or 1024×768 resolution recommended
- A floppy disk drive configured as drive A:
- A properly configured CD-ROM drive
- A properly configured sound card and speakers
- A Pentium processor, preferably 400MHz or faster
- Required RAM depends on the operating system and other loaded programs, but should typically be between 64MB and 256MB
- Computer lab users must have Write rights to the Windows Registry and to the Windows Temporary folder (typically c:\windows\temp).

UNIT A

Computer and Internet Basics

OBJECTIVES

Define computers

Explore computer functions

Categorize computers

Examine personal computer systems

Explore data, information, and files

Introduce application and system software

Define Internet basics

Connect to the Internet

Understand World Wide Web basics

Use browsers

Understand e-mail basics

Tech Talk: The Boot Process

Unit A provides an overview of computer and Internet technologies. The unit begins by defining the basic characteristics of a computer system and then provides a quick overview of data, information, and files. You will be introduced to application software, operating systems, and platform compatibility. You will get a basic overview of the Internet, the Web, and e-mail. The unit concludes with a lesson on the boot process, the sequence of events that happens when you turn on your computer.

Defining computers

Whether you realize it or not, you already know a lot about computers. You've picked up information from commercials and magazine articles, from books and movies, from conversations and correspondence, and perhaps even from using your own computer and trying to figure out why it doesn't always work. This lesson provides an overview designed to help you start organizing what you know about computers, provide you with a basic understanding of how computers work, and get you up to speed with basic computer vocabulary.

DETAILS

- The word "computer" has been part of the English language since 1646, but if you look in a dictionary printed before 1940, you might be surprised to find a computer defined as a person who performs calculations! Prior to 1940, machines that were designed to perform calculations were referred to as calculators and tabulators, not computers. The modern definition and use of the term "computer" emerged in the 1940s, when the first electronic computing devices were developed.

- Most people can formulate a mental picture of a computer, but computers do so many things and come in such a variety of shapes and sizes that it might seem difficult to distill their common characteristics into an all-purpose definition. At its core, a **computer** is a device that accepts input, processes data, stores data, and produces output, all according to a series of stored instructions.

- A **computer system** includes hardware, peripheral devices, and software. Figure A-1 shows a basic computer system. **Hardware** includes the electronic and mechanical devices that process data. The term "hardware" refers to the computer as well as components called peripheral devices. **Peripheral devices** expand the computer's input, output, and storage capabilities.

- An **input device**, such as a keyboard or mouse, gathers input and transforms it into a series of electronic signals for the computer. An **output device**, such as a monitor or printer, displays, prints, or transmits the results of processing from the computer memory.

- A computer requires instructions called **software**, which is a **computer program** that tells the computer how to perform particular tasks.

- A **computer network** consists of two or more computers and other devices that are connected for the purpose of sharing data and programs. A **LAN (local area network)** is simply a computer network that is located within a limited geographical area, such as a school computer lab or a small business.

FYI

The term "personal computer" is sometimes abbreviated as "PC." However, "PC" is usually used for a specific type of personal computer that runs Windows software.

FIGURE A-1: A basic computer system

Exploring computer functions

To really understand computers, you can look at the functions they perform. Figure A-2 illustrates the basic computer functions—accept input, process data, store data, and produce output—and shows the components that work together to accomplish each function.

DETAILS

- Accept input. A computer accepts input. Computer **input** is whatever is put into a computer system. Input can be supplied by a person, by the environment, or by another computer. Examples of the kinds of input that a computer can accept include the words and symbols in a document, numbers for a calculation, pictures, temperatures from a thermostat, music or voice audio signals from a microphone, and instructions from a computer program.

- Process data. A computer processes data. In the context of computing, **data** refers to the symbols that represent facts, objects, and ideas. Computers manipulate data in many ways, and we call this manipulation **processing**. Some of the ways that a computer can process data include performing calculations, sorting lists of words or numbers, modifying documents and pictures, and drawing graphs. The instructions that tell a computer how to carry out the processing tasks are referred to as a **computer program**, or simply a "program." In a computer, most processing takes place in a **microprocessor** called the **central processing unit (CPU)**, which is sometimes described as the "brain" of the computer.

- Store data. A computer stores data so that it will be available for processing. Most computers have more than one location for storing data, depending on how the data is being used. **Memory** is an area of a computer that temporarily holds data waiting to be processed, stored, or output. **Storage** is the area of a computer that holds data on a permanent basis when it is not immediately needed for processing. For example, while you are working on it, a document is in memory; it is not in storage until you save it. After you save the document, it is still in memory until you close the document, exit the program, or turn the computer off. Documents in memory are lost when you turn off the power. Stored documents are not lost when the power is turned off.

- Produce output. **Output** consists of the processing results produced by a computer. Some examples of computer output include reports, documents, music, graphs, and pictures. An output device displays, prints, or transmits the results of processing. Figure A-2 helps you visualize the input, processing, storage, and output activities of a computer.

FIGURE A-2: Basic computer functions

A computer produces output.
You use an output device, such as a printer or display screen, to see the computer outputs—the results of processing

A computer processes data.
The CPU retrieves the numbers and the instruction, and then processes the numbers by performing addition; the result, 9, is temporarily held in memory; from memory, the result can be output or stored

A computer accepts input.
You use an input device, such as a keyboard, to input numbers, such as 2 and 7, along with the instruction ADD; the instruction and the numbers are temporarily held in memory

A computer stores data.
You can permanently store data on disks and CDs

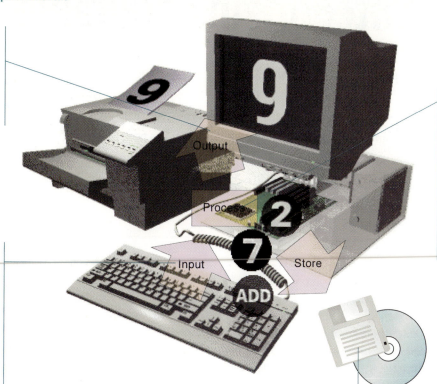

Understanding the importance of stored programs

Early computers were really no more than calculating devices designed to carry out a specific mathematical task. To use one of these devices for another task, it was necessary to rewire or reset its circuits—a task best left to an engineer. In a modern computer, the idea of a **stored program** means that instructions for a computing task can be loaded into a computer's memory. These instructions can easily be replaced by different instructions when it is time for the computer to perform a different task. The stored program concept allows you to use your computer for one task, such as word processing, and then easily switch to a different type of computing task, such as editing a photo or sending an e-mail message. It is the single most important characteristic that distinguishes a computer from other simpler and less versatile devices.

Categorizing computers

Computers are versatile machines, but some types of computers are better suited to certain tasks than others. Computers are categorized to help consumers associate computers with appropriate tasks. Categorizing computers is a way of grouping them according to criteria such as usage, cost, size, and capability. Knowing how a computer has been categorized provides an indication of its best potential use. To reflect today's computer technology, the following categories are appropriate: personal computers, handheld computers, workstations, videogame consoles, mainframes, super-computers, and servers.

DETAILS

- A **personal computer**, also called a **microcomputer**, is designed to meet the computing needs of an individual. It typically provides access to a wide variety of computing applications, such as word processing, photo editing, e-mail, and Internet access. Personal computers include **desktop computers**, as illustrated in Figure A-3, and **notebook computers** (sometimes called "laptop computers"), as illustrated in Figure A-4. A desktop has separate components, while laptops have a keyboard, monitor, and system in one compact unit. Laptops are considerably more expensive than comparable desktops.

- A **handheld computer**, also called a **PDA (Personal Digital Assistant),** shown in Figure A-5, is designed to fit into a pocket, run on batteries, and be used while you are holding it. A PDA is typically used as an electronic appointment book, address book, calculator, and notepad. Inexpensive add-ons make it possible to send and receive e-mail, use maps and global positioning to get directions, maintain an expense account, and make voice calls using cellular service. With its slow processing speed and small screen, a handheld computer is not powerful enough to handle many of the tasks that can be accomplished using desktop or notebook personal computers.

- Computers that are advertised as **workstations** are usually powerful desktop computers designed for specialized tasks such as design tasks. A workstation can tackle tasks that require a lot of processing speed, such as medical imaging and computer-aided design. Some workstations contain more than one micro-processor, and most have circuitry specially designed for creating and displaying three-dimensional and animated graphics. "Workstation" can also mean an ordinary personal computer that is connected to a local area network.

- A **videogame console**, such as the Nintendo® GameCube™, the Sony PlayStation®, or the Microsoft XBox®, is a computer. In the past, a videogame console was not considered a computer because of its history as a dedicated game device that connects

to a TV set and provides only a pair of joysticks for input. Today's videogame consoles, however, contain microprocessors that are equivalent to any found in a fast personal computer, and they are equipped to produce graphics that rival those on sophisticated workstations. Add-ons make it possible to use a videogame console to watch DVD movies, send and receive e-mail, and participate in online activities, such as multiplayer games.

- A **mainframe computer** is a large and expensive computer capable of simultaneously processing data for hundreds or thousands of users. Mainframes are generally used by busi-nesses, universities, or governments to provide centralized stor-age, processing, and management of large amounts of data where reliability, data security, and centralized control are nec-essary. Its main processing circuitry is housed in a closet-sized cabinet. See Figure A-6.

- A computer is a **supercomputer** if, at the time of construc-tion, it is one of the fastest computers in the world. Because of their speed and complexity, supercomputers can tackle tasks that would not be practical for other computers. Typical uses for supercomputers include breaking codes and modeling worldwide weather systems. A supercomputer CPU is con-structed from thousands of microprocessors. As an example, a supercomputer currently under development is designed to use 12,000 microprocessors, which will enable it to operate at speeds exceeding 30 trillion operations per second.

- In the computer industry, the term "server" has several mean-ings. It can refer to computer hardware, to a specific type of software, or to a combination of hardware and software. In any case, the purpose of a **server** is to "serve" the computers on a network (such as the Internet or a LAN) by supplying them with data. Just about any personal computer, workstation, main-frame, or supercomputer can be configured to perform the work of a server.

FIGURE A-3: A desktop personal computer

▶ A desktop computer fits on a desk and runs on power from an electrical wall outlet; the main unit can be housed in either a vertical case (like the one shown) or a horizontal case

FIGURE A-4: A notebook personal computer

▲ A notebook computer is small and lightweight, giving it the advantage of portability; it can run on power supplied by an electrical outlet, or it can run on battery power

FIGURE A-5: A personal digital assistant

▲ Many handheld computers accept writing input; you can "synchronize" a handheld with a personal computer in order to transfer updated or new information between the two

FIGURE A-6: A mainframe computer

▶ This IBM S/390 mainframe computer weighs about 1,400 lbs. and is about 6.5 feet tall; after additional components are added for storage and output

Examining personal computer systems

The term "**computer system**" usually refers to a computer and all of the input, output, and storage devices that are connected to it. Despite cosmetic differences among personal computers, see Figure A-7, a personal computer system usually includes standard equipment or devices. Devices may vary in color, size, and design for different personal computers. Figure A-8 illustrates a typical desktop personal computer system. Refer to Figure A-8 as you read through the list of devices below.

DETAILS

- **System unit**. The system unit is the case that holds the power supply, storage devices, and the circuit boards, including the main circuit board (also called the "motherboard"), which contains the microprocessor. The system unit for most notebook computers also holds a built-in keyboard and speakers.

- **Monitor**. Most desktop computers use a separate monitor as a display (output) device, whereas notebook computers use a flat panel display screen that is attached to the system unit.

- **Keyboard**. Most computers are equipped with a keyboard as the primary input device.

- **Mouse**. A mouse is a common input device designed to manipulate on-screen graphical objects and controls.

- **Storage devices**. Computers have many types of storage devices that are used to store data when the power is turned off. For example: A **floppy disk drive** is a storage device that reads data from and writes data to floppy disks. A **hard disk drive** can store billions of characters of data. It is usually mounted inside the computer's system unit. A small external light indicates when the drive is in use. A **CD-ROM drive** is a storage device that uses laser technology to read data that is permanently stored on data or audio CDs. A **DVD drive** can read data from data CDs, audio CDs, data DVDs, or DVD movie disks. CD-ROM and DVD drives typically cannot be used to write data onto disks. "ROM" stands for "read-only memory" and means that the drive can read data from disks, but cannot be used to store new data on them. Many computers, especially desktop models, include a **CD-writer** that can be used to create and copy CDs.

- **Speakers** and **sound card**. Desktop computers have a rudimentary built-in speaker that's mostly limited to playing beeps. A small circuit board, called a sound card, is required for high-quality music, narration, and sound effects. A desktop computer's sound card sends signals to external speakers. A notebook's sound card sends signals to speakers that are built into the notebook system unit. The sound card is an input and an output device, while speakers are output devices.

- **Modem**. Virtually every personal computer system includes a built-in modem that can be used to establish an Internet connection using a standard telephone line. A modem is both an input and an output device.

- **Printer**. A computer printer is an output device that produces computer-generated text or graphical images on paper.

What's a peripheral device?

The word "peripheral" dates back to the days of mainframes when the CPU was housed in a giant box, and all input, output, and storage devices were housed separately. Today, the term "peripheral device" designates equipment that might be added to a computer system to enhance its functionality. A printer is a popular peripheral device, as is a digital camera, zip drive, scanner, joystick, or graphics tablet. Though a hard disk drive seems to be an integral part of a computer—after all, it's built right into the system unit—by the strictest technical definition, a hard disk drive would be classified as a peripheral device. The same goes for other storage devices and the keyboard, monitor, LCD screen, sound card, speakers, and modem.

FIGURE A-7: Typical personal computer systems

FIGURE A-8: Components of a typical personal computer system

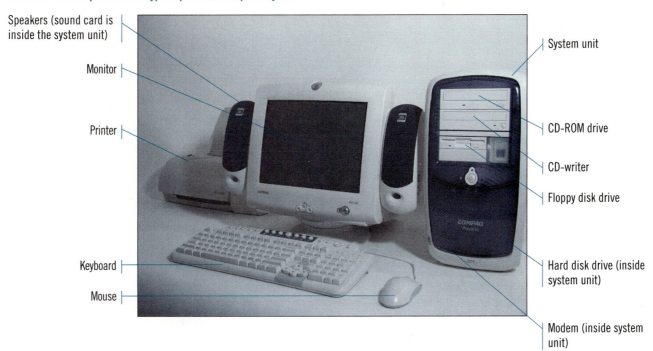

Speakers (sound card is inside the system unit)

Monitor

Printer

Keyboard

Mouse

System unit

CD-ROM drive

CD-writer

Floppy disk drive

Hard disk drive (inside system unit)

Modem (inside system unit)

Exploring data, information, and files

In everyday conversation, people use the terms "data" and "information" interchangeably. Nevertheless, some computer professionals make a distinction between the two terms. They define **data** as the symbols that represent people, events, things, and ideas. Data becomes **information** when it is presented in a format that people can understand and use. As a rule of thumb, remember that data is used by computers; information is used by people. See Figure A-9.

DETAILS

● Have you ever gotten a computer file you couldn't read? It could be because the data has not been converted to information. Computers process and store data using the binary number system and several other codes designed expressly for electronic data. The **binary number system** has only two digits: 0 and 1. The binary number system can represent number data using only 0s and 1s.

● Computers use these codes to store data in a digital format as a series of 1s and 0s. Each 0 or 1 is a **bit**, and 8 bits are called a **byte**. The bits and bytes that are processed and stored by a computer are data. The output results of processing data—the words, numbers, sounds, and graphics—are information.

● A computer stores data in files. A **computer file**, usually referred to simply as a **file**, is a named collection of data that exists on a storage medium, such as a hard disk, a floppy disk, or a CD. Although all files contain data, some files are classified as "data files," whereas other files are classified as "executable files."

● A **data file** contains data. For example, it might contain the text for a document, the numbers for a calculation, the specifications for a graph, the frames of a video, or the notes of a musical passage.

● An **executable file** contains the programs or gives the instructions that tell a computer how to perform a specific task. For example, the word processing program that tells your computer how to display and print text is stored as an executable file.

You can think of data files as passive because the data does not instruct the computer to do anything. Executable files, on the other hand, are active because the instructions stored in the file cause the computer to carry out some action.

● Every file has a name, the **filename**, which often provides a clue to its contents. A file also has a **filename extension** usually referred to simply as an "extension" that further describes a file's contents. For example, in Pbrush.exe, "Pbrush" is the filename and "exe" is the extension. As you can see, the filename is separated from the extension by a period called a "dot." To tell someone the name of this file, you would say, "P brush dot e-x-e."

Executable files typically have .exe extensions. Data files have a variety of extensions, such as .bmp or .tif for a graphic, .mid for synthesized music, or .htm for a Web page. Each software program assigns a specific filename extension to the data files it creates. As a user, you do not decide the extension; rather, it is automatically included when files are created and saved, for example .xls for Excel files or .doc for files created with Word. Depending on your computer settings, you may or may not see the filename extension assigned to a file. Figure A-10 shows a list of files, including the filename extensions.

FIGURE A-9: The difference between data and information

The computer reads the data in the file and produces the output image as information that the viewer can understand

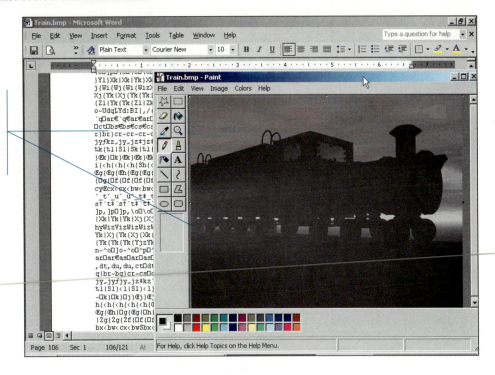

FIGURE A-10: Filenames, including filename extensions

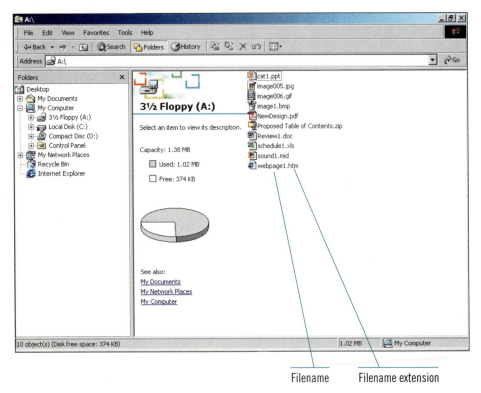

Filename   Filename extension

Introducing application and system software

A computer's application software and operating system make a computer run. As a computer user, you are probably most familiar with application software. In fact, you probably use many different types of application software that are installed on your computer. As a computer user, your computing experience is driven by the operating system. There is usually only one operating system on your computer; the operating system is not another type of application software. You can run many applications at one time, but only one operating system at one time.

Info Web
APPLE COMPUTERS

DETAILS

- **Application software** is a set of computer programs that helps a person carry out a task. Word processing software, for example, helps people create, edit, and print documents. Personal finance software helps people keep track of their money and investments. Video editing software helps people create and edit home movies and even some professional, commercially-released films.

- An operating system is essentially the master controller for all of the activities that take place within a computer. An **operating system** is classified as **system software**, not application software, because its primary purpose is to help the computer system monitor itself in order to function efficiently. Unlike application software, an operating system does not directly help people perform application-specific tasks, such as word processing. Most of the time people interact with the operating system without realizing it. However, people do interact with the operating system for certain operational and storage tasks, such as starting programs and locating data files.

- Popular personal computer operating systems include Microsoft Windows and Mac OS. Microsoft Windows CE and Palm OS control most handheld computers. Linux and UNIX are popular operating systems for servers. Microsoft Windows (usually referred to simply as "Windows") is probably the most widely used operating system for personal computers. As shown in Figure A-11, the Windows operating system displays menus and simulated on-screen controls designed to be manipulated by a mouse.

- Windows software is not the same as the Windows operating system. The term "Windows software" refers to any application software that is designed to run on computers that use Microsoft Windows as their operating system. For example, a program called Microsoft Word for Windows is a word processing program; it is an application program that is referred to as "Windows software."

- An operating system affects compatibility. Computers that operate in essentially the same way are said to be "compatible." Two of the most important factors that influence compatibility and define a computer's platform are the microprocessor and the operating system. A **platform** consists of the underlying hardware and software of the computer system. Today, two of the most popular personal computer platforms are PCs and Macs. See Figure A-12.

  PCs are based on the design for one of the first personal computer "superstars"—the IBM PC. A huge selection of personal computer brands and models based on the original PC design and manufactured by companies such as IBM, Hewlett-Packard, Toshiba, Dell, and Gateway are on the shelves today. The Windows operating system was designed specifically for these personal computers. Because of this, the PC platform is sometimes called the "Windows platform." Most of the examples in this book pertain to PCs because they are so popular.

  Macs are based on a proprietary design for a personal computer called the Macintosh, manufactured almost exclusively by Apple Computer, Inc. The stylish iMac is one of Apple's most popular computers, and like other computers in the Mac platform, it uses Mac OS as its operating system.

- The PC and Mac platforms are not compatible because their microprocessors and operating systems differ. Consequently, application software designed for Macs does not typically work with PCs. When shopping for new software, it is important to read the package to make sure that it is designed to work with your computer platform.

  Different versions of some operating systems have been created to operate with more than one microprocessor. For example, a version of the Linux operating system exists for the PC platform and another version exists for the Mac platform.

FIGURE A-11: The Windows interface

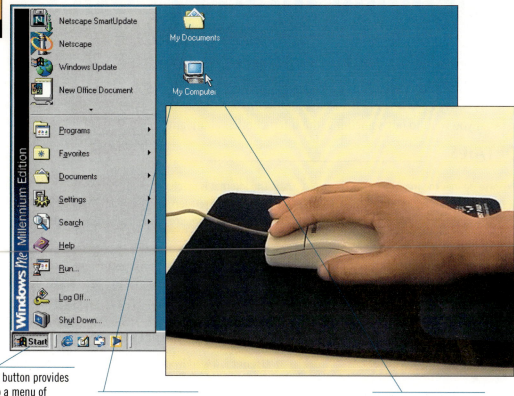

The Start button provides access to a menu of program, document, and customization options

Small pictures called "icons" represent disk drives and documents

An on-screen pointer can be positioned on an object by moving the mouse; you can manipulate an object with the mouse by clicking or dragging the object

FIGURE A-12: The PC and the Mac platforms

Defining Internet basics

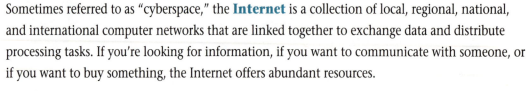

Sometimes referred to as "cyberspace," the **Internet** is a collection of local, regional, national, and international computer networks that are linked together to exchange data and distribute processing tasks. If you're looking for information, if you want to communicate with someone, or if you want to buy something, the Internet offers abundant resources.

DETAILS

- The **Internet backbone** defines the main routes of the Internet. See Figure A-13. Analogous to interstate highways, the Internet backbone is constructed and maintained by major telecommunications companies. These telecommunications links can move huge amounts of data at incredible speeds.

- In addition to the backbone, the Internet encompasses an intricate collection of regional and local communications links. These links can include local telephone systems, cable television lines, cellular telephone systems, and personal satellite dishes that transport data to and from millions of computers and other electronic devices.

- Communication among all of the different devices on the Internet is made possible by **TCP/IP (Transmission Control Protocol/Internet Protocol)**, which is a standard set of rules for electronically addressing and transmitting data.

- Most of the information that is accessible on the Internet is stored on servers. These servers use special **server software** to locate and distribute data requested by Internet users.

- Every device that's connected to the Internet is assigned a unique number, called an **IP address** that pinpoints its location in cyberspace. To prepare data for transport, a computer divides the data into small chunks called **packets**. Each packet is labeled with the IP address of its destination and then transmitted. When a packet reaches an intersection in the Internet's communications links, a device called a **router** examines the packet's address. The router checks the address in a routing table and then sends the packet along the appropriate link towards its destination. As packets arrive at their destinations, they are reassembled into a replica of the original file.

- A **Web site** can provide information, collect information through forms, or provide access to other resources, such as search engines and e-mail.

- The Internet is revolutionizing business by directly linking consumers with retailers, manufacturers, and distributors through electronic commerce, or **E-commerce**. See Figure A-14.

- Electronic mail, known as **e-mail**, allows one person to send an electronic message to another person or to a group of people. A variation of e-mail called a **mailing list server**, or "listserv," maintains a public list of people who are interested in a particular topic. Messages sent to the list server are automatically distributed to everyone on the mailing list.

- **Usenet** is a worldwide bulletin board system that contains thousands of discussion forums on every imaginable topic called **newsgroups**. Newsgroup members post messages based on their interests to the bulletin board; these messages can be read and responded to by other group members.

- The Internet allows real-time communication. For example, a **chat group** consists of several people who connect to the Internet and communicate in real time by typing comments to each other. A private version of a chat room, called **instant messaging**, allows people to send typed messages back and forth. **Internet telephony** allows telephone-style conversations to travel over the Internet. Internet telephony requires special software at both ends of the conversation and, instead of a telephone, it uses a microphone connected to a computer.

- The Internet carries radio shows and teleconferences that can be **broadcast** worldwide. Internet radio is popular because broadcasts aren't limited to a small local region.

- Internet servers store a variety of files including documents, music, software, videos, animations, and photos. The process of transferring one of these files from a remote computer, such as a server, to a local computer, such as your personal computer, is called **downloading**. Sending a file from a local computer to a remote computer is called **uploading**. See Figure A-15.

FIGURE A-13: The Internet backbone

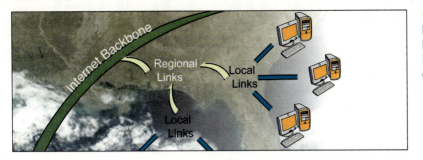

◄ Personal computers are connected to regional and local communications links, which in turn connect to the Internet backbone; data transport works seamlessly between any two platforms—between PCs and Macs, and even between personal computers and mainframes

FIGURE A-14: Online auctions

◄ E-commerce includes activities such as online shopping, linking businesses to other businesses (sometimes called e-business or B2B), online stock trading, and electronic auctions

FIGURE A-15: Web sites provide files

◄ Many Web sites provide files that the public can download to personal computers; uploads, on the other hand, are limited to people who have password access to the site

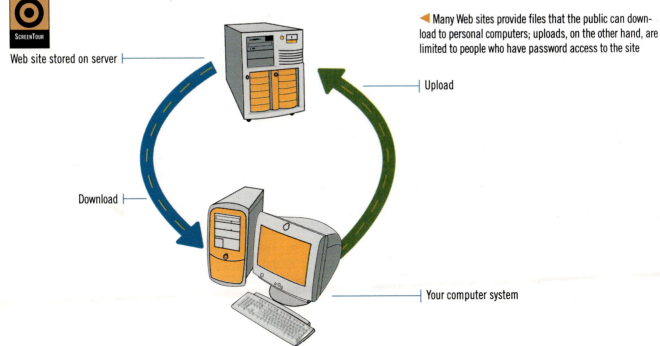

Web site stored on server

Upload

Download

Your computer system

Connecting to the Internet

To take advantage of the Internet, you'll have to establish a communications link between your computer and the Internet. Possibilities include using your existing telephone line, a cable television line, a personal satellite link, wireless or cell phone service, or special high-speed telephone services. Being on the Internet is often referred to as being **online**.

National ISPs   Making a Dial Up Connection

DETAILS

- A **dial-up connection** requires a device called a **voice band modem**, or "modem," which converts your computer's digital signals into a type of signal that can travel over telephone lines. Figure A-16 shows various types of computer modems.

  To establish a dial-up connection, your computer's modem dials a special access number, which is answered by an Internet modem. Once the connection is established, your computer is "on the Internet." When you complete an Internet session, you must "hang up" your modem. You can choose to disconnect automatically or manually; either way the connection is discontinued until the next time you dial in.

  Theoretically, the top speed of a dial-up connection is 56 K, meaning that 56,000 bits of data are transmitted per second. Actual speed is usually reduced by distance, interference, and other technical problems, however, so the speed of most 56 K dial-up connections is more like 45 K. This speed is useable for e-mail, e-commerce, and chat. It is not, however, really optimal for applications that require large amounts of data to be transferred quickly over the Internet.

- **Cable modem service** is offered to a cable company's customers for an additional monthly charge and usually requires two pieces of equipment: a network card and a cable modem. A **network card** is a device that's designed to connect a personal computer to a local area network. A **cable modem** is a device that changes a computer's signals into a form that can travel over cable TV links.

  Cable modem access is referred to as an **always-on connection**, because your computer is, in effect, always connected to the Internet, unlike a dial-up connection that is established only when the dialing sequence is completed. A cable modem receives data more than 25 times faster than a dial-up connection. This speed is suitable for most Internet activities, including real-time video and teleconferencing.

- Many telephone and independent telecommunications companies offer high-speed, always-on connections. **ISDN (Integrated Services Digital Network)** provides data transfer speeds of either 64 K (bits per second, or bps) or 128 K (bps). Given data transfer speeds that are only marginally better than a 56 K dial-up

connection and substantial monthly fees, ISDN ranks low on the list of high-speed Internet options for most consumers. **DSL (Digital Subscriber Line)** and **xDSL** are generic names for a family of high-speed Internet links, including ADSL, SDSL, and DSL lite. Each type of DSL provides different maximum speeds from twice as fast to approximately 125 times faster than a 56 K dial-up connection. Both ISDN and DSL connections require proximity to a telephone switching station, which can be a problem for speed-hungry consumers who don't live near one.

- Another Internet connection option is **DSS (Digital Satellite Service)**, which today offers two-way Internet access at an average speed of about 500 K. Consumers are required to rent or purchase a satellite dish and pay for its installation.

- An **ISP (Internet Service Provider)** is a company that maintains Internet computers and telecommunications equipment in order to provide Internet access to businesses, organizations, and individuals. Some parts of the Internet (such as military computers) are off limits to the general public. Other parts of the Internet (such as the New York Times archives) limit access to paid members. Many parts of the Internet encourage memberships and offer additional perks if you sign up.

- User IDs and passwords are designed to provide access to authorized users and to prevent unauthorized access. A **user ID** is a series of characters, letters, and possibly numbers that becomes a person's unique identifier, similar to a social security number. A **password** is a different series of characters that verifies the user ID, sort of like a PIN (personal identification number) verifies your identity at an ATM machine.

- Typically, your ISP provides you with a user ID and password that you use to connect to the Internet. You will accumulate additional user IDs and passwords from other sources for specific Internet activities, such as reading New York Times articles, or participating in an online auction. The process of entering a user ID and password is usually referred to as "logging in" or "logging on." See Figure A-17. The rules for creating a user ID are not consistent throughout the Internet, so it is important to read all of the instructions carefully before finalizing your ID.

FIGURE A-16: Computer modems

▲ To determine whether a computer has a modem, look for a place to plug in a standard phone cable

▲ An external modem (top left) connects to the computer with a cable; an internal modem (top right) is installed inside the computer's system unit; a PC card modem (bottom center) is typically used in a notebook computer

▲ A modem card slides into a notebook computer's PC card slot

FIGURE A-17: Entering a password

◀ Don't share your password with anyone, or write it down where it could be found; your password should be a sequence of characters and numbers that is easy for you to remember, but would be difficult for someone else to guess

Typically, when you log in and enter your password, a series of asterisks appears on the screen

What service does an Internet service provider provide?

To access the Internet, you do not typically connect your computer directly to the backbone. Instead, you connect it to an ISP that in turn connects to the backbone. An ISP is a point of access to the Internet. An ISP typically provides a connection to the Internet and an e-mail account. ISP customers arrange for service, in this case for Internet access, for which they pay a monthly fee. In addition to a monthly fee, an ISP might also charge an installation fee. In Europe, subscribers may also be required to pay per-minute fees, similar to cell phone charges. The ISP that you select should provide service in the places that you typically use your computer. If your work takes you on the road a lot, you'll want to consider a national ISP that provides local access numbers in the cities that you visit. An ISP usually specializes in one type of service. The quality of dial-up and cable modem services tends to decrease as the number of customers increases due to increased traffic.

Understanding World Wide Web basics

In the 1960s, long before personal computers or the Internet existed, a Harvard student named Ted Nelson wrote a term paper in which he described a set of documents, called **hypertext**, that would be stored on a computer. While reading a document in hypertext, a person could use a set of "links" to view related documents. A revolutionary idea for its time, today hypertext is the foundation for a part of the Internet that's often called "the Web" by the millions of people who use it every day.

DETAILS

● One of the Internet's most captivating attractions, the **Web** (short for "World Wide Web") is a collection of files that are interconnected through the use of hypertext. Many of these files produce documents called **Web pages**. Other files contain photos, videos, animations, and sounds that can be incorporated into specific Web pages. Most Web pages contain **links** (sometimes called "hyperlinks") to related documents and media files. See Figure A-18.

● A series of Web pages can be grouped into a **Web site**—a sort of virtual "place" in cyberspace. Every day, thousands of people shop at online department stores featuring clothing, shoes, and jewelry; visit research Web sites to look up information; and go to news Web sites, not only to read about the latest news, sports, and weather, but also to discuss current issues with other readers. The Web encompasses these and many other types of sites.

● Web sites are hosted by corporations, government agencies, colleges, and private organizations all over the world. The computers and software that store and distribute Web pages are called **Web servers**.

● Every Web page has a unique address called a **URL (uniform resource locator)**. For example, the URL for the Cable News Network Web site is http://www.cnn.com. Most URLs begin with http://. **HTTP (Hypertext Transfer Protocol)** is the communications standard that's instrumental in ferrying Web documents to all corners of the Internet. When typing a URL, the http:// can usually be omitted, so www.cnn.com works just as well as http://www.cnn.com.

● Most Web sites have a main page that acts as a doorway to the rest of the pages at the site. This main page is sometimes referred to as a **home page**. The URL for a Web site's main page is typically short and to the point, like www.cnn.com.

The site might then be divided into topic areas that are reflected in the URL. For example, the CNN site might include a weather center www.cnn.com/weather/ and an entertainment desk www.cnn.com/showbiz/. A series of Web pages will then be grouped under the appropriate topic. For example, you might find a page about hurricanes at the URL www.cnn.com/weather/hurricanes.html or a page about el niño at www.cnn.com/weather/elnino.htm. The filename of a specific Web page always appears last in the URL—hurricanes.html and elnino.htm are the names of two Web pages. Web page filenames usually have an .htm or .html extension, indicating that the page was created with **HTML** (Hypertext Markup Language), a standard format for Web documents. Figure A-19 identifies the parts of a URL.

● A URL never contains a space, even after a punctuation mark. An underline character is sometimes used to give the appearance of a space between words, as in the URL www.detroit.com/restaurants/best_restaurants.html. Be sure to use the correct type of slash—always a forward slash (/)—and duplicate the URL's capitalization exactly. The servers that run some Web sites are case sensitive, which means that an uppercase letter is not the same as a lowercase letter. On these servers, typing www.cmu.edu/Overview.html (with an uppercase "O") will not locate the page that's stored as www.cmu.edu/overview.html (with a lowercase "o").

FIGURE A-18: A Web page

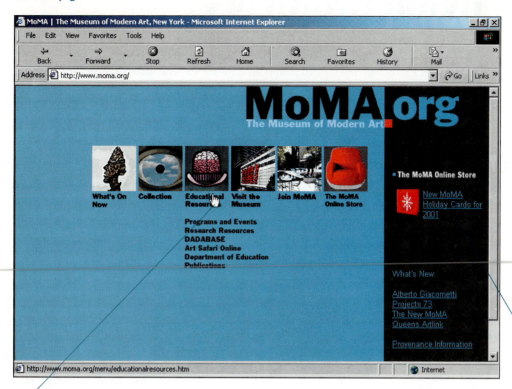

To determine whether an object is a link, position the pointer on it; if the pointer changes to a hand shape, the object is a link; to activate a link, simply click it

On most Web pages, underlined text indicates a link

FIGURE A-19: A URL

http://www.cnn.com/showbiz/movies.htm

Web
protocol
standard

Web
server
name

Folder
name

Document name
and filename
extension

◀ The URL for a Web page indicates the computer on which it is stored, its location on the Web server, a folder name, its filename, and its filename extension

Using browsers

A Web browser, usually referred to simply as a **browser**, is a software program that runs on your computer and helps you access Web pages. A browser fetches and displays Web pages. Two of today's most popular browsers are Microsoft Internet Explorer® (IE) and Netscape Navigator® (Navigator). Browser software provides a set of tools for viewing and navigating Web pages.

DETAILS

● Whether it's called a "URL box," an "Address box," a "Location box," or a "Netsite box," most browsers provide a space for entering URLs.

● If you want to view the Web page located at www.dogs.com/boxer.html, you enter the URL into the Address box provided by your browser. When you press [Enter] on the keyboard, the browser contacts the Web server at www.dogs.com and requests the boxer.html page. The server sends your computer the data stored in boxer.html. This data includes two things: the information that you want to view and embedded codes, called **HTML tags**, that tell your browser how to display the information. The tags specify details such as the color of the background, the text color and size, and the placement of graphics. Figure A-20, which shows a page in Internet Explorer and the HTML code used to display the page, shows that a browser assembles a document on your computer screen according to the specifications contained in the HTML tags.

● Web browsers offer a remarkably similar set of features and capabilities. HTML tags make it possible for Web pages to appear similar from one browser to the next.

● After you look at a sequence of pages, the browser's Back button lets you retrace your steps to view pages that you've seen previously. Most browsers also have a Forward button, which shows you the page that you were viewing before you pressed the Back button.

● Your browser lets you select a **home page**, which is the Web page that appears every time you start your browser. The idea is that you'll select a home page that contains links or information

that you use often. Whenever you click the Home button, your browser displays your home page. This home page is different than the home page of a Web site which was defined earlier.

● Typically, a browser provides access to a print option from a button or a menu, allowing you to print the contents of a Web page. You should always preview before printing because a Web page on the screen may print out as several printed pages. Most browsers let you save a copy of a Web page and place it at the storage location of your choice, and allow you to save a copy of a graphic or sound that you find on a Web page. Most browsers also provide a Copy command that allows you to copy a section of text from a Web page, which you can then paste into one of your own documents. To keep track of the source for each insertion, you can also use the Copy command to copy the Web page's URL from the Address box and then paste the URL into your document.

● To help you revisit sites from previous sessions, your browser provides a **History list**. You can display this list by clicking a button or menu option provided by your browser. To revisit any site in the History list, click its URL. Many browsers allow you to specify how long a URL will remain in the History list.

● If you find a great Web site and you want to revisit it sometime in the future, you can add the URL to a list, typically called **Favorites** or **Bookmarks** so you can simply click its URL to display it.

● Sometimes a Web page takes a very long time to appear on your screen. If you don't want to wait for a page, click the Stop button.

● If you're looking for specific information on a "long" Web page, you can save yourself a lot of reading by using the Find option on your browser's Edit menu to locate a particular word or phrase.

Using search engines

The term "**search engine**" popularly refers to a Web site that provides a variety of tools to help you find information on the Web. A **keyword** is any word or phrase that you type to describe the information that you're trying to find. Based on your input, the search engine provides a list of pages. Depending on the search engine that you use, you may be able to

find information by entering a description, filling out a form, or clicking a series of links to review a list of topics and subtopics (Topic Directory). See Figure A-21. Without search engines, using the Internet would be like trying to find a book in the Library of Congress by wandering around the stacks. To discover exactly how to use a particular search engine effectively, refer to its Help pages.

FIGURE A-20: Internet Explorer browser

```
<HTML>
<HEAD><TITLE>From the North Woods</TITLE></HEAD>
<BODY>
<CENTER>
<FONT SIZE=+3>North Woods Update</FONT><BR>
<B>Brought to you by Frank Parker, Forestry Student</B>
</CENTER>
<BR>
<OL>
<LI> Never place your tongue on frozen  metal.
<LI> Always take your boots off in the sauna.
</OL>
<HR>
<IMG SRC="Chevy.jpg
Today's Feature:
<A HREF = "parker/e
Chevrolet </A>
</BODY>
<HTML>
```

An HTML document is basically a running string of text with embedded HTML tags, such as this tag that instructs the browser to center a line of text

When the browser displays the Web page, the specified text is centered

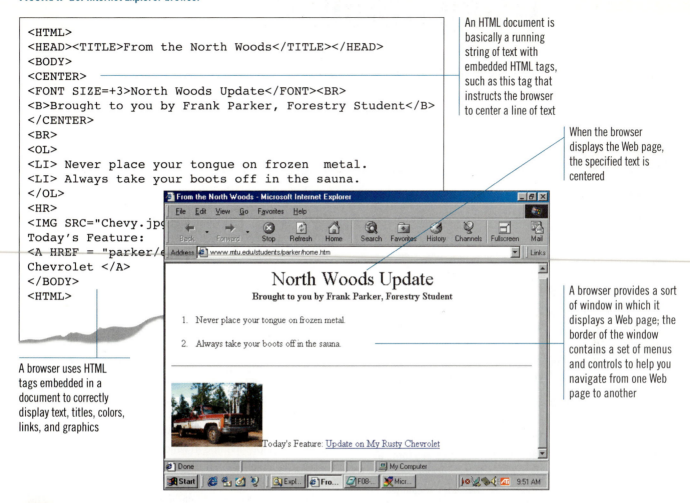

A browser provides a sort of window in which it displays a Web page; the border of the window contains a set of menus and controls to help you navigate from one Web page to another

A browser uses HTML tags embedded in a document to correctly display text, titles, colors, links, and graphics

FIGURE A-21: Search engines

The search engine displays the total number of relevant pages

Underlined links make it easy to quickly connect to any of the Web pages in the list

The search was for railroad cars

Search results are typically arranged in order of relevancy, so that the most promising Web pages should be at the top of the list; a brief description of the page helps you determine whether you want to view it

Understanding e-mail basics

The Internet really took off when people discovered electronic mail. Billions of e-mail messages speed over the Internet each year. E-mail can refer to a single electronic message or to the entire system of computers and software that transmits, receives, and stores e-mail messages. Any person with an e-mail account can send and receive e-mail.

DETAILS

- An **e-mail account** provides the rights to a storage area, or mailbox, supplied by an e-mail provider, such as an ISP. Each mailbox has a unique address that typically consists of a user ID, an @ symbol, and the name of the computer that maintains the mailbox. For example, suppose that a university student named Dee Greene has an electronic mailbox on a computer called rutgers.edu. If her user ID is "dee_greene," her **e-mail address** would be dee_greene@rutgers.edu.

- An **e-mail message** is a document that is composed on a computer and transmitted in digital or "electronic" form to another computer. Every message includes a message header and the body of the message, usually displayed in a form, as shown in Figure A-22. Basic e-mail activities include writing, reading, replying to, and forwarding messages. Messages can be printed, kept for later reference, or deleted.

- Any file that travels with an e-mail message is called an **e-mail attachment**.

- After you receive an e-mail message, you can use the Forward feature to pass it on to other people. When you initiate the forward process, the original e-mail message is copied into a new message window, complete with the address of the original sender. You can then enter the address of the person to whom you are forwarding the message. You can also add a note about why you are passing the message along.

- By default, e-mail messages are stored in a simple format called ASCII text. No fancy formatting is allowed, no variation in font type or color, no underlining or boldface, and of course, no pictures or sounds.

- Today, most e-mail software allows you to create e-mail messages in HTML format. Why use HTML format for your mail? HTML messages can contain fancy formatting. The only limitation is that your e-mail recipients must have HTML-compliant e-mail software; otherwise, your message will be delivered as plain old ASCII text.

- Although e-mail is delivered quickly, it is important to use proper netiquette when composing a message. **Netiquette** (Internet etiquette) is a series of customs or guidelines for maintaining civilized and effective communications in online discussions and e-mail exchanges. For example, typing in all caps, such as "WHAT DID YOU DO?" is considered shouting and rude.

- An **e-mail system** is the equipment and software that carries and manipulates e-mail messages. It includes computers and software called **e-mail servers** that sort, store, and route mail.

- E-mail is based on **store-and-forward technology**, a communications method in which data that cannot be sent directly to its destination will be temporarily stored until transmission is possible. This technology allows e-mail messages to be routed to a server and held until they are forwarded to the next server or to a personal mailbox.

- Three types of e-mail systems are widely used today: POP, IMAP, and Web-based mail. **POP** (**Post Office Protocol**) temporarily stores new messages in your mailbox on an e-mail server. See Figure A-23. Most people who use POP have obtained an e-mail account from an ISP. Such an account provides a mailbox on the ISP's **POP server**, which is a computer that stores your incoming messages until they can be transferred to your hard disk. Using POP requires e-mail client software. This software, which is installed on your computer, provides an Inbox and an Outbox. When you ask the e-mail server to deliver your mail, all of the messages stored in your mailbox on the POP server are transferred to your computer, stored on your computer's disk drive, and listed as new mail in your Inbox. You can then disconnect from the Internet, if you like, and read the new mail at your leisure.

  IMAP (**Internet Messaging Access Protocol**) is similar to POP, except that you have the option of downloading your mail or leaving it on the server. **Web-based e-mail**, the most commonly used, keeps your mail at a Web site rather than transferring it to your computer. Examples of Web-based e-mail are Yahoo mail and Hotmail. Before you can use Web-based e-mail, you'll need an e-mail account with a Web-based e-mail provider.

FIGURE A-22: Composing an e-mail message

When you compose an e-mail message, you'll begin by entering the address of one or more recipients and the subject of the message

You can also specify one or more files to attach to the message

The body of the e-mail message contains the message itself

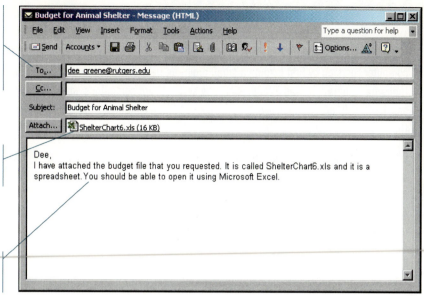

When the message is sent, your e-mail software adds the date and your e-mail address to identify you as the sender

FIGURE A-23: Incoming and outgoing mail

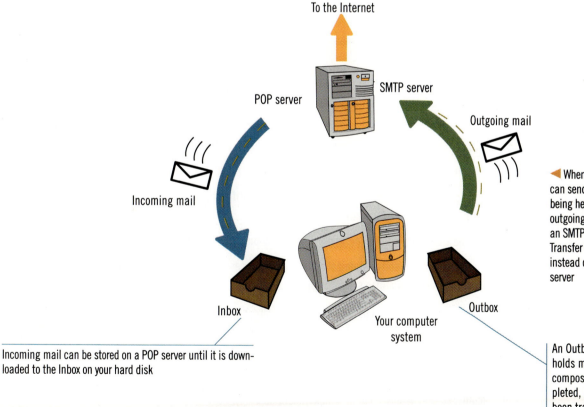

When you go online, you can send all the mail that's being held in your Outbox; outgoing mail is routed by an SMTP (Simple Mail Transfer Protocol) server, instead of by the POP server

Incoming mail can be stored on a POP server until it is downloaded to the Inbox on your hard disk

An Outbox temporarily holds mesages that you composed and completed, but that haven't been transmitted over the Internet

The Boot Process

The sequence of events that occurs between the time that you turn on a computer and the time that it becomes ready to accept commands is referred to as the **boot process** or "booting" your computer. Your computer boots up by first loading a small program, called a "bootstrap" program, into memory, then it uses that small program to load a large operating system. Your computer's small bootstrap program is built into special ROM (read-only memory) circuitry housed in the computer's system unit. When you turn on a computer, the ROM circuitry receives power and it begins the boot process.

What is the purpose of the boot process? The boot process involves a lot of flashing lights, whirring noises, and beeping as your computer performs a set of diagnostic tests called the **power-on self-test (POST)**. The good news is that these tests can warn you if certain crucial components of your computer system are out of whack. The bad news is that these tests cannot warn you of impending failures. Also, problems identified during the boot process usually must be fixed before you can start a computing session.

The boot process serves an additional purpose—loading the operating system from the hard disk and into memory so that it can help the computer carry out basic operations. Without the operating system, a computer's CPU is basically unable to communicate with any input, output, or storage devices. It can't display information, accept commands, store data, or run any application software. Therefore, loading the operating system is a crucial step in the boot process.

Most of a computer's memory is "volatile" random access memory (RAM), which cannot hold any data when the power is off. Although a copy of the operating system is housed in RAM while the computer is in operation, this copy is erased as soon as the power is turned off. Given the volatility of RAM, computer designers decided to store the operating system on a computer's hard disk. During the boot process, a copy of the operating system is copied into RAM, where it can be accessed quickly whenever the computer needs to carry out an input, output, or storage operation. The operating system remains in RAM until the computer is turned off.

Six major events happen during the boot process:

1. Power up. When you turn on the power switch, the power light is illuminated, and power is distributed to the computer circuitry.

2. Start boot program. The microprocessor begins to execute the bootstrap program that is stored in ROM.

3. Power-on self-test. The computer performs diagnostic tests of several crucial system components.

4. Identify peripheral devices. The operating system identifies the peripheral devices that are connected to a computer and checks their settings.

5. Load operating system. The operating system is copied from the hard disk to RAM.

6. Check configuration and customization. The microprocessor reads configuration data and executes any customized startup routines specified by the user.

What if I turn on a computer and nothing happens? The first step in the boot process is the power-up stage. Power from a wall outlet or battery activates a small power light. If the power light does not come on when you flip the "on" switch, you should check all the power connections and be sure everything is plugged in properly.

What kinds of problems are likely to show up during the power-on self-test? The POST checks your computer's main circuitry, screen display, memory, and keyboard. It can identify when one of these devices has failed, but it cannot identify intermittent problems or impending failures. The POST notifies you of a hardware problem by displaying an error message on the screen or by emitting a series of beeps. A **beep code** provides your computer with a way to signal a problem, even if the screen is not functioning. You can check the documentation or Web site for your computer to find the specific meaning of numeric error codes. The printed or online reference manual for a computer usually explains the meaning of each beep code.

Should I try to fix these problems myself? If a computer displays error messages, emits beep codes, or seems to freeze up during the boot process, you can take some simple steps that might fix it. First, turn the computer off, check all the cables, wait five seconds, then try to start the computer again. Refer to Figure A-24 for a power-up checklist. If you still encounter a boot error after trying to restart the computer several times, contact a technical support person.

What's the long list of stuff that appears on my screen during the boot process? After the POST, the bootstrap program tries to identify all of the devices that are connected to the computer. The settings for each device appear on the screen, creating a list of rather esoteric information.

On occasion, a device gets skipped or misidentified during the boot process. An error message is not produced, but the device doesn't seem to work properly. To resolve this problem, shut down the computer and reboot it. If a device is causing persistent problems, you may need to check the manufacturer's Web site to see if a new software patch will improve its operation.

Do computers have trouble loading the operating system or applying customization settings? Problems during the last stages of the boot process are rare, except when a disk has been inadvertently left in the floppy disk drive. Before computers were equipped with hard disk drives, floppy disks were used to store the operating system and application software. As a legacy from these early machines, today's computers first check the floppy disk drive for a disk containing the operating system. If it doesn't find a disk in the drive, it proceeds to look for the operating system on the hard disk. However, if a floppy disk happens to be left in drive A, the computer will assume that you want to boot from it and will look for the operating system on that disk. The error message "Non-system disk or disk error" is the clue to this problem. Remove the floppy disk and press any key to resume the boot process.

How do I know when the boot process is finished? The boot process is complete when the computer is ready to accept your commands. Usually, the computer displays an operating system prompt or main screen. The Windows operating system, for example, displays the Windows desktop when the boot process is complete.

If Windows cannot complete the boot process, you are likely to see a menu that contains an option for Safe Mode. **Safe Mode** is a limited version of Windows that allows you to use your mouse, monitor, and keyboard, but not other peripheral devices. This mode is designed for troubleshooting, not for real computing tasks. If your computer enters Safe Mode at the end of the boot process, you should use the Shut Down command on the Start menu to shut down and turn off your computer properly. You can then turn on your computer again. It should complete the boot process in regular Windows mode. If your computer enters Safe Mode again, consult a technician.

FIGURE A-24: Power-Up checklist

> ☑ **Make sure that the power cable is plugged into the wall and into the back of the computer.**
>
> ☑ **Check batteries if you're using a notebook computer.**
>
> ☑ **Try to plug your notebook into a wall outlet.**
>
> ☑ **Make sure that the wall outlet is supplying power (plug a lamp into it and make sure that you can turn it on).**
>
> ☑ **If the computer is plugged into a surge strip, extension cord, or uninterruptible power supply, make sure that it is turned on and functioning correctly.**
>
> ☑ **Can you hear the fan in your desktop computer? If not, the computer's power supply mechanism might have failed.**

When you drop an envelope in the corner mailbox, you probably expect it to arrive at its destination unopened, and with its contents kept safe from prying eyes. When you make a phone call, you might assume that your conversation will proceed unmonitored by wiretaps or other listening devices. Can you also expect an e-mail message to be read only by the person to whom it is addressed?

In the U.S., The Electronic Communications Privacy Act of 2000 prohibits the use of intercepted e-mail as evidence unless a judge approved a search warrant. That doesn't mean, however, that the government can't or isn't reading your mail. The FBI developed a technology called Carnivore that scans through messages entering and leaving an ISP's e-mail system and looks for e-mail associated with a person who is under investigation. Privacy advocates are concerned because Carnivore scans all of the messages that pass through an ISP, not just those messages destined for a particular individual.

Law enforcement agencies are required to obtain a search warrant before intercepting e-mail. No such restriction, however, exists for employers who want to monitor employee e-mail. According to the American Management Association, 27 percent of U.S. businesses monitor employee e-mail. But this intentional eavesdropping is only one way in which the contents of your e-mail messages might become public. The recipient of your e-mail can forward it to one or more people, people you never intended to read it. Your e-mail messages can pop up on a technician's screen in the course of system maintenance or repairs. Also, keep in mind that e-mail messages, including those that you delete from your own PC, can be stored on backups of your ISP's e-mail server.

The United States Omnibus Crime Control and Safe Streets Act of 1968 and the Electronic Communications Privacy Act of 1986 prohibit public and private employers from engaging in surreptitious surveillance of employee activity through the use of electronic devices. However, two exceptions to these privacy statutes exist. The first exception permits an employer to monitor e-mail if one party to the communication consents to the monitoring. An employer must inform employees of this policy before undertaking any monitoring. The second exception permits employers to monitor their employees' e-mail if a legitimate business need exists and the monitoring takes place within the business-owned e-mail system.

Employees have not been successful in defending their rights to e-mail privacy. For example, in 1996, a Pillsbury employee was fired from his job for making unprofessional comments in an e-mail to his supervisor. Like employees of a business, students who use a school's e-mail system cannot be assured of e-mail privacy. When a CalTech student was accused of sexually harassing a female student by sending lewd e-mail to her and her boyfriend, investigators retrieved all of the student's e-mail from the archives of the e-mail server. The student was expelled from the university even though he claimed that the e-mail had been "spoofed" to make it look as though he had sent it, when it had actually been sent by someone else.

Why would an employer want to know the contents of employee e-mail? Why would a school be concerned with the correspondence of its students? An organization that owns an e-mail system can be held responsible for the consequences of actions related to the contents of e-mail messages on that system.

Many schools and businesses have established e-mail privacy policies that explain the conditions under which you can and cannot expect your e-mail to remain private. Court decisions, however, seem to support the notion that because an organization owns and operates its e-mail system, the organization owns the e-mail messages that are generated on its system. The individual who authors an e-mail message does not own it and therefore has no rights related to it. A company can therefore legally monitor your e-mail.

You should use your e-mail account with the expectation that some of your mail will be read from time to time. Think of your e-mail as a postcard, rather than a letter, and save your controversial comments for face-to-face conversations.

▼ INTERACTIVE QUESTIONS

○ Yes ○ No ○ Not sure
1. Do you think that most people believe that their e-mail is private?

○ Yes ○ No ○ Not sure
2. Do you agree with CalTech's decision to expel the student who was accused of sending harassing e-mail to another student?

○ Yes ○ No ○ Not sure
3. Should the laws be changed to make it illegal for employers to monitor e-mail without court approval?

○ Yes ○ No ○ Not sure
4. Would you have different privacy expectations regarding an e-mail account at your place of work as opposed to an account that you purchase from an e-mail service provider?

▼ EXPAND THE IDEAS

1. How private do you think your e-mail is? Discuss in class. Support your ideas with concrete examples.

2. Would you have different privacy expectations regarding an e-mail account at your place of work than you would for an account that you purchase from an e-mail service provider? Write a short paper in which you present your opinions.

3. Do you agree that a college should be able to expel a student accused of sending harassing e-mail to another student? Research cases where this might have occurred. Write a short paper that details at least one recent case. Include at least one paragraph presenting your view on the issue: whether or not you agree with the outcome of the case. Be sure to include your sources.

End of Unit Exercises

▼ KEY TERMS

Always-on connection
Application software
Beep code
Binary number system
Bit
Bookmarks
Boot process
Browser
Byte
Cable modem
Cable modem service
CD-ROM drive
CD-writer
Central processing unit (CPU)
Chat group
Computer
Computer file
Computer network
Computer program
Computer system
Data
Data file
Desktop computer
Dial-up connection
Downloading
DSL
DSS
DVD drive
E-commerce
E-mail

E-mail account
E-mail address
E-mail attachment
E-mail message
E-mail servers
E-mail system
Executable file
Favorites
File
Filename
Filename extension
Floppy disk drive
Handheld computer
Hard disk drive
Hardware
History list
Home page
HTML
HTML tags
HTTP
Hypertext
IMAP
Information
Input
Input device
Instant messaging
Internet
Internet backbone
Internet telephony
IP address

ISDN
ISP
Keyboard
Keyword
LAN (local area network)
Links
Macs
Mailing list server
Mainframe computer
Memory
Microcomputer
Microprocessor
Modem
Monitor
Mouse
Netiquette
Network card
Newsgroups
Notebook computer
Online
Operating system
Output
Output device
Password
PDA
Peripheral device
Personal computer (PC)
Platform
POP
POP server

Power-on self-test (POST)
Printer
Processing
Router
Safe Mode
Search engine
Server
Server software
Software
Sound card
Speakers
Storage
Store-and-forward technology
Stored program
Supercomputer
System software
System unit
TCP/IP
Uploading
URL
Usenet
User ID
Videogame console
Voice band modem
Web
Web pages
Web servers
Web site
Web-based e-mail
Workstation

▼ UNIT REVIEW

1. Make sure that you can define each of the key terms in this unit in your own words. Select 10 of the terms with which you are unfamiliar and write a sentence for each of them.

2. Explain the basic functions of a computer: inputting, processing, storing, and outputting. Explain why the stored program concept is important to all of this.

3. Identify and describe each of the components of a basic personal computer system.

4. Describe the difference between an operating system and application software.

5. Define computer platform. Then discuss what makes two computer platforms compatible or incompatible.

6. List at least five resources that are provided by the Internet and identify those that are most popular.

7. Make a list of the ways to connect to the Internet presented in this unit and specify characteristics of each.

8. Describe the components of a URL and of an e-mail address.

9. Make a list of the rules that you should follow when typing a URL.

10. Define "browser," then describe how a browser helps you navigate the Web.

▼ FILL IN THE BEST ANSWER

1. The basic functions of a computer are to accept _____, process data, store data, and produce output.

2. A computer processes data in the _____ processing unit.

3. The idea of a(n) _____ program means that instructions for a computing task can be loaded into a computer's memory.

4. The _____ unit is the case that holds the main circuit boards, microprocessor, power supply, and storage devices for a personal computer system.

5. A device that is an integral part of a computer but that can be added to a computer is called a(n) _____ device.

6. Executable files usually have a(n) _____ extension.

7. A(n) _____ system is the software that acts as the master controller for all of the activities that take place within a computer system.

8. The main routes of the Internet are referred to as the Internet _____.

9. Communication between all of the different devices on the Internet is made possible by _____ /IP.

10. Most of the "stuff" that's accessible on the Internet is stored on _____ that are maintained by various businesses and organizations.

11. A dial-up connection requires a device called a(n) _____ band modem.

12. To use a cable Internet connection you need a cable modem and a(n) _____.

13. A cable modem provides an always _____ connection to the Internet.

14. The process of entering a user ID and password is referred to as _____.

15. Every Web page has a unique address called a(n) _____.

16. A browser assembles a Web page on your computer screen according to the specifications contained in the _____ tags.

17. Whenever you start your browser, it displays your _____ page.

18. A(n) _____ fetches and displays Web pages.

19. Store-and-forward technology stores messages on an e-mail _____ until they are forwarded to an individual's computer.

20. For many e-mail systems, a(n) _____ server handles incoming mail, and a(n) _____ server handles outgoing mail.

▼ PRACTICE TESTS

When you use the Interactive CD, you can take Practice Tests that consists of 10 multiple-choice, true/false, and fill-in-the blank questions. The questions are selected at random from a large test bank, so each time you take a test, you'll receive a different set of questions. Your tests are scored immediately, and you can print study guides to determine which questions you answered incorrectly. If you are using a Tracking Disk, insert it in the floppy disk drive to save your test scores.

▼ INDEPENDENT CHALLENGE 1

When discussing computers and computer concepts it is important to use proper terminology. Unit A presented you with many computer terms that describe computer equipment. If you would like to explore any of the terms in more detail, there are online dictionaries that can help you expand your understanding of these terms.

1. For this independent challenge, write a one-page paper that describes the computer that you use most frequently.

2. Refer to the Key Terms used in this unit and use terms from this unit to describe your computer components and the functions they perform.

3. In your final draft, underline each Key Term that you used in your paper. Follow your professor's instructions for submitting your paper as an e-mail attachment or as a printed document.

▼ INDEPENDENT CHALLENGE 2

Suppose that producers for a television game show ask you to help them create a set of computer-related questions for the next show. You will compose a set of 10 questions based on the information provided in Unit A. Each question should be in multiple-choice format with four possible answers.

1. Write 10 questions: two very simple questions, five questions of medium difficulty, and three difficult questions. Each question should be on an index card.

2. For each question, indicate the correct answer on the back of each card and the page in this book on which the answer can be found.

3. Gather in small groups and take turns asking each other the questions.

▼ INDEPENDENT CHALLENGE 3

The Issue section of this unit focused on how much (or how little) privacy you can expect when using an e-mail account. For this independent challenge, you will write a two- to five-page paper about e-mail privacy based on information that you gather from the Internet.

1. To begin this Independent Challenge, consult the E-mail Privacy InfoWeb and link to the recommended Web pages to get an in-depth overview of the issue.

2. Determine the viewpoint that you will present in your paper about e-mail privacy. You might, for example, decide to present the viewpoint of a student who believes that e-mail should be afforded the same privacy rights as a sealed letter. Or you might present the viewpoint of an employer who wants to explain why your business believes that it is necessary to monitor employee e-mail. Whatever viewpoint you decide to present, make sure that you can back it up with facts and references to authoritative articles and Web pages.

3. Place citations to your research (include the author's name, article title, date of publication, and URL) at the end of your paper as endnotes, on each page as footnotes, or along with the appropriate paragraphs using parentheses. Follow your professor's instructions for submitting your paper via e-mail or as a printed document.

▼ INDEPENDENT CHALLENGE 4

A new ISP is getting ready to open in your area, and the president of the company asks you to design a print ad. Your ad must communicate all pertinent information about the ISP.

1. Before starting on the design, use your favorite search engine to find out more about ISPs in your area. Gather information to use in your ad, such as the type of services offered (dial-up, cable modem, etc.), the speed of service, the geographical coverage, price, and special or proprietary services.

2. Make up a name for your ISP. Design a print ad for the company using a computer or freehand tools. Submit your ad design along with a short written summary that describes how this ad reflects the ISP and the services it offers.

▼ LAB: MAKING A DIAL-UP CONNECTION

1. Start the interactive part of the lab. Insert your Tracking Disk if you want to save your QuickCheck results. Perform each of the lab steps as directed and answer all of the lab QuickCheck questions. When you exit the lab, your answers are automatically graded and your results are displayed.

2. Make a list of at least five ISPs that are available in your area. If possible, include both local and national ISPs in your list.

3. Suppose that you intend to create manually a dial-up connection icon for AT&T WorldNet. What's missing from the following information?

   - AT&T's dial-in telephone number and country

   - AT&T's IP address

   - Your password

4. Provide the following information about the Internet connection that you typically use: Name of ISP, type of Internet connection (dial-up, DSL, cable modem, ISDN, DSS, school network, or business network), connection speed, and monthly fee. (If you don't currently have Internet access, describe the type of connection that you would like to use.)

▼ LAB: BROWSING AND SEARCHING

1. Start the interactive part of the lab. Insert your Tracking Disk if you want to save your QuickCheck results. Perform each of the lab steps as directed and answer all of the lab QuickCheck questions. When you exit the lab, your answers are automatically graded and your results are displayed.

2. Make a note of the brand and location of the computer that you're using to complete these lab assignments.

3. Examine the Favorites or Bookmarks list. How many pages are included in this list? Link to three of the pages, and provide their URLs and a brief description of their contents.

4. Suppose that you want to make your own trail mix, but you need a recipe. In three different search engines, enter the query: "trail mix" AND "recipe". (Refer to the Search Engines InfoWeb for a list of popular search engines.) Describe the similarities and differences in the results lists produced by each of the three search engines.

5. Conduct a second search to find the blue book price for a Taurus. Use the search engine of your choice to determine whether the query: "Blue book price" Taurus -"used car" provides the same results as the query: Blue book price Taurus -"used car".

   Make sure that you enter each query exactly as specified, including the quotation marks and no space after the hyphen. Explain the similarities and differences in the query results.

▼ LAB: USING E-MAIL

1. Start the interactive part of the lab. Insert your Tracking Disk if you want to save your QuickCheck results. Perform each of the lab steps as directed and answer all of the lab QuickCheck questions. When you exit the lab, your answers are automatically graded and your results are displayed.

2. Using the e-mail software of your choice, send an e-mail message to kendra_hill@cciw.com. In the body of your message, ask for a copy of the "Most Influential Person Survey."

3. Wait a few minutes after sending the message to Kendra Hill, then check your mail. You should receive a survey from Kendra Hill. Reply to this message and Cc: your instructor. In your reply, answer each question in the survey, interspersing your answers with the original text. Send the reply, following the procedures required by your e-mail provider.

4. Examine the address book offered by your e-mail software. Describe how much information (name, home address, business address, birth date, telephone number, fax number, etc.) you can enter for each person. In your opinion, would this address book be suitable for a businessperson to use for storing contact information? Why or why not? Send the descriptions and answers to these questions to your instructor in an e-mail.

▼ VISUAL WORKSHOP

The digital divide is defined as the difference in rates of access to computers and the Internet among different demographic groups. With the explosion of the Internet and the technology that drives the information age, forward-thinking social reformers recognized early on the potential for a divide between the "haves" and the "have nots." Not-for-profit organizations, concerned with the impact of the digital divide, designed studies to help them analyze the causes and effects of this phenomenon. These studies have been conducted for the past few decades.

FIGURE A-25

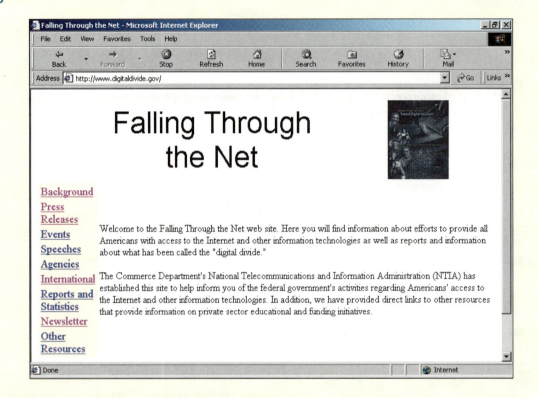

1. Is there a solution to the digital divide? Connect to the Internet and use your favorite search engine to search on the key phrase "digital divide." Among the sites you should find is the Digital Divide Web site at www.digitaldivide.gov, which is shown in Figure A-25. This site includes links to articles and research studies that address the digital divide. Review the findings for two studies or articles. Write a short paper summarizing these studies or articles. In your conclusion, comment on how you feel the digital divide affects our society and what we as a society should do about it, if anything.

2. Could you live without computers? Computers are ubiquitous; beyond the obvious applications, such as using your word processor to write a report, you come in contact with them during the course of your day in simple activities such as shopping in a supermarket or getting cash from your bank's ATM machine. Create a log to track your daily activities that involve computers. Keep the log for one week. At the end of the week, write a summary of any surprises or insights you have as to how computers affect your life.

3. Is there a digital divide in your community? Create a survey that will determine Internet access and computer ownership among people that you know. The survey should consist of 5-10 questions. You want to find out, within a chosen sector, who owns a computer, if they own more than one, what they use the computer(s) for, if they have Internet access, and if they access the Internet from their home or elsewhere. Be sure to survey at least 20 people. The survey should be anonymous but include demographic information. Compile the results of your survey into a chart and write a short summary explaining your findings.

UNIT B

Computer Hardware

OBJECTIVES

Introduce storage technology
Compare storage technologies
Compare storage media and devices
Explore floppy disk technology
Explore hard disk technology
Explore CD/DVD technology
Understand expansion slots, cards, ports, and cables
Compare display devices
Compare printers
Examine keyboards
Explore peripheral devices
Tech Talk: The Windows Registry

This unit discusses computer hardware, with several lessons focusing on the various technologies that enable a computer to store and retrieve data and programs. Storage technology defines how computers store data and program files. You will learn the difference between magnetic storage and optical storage. You will learn about the components of a computer's expansion bus, including various types of expansion slots and cables and how to use the expansion bus to add devices to a computer. You will learn about input and output devices such as popular printer and display technologies, and you will get an in-depth look at the keyboard. You will learn about a variety of peripheral devices including how to install them, and how the Windows Registry tracks installed devices.

Introducing storage technology

The basic functions of a computer are to accept input, process data, store data, and produce output. When you want to store data permanently, you save the data to a storage device. Computers can be configured with a variety of storage devices, such as a floppy disk drive, hard disk drive, CD drive, or DVD drive. While one storage technology might provide extremely fast access to data, it might also be susceptible to problems that could wipe out all of your data. A different storage technology might be more dependable, but it might also have the disadvantage of providing relatively slow access to data. Understanding the strengths and weaknesses of each storage technology will enable you to use each device appropriately and with maximum effectiveness.

LAB
WORKING WITH
BINARY NUMBERS **DETAILS**

- The term **storage technology** refers to data storage systems. Each data storage system has two main components: a storage medium and a storage device. A **storage medium** (storage media is the plural) is the disk, tape, CD, DVD, paper, or other substance that holds data. See Figure B-1. A **storage device** is the mechanical apparatus that records and retrieves data from a storage medium. Storage devices include floppy disk drives, Zip drives, hard disk drives, tape drives, CD drives, and DVD drives. See Figure B-2.

- Data is copied from a storage device into RAM, where it waits to be processed. **RAM** (random access memory) is a temporary holding area for the operating system, the file you are working on (such as a word processing document), and application program instructions. RAM is not permanent storage, in fact RAM is very **volatile**, which means data in RAM can be lost easily. That is why it is important to store data permanently.

- RAM is important to the storage process. You can think of RAM as the connection between your computer's storage devices and their storage media. After data is processed in RAM, it is usually copied to a storage medium for more permanent safekeeping.

- The process of storing data is often referred to as "writing data" or "saving a file" because the storage device writes the data on the storage medium to save it for later use. The process of retrieving data is often referred to as "reading data," "loading data," or "opening a file."

- A computer works with data that has been coded and can be represented by 1s and 0s. When data is stored, these 1s and 0s must be converted into a signal or mark that's fairly permanent but that can be changed when necessary. The data is not literally written as "1" or "0." Instead, the 1s and 0s must be transformed to change the surface of a storage medium. Exactly how this transformation happens depends on the storage technology. For example, floppy disks store data in a different way than CD-ROMs.

The science of data representation

Letters, numbers, musical notes, and pictures don't pass from the keyboard through the circuitry of a computer and then jump out onto the screen or printer. So how is it that a computer can work with documents, photos, videos, and sound recordings? The answer to that question is what data representation and digital electronics are all about. Data representation is based on the binary number system, which uses two numbers, 1 and 0, to represent all data. Data representation makes it possible to convert letters, sounds, and images into electrical signals. Digital electronics makes it possible for a computer to manipulate simple "on" and "off" signals, which are represented by the 0s and 1s, to perform complex tasks.

FIGURE B-1: Examples of storage media

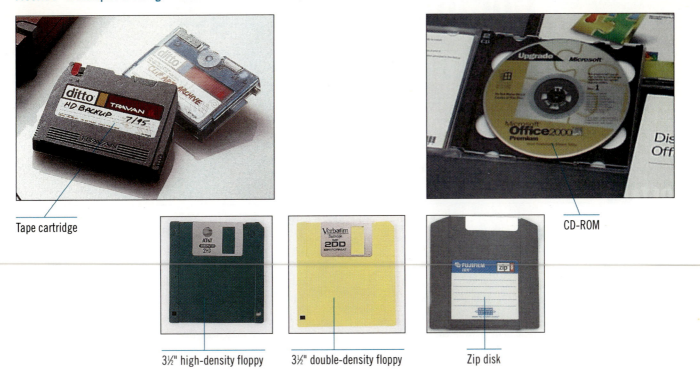

Tape cartridge

CD-ROM

3½" high-density floppy

3½" double-density floppy

Zip disk

FIGURE B-2: Examples of storage devices in a system unit

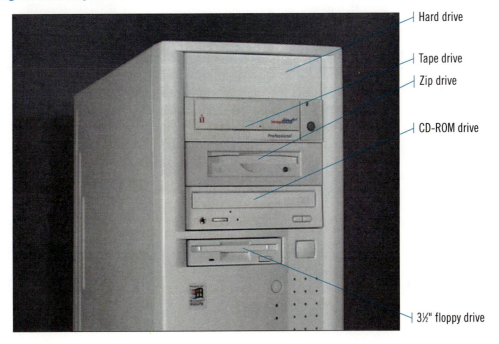

Hard drive

Tape drive

Zip drive

CD-ROM drive

3½" floppy drive

Comparing storage technologies

Currently there are two main categories of storage technologies: magnetic and optical. Each storage technology has advantages and disadvantages. To compare storage devices, you need to understand how each one works.

DETAILS

- Hard disk, floppy disk, Zip disk, and tape storage technologies can be classified as **magnetic storage**, which stores data by magnetizing microscopic particles on the disk or tape surface. The particles retain their magnetic orientation until that orientation is changed, thereby making disks and tape fairly permanent but modifiable storage media. A **read-write head** mechanism in the disk drive reads and writes the magnetized particles that represent data. Figure B-3 shows how a computer stores data on magnetic media.

- Before data is stored, the particles on the surface of the disk are scattered in random patterns. The disk drive's read-write head magnetizes the particles and orients them in either a positive or negative direction. These patterns of magnetized particles are interpreted as the 0s and 1s that represent data. Data stored magnetically can be changed or deleted simply by altering the magnetic orientation of the appropriate particles on the disk surface. This feature of magnetic storage provides flexibility for editing data and reusing areas of a storage medium containing data that is no longer needed.

- Magnetic media is not very durable. Data stored on magnetic media such as floppy disks can be altered by magnetic fields, dust, mold, smoke particles, heat, and mechanical problems with a storage device. For example, a magnet should never be placed on or near a floppy disk because it will destroy the magnetic particles on the disk. Magnetic media gradually lose their magnetic charge, which results in lost data. Some experts estimate that the reliable life span of data stored on magnetic media is about three years.

- CD and DVD storage technologies make use of **optical storage**, which stores data as microscopic light and dark spots on the disk surface. The dark spots are called **pits**, and it is possible to see the data stored on a CD or DVD storage medium using a high-powered microscope. See Figure B-4. The lighter, non-pitted surface areas of the disk are called **lands**. This type of storage is called optical storage because a low-power laser light is used to read the data stored on an optical disk. When the beam strikes a pit, no light is reflected. When the laser strikes a reflective surface, light bounces back into the read head. The patterns of light and dark between pits and lands are interpreted as the 1s and 0s that represent data. Data recorded on optical media is generally considered to be less susceptible to environmental damage than data recorded on magnetic media. The useful life of a CD-ROM disk is estimated to exceed 500 years.

FIGURE B-3: Magnetic storage

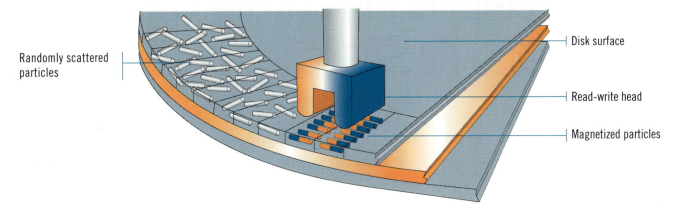

Randomly scattered particles

Disk surface

Read-write head

Magnetized particles

FIGURE B-4: Optical storage

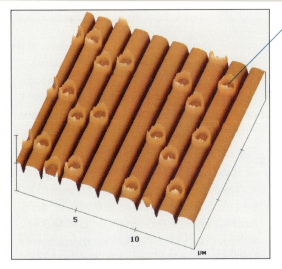

The pits on an optical storage disk as seen through an electron microscope; each pit is 1 micron in diameter

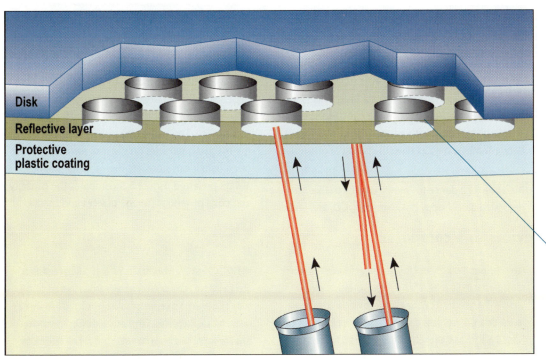

Disk

Reflective layer

Protective plastic coating

When a CD-ROM disk is manufactured, a laser burns pits into a reflective surface; these pits become dark non-reflective areas on the disk

Comparing storage media and devices

When trying to determine the best storage media for a job, it is useful to apply four criteria: versatility, durability, speed, and capacity. Versatility is the ability of a device and its media to work in more than one way. After storing data using this storage technology, can that data be changed? Durability determines the ability of the device or media to last. How long will it work? How long will the data be accessible? Speed is the time it takes to retrieve or access the data, a factor that is very important in determining how efficiently you work. Finally, capacity is the amount of data each technology can store.

DETAILS

- **Versatility.** Some storage devices can access data from only one type of medium. More versatile devices can access data from several different media. A floppy disk drive, for example, can access only floppy disks, but a DVD drive can access data DVDs, DVD movies, audio CDs, data CDs, and CD-Rs.

- **Durability.** Most storage technologies are susceptible to damage from mishandling or other environmental factors, such as heat and moisture. Some technologies are less susceptible than others. Optical technologies tend to be less susceptible than magnetic technologies to damage that could cause data loss.

- **Speed.** Not surprisingly, fast storage devices are preferred over slower ones. **Access time** is the average time it takes a computer to locate data on the storage medium and read it. Access time for a personal computer storage device, such as a disk drive, is measured in **milliseconds** (thousandths of a second). Lower numbers indicate faster access times. For example, a drive with a 6 ms access time is faster than a drive with an access time of 11 ms. Random-access devices have the fastest access times.

  Random access (also called "direct access") is the ability of a device to "jump" directly to the requested data. Floppy disk, hard disk, CD, and DVD

drives are random-access devices. A tape drive, on the other hand, must use slower **sequential access**, which reads through the data from the beginning of the tape. The advantage of random access becomes clear when you consider how much faster and easier it is to locate a song on a CD (random access) than on a cassette tape (sequential access).

  Data transfer rate is the amount of data that a storage device can move from the storage medium to the computer per second. Higher numbers indicate faster transfer rates. For example, a CD-ROM drive with a 600 KBps (kilobytes per second) data transfer rate is faster than one with a 300 KBps transfer rate.

- **Capacity. Storage capacity** is the maximum amount of data that can be stored on a storage medium, measured in kilobytes (KB), megabytes (MB), gigabytes (GB), or terabytes (TB). The amount of data that a disk stores—its capacity—depends on its density. **Disk density** refers to the closeness and size of the magnetic particles on the disk surface. The higher the disk density, the smaller the magnetic particles on the disk surface, and the more data it can store. Higher capacity is almost always preferred. Figure B-5 compares the capacity and costs of various storage devices and media.

FYI

Storage media is divided into tracks and then into sectors to create electronic "addressable bins" in which to store data.

Adding storage devices to a computer

Computer users frequently want to upgrade their hard drive to gain capacity or to add CD or DVD drives to make their system more versatile. The system unit case for a desktop computer contains several storage device "parking spaces" called **drive bays**. See Figure B-6. If you have an empty bay that is the right type and size, you can add a storage device. Bays come in two widths—5 ¼"

and 3½". CD and DVD drives require 5¼" bays; a floppy disk drive fits in a 3½" bay. Some drive bays provide access from the outside of the system unit, a necessity for a storage device with removable media, such as floppy disks, CDs, tapes, and DVDs. Internal drive bays are located deep inside the system unit and are designed for hard disk drives, which don't use removable storage media.

FIGURE B-5: Storage capacities of backup media

	DEVICE COST	MEDIA COST	CAPACITY	COMMENTS
Floppy disk	$40-99	30¢	1.44 MB	Low capacity means that you have to wait around to feed in disks
Zip disk	$139 (average)	$11.00	250 MB	Holds much more than a floppy but a backup still requires multiple disks
Fixed hard disk	$150 (average)	-NA-	40 GB (average)	Fast and convenient, but risky because it is susceptible to damage or theft of your computer
Removable hard disk	$149 (average)	$30.00	2.2 GB (average)	Fast, limited capacity, but disks can be removed and locked in a secure location
CD-R	$130-200	50¢	680 MB	Limited capacity, can't be reused, long shelf life
CD-RW	$130-200	$1.50	680 MB	Limited capacity, reusable, very slow
Writable DVD	$500 (average)	$25.00	5.2 GB	Good capacity, not yet standardized
Tape	$199 (average)	$50.00	30 GB (average)	Great capacity, reasonable media cost, convenient—you can let backups run overnight

 FIGURE B-6: Drive bays

An empty 5¼" drive bay located on the front of a desktop computer

An empty 3½" drive bay

An empty drive bay located on the side of a notebook computer

Exploring floppy disk technology

A **floppy disk** is a round piece of flexible mylar plastic covered with a thin layer of magnetic oxide and sealed inside a protective casing. If you broke open the disk casing (something you should never do unless you want to ruin the disk), you would see that the mylar disk inside is thin and literally floppy. See Figure B-7. Floppy disks are also referred to as "floppies" or "diskettes." It is not correct to call them "hard disks" even though they seem to have a "hard" or rigid plastic casing. The term "hard disk" refers to an entirely different storage technology.

Info Web
FLOPPY DISK DRIVES

DETAILS

- Floppy disks come in many sizes and capacities. The floppies most commonly used on today's personal computers are 3½" disks with a capacity of 1.44 MB, which means they can store 1,440,000 bytes of data.

- A floppy disk features a **write-protect window**, which is a small square opening that can be covered by a moveable plastic tab on the disk. When you open the window, the disk is "write-protected," which means that a computer cannot write or save data on the disk.

- Two additional storage systems use floppy disk technology. **Zip disks**, manufactured by Iomega, are available in 100 MB and 250 MB versions. **SuperDisks**, a technology manufactured by Imation, have a capacity of 120 MB. Although the increased storage capacity of these types of disks is attractive, they require special disk drives; a standard floppy disk drive will not read them. SuperDisks, however, are backward-compatible with standard floppy disk technology, which means you can use a SuperDisk drive to read and write to standard floppy disks. Three types of floppy disk drives are shown in Figure B-8.

- The major advantage of floppy disks is their portability. Floppies are still used in many school computer labs so that students can transport their data to different lab machines or to their personal computers.

- A major disadvantage of standard 3½" floppy disks is their relatively low storage capacity. Files that students are creating, such as presentations with graphics and databases, are large. Often, these files will not fit on a 3½" floppy disk, making Zip disks, SuperDisks, or CDs that you can read from and write to (called CD-Rs) more attractive.

- Another disadvantage is that a standard 3½" floppy disk drive is not a particularly speedy device. It takes about 0.5 second for the drive to spin the disk up to maximum speed and find a specific sector that contains data. A Zip drive is about 20 times faster, but both are significantly slower than a hard disk drive.

- The limited storage capacity of floppy disks also makes them less attractive as a distribution medium. In the past, software was distributed on floppy disks. Today, most software vendors use CD-ROM or DVD-ROM disks instead. The Internet has also made it easy to share data files so floppy disks are shipped less frequently.

What HD DS and HDD mean

Today's floppies are "high-density disks" (HD or HDD). When you see "HD DS" on a box of floppy disks it means "high-density double-sided." Although the storage capacity of a standard floppy disk pales beside that of Zip and SuperDisks, there was a time when floppies stored even less. At one time, floppy disks stored data only on one side. Today, however, most store data on both sides. Read-write heads above and below the disk read both sides so that you don't have to turn the disk over.

FIGURE B-7: A 3½" floppy disk

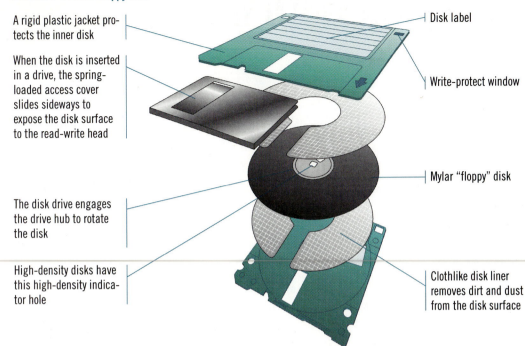

A rigid plastic jacket protects the inner disk

When the disk is inserted in a drive, the spring-loaded access cover slides sideways to expose the disk surface to the read-write head

The disk drive engages the drive hub to rotate the disk

High-density disks have this high-density indicator hole

Disk label

Write-protect window

Mylar "floppy" disk

Clothlike disk liner removes dirt and dust from the disk surface

FIGURE B-8: Inserting a floppy disk, a Zip disk, or a SuperDisk

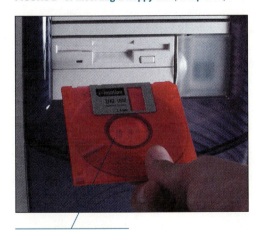

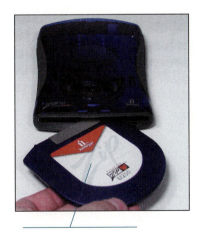

The storage device that records and retrieves data on a floppy disk is a floppy disk drive, shown here with a 3½" floppy disk

A Zip disk requires special disk drives, but is transportable and provides more storage capacity than a floppy disk

A SuperDisk provides an alternative high-capacity, transportable storage option; SuperDisk drives can read standard floppy disks, but a SuperDisk cannot be used in a standard floppy disk drive

Exploring hard disk technology

Hard disk technology is the preferred type of main storage for most computer systems. Hard disks provide more than enough storage capacity for most users and provide faster access to files than floppy disk drives do. In addition, hard disks are more economical than floppy disks. A hard disk typically stores millions of times more data than a floppy disk, but a hard disk drive might cost only three times as much as a floppy disk drive.

DETAILS

● A **hard disk** is one or more platters and their associated read-write heads. A **hard disk platter** is a flat, rigid disk made of aluminum or glass and coated with magnetic iron oxide particles. Personal computer hard disk platters are typically 3½" in diameter. This is the same size as the circular mylar disk in a floppy, but the density of the surface particles on hard disk platters far exceeds that of a floppy disk. You will frequently see the terms "hard disk" and "hard disk drive" used interchangeably. You might also hear the term "fixed disk" used to refer to hard disks.

● The data storage capacity of a hard disk far exceeds that of a floppy disk. Hard disk storage capacities of 40 GB and access times of 6 to 11 ms are not uncommon.

● The access time for a hard disk is significantly faster than that for a floppy disk. Hard disk drive speed is sometimes measured in **revolutions per minute** (rpm). The faster a drive spins, the more rapidly it can position the read-write head over specific data. For example, a 7,200 rpm drive is able to access data faster than a 5,400 rpm drive.

● Hard disk platters are divided into tracks and sectors into which data is written. You might guess that a hard disk drive would fill one platter before storing data on a second platter. However, it is more efficient to store data at the same track and sector locations on all platters before moving the read-write heads to the next sector. A vertical stack of tracks is called a **cylinder**, which is the basic storage bin for a hard disk drive. Figure B-9 provides more information on how a hard disk drive works.

● A hard drive storage device includes a circuit board, called a **controller,** which positions the disk and read-write heads to locate data. Disk drives are classified according to the type of controller they use. Popular drive controllers include Ultra ATA,

EIDE, and SCSI. **Ultra ATA (AT attachment)** and **EIDE (enhanced integrated drive electronics)** use essentially the same drive technology and feature high storage capacity and fast data transfer. Ultra ATA drives, which are commonly found in today's PCs, are twice as fast as their EIDE counterparts. **SCSI (small computer system interface)** drives provide a slight performance advantage over EIDE drives and are typically found in high-performance workstations and servers.

● Hard disks are not as durable as many other storage technologies. The read-write heads in a hard disk hover a microscopic distance above the disk surface. If a read-write head runs into a dust particle or some other contaminant on the disk, or if the hard disk is jarred while it is in use, it might cause a **head crash**. A head crash damages some of the data on the disk. To help prevent contaminants from contacting the platters and causing head crashes, a hard disk is sealed in its case.

● Removable hard disks or hard disk cartridges contain platters and read-write heads that can be inserted and removed from the drive much like floppy disks. Removable hard disks increase the storage capacity of your computer system, although the data is available on only one disk at a time. Removable hard disks also provide security for data by allowing you to remove the hard disk cartridge and store it separately from the computer.

● **RAID (redundant array of independent disks)** is another category of disk drive storage devices. RAID combines two or more drives containing many disk platters to provide redundancy and achieve faster data access than conventional hard disks. The redundancy feature of RAID technology protects data from media failures by recording the same data on more than one disk platter simultaneously. RAID is a popular option for mainframe and server storage but is less popular for personal computers.

FIGURE B-9: How a hard disk works

The drive spindle supports one or more hard disk platters; both sides of the platter are used for data storage; more platters mean more data storage capacity; hard disk platters rotate as a unit on the spindle to position read-write heads over specific data; the platters spin continuously, making thousands of rotations per minute

▲ Each data storage surface has its own read-write head, which moves in and out from the center of the disk to locate data; the head hovers only a few microinches above the disk surface, so the magnetic field is much more compact than on a floppy disk; as a result, more data is packed into a smaller area on a hard disk platter

Understanding tape storage

Tape is another type of storage technology; it consists of a tape for the storage medium and a tape drive for the storage device. Tape is a sequential, rather than a random-access, storage medium. Data is arranged as a long sequence of bits that begins at one end of the tape and stretches to the other end. As a result, tape access is much slower than hard drive access. In fact, access times for a tape are measured in seconds rather than in milliseconds. A tape may contain hundreds, or in the case of a mainframe, thousands of feet of tape.

The most popular types of tape drives for personal computers use tape cartridges for the storage medium. A **tape cartridge** is a removable magnetic tape module similar to a cassette tape. Figure B-10 shows several different kinds of tape used with personal computer tape drives.

Tape drives are available in either internal or external models. An internal tape drive fits into a standard drive bay. An external model is a stand-alone device that you can connect to your computer with a cable.

FIGURE B-10

DDS (digital data storage) Ditto Travan ADR (advanced digital recording)

Exploring CD/DVD technology

A CD-ROM drive is an optical storage device that is usually installed in one of the system unit's drive bays. **CD-ROM (compact disc read-only memory)** is based on the same technology as the audio CDs that contain your favorite music. Your computer can read data from a CD-ROM, but you can't store or record any of your own data on a CD-ROM disk. Two CD-writer technologies called CD-R and CD-RW allow you to create your own CDs. **DVD** ("digital video disc" or "digital versatile disk") is a variation of CD technology that was originally designed as an alternative to VCRs, but was quickly adopted by the computer industry to store data.

DETAILS

● A computer **CD-ROM disk**, like its audio counterpart, contains data that was stamped on the disk surface when it was manufactured. Today, when you purchase software from a computer store, the box typically contains CDs. Therefore, unless you plan to download all of your new software from the Internet, your computer should have a CD drive so that you can install new software. Figure B-11 shows how to place a CD in the drive. Figure B-12 illustrates how a CD-ROM drive uses laser technology to read data.

● CD-ROM technology provides a far larger storage capacity than floppy disks, Zip disks, or SuperDisks. A single CD-ROM disk holds up to 680 MB, equivalent to more than 300,000 pages of text. The surface of the disk is coated with a clear plastic, making the disk quite durable. Unlike magnetic media, the data on a CD-ROM is not susceptible to permanent damage by humidity, fingerprints, dust, or magnets.

● The original CD-ROM drives were able to access 150 KB of data per second. The next generation of drives doubled the data transfer rate and was consequently dubbed "2X"; and transfer rates are continually increasing. A 24X CD-ROM drive, for example, would transfer data at a rate of 24 × 150 KB, or 3,600 KB per second.

● A **CD-R (compact disc recordable)** drive records data on a special CD-R disk. The drive mechanism includes a laser that changes the reflectivity of a dye layer on a blank CD-R disk. As a result, the data on the disk is not actually stored in pits. Dark spots in the dye layer, however, play the same role as pits to represent data and allow the disks that you create to be read by not only a CD-R drive, but also by a standard CD-ROM or DVD

drive. The data on a CD-R cannot be erased or modified once recorded, but most CD-R drives allow you to record your data in multiple sessions.

● **CD-RW (compact disc rewritable)** technology allows you to write data on a CD and change that data at a later time. The process requires special CD-RW disks and a CD-RW drive, which uses phase change technology to alter the crystal structure on the disk surface. Altering the crystal structure creates patterns of light and dark spots similar to the pits and lands on a CD-ROM disk. The crystal structure can be changed from light to dark and back again many times, making it possible to record and modify data much like you can with a hard disk or a floppy disk. However, accessing, saving, and modifying data on a CD-RW disk is slower than on a hard disk.

● Both CD-R and CD-RW technologies are quite useful for archiving data and distributing large files. **Archiving** refers to the process of removing infrequently used data from a primary storage device to another storage medium, such as a CD-R.

● A computer's DVD drive can read disks that contain computer data (often called **DVD-ROM** disks) and disks that contain DVD movies (sometimes called DVD-Video disks). A DVD holds about 4.7 GB (4,700 MB), compared with 680 MB on a CD-ROM. Like a CD-ROM disk, a DVD-ROM disk is permanently stamped with data at the time of manufacture, so you cannot add or change data. The speed of a DVD drive is measured on a different scale than a CD drive. A 1X DVD drive is about the same speed as a 9X CD drive. Table B-1 provides additional speed equivalents.

Using DVD technologies

A computer DVD drive is not exactly the same as one that's connected to a television set. Even with the large storage capacity of a DVD, movie files are much too large to fit on a disk unless they are compressed, using a special type of data coding called **MPEG-2**. The DVD player that you connect to your television includes MPEG decoding circuitry, which is not included on your computer's

DVD drive. When you play DVD movies on your computer, it uses the CPU as an MPEG decoder. The necessary decoder software is included with Windows, or can be located on the DVD itself. You cannot play DVDs on your CD-ROM drive, but you can play CD-ROM, most CD-R, and most CD-RW disks on your DVD drive.

FIGURE B-11: Inserting a CD-ROM

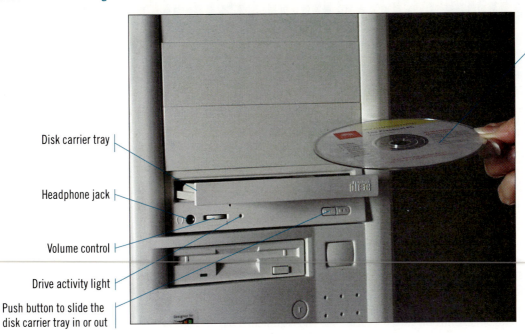

Disk carrier tray

Headphone jack

Volume control

Drive activity light

Push button to slide the disk carrier tray in or out

Data is stored on the bottom of a CD-ROM disk in one continuous track that spirals out from the center of the disk; the track is divided into equal-length sectors; the printed side of the disk does not contain data; it should be face up when you insert the disk because the lasers read the bottom of the disk

FIGURE B-12: How a CD-ROM drive works

Laser lens directs a beam of light to the underside of the CD-ROM disk

Tracking mechanism positions a disk track over the laser lens

Drive spindle spins disk

Laser pickup assembly senses the reflectivity of pits and lands

TABLE B-1: Comparing DVD and CD speeds

DVD DRIVE SPEED	DATA TRANSFER RATE	CD SPEED
1X	11.08 Mbps	9X
2X	22.16 Mbps	18X
4X	44.32 Mbps	36X
5X	55.40 Mbps	46X

Understanding expansion slots, cards, ports, and cables

Within a computer, data travels from one component to another over circuits called a **data bus**. One part of the data bus runs between RAM and the microprocessor; the other part runs between RAM and various storage devices. The segment of the data bus between RAM and peripheral devices is called the **expansion bus**. As data moves along the expansion bus, it may travel through expansion slots, cards, ports, and cables.

DETAILS

● An **expansion slot** is a long, narrow socket on the motherboard into which you can plug an expansion card. The motherboard is the main board in the computer that holds the components that control the processing functions. An **expansion card** is a small circuit board that provides a computer the ability to control a storage device, an input device, or an output device. Expansion cards are also called "expansion boards," "controller cards," or "adapters." To insert an expansion card, you slide it into an expansion slot, where it can be secured with a small screw. See Figure B-13.

● Most desktop computers have four to eight expansion slots, but some of the slots usually contain expansion cards. A **graphics card** (sometimes called a "video card") provides a path for data traveling to the monitor. A **modem card** provides a way to transmit data over phone lines or cable television lines. A **sound card** carries data out to speakers and headphones, or back from a microphone. A **network card** allows you to connect your computer to a local area network. You might add other expansion cards if you want to connect a scanner or download videos from a camera or VCR.

● A desktop computer may have up to three types of expansion slots. Each expansion card is built for only one type of slot. AGP, PCI, and ISA slots are different lengths so you can easily identify them by opening your computer's system unit and looking at the motherboard. See Figure B-14. **ISA (industry standard architecture)** slots are an old technology, used today only for some modems and other relatively slow devices. **PCI (peripheral component interconnect)** slots offer fast transfer speeds and a 32-bit or 64-bit data bus. This type of slot typically houses a graphics card, sound card, video capture card, modem, or network interface card. **AGP (accelerated graphics port)** slots provide a high-speed data pathway that is primarily used for graphics cards.

● Most notebook computers are equipped with a special type of external slot called a **PCMCIA slot (personal computer memory card international association)**. Typically, a notebook computer has only one of these slots, but the slot can hold more than one PC card (also called "PCMCIA expansion cards" or "Card Bus cards"). PCMCIA slots are classified according to their thickness. Type 1 slots accept only the thinnest PC cards, such as memory expansion cards. Type II slots accept most of the popular PC cards such as those that contain modems, sound cards, and network cards. Type III slots commonly included with today's notebook computers accept the thickest PC cards, which contain devices such as hard disk drives. A Type III slot can also hold two Type 1 cards, two Type II cards, or a Type 1 and a Type II card. Figure B-15 shows a PCMCIA slot and a PC card.

● An **expansion port** is any connector that passes data in and out of a computer or peripheral device. See Figure B-16. Ports are sometimes called "jacks" or "connectors," but the terminology is inconsistent. An expansion port is often housed on an expansion card so that it is accessible through an opening in the back of the computer's system unit. A port might also be built into the system unit case of a desktop or notebook computer. The built-in ports on a computer usually include a mouse port, keyboard port, serial port, and USB port. Ports that have been added with expansion cards usually protrude through rectangular cutouts in the back of the case.

● If a **cable** is supplied with a peripheral device, you can usually figure out where to plug it in by matching the shape of the cable connector to the port. If you need to purchase a cable, be sure the cable matches the available ports.

FIGURE B-13: Inserting an expansion card

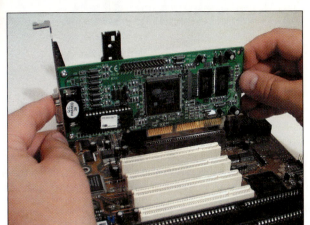

FIGURE B-14: Types of expansion slots

ISA slot   PCI slot   AGP slot

FIGURE B-15: PC card for a notebook computer

PC card

FIGURE B-16: Expansion ports on a typical desktop computer

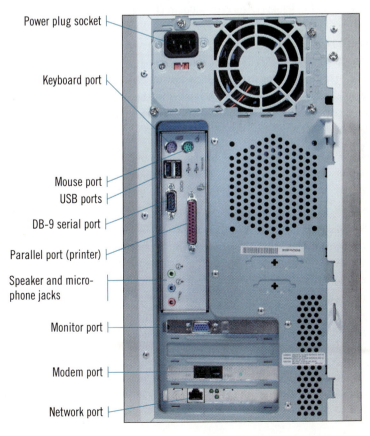

Power plug socket

Keyboard port

Mouse port

USB ports

DB-9 serial port

Parallel port (printer)

Speaker and micro-
phone jacks

Monitor port

Modem port

Network port

Comparing display devices

A computer display system is the main output device for a computer. Two key components of a computer display system are a graphics card and a display device, such as a monitor or LCD screen.

Info Web
DISPLAY DEVICES

DETAILS

- A **graphics card** (also called a "graphics board" or a "video card") contains circuitry that generates the signals for displaying an image on the screen. It also contains special video memory, which stores screen images as they are processed before they are displayed. Today's fastest graphics cards fit in an AGP expansion slot. PCI graphics cards typically take a bit longer to update the screen. Many graphics cards contain special graphics accelerator technology to boost performance for 3-D graphics applications, including computer games.

- For many years, CRT monitors were the only game in town for desktop computer displays. **CRT (cathode ray tube)** technology uses gun-like mechanisms to direct beams of electrons toward the screen and activate individual dots of color that form an image—much like a color TV. CRT monitors offer an inexpensive and dependable computer display.

- As an alternative to CRT monitors, an **LCD (liquid crystal display)** monitor produces an image by manipulating light within a layer of liquid crystal cells. Modern LCD technology is compact in size, lightweight, and easy to read. While LCDs are standard equipment on notebook computers, newer notebooks feature an **active matrix screen**, sometimes referred to as **"TFT" (thin film transistor)**, which updates rapidly and is essential for crisp display of animations and video. Consumers might pay more for a notebook with TFT technology. Recently, stand-alone LCDs, referred to as "LCD monitors" or "flat panel displays," have also become available for desktop computers.

- The advantages of an LCD monitor include display clarity (even in sunlit rooms), low radiation emission, portability, and compactness. However, there are several disadvantages. An LCD monitor can be triple the price of an equivalent CRT monitor. LCD monitors have a limited viewing angle; the brightness and color tones that you see depend on the angle from which you view the screen because of the way that light reflects off the LCD screen. Graphic artists prefer CRT technology, which displays uniform color from any viewing angle.

- Image quality is determined by screen size, dot pitch, resolution, and color depth. **Screen size** is the measurement in inches from one corner of the screen diagonally across to the opposite corner. Typical monitor screen sizes range from 13" to 21". On most

monitors, the viewable image does not stretch to the edge of the screen. Instead, a black border makes the viewing area smaller than the screen size. Many computer ads now include a measurement of the **viewable image size (vis)**. A 15" monitor has an approximately 13.9" vis, as shown in Figure B-17.

- **Dot pitch** (dp) is a measure of image clarity. A smaller dot pitch means a crisper image. Technically, dot pitch is the distance in millimeters between like-colored pixels, the small dots of light that form an image. A dot pitch between .26 and .23 is typical for today's monitors.

- The computer's graphics card sends an image to the monitor at a specific **resolution**, defined as the maximum number of horizontal and vertical pixels that are displayed on the screen. Standard resolutions include 640 × 480, 800 × 600, and 1024 × 768. Even higher resolutions, such as 1600 × 1200, are possible given enough memory on the graphics card and a monitor capable of displaying that resolution. At higher resolutions, the computer displays a larger work area, such as an entire page of a document, but text and other objects appear smaller. The two screen shots in Figure B-18 help you compare a display at 640 × 480 resolution with a display at 1024 × 768 resolution.

- The number of colors that a monitor and graphics card can display is referred to as **color depth** or "**bit depth**." Most PCs have the capability to display millions of colors. When you set the resolution at 24-bit color depth (sometimes called "True Color"), your PC can display more than 16 million colors and produce what are considered photographic-quality images. Windows allows you to select resolution and color depth simply by right-clicking an empty area of the desktop, selecting Properties on the shortcut menu, selecting the Settings tab, and then changing the settings to meet your needs. Most desktop owners choose 24-bit color at 1024 × 768 resolution.

- Although you can set the color depth and resolution of your notebook computer display, you might not have as many options as you do with a desktop computer. Typically, the graphics card circuitry is built into the motherboard of a notebook computer, making it difficult to upgrade and gain more video memory for additional resolution and color depth.

FIGURE B-17: Viewable image size of a monitor

15 inches

13.9 inches vis

FIGURE B-18: Comparing screen resolutions

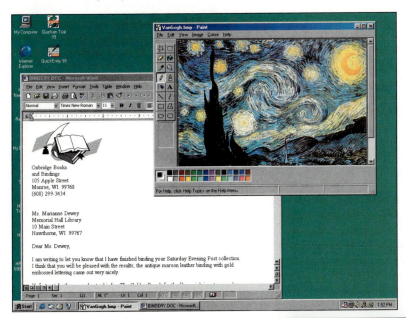

◀ Computer display set at 1024 × 768 resolution

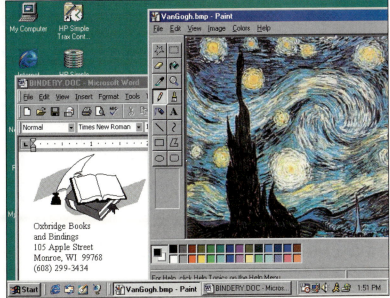

▶ Computer display set at 640 × 480 resolution; text and other objects appear larger than on the high-resolution screen, but you see a smaller portion of the screen-based desktop

Comparing printers

Printer technologies include ink jet, solid ink, thermal transfer, dye sublimation, laser, and dot matrix. Printers differ in resolution and speed, both of which affect the print quality and price. Most ink jet printers are small, lightweight, and inexpensive, yet produce very good quality color output. Laser printers are a popular technology for situations that require high-volume output or good-quality printouts. A dot matrix printer uses a grid of thin wires to strike a ribbon and create an image on paper. Unlike laser and ink-jet technologies, a dot matrix printer actually strikes the paper and, therefore, can print multipart carbon forms.

Info Web
PRINTER BUYER'S GUIDE

DETAILS

- The quality or sharpness of printed images and text depends on the printer's resolution, the density of the grid of dots that create an image. Printer resolution is measured by the number of dots it can print per linear inch, abbreviated as **dpi**. At normal reading distance, a resolution of about 900 dots per inch appears solid to the human eye, but a close examination of color sections will reveal a dot pattern. Expensive coffee-table books are typically produced on printers with 2,400 dpi or higher.

- Printer speeds are measured either by pages per minute (ppm) or characters per second (cps). Color printouts typically take longer than black-and-white printouts. Pages that contain mostly text tend to print more rapidly than pages that contain graphics. Ten pages per minute is a typical speed for a personal computer printer.

- Ink jet printers (see Figure B-19) outsell all of the others because they produce low-cost color or black-and-white printouts. An **ink jet printer** has a nozzle-like print head that sprays ink onto paper to form characters and graphics. You must periodically replace the black ink cartridge and a second cartridge that carries the colored inks. Ink jet printers have excellent resolution, which can range from 600 dpi to 2,880 dpi, depending on the model. Some ink jet printers can produce ultra-high resolution by making multiple passes over the paper.

- A **solid ink printer** melts sticks of crayon-like ink and then sprays the liquefied ink through the print head's tiny nozzles. The ink solidifies before the paper can absorb it, and a pair of rollers finishes fusing the ink onto the paper. A solid ink printer produces vibrant colors on most types of paper, so unlike an ink jet printer, it does not require special, expensive paper to produce photographic-quality images.

- A **thermal transfer printer** uses a page-sized ribbon that is coated with cyan, magenta, yellow, and black wax. The print head consists of thousands of tiny heating elements that melt the wax onto specially coated paper or transparency film (the kind used for overhead projectors). This type of printer excels at printing colorful transparencies for presentations, but the fairly

expensive per-page costs and the requirement for special paper make this a niche market printer used mainly by businesses.

- A **dye sublimation printer** uses technology similar to wax transfer. The difference is that the page-sized ribbon contains dye instead of colored wax. Heating elements in the print head diffuse the dye onto the surface of specially coated paper. Dye sublimation printers produce excellent color quality—perhaps the best of any printer technology. A high cost per page, however, makes these printers a bit pricey.

- A **laser printer** (see Figure B-20) uses the same technology as a photocopier to produce dots of light on a light-sensitive drum. Personal laser printers produce six to eight ppm (pages per minute) at a resolution of 600 dpi. Professional models pump out 15 to 25 ppm at 1,200 dpi. A personal laser printer has a duty cycle of about 3,000 pages per month, which means roughly 100 pages per day.

    Laser printers accept print commands from a personal computer, but use their own printer language to construct a page before printing it. **Printer Control Language (PCL)** is the most widely used printer language, but some printers use the PostScript language, which is preferred by many publishing professionals. Printer languages require memory, and most laser printers have between 2 MB and 8 MB. A large memory capacity is required to print color images and graphics-intensive documents. A laser printer comes equipped with enough memory for typical print jobs. If you find that you need more memory, check the printer documentation for information.

- When PCs first began to appear in the late 1970s, dot matrix printers were the technology of choice, and they are still available today. A **dot matrix printer** (see Figure B-21) produces characters and graphics by using a grid of fine wires. Dot matrix speed is typically measured in characters per second (cps). A fast dot matrix device can print at speeds up to 455 cps or about five pages per minute. Today dot matrix printers are used primarily for "back-office" applications that demand low operating cost and dependability but not high print quality.

FIGURE B-19: Ink jet printer

▶ The print head in a color ink jet printer consists of a series of nozzles, each with its own ink cartridge; most ink jet printers use **CMYK color**, which requires only cyan (blue), magenta (pink), yellow, and black inks to create a printout that appears to have thousands of colors; alternatively, some printers use six ink colors to print midtone shades that create slightly more realistic photographic images

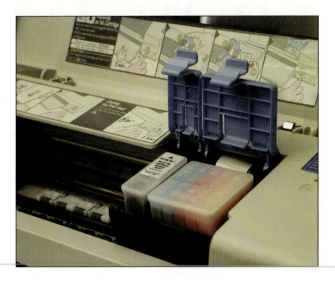

FIGURE B-20: Laser printer

Electrostatically charged ink is applied to the drum, then transferred to paper

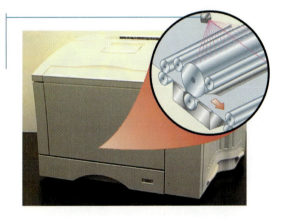

FIGURE B- 21: A dot matrix printer

◀ Dot matrix printers can print text and graphics; some even print in color using a multicolored ribbon; with a resolution of 140 dpi, a dot matrix printer produces low-quality output with clearly discernible dots forming lettters and graphics

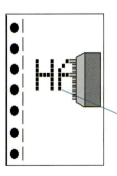

As the print head moves across the paper, the wires strike the ribbon and paper in a pattern prescribed by your PC

Examining keyboards

Most computers are equipped with a keyboard as the primary input device. A computer keyboard includes keys or buttons with letters and numbers as well as several keys with special characters and special words to control computer-specific tasks. Virtually every computer user interface requires you to use a keyboard. Although you don't have to be a great typist to use a computer effectively, you should be familiar with the computer keyboard and its special keys. Figure B-22 shows the location of the keys on a standard computer keyboard.

DETAILS

● You use the keys to input commands, respond to prompts, and type the text of documents. A cursor or an insertion point indicates where the characters you type will appear. The **cursor** appears on the screen as a flashing underline. The **insertion point** appears on the screen as a flashing vertical bar. You can change the location of the cursor or insertion point using the arrow keys or the mouse.

● The **numeric keypad** provides you with a calculator-style input device for numbers and arithmetic symbols. You can type numbers using either the set of number keys at the top of the keyboard or the keys on the numeric keypad. Notice that some keys on the numeric keypad contain two symbols. When the Num Lock key is activated, the numeric keypad will produce numbers. When the Num Lock key is not activated, the keys on the numeric keypad move the cursor in the direction indicated by the arrows on the keys.

The Num Lock key is an example of a toggle key. A **toggle key** switches back and forth between two modes. The Caps Lock key is also a toggle key. When you press the Caps Lock key, you switch or "toggle" into uppercase mode. When you press the Caps Lock key again you toggle back into lowercase mode.

● **Function keys**, those keys numbered F1 through F12, are located either at the top or along the side of your keyboard. They were added to computer keyboards to help you initiate commands.

For example, with many software packages, you press the [F1] key to get help. The problem with function keys is that they are not standardized. In one program, you might press [F7] to save a document; but in another program, you might press [F5] to perform the same task.

● **Modifier keys**, the [Ctrl] (Control), [Alt], and [Shift] keys are located at the periphery of the typing keypad. There are 12 function keys, but you usually need more than 12 commands to control software. Therefore, you can use the [Ctrl], [Alt], and [Shift] keys in conjunction with the function keys to expand the repertoire of available commands. The [Alt] and [Ctrl] modifier keys also work in conjunction with the letter keys. Instead of using the mouse, you might use the [Alt] or [Ctrl] keys in combination with letter keys to access menu options. Such combinations are called **keyboard shortcuts**. If you see Alt+F1, [Alt F1], Alt-F1, or Alt F1 on the screen or in an instruction manual, it means to hold down the [Alt] key and press [F1] at the same time. You might see similar notations for using the [Ctrl] or [Shift] keys. In many Windows programs, [Ctrl]+X works as a keyboard shortcut to cut a selection and place it on the Clipboard, [Ctrl]+V works as a keyboard shortcut to paste the contents of the Clipboard at the insertion point, and [Ctrl]+C works as a keyboard shortcut to copy selected contents so that you can paste that information at the insertion point.

FIGURE B-22: The computer keyboard

The **Esc** or "escape" key cancels an operation

Each time you press the **Backspace** key, one character to the left of the insertion point is deleted

The **Print Screen** key either prints the contents of the screen or stores a copy of your screen in memory that you can manipulate or print with graphics software

The function of the **Scroll Lock** key depends on the software you are using; this key is rarely used with today's software

Indicator lights show you the status of each toggle key: Num Lock, Caps Lock, and Scroll Lock; the Power light indicates whether the computer is on or off

Function keys execute commands, such as saving a document; the command associated with each function key depends on the software you are using

The **Insert** key toggles between insert mode and typeover mode

The **Num Lock** key is a toggle key that switches between number keys and arrow keys on the numeric keypad

The **Caps Lock** key capitalizes all the letters you type when it is engaged, but does not produce the top symbol on keys that contain two symbols

You hold down the **Ctrl** or the **Alt** key while you press another key; the result of Ctrl key or Alt key combinations depends on the software you are using

The **arrow** keys move the insertion point

The **Page Up** key displays the previous screen of information; the **Page Down** key displays the next screen of information

The **Home** key takes you to the beginning of a line or the beginning of a document, depending on the software you are using

You hold down the **Shift** key while you press another key; the Shift key capitalizes letters and produces the top symbol on keys that contain two symbols

The **End** key takes you to the end of the line or the end of a document, depending on the software you are using

Alternative keyboard designs

In addition to the standard keyboard, innovative alternatives are becoming available. For example, some keyboards come with Internet hot keys. These keyboards have special keys that let you instantly access favorite Internet activities such as e-mailing, shopping, or searching the Web. Another alternative is an ergonomically designed keyboard, such as the one shown in Figure B-23, which may prevent computer, stress-related wrist injuries.

FIGURE B-23

▼ INDEPENDENT CHALLENGE 2

Storage technology has a fascinating history. Mankind has evolved many ways to retain and store data. From the ancient days when Egyptians were writing on papyrus to modern day holographic technologies, societies have found ways to retain more and more information in permanent and safe ways.

1. To complete this independent challenge you will research the history of storage technologies and create a timeline that shows the developments. Be sure to include such items as 78-rpm records and 8-track tapes. Your research should yield some interesting technologies and systems.

2. For each technology, list the media, the device used to retrieve the information, two significant facts about the technology, the era in which it was used or popular, and what lead to its demise or obsolescence.

3. You can create the timeline using images or just words. This is a creative project. Your best research, artistic, and communication skills come together to create this timeline.

▼ INDEPENDENT CHALLENGE 3

It is important that you are familiar with the type of computer you use daily. You may need to consult your technical resource person to help you complete this independent challenge.

1. Identify the components on your computer. What type of computer are you using? What kind of system unit do you have?

2. What peripheral devices are attached to your computer? List the name brand and model number if available.

3. Draw a sketch of your computer. Label each component and identify what it does.

▼ INDEPENDENT CHALLENGE 4

 In this unit you learned about peripheral devices. Some of these are standard peripheral devices such as monitors and printers. If your office is tight for space, you might consider purchasing a multifunction device. For this project, use your library and Web resources to research information about multifunction devices.

1. Research and find the types of multifunction devices available. Categorize them by their functions: scanners, fax, phone, copiers, color or black-and-white printing, laser or inkjet. Different manufacturers bundle different capabilities into their devices. The more features a unit has, typically, the more expensive it will be.

2. Research and find the manufacturers and model numbers for three devices you would consider buying. Write a comparison of the features, strengths, and weaknesses of each model.

▼ INDEPENDENT CHALLENGE 5

 For this project, use your library and Web resources to research information in order to compare printers.

1. Use the information in this unit as well as your own resources to create a comparative table of printers.

2. Your column heads might address these questions: What types are available? What technology is used? What is the duty cycle? What is the cost range? What is the average cost per page? Who is the market for this type of printer?

3. Provide a summary statement indicating which printer you would buy and why, based on the information in your table.

▼ INDEPENDENT CHALLENGE 6

 The Issue section of this unit focused on the potential for discarded computers and other electronic devices to become a significant environmental problem. For this independent challenge, you will write a short paper about recycling computers based on information that you gather from the Internet.

1. To begin this independent challenge, consult the Internet and use your favorite search engine to search for and find Web pages to get an in-depth overview of the issue.

2. Determine the specific aspect of the issue that you will present in your paper. You might, for example, decide to focus on the toxic materials contained in computers that end up in landfills. Or you might tackle the barriers that discourage the shipment of old computers across national borders. Whatever aspect of the issue you decide to present, make sure that you can back up your discussion with facts and references to authoritative articles and Web pages.

3. You can place citations to these pages (include the author's name, article title, date of publication, and URL) at the end of your paper as endnotes, on each page as footnotes, or along with the appropriate paragraphs using parentheses. Follow your professor's instructions for submitting your paper via e-mail or as a printed document.

▼ LAB: WORKING WITH BINARY NUMBERS

1. Start the interactive part of the lab. Insert your Tracking disk if you want to save your QuickCheck results. Perform each of the lab steps as directed and answer all of the lab QuickCheck questions. When you exit the lab, your answers are automatically graded and your results are displayed.

2. Using paper and pencil, manually convert the following decimal numbers into binary numbers. Your instructor might ask you to show the process that you used for each conversion.

   a. 100   b. 1,000   c. 256   d. 27

   e. 48   f. 112   g. 96   h. 1,024

3. Using paper and pencil, manually convert the following binary numbers into decimal numbers. Your instructor might ask you to show the process that you used for each conversion.

   a. 100   b. 101   c. 1100   d. 10101

   e. 1111   f. 10000   g. 1111000   h. 110110

4. Describe what is wrong with the following sequence:

   10 100 110 1000 1001 1100 1110 10000

5. What is the decimal equivalent of 2^0? 2^1? 2^8?

▼ LAB: OPERATING A PERSONAL COMPUTER

1. Start the interactive part of the lab. Insert your Tracking Disk if you want to save your QuickCheck results. Perform each of the lab steps as directed and answer all of the lab QuickCheck questions. When you exit the lab, your answers are automatically graded and your results are displayed.

2. Make a note of the brand and location of the computer that you're using to complete these lab assignments.

3. Use the Start button to access your computer's Control Panel folder. Describe the status of your computer's power saver settings.

4. Preview the screen savers that are available on the computer that you use most frequently. Select the screen saver that you like the best and describe it in a few sentences.

5. What is the purpose of an Fn key? Does your computer keyboard include an Fn key? Explain why or why not.

6. In your own words, describe what happens when you (a) click the Close button, (b) hold down the Ctrl, Alt, and Del keys, (c) press the reset button, and (d) select the Shut Down option.

Exercises

▼ VISUAL WORKSHOP

If you thought a holograph was just the image of Princess Leia saying "Obi-Wan Kenobi, you are my only hope," think again. Holographic storage devices are in development as a means to respond to the growing need for large-volume data storage. Holographic technologies promise data retrieval speeds far exceeding magnetic or optical storage and capacities far beyond anything currently available. Researchers are working to make this technology an affordable reality. Figure B-28 shows a Web page from the IBM Science and Technology Center at Almaden that researches holographic technologies.

FIGURE B-28

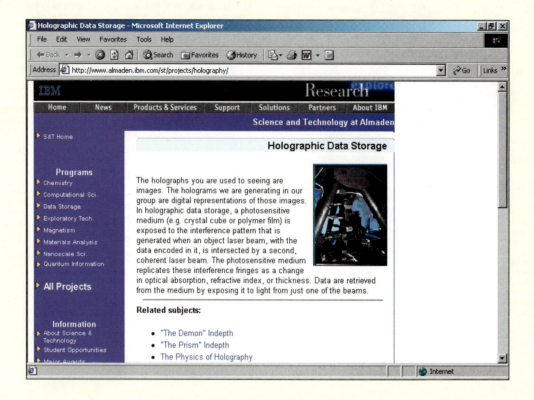

1. Use your favorite search engine to find and read the May 2000 edition of Scientific American (www.sciam.com), which included a feature article about holographic storage. Write a brief summary of the article and, based on what you read, explain the basics of how holographic memory works.

2. Research the current trends in holographic development. Are there any existing applications? How far has the technology come? What companies are working to develop these technologies? How far are we from using holocubes for data storage?

3. Write a scenario that includes the requirements and applications for holographic storage. Under what circumstances do you think such technologies would be useful, and what types of data do you think would best take advantage of this new technology?

UNIT C
Computer Software

OBJECTIVES

A computer's versatility is possible because of software—the instructions that tell a computer how to perform a specific type of task. This unit begins with the components of a typical software package and explains how these components work together. Next, you will learn about a computer's most important system software, its operating system. You will get an overview of software applications, including document production, spreadsheets, data management, graphics, music, video editing, and games. Finally, the unit wraps up with important practical information on software copyrights and licenses and installing and uninstalling software.

Introducing computer software

In common practice, the term "software" is used to describe a commercial product. Computer software determines the types of tasks that a computer can help you accomplish. For example, some software helps you create documents, while other software helps you create presentations, prepare your tax return, or design the floor plan for a new house. You will learn about the components of computer software and how these components work together to help you complete tasks.

DETAILS

- Software is categorized as either application software or system software. **Application software** helps you carry out tasks—such as creating documents, crunching numbers, and editing photographs—using a computer. **System software**—your computer's operating system, device drivers, and utilities—helps your computer carry out its basic operating functions. Figure C-1 shows the types of software that fall into the system software and application software categories.

- **Software** consists of computer programs, support modules, and data modules that work together to provide a computer with the instructions and data necessary for carrying out a specific type of task, such as document production, video editing, or Web browsing.

- Software typically includes files that contain computer programs. A **computer program**, or "program," is a set of self-contained instructions that tells a computer how to solve a problem or carry out a task. A key characteristic of a computer program is that it can be started or "run" by a computer user. For example, the **main executable file** is a program that you run to start the software. Another file might contain the program that you use to install the software. Still another file might contain the program that you run to uninstall the software. Program files often use the .exe filename extension.

- A **support module** provides an auxiliary set of instructions that can be used in conjunction with the main software program. Each module is stored in its own file. Unlike a program file, a support module is not designed to be run by the computer user.

Instead, these modules are "called" by the computer program, as needed. For example, when you use the spelling checker in a word processing program, the word processing program calls on support modules to run the spelling checker. Support modules often use the .dll filename extension.

- A **data module** contains any data that is necessary for a task, but that is not supplied by the user. For example, word processing software checks spelling by comparing the words in a document with the words in a dictionary file. This dictionary file is a data module that is supplied by the software, not by the user.

- Most software packages include at least one executable program file, several support modules, and one or more data modules. See Figure C-2. The use of a main program file plus several support modules and data modules provides a great deal of flexibility and efficiency for programmers. For example, many of the support modules contain "generic" program instructions that can be adapted to work with a wide variety of programs. Instead of writing these instructions "from scratch," a programmer can simply plug in a generic support module.

- Most software is designed to provide a task-related environment, which includes a screen display, a means of collecting commands and data from the user, the specifications for processing data, and a method for displaying or outputting data. Figure C-3 illustrates a very simple computer program that converts a Fahrenheit temperature to Celsius and displays the result.

FIGURE C-1: Software categories

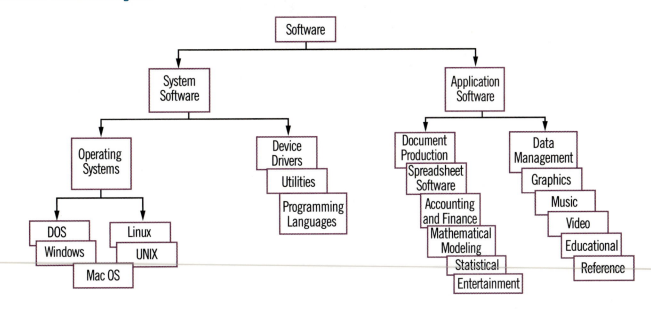

FIGURE C-2: Installed files for a software program

▶ A list of the main files required by the VideoFactory software includes program files, support modules, and data modules

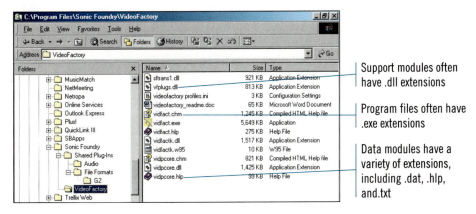

Support modules often have .dll extensions

Program files often have .exe extensions

Data modules have a variety of extensions, including .dat, .hlp, and.txt

FIGURE C-3: A simple computer program

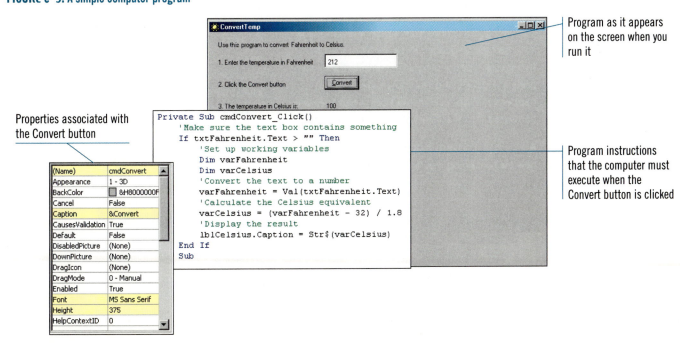

Program as it appears on the screen when you run it

Properties associated with the Convert button

Program instructions that the computer must execute when the Convert button is clicked

Explaining how computers interpret software

Computer programmers write the instructions for the computer programs and support modules that become the components of a computer software product. The finished software product is then distributed by the programmers themselves, or by software publishers, companies that specialize in packaging, marketing, and selling commercial software. Most businesses, organizations, and individuals purchase commercial software to avoid the time and expense of writing their own. Learning how programmers write the instructions and how a computer's microprocessor translates these instructions will help you understand how software works.

DETAILS

A **computer language** provides the tools that a programmer uses to create software. These languages help the programmer produce a lengthy list of instructions called **source code**. Most programmers today prefer to use **high-level languages**, such as C++, Java, COBOL, and Visual Basic, which have some similarities to human languages and produce programs that are fairly easy to test and modify.

A computer's microprocessor interprets the programmer's instructions, but the microprocessor can only understand **machine language**—the instruction set that is "hard wired" within the microprocessor's circuits. Instructions written in a high-level language must be translated into machine language before a computer can use them.

Translating instructions from a high-level language into machine language can be accomplished by two special types of programs: compilers and interpreters. Figure C-4 gives you an idea of what happens to high-level instructions when they are converted into machine language instructions.

A **compiler** converts high-level instructions into a new file containing machine language instructions.

A compiler translates all of the instructions in a program as a single batch, and the resulting machine language instructions, called **object code**, are placed in a new file. See Figure C-5.

As an alternative to a compiler, an **interpreter** converts one instruction at a time while the program is running. An interpreted program runs more slowly than a compiled program because the translation process happens while the program is running. This method of converting high-level instructions into machine language is more common with Web-based programs called **scripts**, written in languages such as JavaScript and VBScript. These scripts contain high-level instructions that arrive as part of a Web page. An interpreter reads the first instruction in a script, converts it into machine language, and then sends it to the microprocessor. The interpreter continues in this way to convert instructions until all instructions are interpreted. See Figure C-6. To run a script, your computer must have the corresponding interpreter program, which is typically supplied with Web browser software or is available as a download from the Web.

FIGURE C-4: Converting a high-level instruction to machine code

High-level Language Instruction	Machine Language Equivalent	Description of Machine Language Instructions
Answer = FirstNumber + SecondNumber	10001000 00011000 010000000	Load FirstNumber into Register 1
	10001000 00010000 00100000	Load SecondNumber into Register 2
	00000000 00011000 00010000	Perform ADD operation
	10100010 00111000	Move the number from the accumulator to the RAM location called Answer

FIGURE C-5: What the compiler does

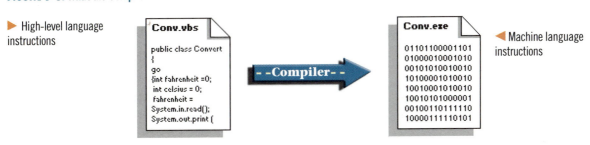

▶ High-level language instructions

◀ Machine language instructions

FIGURE C-6: The interpreter converts instructions one instruction at a time

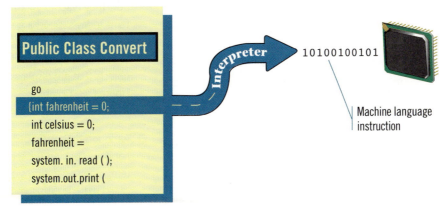

Machine language instruction

Exploring operating systems

The term **operating system** (OS) is defined as system software that acts as the master controller for all of the activities that take place within a computer system. If you understand how an operating system works, you will understand how your computer performs its many functions. For example, when you issue a command using application software, the application software tells the operating system what to do. See Figure C-7. While you interact with application software, your computer's operating system is busy behind the scenes with tasks such as identifying storage space, allocating memory, and communicating with your peripheral devices.

DETAILS

- The operating system interacts with application software, device drivers, and hardware to manage a computer's resources. For example, your operating system stores and retrieves files from your disks and CDs. It remembers the names and locations of all your files and keeps track of empty spaces where new files can be stored. It communicates with device driver software so that data can travel smoothly between the computer and the peripheral resources. If a peripheral device or driver is not performing correctly, the operating system makes a decision about what to do; usually it displays an on-screen warning about the problem.

- Many activities called "processes" compete for the attention of your computer's microprocessor. For example, commands are arriving from programs that you're using while input is arriving from the keyboard and mouse. At the same time, data must be sent to the display device or printer, and Web pages are arriving from your Internet connection. To manage all of these competing processes, your computer's operating system helps the microprocessor switch tasks. From the user's vantage point, everything seems to be happening at the same time. This is because the operating system makes sure that the microprocessor doesn't stop processing while it is waiting for instructions for a different processing task.

- When you want to multitask—run more than one program at a time—the operating system has to allocate specific areas of memory for each program. While multiple programs are running, the OS must ensure that instructions and data from one area of memory don't "leak" into an area

allocated to another program. If an OS falls down on the job and fails to protect each program's memory area, data can get corrupted, programs can "crash," and your computer will display error messages, such as "General Protection Fault." Your PC can sometimes recover from memory leak problems if you use the Ctrl-Alt-Del key sequence to close the corrupted program.

- Your computer's operating system ensures that input and output proceed in an orderly manner, using queues to collect data and buffers to hold data while the computer is busy with other tasks. By using a keyboard buffer, for example, your computer never misses one of your keystrokes, regardless of how fast you type or what else is happening within your computer system at the same time.

- Many operating systems also influence the "look and feel" of your software by determining the kinds of menus, toolbars, and controls that are displayed on the screen for all of its compatible software, and how they react to your input. Most operating systems today support a **graphical user interface**, which provides a way to point and click a mouse to select menu options and manipulate graphical objects that are displayed on the screen. See Figure C-8. Graphical user interface is sometimes abbreviated "GUI" and referred to as a "gooey."

- Although their main purpose is to control what happens "behind the scenes" of a computer system, many operating systems provide helpful tools, called **utilities**, that you can use to control and customize your computer equipment and work environment. Table C-1 lists some OS utilities.

FIGURE C-7: How the operating system interacts with the application software

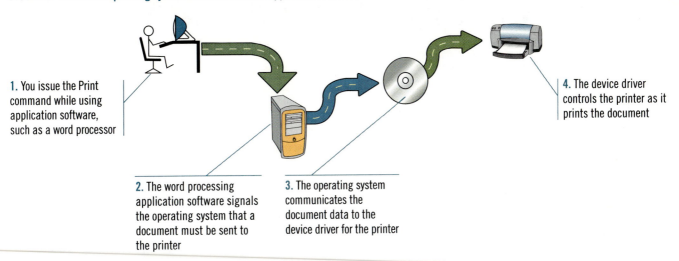

1. You issue the Print command while using application software, such as a word processor

2. The word processing application software signals the operating system that a document must be sent to the printer

3. The operating system communicates the document data to the device driver for the printer

4. The device driver controls the printer as it prints the document

FIGURE C-8: Example of a graphical user interface (GUI)

▶ A graphical user interface features menus and icons that you can manipulate with the click of a mouse

TABLE C-1: Examples of Windows operating system utilities

UTILITY USED TO	WHAT WINDOWS PROVIDES
Launch programs	When you start your computer, Windows displays a "desktop" that contains a collection of graphical objects, such as the Start menu, which you can manipulate to start programs.
Manage files	Windows Explorer allows you to view a list of files, move them to different storage devices, copy them, rename them, and delete them.
Get help	Windows provides a Help system that you can use to find out how various commands work.
Customize the user interface	The Control Panel, accessible from the Start menu, provides utilities that help you customize your screen display and work environment.
Configure equipment	The Windows Control Panel also provides access to utilities that help you set up and configure your computer's hardware and peripheral devices.

Comparing operating systems

The operating system is the master controller of your computer system. It determines how you interact with your computer. This lesson discusses categories of operating systems and compares the main features of popular operating systems.

DETAILS

- Operating systems are informally categorized using one or more of the following terms:

  A **single-user operating system** expects to deal with one set of input devices—those that can be controlled by one user at a time. Operating systems for handheld computers and many personal computers fit into the single-user category.

  A **multiuser operating system** is designed to deal with input, output, and processing requests from many users at the same time. One of its most difficult responsibilities is to schedule all of the processing requests that must be performed by a centralized computer, often a mainframe.

  A **network operating system**, or **server operating system**, provides communications and routing services that allow computers to share data, programs, and peripheral devices. While a multiuser OS and a network OS may sound the same, a multiuser operating system schedules requests for processing on a centralized computer; a network operating system simply routes data and programs to each user's local computer, where the actual processing takes place.

  A **desktop operating system** is one that's designed for either a desktop or notebook personal computer. The computer that you typically use at home, at school, or at work is most likely configured with a desktop operating system. Typically, these operating systems are designed to accommodate a single user, but may also provide networking capability.

  Today's desktop operating systems invariably provide multitasking services. A **multitasking operating system** provides process and memory management services that allow two or more programs to run simultaneously. Most of today's personal computers use operating systems that offer multitasking services.

- **Microsoft Windows** is installed on over 80 percent of the world's personal computers. Since its introduction, Windows has evolved through several versions. Windows 95, Windows 98, Windows ME, and Windows XP are classified as desktop operating systems that provide basic networking capabilities. Windows NT, Windows 2000, and Windows XP Professional are typically classified as server operating systems, because they are designed to handle the demands of medium-size to large-size networks.

- Like Windows, **Mac OS** has been through a number of revisions, including OS X (X means version 10), which made its debut in 2001.

- Both Mac OS for the Apple Macintosh computer and Windows base their user interfaces on the graphical model that was pioneered at Xerox. A quick comparison of Figure C-9 and Figure C-10 shows that both Mac and Windows interfaces use a mouse to point and click various icons and menus. Both interfaces feature rectangular work areas for multitasking services and provide basic networking services. Many of the most prolific software publishers produce one version of their software for Windows and another version for Mac OS.

- The **UNIX** operating system was developed in 1969 at AT&T's Bell Labs. It gained a good reputation for its dependability in multiuser environments. Many versions of it became available for mainframes and microcomputers.

- In 1991, a young Finnish student named Linus Torvalds developed the **Linux** operating system, based on a version of UNIX. Linux is rather unique because it is distributed under the terms of a General Public License (GPL), which allows everyone to make copies for their own use, to give it to others, or to sell it. This licensing policy has encouraged programmers to develop Linux utilities, software, and enhancements. Linux is primarily distributed over the Web.

  The Linux operating system includes such features as multitasking, TCP/IP drivers, and multiuser capabilities. These features make Linux a popular operating system for e-mail and Web servers, as well as for local area networks. Linux has been gaining popularity as a desktop operating system. See Figure C-11. Some new personal computers come configured with Linux instead of Windows or Mac OS.

- **DOS** stands for Disk Operating System. It was developed by Microsoft, the same company that later produced Windows. It was introduced on the original IBM PC in 1982. Although IBM called this operating system PC-DOS, Microsoft marketed it to other companies under the name MS-DOS. After more than 20 years, the remnants of DOS still linger as part of the operating system for Windows versions 3.1, 95, 98, and ME. Today, users rarely interact with DOS.

FIGURE C-9: Microsoft Windows

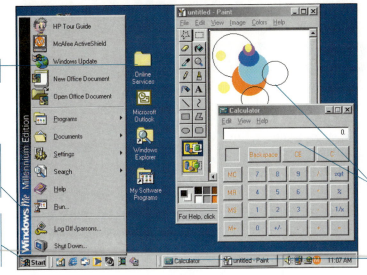

Icons represent computer hardware and software

The left side of the Start menu usually displays the version of the Windows OS that is in use

The Start button provides access to a menu of programs, documents, and utilities

◀ The Windows operating system gets its name from the rectangular work areas that appear on the screen-based desktop; each work area can display a different document or program, providing a visual model of the operating system's multitasking capabilities

Two different programs can run in two separate windows

The taskbar indicates which programs are running

FIGURE C-10: Mac OS

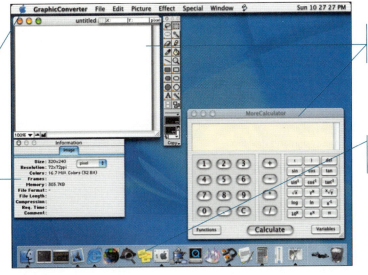

The Apple logo provides access to a menu

Menus and other on-screen objects are manipulated by using a mouse

Two different programs can run in two separate windows

Icons represent computer hardware components and software

FIGURE C-11: Linux

Desktop icons look similar to those on the Windows and Macintosh desktops

A horizontal option bar combines features of the Windows Start menu, Control Panel, and taskbar

◀ Linux users can choose from several graphical interfaces; this is the popular KDE (K Desktop Environment)

Two different programs can run in two separate windows

Defining document production software

Whether you are writing a 10-page paper, writing software documentation, designing a brochure for your new startup company, or laying out the school newspaper, you will probably use some form of **document production software**. This software assists you with composing, editing, designing, printing, and electronically publishing documents.

DETAILS

⬤ Three popular types of document production software:

Word processing software is used to produce documents such as reports, letters, and manuscripts. Word processing software gives you the ability to compose a document on the screen before you commit it to paper. Refer to Figure C-12.

Desktop publishing software (DTP) takes word processing software one step further by helping you use graphic design techniques to enhance the format and appearance of a document. Although today's word processing software offers many page layout and design features, desktop publishing software provides more sophisticated features to help you produce professional-quality output for publications.

Web authoring software helps you design and develop Web pages that you can publish electronically on the Internet. Web authoring software provides easy-to-use tools for composing the text for a Web page, assembling graphical elements, and automatically generating HTML tags.

⬤ Table C-2 describes common features of document production software. None of these automated features, however, can substitute for a thorough proofreading of your document.

⬤ The **format** for a document refers to how all text, pictures, titles, and page numbers are arranged on the page. The look of your document will depend on formatting factors, such as font style, paragraph style (see Figure C-13), and page layout.

⬤ **Page layout** refers to the physical position of each element on a page. A **header** is text that you specify to appear in the top margin of every page automatically. A **footer** is text that you specify to appear in the bottom margin of every page automatically. **Clip art** is a collection of drawings and photos designed to be inserted into documents. A **table** is a grid-like structure that can hold text or pictures. For printed documents, tables are a popular way to provide easy-to-read columns of data and to position graphics. For Web pages, tables provide one of the few ways to position text and pictures precisely.

⬤ Frame-oriented software allows you to divide each page into several rectangular-shaped **frames** that you can fill with either text or pictures. See Figure C-14. Frames provide you with finer control over the position of elements on a page, such as a figure and a caption on top of it. DTP software is usually frame oriented.

TABLE C-2: Some features of document production software

FEATURE	DESCRIPTION
alignment	determines position of text as left, right, centered, or full justified
autocorrect	automatically changes a typo, such as "teh" to "the"
find and replace	finds all occurrences of a word or phrase and lets you replace it with another word or phrase, such as changing May to August
formatting options	allows you change font, font size, font style
line spacing	determines the space between lines of type, such as single space
mail merge	creates personalized letters by automatically combining information in a mailing list with a form letter
spelling checker/ grammar checker	marks words in a document as misspelled if they do not match words in the spelling dictionary; reads through your document and points out potential grammatical trouble spots, such as run-on sentences
style	saved set of formatting options that you apply to text; you can create character, paragraph, table, and list styles

FIGURE C-12: Microsoft Word

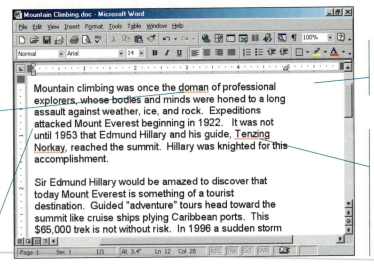

As you type, the spelling checker compares your words with a list of correctly spelled words; words not included in the list are marked with a wavy line as possible misspellings

Even after you type an entire document, adjusting the size of your right, left, top, and bottom margins is simple

Document production software uses word wrap automatically to fit your text within the margins

Proper nouns and scientific, medical, and technical words are likely to be flagged as misspelled even if you spell them correctly because they do not appear in the spelling checker's dictionary

FIGURE C-13: Applying a style

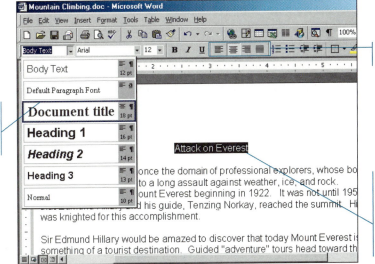

The style called Document title specifies Times New Roman font, size 18, bold, and centered

Paragraph alignment buttons

Applying the formats assigned to a style simply requires you to highlight the text, then click a style from the list, such as the Document title style

FIGURE C-14: Using frames

One frame holds the centered title and author's byline

A frame can be positioned anywhere on the page—even in the center of two text columns

Wrapping text around a frame adds interest to the layout

Attack on Everest

by Janell Chalmers

Mountain climbing was once the domain of professional explorers, whose bodies and minds were honed to a long assault against weather, ice, and rock. Expeditions attacked Mount Everest beginning in 1922. It was not until 1953 that Edmund Hillary and his guide, Tenzing Norkay, reached the summit. Hillary was knighted for this accomplishment.

Sir Edmund Hillary would be amazed to discover that today Mount Everest is something of a tourist destination. Guided "adventure" tours head toward the

summit like cruise ships plying Caribbean ports. This $65,000 trek is not without risk. In 1996 a sudden storm killed eight climbers.

Back in 1923, British mountaineer, George Mallory was asked, why climb Everest? His reply, "Because it's there." A new answer to this question, "Because we can" may be largely attributable to new high-tech mountain gear. Nylon, polypropylene and Gore-Tex clothing provide light, yet warm protection from the elements. Ultraviolet lenses protect eyes from dangerous "snow-blindness."

"Because it's there."
George Mallory

Graphical elements such as photos, diagrams, graphs, and pie charts can be incorporated in your documents using frames

Defining spreadsheet software

Spreadsheet software, used for numerical calculations, was initially popular with accountants and financial managers who dealt with paper-based spreadsheets, but found the electronic version far easier to use and less prone to errors than manual calculations. Other people soon discovered the benefits of spreadsheets for projects that require repetitive calculations: budgeting, maintaining a grade book, balancing a checkbook, tracking investments, calculating loan payments, and estimating project costs. You can use spreadsheets to make other calculations too, based on simple equations or more complex formulas. Spreadsheet software can turn your data into a variety of colorful graphs and charts.

DETAILS

- A **spreadsheet** uses rows and columns of numbers to create a model or representation of a real situation. For example, your checkbook register is a type of spreadsheet because it is a numerical representation of the cash flowing in and out of your bank account. **Spreadsheet software** provides tools to create electronic spreadsheets.

FYI

Spreadsheet software is useful for what-if analyses, such as, "Is it better to take out a 30-year mortgage at 8.5% interest or a 15-year mortgage at 7.75% interest?"

- You use spreadsheet software to create an on-screen **worksheet** like the one shown in Figure C-15. A worksheet is based on a grid of columns and rows. Each **cell** in the grid can contain a value, label, or formula and has a unique **cell reference**, or "address," derived from its column and row location. For example, A1 is the cell reference for the upper-left cell in a worksheet because it is in column A and row 1. You can select any cell and make it the active cell by clicking it. Once a cell is active, you can enter data into it. A **value** is a number that you want to use in a calculation. A **label** is any text that is used to describe data.

QUICK TIP

You can format the labels and values on a worksheet by changing fonts and font size, selecting a font color, and selecting a font style, such as bold.

- The values contained in a cell can be manipulated by formulas that are placed in other cells. A **formula** works behind the scenes to tell the computer how to use the contents of cells in calculations. You can enter a simple formula in a cell to add, subtract, multiply, or divide numbers. Figure C-16 illustrates how a formula might be used in a simple spreadsheet to calculate savings. More complex formulas can be designed to perform just about any calculation you can imagine. You can enter a formula "from scratch" by typing it into a cell, or you can use a

function, which is a predefined formula built into the spreadsheet software.

- Unless you specify otherwise, a cell reference is a **relative reference**—a reference that can change if cells are deleted or inserted and the data or a formula moves. See Figure C-17. If you don't want a cell reference to change, you can use an absolute reference. An **absolute reference** never changes when you delete or insert cells or copy or move formulas. Understanding when to use absolute references is one of the key aspects to developing spreadsheet design expertise.

- When you change the contents of any cell in a worksheet, all of the formulas are recalculated. This **automatic recalculation** feature assures you that the results in every cell are accurate with regard to the information currently entered in the worksheet. Your worksheet is also automatically updated to reflect any rows or columns that you add, delete, or copy within the worksheet.

- Most spreadsheet software includes a few templates or wizards for predesigned worksheets, such as invoices, income-expense reports, balance sheets, and loan payment schedules. Additional templates are available on the Web. These templates are typically designed by content professionals and contain all of the necessary labels and formulas. To use a template, you simply plug in the values for your calculation.

FIGURE C-15: An on-screen worksheet

Each column is lettered

Cell A1

Each row is numbered

Values in these cells can be used for calculations

Labels, such as Profit and Expenses, identify data

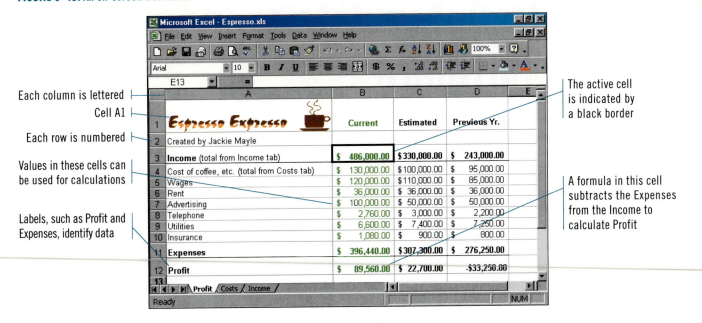

The active cell is indicated by a black border

A formula in this cell subtracts the Expenses from the Income to calculate Profit

FIGURE C-16: How formulas work

When a cell contains a formula, it displays the result of the formula, rather than the formula itself

The number that appears in cell B6 was calculated by the spreadsheet based on the formula typed in the cell

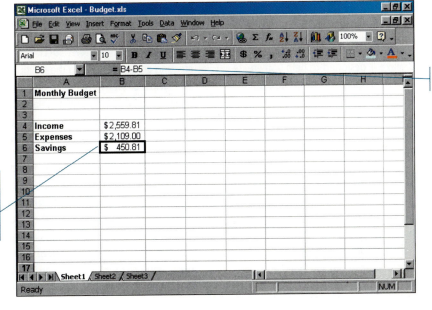

The formula for cell B6 is shown on the Formula bar

FIGURE C-17: Relative vs. absolute references

Relative references within a formula can change when you insert or delete rows and columns or when you copy or move formulas; an absolute reference is "anchored" so that it always refers to a specific cell

Two blank rows

The original formula =B4-B5 uses relative references

When row 3 is deleted, the Income and Expenses values move up one row, which means that these values have new cell references; the formula changes to =B3-B4 to reflect the new cell references

Defining data management software

Data management software helps you to store, find, organize, update, and report information. Several types of data management software exist, including file management software and database management software. This lesson provides background on structured files and the file management software designed for these files, as well as a discussion of databases and the database management software designed for databases.

DETAILS

● A **structured file** is a collection of records, each with the same set of fields that can hold data. Each **record** holds data for a single entity—a person, place, thing, or event. A **field** holds one item of data relevant to a record. Figure C-18 illustrates records and fields in a structured file. A single file, sometimes called a **flat file**, can be a useful repository for simple lists of information, such as e-mail addresses, holiday card addresses, doctor visits, appointments, or household valuables.

● **File management software** is designed to help you create, modify, search, sort, and print simple lists, or flat files. Some file management software is tailored to special applications. A **personal information manager**, for example, is a specialized file system that keeps track of daily appointments, addresses, and To Do lists.

● In contrast to a single flat file, a **database** is a collection of files that can be treated as a single unit, sometimes referred to as a table. For example, suppose you have one computer file containing video information and another containing information about performers. Database software lets you join the two files together to display the information about the video and performers at the same time.

Most of today's databases are based on either a relational model or an object-oriented model. A **relational database** structures each file as a table in which each column is a field and each

row is a record. Relationships can be established between tables to join the tables together so that they can be treated as one, as shown in Figure C-19. An **object-oriented database** treats each record as a unit that can be manipulated using program instructions called methods. For example, a university database containing information about its students might include an object called "Course Grades" and a method called "Calculate GPA."

● **Database management software** (DBMS) is designed for creating and manipulating the multiple files that form a database. Most of today's database management software is designed for creating and manipulating relational databases. Special object-oriented database management software is required for creating and manipulating object-oriented databases.

● Your data management software, whether it is file management software or database management software, requires you to create a file structure. A **file structure** is somewhat like a fill-in form that contains a list of fields and their data types that define the data in the file. See Figure C-20. Once you create a file structure, you can enter the data for each of your records. With the data in place, you can modify the data in individual records to keep it up to date. Your data management software also will help you print reports, export data to other programs (such as to a spreadsheet, where you can graph the data), convert the data to other formats (such as HTML, so that you can post the data on the Web), and transmit data to other computers.

Searching flat files and databases

Many flat files and databases contain hundreds or thousands of records. If you want to find a particular record or a group of records, scrolling through every record is much too cumbersome. Instead, you can enter search specifications called a **query**, and the computer will quickly locate the records you seek. Most data management software provides one or more methods for making queries. A **query language** provides a set of commands for locating and manipulating data. **SQL** (Structured Query Language) is a popular query language used by numerous data

management software packages. In addition to a formal query language, some data management software provides **natural language query** capabilities. To make such queries, you don't have to learn an esoteric query language. Instead, you can simply enter questions using natural language. As an alternative to a query language or a natural language query, your data management software might allow you to **query by example** (QBE), simply by filling out a form with the type of data that you want to locate.

FIGURE C-18: A structured file

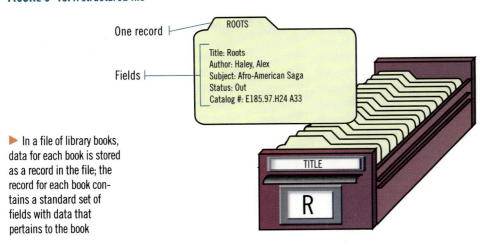

One record

Fields

ROOTS

Title: Roots
Author: Haley, Alex
Subject: Afro-American Saga
Status: Out
Catalog #: E185.97.H24 A33

TITLE

R

▶ In a file of library books, data for each book is stored as a record in the file; the record for each book contains a standard set of fields with data that pertains to the book

FIGURE C-19: A relational database

▶ A relational database can contain multiple files, which are represented by tables; equivalent fields in each table can be used to join the records in these tables so that you can see the data in both tables at the same time

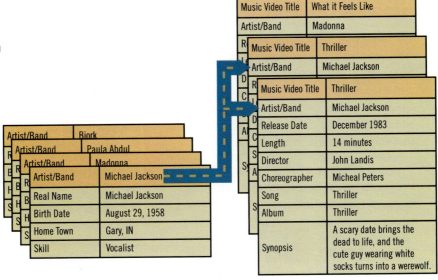

Music Video Title	What it Feels Like
Artist/Band	Madonna

Music Video Title	Thriller
Artist/Band	Michael Jackson

Music Video Title	Thriller
Artist/Band	Michael Jackson
Release Date	December 1983
Length	14 minutes
Director	John Landis
Choreographer	Micheal Peters
Song	Thriller
Album	Thriller
Synopsis	A scary date brings the dead to life, and the cute guy wearing white socks turns into a werewolf.

Artist/Band	Biork

Artist/Band	Paula Abdul

Artist/Band	Madonna

Artist/Band	Michael Jackson
Real Name	Michael Jackson
Birth Date	August 29, 1958
Home Town	Gary, IN
Skill	Vocalist

FIGURE C-20: Database management software

CD
ScreenTour

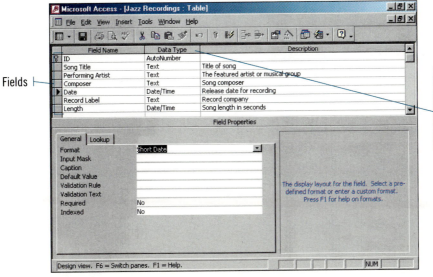

Fields

When you define a field, you can specify its data type as either character data, numeric data, date data, logical data, hyperlink data, or memo data

Defining graphics software

In computer lingo, the term **graphics** refers to any picture, drawing, sketch, photograph, image, or icon that appears on your computer screen. **Graphics software** is designed to help you create, display, modify, manipulate, and print graphics. Many kinds of graphics software exist, and each one typically specializes in a particular type of graphic. If you are really interested in working with graphics, you will undoubtedly end up using more than one graphics software package.

DETAILS

- **Paint software** (sometimes called "image editing software") provides a set of electronic pens, brushes, and paints for painting images on the screen. Graphic artists, Web page designers, photographers, and illustrators use paint software as their primary computer-based graphics tool.

- **Photo editing software** includes features specially designed to fix poor-quality photos by modifying contrast and brightness, cropping out unwanted objects, and removing "red eye." Photos can also be edited using paint software, but photo editing software typically provides tools and wizards that simplify common photo editing tasks.

- **Drawing software** provides a set of lines, shapes, and colors that can be assembled into diagrams, corporate logos, and schematics. The drawings created with this type of software tend to have a "flat" cartoon-like quality, but they are very easy to modify and look good at just about any size. Figure C-21 provides more information on paint, photo editing, and drawing software.

- **3-D graphics software** provides a set of tools for creating "wireframes" that represent three-dimensional objects. A wireframe acts much like the framework for a pop-up tent. Just as you would construct the framework for the tent, then cover it with a nylon tent cover, 3-D graphics software can cover a wireframe object with surface texture and color to create a graphic of a 3-D object. See Figure C-22.

- **CAD software** (computer-aided design software) is a special type of 3-D graphics software designed for architects and engineers who use computers to create blueprints and product specifications. Scaled-down versions of professional CAD software provide simplified tools for homeowners who want to redesign their kitchens, examine new landscaping options, or experiment with floor plans.

- **Presentation software** provides all of the tools you need for combining text, graphics, graphs, animations, and sound into a series of electronic **slides**. You can display the electronic slides on a color monitor for a one-on-one presentation or use a computer projection device, like the one shown in Figure C-23, for group presentations. You can also output the presentation as overhead transparencies, paper copies, or 35-mm slides.

FIGURE C-21: Images created using paint, photo editing, and drawing software

▲ Paint software works well with realistic art and photos

▲ Photo editing software includes special features for touching up photographs

▲ Drawing software tends to create two-dimensional "cartoon-like" images

FIGURE C-22: 3-D graphics tools

▶ Some 3-D software specializes in drawing figures

▲ 3-D graphics software provides tools for creating a wireframe that represents a three-dimensional object

FIGURE C-23: A computer-based presentation

▲ A presentation can be displayed for a group by using a projection device

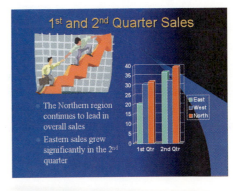

▲ A computer-based presentation consists of a series of slides that can include graphics, bulleted lists, and charts

Defining business and science software

The terms business software and science software provide a broad umbrella for several types of software that are designed to help businesses and organizations accomplish routine or specialized tasks. These types of software provide a structured environment dedicated to a particular number-crunching task, such as money management, mathematical modeling, or statistical analysis.

Info Web

NUMERIC SOFTWARE

DETAILS

- **Accounting and finance software** helps you keep a record of monetary transactions and investments. In this software category, **personal finance software** (Figure C-24) is geared toward individual finances. **Tax preparation software** is a specialized type of personal finance software designed to help you gather your annual income and expense data, identify deductions, and calculate your tax payment.

- Some accounting and finance software is geared toward business. If you're an entrepreneur, **small business accounting software** can be a real asset. These easy-to-use programs don't require more than a basic understanding of accounting and finance principles. This type of software helps you invoice customers and keep track of what they owe. It stores additional customer data, such as contact information and purchasing history. Inventory functions keep track of the products that you carry. Payroll capabilities automatically calculate wages and deduct federal, state, and local taxes.

- **Vertical market software** is designed to automate specialized tasks in a specific market or business. Examples include patient management and billing software specially designed for hospitals, job estimating software for construction businesses, and student record management software for schools. Today, almost every business has access to some type of specialized vertical market software designed to automate, streamline, or computerize key business activities.

- **Horizontal market software** is generic software that can be used by just about any kind of business. **Payroll software** is a good example of horizontal market software. Almost every business has employees and must maintain payroll records. No matter what type of business uses it, payroll software must collect similar data and make similar calculations in order to produce payroll checks and W2 forms. Accounting software and project management software are additional examples of horizontal market software. **Accounting software** helps a business keep track of the money flowing in and out of various accounts. **Project management software** is an important tool for planning large projects, scheduling project tasks, and tracking project costs.

- **Groupware**, another umbrella term in the world of business software, is designed to help several people collaborate on a single project using network or Internet connections. It usually provides the capability to maintain schedules for all of the group members, automatically select meeting times for the group, facilitate communication by e-mail or other channels, distribute documents according to a prearranged schedule or sequence, and allow multiple people to contribute to a single document.

- One type of science-related software is **statistical software**, which helps you analyze large sets of data to discover relationships and patterns. It is a helpful tool for summarizing survey results, test scores, experiment results, or population data. Most statistical software includes graphing capability so that you can display and explore your data visually.

- **Mathematical modeling software**, such as MathCAD and Mathematica, provides tools for solving a wide range of math, science, and engineering problems. See Figure C-25. Students, teachers, mathematicians, and engineers, in particular, appreciate how this software helps them recognize patterns that can be difficult to identify in columns of numbers.

FIGURE C-24: Personal finance software

▶ Personal finance software helps you keep track of bank accounts, investments, credit card balances, and bills; some packages also support online banking, a way to use your computer and modem to download transactions directly from your bank, transfer funds between accounts, and pay bills

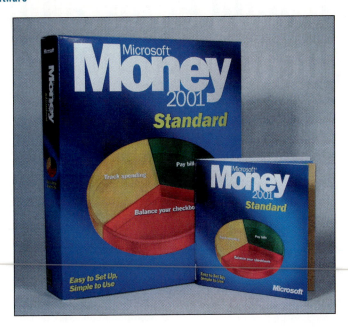

FIGURE C-25: Visualization of equation using mathematics software

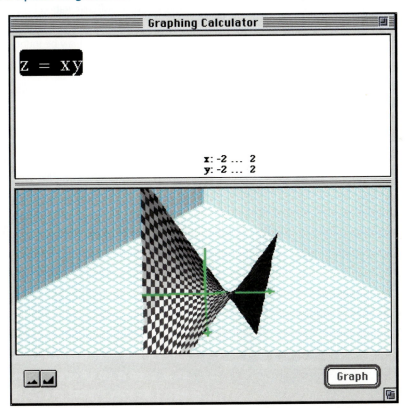

Why spreadsheet software is not always the best software for businesses

Spreadsheet software provides a tool to work with numeric models by using values, labels, and formulas. The advantage of spreadsheet software is its flexibility. You can create customized calculations according to your exact specifications. The disadvantage of spreadsheet software is that, aside from a few pre-designed templates, you are responsible for entering formulas and selecting functions for calculations. If you don't know the formulas, or don't understand the functions, you would do much better to purchase a business software package with those functions to meet your specific needs.

Defining entertainment and education software

The computer can provide entertainment in many formats, including listening to music, watching videos, and playing games. Computer games are the most popular type of entertainment software. Over $6 billion of computer and video games are sold each year in the U.S. Software classified as educational can also be entertaining; these software categories often overlap.

DETAILS

● It is easy to make your own digital voice and music recordings and store them on your computer's hard disk. Windows and Mac OS operating system utilities typically supply the necessary **audio editing software**, including Sound Recorder on PCs (see Figure C-26), and iTunes on iMacs. Audio editing software typically includes playback as well as recording capabilities. A specialized version of this software called Karaoke software integrates music files and on-screen lyrics; everything you need to sing along with your favorite tunes.

● **MP3** is a music compression file format that stores digitized music in such a way that the sound quality is excellent, but the file size remains relatively small—small enough to be easily downloaded from the Web. To listen to MP3 music on your computer, you need an **MP3 player**. Versions of MP3 player software are available for many handheld computers and for personal computers running Windows, Mac OS, and Linux.

● **Ear training software** targets musicians and music students who want to learn to play by ear, develop tuning skills, recognize notes and keys, and develop other musical skills. **Notation software** is the musician's equivalent of a word processor. It helps musicians compose, edit, and print the notes for their compositions. For non-musicians, **computer-aided music software** is designed to generate unique musical compositions simply by selecting the musical style, instruments, key, and tempo. **MIDI sequencing software** and software synthesizers are an important part of the studio musician's toolbox. They're great for sound effects and for controlling keyboards and other digital instruments.

● The growing popularity of computer-based video editing can be attributed to video editing software, such as Windows Movie Maker and Apple iMovie, now included with Windows computers and iMacs. **Video editing software** provides a set of tools for transferring video footage from a camcorder to a computer, clipping out unwanted footage, assembling video segments in

any sequence, adding special visual effects, and adding a sound track. Despite an impressive array of features, video editing software is relatively easy to use, as explained in Figure C-27.

● Computer games are generally classified into subcategories, such as role-playing, action, adventure, puzzles, simulations, and strategy/war games. Since it was established in 1994, the Entertainment Software Rating Board (ESRB) has rated more than 7,000 video and computer games. Rating symbols, shown in Figure C-28, can usually be found on the game box.

● **Educational software** helps you learn and practice new skills. For the youngest students, educational software, such as MindTwister Math and 3-D Froggy Phonics, teaches basic arithmetic and reading skills. Instruction is presented in game format, and the levels of play are adapted to the player's age and ability. For older students and adults, software is available for such diverse educational endeavors as learning languages, training yourself to use new software, learning how to play the piano or guitar, preparing for standardized tests, improving keyboarding skills, and even learning managerial skills for a diverse workplace. Exam preparation software is available for standardized tests such as the SAT, GMAT, and LSAT.

● **Reference software** provides you with a collection of information and a way to access that information. The reference software category spans a wide range of applications from encyclopedias to medical references, from map software to trip planners, and from cookbooks to telephone books. The options are as broad as the full range of human interests. Reference software is generally shipped on a CD-ROM because of the quantity of data it includes. Many of these products provide links to Web sites that contain updates for the information on the CD-ROM. Other software publishers have eliminated the CD-ROM entirely and have placed all of their reference materials on the Web. Access to that information often requires a fee or a subscription.

FIGURE C-26: Music editing software

Menus provide additional digital editing features, such as speed control, volume adjustments, clipping, and mixing

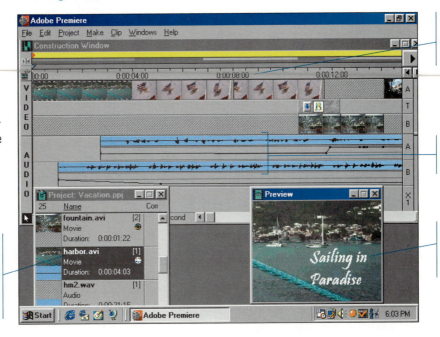

Audio editing software, such as Sound Recorder, provides controls much like a tape recorder

Rewind to beginning

Fast Forward to end   Play   Stop   Record

FIGURE C-27: Video editing software

▶ Video editing software, such as Adobe Premiere, helps you import a series of video clips from a camera or VCR, arrange the clips in the order of your choice, add transitions between clips, and add an audio track

Use the timeline to indicate the sequence for your video clips and transitions

Arrange the audio tracks to synchronize with each video clip

The video and sound clips that you import for the project are displayed in a list so that you can easily select them in sequence

Preview your video to see how the clips, transitions, and soundtrack all work together

FIGURE C-28: ESRB ratings and symbols

TEEN
Suitable for 13 and older. May contain violent content, mild or strong language, and/or suggestive themes.

MATURE
Suitable for 17 and older. May contain mature sexual themes or more intense violence or language.

EARLY CHILDHOOD
Suitable for ages 3 and older. Contains no material that parents would find inappropriate.

EVERYONE
Suitable for ages 6 and older. May contain minimal violence, some comic mischief, or crude language.

ADULTS ONLY
Content suitable only for adults. May include graphic depictions of sex and/or violence.

RATING PENDING
Product has been submitted, but a rating has not yet been assigned.

Understanding licenses and copyrights

Once you purchase a software package, you might assume that you can install it and use it in any way that you like. In fact, your "purchase" entitles you to use the software only in certain pre-scribed ways. In most countries, computer software, like a book or movie, is protected by a copyright. In addition to copyright protection, computer software is often protected by the terms of a software license. Copyright laws provide fairly severe restrictions on copying, distributing, and reselling software. However, a license agreement may offer some rights to consumers as well. The licenses for commercial software, shareware, freeware, open source, and public domain software provide different levels of permission for software use, copying, and distribution.

DETAILS

● A **software license**, or "license agreement," is a legal contract that defines the ways in which you may use a computer program. For personal computer software, you will find the license on the outside of the package, on a separate card inside the package, on the CD packaging, or in one of the program files.

● A **copyright** is a form of legal protection that grants the author of an original work an exclusive right to copy, distribute, sell, and modify that work, except under special circumstances described by copyright laws. Exceptions include the purchaser's right to copy software from a distribution disk or Web site to a computer's hard disk in order to install it; to make an extra, or backup, copy of the software in case the original copy becomes erased or damaged; and to copy and distribute sections of a software program for use in critical reviews and teaching.

● Most software displays a **copyright notice**, such as "© 2002 eCourseWare," on one of its screens. However, because this notice is not required by law, programs without a copyright notice are still protected by copyright law. People who circumvent copyright law and illegally copy, distribute, or modify software are sometimes called software pirates, and their illegal copies are referred to as pirated software.

● Most legal contracts require signatures before the terms of the contract take effect. This requirement becomes unwieldy with software; imagine having to sign a license agreement and return it before you can use a new software package. To circumvent the signature requirement, software publishers typically use two techniques to validate a software license: shrink-wrap licenses and

installation agreements. When you purchase computer software, the distribution disks, CDs, or DVDs are usually sealed in an envelope, plastic box, or shrink wrapping. A **shrink-wrap license** goes into effect as soon as you open the packaging. Figure C-29 explains more about the mechanics of a shrink-wrap license.

● An **installation agreement** is displayed on the screen when you first install the software. After reading the software license on the screen, you can indicate that you accept the terms of the license by clicking a designated button usually labeled "OK," "I agree," or "I accept."

● Software licenses are often lengthy and written in legalese, but your legal right to use the software continues only as long as you abide by the terms of the software license. Therefore, you should understand the software license for any software you use. When you read a software license agreement, look for answers to the following questions:

- Am I buying the software or licensing it?
- When does the license go into effect?
- Under what circumstances can I make copies?
- Can I rent the software?
- Can I sell the software?
- What if the software includes a distribution CD and a set of distribution disks?
- Does the software publisher provide a warranty?
- Can I loan the software to a friend?

FIGURE C-29: A shrink-wrap license

▶ When software has a shrink-wrap license, you agree to the terms of the software license by opening the package; if you do not agree with the terms, you should return the software in its unopened package

Examining copyright protections for software

Commercial software is typically sold in computer stores or at Web sites. Although you buy this software, you actually purchase only the right to use it under the terms of the software license. A license for commercial software typically adheres closely to the limitations provided by copyright law, although it might give you permission to install the software on a computer at work and on a computer at home, provided that you use only one of them at a time.

Shareware is copyrighted software marketed under a try before you buy policy. It typically includes a license that permits you to use the software for a trial period. To use it beyond the trial period, you must send in a registration fee. A shareware license usually allows you to make copies of the software and distribute them to others. If they choose to use the software, they must send in a registration fee as well. These shared copies provide a low-cost marketing and distribution channel.

Registration fee payment relies on the honor system, so unfortunately many shareware authors collect only a fraction of the money they deserve for their programming efforts. Thousands of shareware programs are available, encompassing just about as many applications as commercial software.

Freeware is copyrighted software that is available without a fee. Because the software is protected by copyright, you cannot do anything with it that is not expressly allowed by copyright law or by the author. Typically, the license for freeware permits you to use the software, copy it, and give it away, but does not permit you to alter it or sell it. Many utility programs, device drivers, and some games are available as freeware.

Open source software makes the uncompiled program instructions available to programmers who want to modify and improve the software. Open source software may be sold or distributed free of charge, but it must, in every case, include the uncompiled source code. Linux is an example of open source software, as is FreeBSD—a version of UNIX designed for personal computers.

Public domain software is not protected by copyright because the copyright has expired or the author has placed the program in the public domain, making it available without restriction. Public domain software may be freely copied, distributed, and even resold. The primary restriction on public domain software is that you are not allowed to apply for a copyright on it.

Installing Software

No matter how you obtain a new software package, you must install it on your computer before you can use it. From time to time, you might also want to uninstall some of the software that exists on your computer. This Tech Talk looks at the process of installing and uninstalling software.

The ingredients necessary to install new software are the files that contain the programs, support modules, and data modules. These files might be supplied on **distribution disks**, one or more CDs, or a series of floppy disks that are packaged in a box, along with an instruction manual. Software downloaded over the Internet typically arrives as one huge file that contains the program modules and the text of the instruction manual.

Printed on the software package, or tucked away at the software publisher's Web site, you'll find a set of **system requirements**, which specifies the operating system and minimum hardware capacities for a software product to work correctly.

When you **install** software, the new software files are placed in the appropriate folders on your computer's hard disk, and then your computer performs any software or hardware configurations necessary to make sure the program is ready to run. The installation process usually includes the following activities:

- Copy files from distribution disks to specified folders on the hard disk

- Uncompress files if they have been distributed in a compressed format, such as WinZip

- Analyze the computer's resources, such as processor speed, RAM capacity, and hard disk capacity, to verify that they meet or exceed the minimum system requirements

- Analyze hardware components and peripheral devices to select appropriate device drivers

- Look for any system files and players, such as Windows Media Player or Internet Explorer, that are required to run the program but are not supplied on the distribution disks

- Update necessary system files, such as the Windows Registry and the Windows Program menu, with information about the new software

With Windows and other operating systems, application software programs share some common files. These files are often supplied by the operating system and perform routine tasks, such as displaying the Print dialog box that allows you to select a printer and specify how many copies of a file you want to print. These "shared" files are not typically provided on the distribution disks for a new software program because the files should already exist on your computer. The installation routine attempts to locate these files and will notify you if any of them are missing.

As part of the installation process, you will be asked to specify the folder that will hold the files for the new software. The main executable files and data modules for the software will be placed in the folder you specify.

Installing downloaded software

Downloaded software is usually one of the following compressed file types: - self-installing executable file, self-executing zip files, or zipped files. The self-installing executable file automatically unzips itself and starts the setup program. Simply follow the setup program prompts to acknowledge the license agreement, indicate the folder for the software files, and complete the installation. A self-executing zip file automatically unzips the software's files, but does not automatically start the setup program. Under this installation system, you start the executable file to unzip the files for the new software. One of these files will be the Setup.exe program. Next, you manually start the setup program and follow its prompts to complete the installation. A zip file must be opened with a program such as WinZip. You then must run the setup program to acknowledge the license agreement, indicate the folder for the software files, and complete the installation.

Installation procedures vary depending on a computer's operating system. Windows software typically contains a **setup program** that guides you through the installation process. Figure C-30 shows you what to expect when you use a setup program.

Operating systems, such as Windows and Mac OS, provide access to an **uninstall routine** that deletes the software's files from various directories on your computer's hard disk. The uninstall routine also removes references to the program from the desktop and from operating system files, such as the file system and, in the case of Windows, from the Windows Registry. With Windows software, you can typically find the uninstall routine on the same menu as the program. If an uninstall routine is not provided by the software, you can use the one provided by the operating system. In Windows, the Add/Remove Programs icon is located in the Control Panel, accessible from the Start menu.

FIGURE C-30: Installing software from a distribution CD

1. Insert the distribution disk, CD, or DVD. The setup program should start automatically. If it does not, look for a file called *Setup.exe* and then run it.

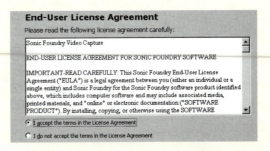

2. Read the license agreement, if one is presented on the screen. By agreeing to the terms of the license, you can proceed with the installation.

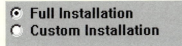

3. Select the installation option that best meets your needs. If you select a full installation, the setup program copies all files and data from the distribution medium to the hard disk of your computer system. A full installation provides you with access to all features of the software.

If you select a custom installation, the setup program displays a list of software features for your selection. After you select the features you want, the setup program copies only the selected program files, support modules, and data modules to your hard disk. A custom installation can save space on your hard disk.

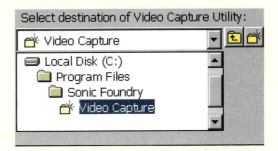

4. Follow the prompts provided by the setup program to specify a folder to hold the new software program. You can typically create a new folder during the setup process if you did not prepare a folder ahead of time.

5. If the software includes multiple distribution disks, insert each one in the specified drive when the setup program tells you to do so.

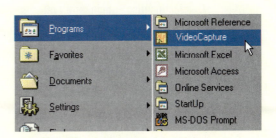

6. When the setup is complete, start the program that you just installed to make sure it works.

Issue   Is Piracy a Problem?

Software is easy to steal. You don't have to walk out of a CompUSA store with a Microsoft Office XP box under your shirt. You can simply borrow your friend's CD-ROM and install a copy of the program on your computer's hard disk. It seems so simple that it couldn't be illegal. But it is.

In many countries, including the United States, software pirates are subject to criminal prosecution. And yet, piracy continues to grow. According to the Software and Information Industry Association (SIIA), a leading anti-piracy watchdog, revenue losses from business software piracy typically exceed $12 billion per year. This figure reveals only a part of the piracy problem; it does not include losses from rampant game and educational software piracy.

A small but vocal minority of software users, such as members of GNU (which stands for "Gnu's Not UNIX"), believe that data and software should be freely distributed. Richard Stallman writes in the GNU Manifesto, "I consider that the golden rule requires that if I like a program I must share it with other people who like it. Software sellers want to divide users and conquer them, making each user agree not to share with others. I refuse to break solidarity with other users in this way. I cannot in good conscience sign a nondisclosure agreement or a software license agreement."

Is software piracy really damaging? Who cares if you use Microsoft Office without paying for it? As a consumer you should care if someone is using software they didn't pay for. Software piracy is damaging because it has a negative effect on the economy. Software production is the third largest industry in the United States, employing more than 2 million people and growing at a phenomenal rate of 5.8 percent per year. This industry, however, is losing an estimated $32 million every day, which translates to over 130,000 lost jobs and billions in lost tax revenues annually.

Decreases in software revenues can have a direct effect on consumers too. When software publishers must cut corners, they tend to reduce customer service and technical support. As a result, you, the consumer, get put on hold when you call for technical support, you find fewer free technical support sites, and you encounter customer support personnel who are only moderately knowledgeable about their products. The bottom line is that software piracy negatively affects customer service.

As an alternative to cutting support costs, some software publishers might build the cost of software piracy into the price of the software. The unfortunate result is that those who legitimately license and purchase software pay an inflated price.

Software piracy is a global problem. Although the United States accounts for the highest dollar amount of software piracy, approximately two-thirds of the piracy occurs outside the United States. The countries with the highest piracy rates are China, Japan, Korea, Germany, France, Brazil, Italy, Canada, and the United Kingdom. But piracy is also a problem in other countries. By some estimates, more than 90 percent of all business software used in Bulgaria, Indonesia, Russia, and Vietnam is pirated.

As a justification of high piracy rates, some observers point out that people in many countries simply might not be able to afford software that is priced for the U.S. market. This argument would make sense in China, where the average annual income is equivalent to about $3,500, and in North Korea, where the average income is only $900. A Korean who legitimately purchases Microsoft Office for $250 would be spending more than one-quarter of his or her annual income. Most of the countries with a high incidence of software piracy, however, have strong economies and respectable per capita incomes. To further discredit the theory that piracy stems from poverty, India—which has a fairly large computer-user community but a per capita income of only $1,600—is not among the top 10 countries with high rates of software piracy.

If economic factors do not account for the pervasiveness of software piracy, what does? Some analysts suggest that people need more education about software copyrights and the economic implications of piracy. Other analysts believe that copyright enforcement must be increased by supporting and implementing more vigorous efforts to identify and prosecute pirates.

▼ INTERACTIVE QUESTIONS

○ Yes ○ No ○ Not sure **1.** Do you believe that software piracy is a serious issue?

○ Yes ○ No ○ Not sure **2.** Do you know of any instances of software piracy?

○ Yes ○ No ○ Not sure **3.** Do you think that most software pirates understand that they are doing something illegal?

○ Yes ○ No ○ Not sure **4.** Should software publishers try to adjust software publishing for local markets?

▼ EXPAND THE IDEAS

1. Do you believe that software piracy is a serious issue? Write a two-page paper supporting your position. Include the opposing side's arguments in your report. Be sure to include your resources.

2. Do you think there are ways that software publishers can control piracy in the United States? In other countries? Do you know of any recent attempts at doing so? Work in a small group to brainstorm ideas and research recent trends or events. Compile your ideas and findings into a short presentation to give to the class. Include handouts for the audience and cite any sources you used.

3. Do you think that most software pirates understand that they are doing something illegal? Design a marketing campaign that could be used to educate the public about the issue. Create a poster that could be used in the campaign.

4. Should software publishers try to adjust software pricing for local markets? How would you propose such a pricing structure? How would these policies be enforced? Can you think of any other industry that adjusts prices for local markets? Write a two-page paper discussing your proposals and explaining your findings. Be sure to cite your sources.

End of Unit Exercises

▼ KEY TERMS

Absolute reference
Application software
Automatic recalculation
Cell
Cell reference
Clip art
Commercial software
Compiler
Computer language
Computer program
Computer programmer
Copyright
Copyright notice
Data management software
Data module
Database
Desktop operating system
Distribution disk
DOS
Field

File management software
File structure
Flat file
Formula
Frames
Freeware
Function
Graphical user interface (GUI)
Graphics
Graphics software
High-level languages
Horizontal market software
Install
Installation agreement
Interpreter
Label
Linux
Mac OS
Machine language
Main executable file

Microsoft Windows
MP3
MP3 player
Multitasking operating system
Multiuser operating system
Natural language query
Network operating system
Object code
Object-oriented database
Open source software
Operating system
Page layout
Public domain software
Query
Query by example
Query language
Record
Relational database
Relative reference
Scripts

Setup program
Shareware
Shrink-wrap license
Single-user operating system
Software
Software license
Source code
Spreadsheet
Spreadsheet software
SQL
Structured file
Support module
System requirements
System software
Table
Uninstall routine
UNIX
Utilities
Value
Vertical market software
Worksheet

▼ UNIT REVIEW

1. Use your own words to define each of the bold terms that appear throughout the unit. List 10 of the terms that are least familiar to you and write a sentence for each of them.

2. Make sure that you can list and describe the three types of files that are typically supplied on a software distribution disk.

3. Explain the difference between a compiler and an interpreter.

4. List three types of system software and at least five categories of application software.

5. Describe how an operating system manages resources.

6. Sketch a simple worksheet like one you might find in a spreadsheet software program and label the following: columns, rows, cell, active cell, values, labels, formulas, and Formula bar.

7. List three types of "number crunching" software that you can use instead of spreadsheet software and tell how you might use each one.

8. Describe when you would use each type of graphics software described in this unit.

9. Create a table with these column headings: single-user, multiuser, network, multitasking, and desktop operating system. List Linux, UNIX, Mac OS, and each version of Windows down the side of the table. Use a check mark to indicate which characteristics fit each operating system.

10. In your own words, explain what each of the ESRB ratings mean and how they would help you purchase software.

▼ FILL IN THE BEST ANSWER

1. Software can be divided into two major categories: application software and _____ software.

2. Software usually contains support modules and data modules, in addition to a main _____ file that you run to start the software.

3. Instructions that are written in a _____ -level language must be translated into _____ language before a computer can use them.

4. A(n) _____ translates all of the instructions in a program as a single batch, and the resulting machine language instructions are placed in a new file.

5. To run more than one program at a time, the operating system must allocate specific areas of _____ for each program.

6. A(n) _____ user interface provides a way for a user to interact with the software using a mouse and graphical objects on the screen.

7. A(n) _____ operating system is designed to deal with input, output, and processing requests from many users.

8. A(n) _____ operating system provides communications and routing services that allow computers to share data, programs, and peripheral devices.

9. Windows 2000 and Linux are classified as _____ operating systems, whereas Windows ME and Mac OS are classified as _____ operating systems.

10. Various kinds of document _____ software provide tools for creating and formatting printed and Web-based documents.

11. _____ management software is useful for working with flat files, whereas _____ management software works well with multiple files.

12. _____ software helps you work with wireframes, CAD drawings, photos, and slide presentations.

13. In a spreadsheet the rows are identified with _____ and the columns are identified with _____.

14. _____ market software is designed to automate specialized tasks in a specific market or business.

15. _____ art is a collection of drawings and photos designed to be inserted into documents.

16. _____ is a music compression file that stores digitized music in such a way that quality is excellent but the file size is relatively small.

17. _____ laws provide software authors with the exclusive right to copy, distribute, sell, and modify that work, except under special circumstances.

18. _____ is copyrighted software that is marketed with a "try before you buy" policy.

19. Linux is an example of open _____ software.

20. Public _____ software is not copyrighted, making it available for use without restriction, except that you cannot apply for a copyright on it.

▼ PRACTICE TESTS

When you use the Interactive CD, you can take Practice Tests that consist of 10 multiple-choice, true/false, and fill-in-the blank questions. The questions are selected at random from a large test bank, so each time you take a test, you'll receive a different set of questions. Your tests are scored immediately, and you can print study guides to determine which questions you answered incorrectly. If you are using a Tracking Disk, insert in the floppy disk drive to save your test scores.

▼ INDEPENDENT CHALLENGE 1

The word processor is one of the most widely used types of application software. Chances are, if you are learning to use the computer, you are also learning how to create documents with some word processing program. Based on your experience with word processing and your reading about document production software in this unit, complete the following independent challenge by writing a short paper discussing the following.

1. Describe the features of the word processing software that you use most often.

2. Explain how a spelling checker works and why it is not a substitute for proofreading.

3. Describe the strengths of word processing software.

4. Describe the weaknesses of word processing software.

▼ INDEPENDENT CHALLENGE 2

Word processing software, in particular, provides several features that automate tasks and allow you to work more productively. For example, suppose that you want to send prospective employers a letter and your resume. Rather than composing and addressing each letter individually, your software can perform a mail merge that automatically creates personalized letters by combining the information in a mailing list with a form letter.

1. Research document productivity software to identify automated features.

2. Create a table listing automated features as column heads and types of productivity software as row labels.

3. Use your research to complete the chart, using Xs to identify automated features available in various document production software.

4. Summarize your findings by writing a few paragraphs to answer the question: Does document production software increase productivity?

▼ INDEPENDENT CHALLENGE 3

How you acquire software varies based on the software and your needs. If you have a home computer and own or have purchased software, complete the following independent challenge by writing a short paper discussing the issues raised below.

1. What software is installed on your computer? How did you acquire the software? What type of software does each package fall into based on the categories outlined in this unit?

2. Explain the differences between commercial software, shareware, open source software, freeware, and public domain software. Do you have any of these? If so, which ones? Why did you select one type over the other?

3. If possible, describe one experience installing software, describe the process of installing software from a distribution CD, and contrast it with the process of installing downloaded software.

4. Have you used software that has an ESRB rating? Based on your experience with the software, did you find that the rating was adequate and fair? Why or why not?

▼ INDEPENDENT CHALLENGE 4

When you use a software package, it is important to understand the legal restrictions on its use. For this independent challenge, make a photocopy of the license agreement for any software package. Read the License agreement, then answer these questions:

1. Is this a shrink-wrap license? Why or why not?

2. After you pay your computer dealer for the program covered by this license, who owns the program?

3. Can you legally have one copy of the program on your computer at work and another copy of the program on your computer at home if you use the software only in one place at a time?

4. Can you legally sell the software? Why or why not?

5. Under what conditions can you legally transfer possession of the program to someone else?

6. If you were the owner of a software store, could you legally rent the program to customers if you were sure they did not keep a copy after the rental period was over?

7. Can you legally install this software on one computer, but give more than one user access to it?

8. If you use this program for an important business decision and later find out that a mistake in the program caused you to lose $500,000, what legal recourse is provided by the license agreement?

▼ INDEPENDENT CHALLENGE 5

 There are so many software packages on the market today that it is often overwhelming to make a wise purchasing decision. The breadth of software available in each category is quite large, and no two packages claim all the same features. Do you base your decision to buy a new application package on word of mouth? Reviewer comments in professional magazines? Trying it out? To complete this independent challenge, you will research a type of software package that you intend to purchase.

1. Determine the type of package you want to select (graphics, DTP, word processing, Web development, e-mail, scheduling, or data management) and which operating system you plan to use.

2. Locate vendor ads either on the Internet or in local papers or trade magazines that sell software.

3. Read comparison reviews of the products. Create a chart detailing the features and prepare a competitive analysis of the three top candidates for your purchase.

4. Write a short summary of your findings, indicating which package you would buy and why.

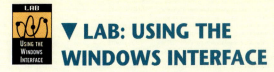

▼ LAB: USING THE WINDOWS INTERFACE

1. Start the interactive part of the lab. Insert your Tracking Disk if you want to save your QuickCheck results. Perform each of the lab steps as directed and answer all of the lab QuickCheck questions. When you exit the lab, your answers are automatically graded and your results are displayed.

2. Draw a sketch or print a screenshot of the Windows desktop on any computer that you use. Use ToolTips to identify all of the icons on the desktop and the taskbar.

3. Use the Start button and Accessories menu to start an application program called Paint. (If Paint is not installed on your computer, you can use any application software, such as a word processing program.) Draw a sketch or print a screenshot of the Paint (or other application) window and label the following components: Window title, title bar, Maximize/Restore button, Minimize button, Close button, menu bar, toolbar, and scroll bar.

4. Look at each of the menu options provided by the Paint software (or other application). Make a list of those that seem to be standard Windows menu options.

5. Draw a sketch of Paint's Print dialog box (or another application's Print dialog box). Label the following parts: buttons, spin bar, pull-down list, option button, and check boxes.

▼ LAB: INSTALLING AND UNINSTALLING SOFTWARE

1. Start the interactive part of the lab. Insert your Tracking Disk if you want to save your QuickCheck results. Perform each of the lab steps as directed and answer all of the lab QuickCheck questions. When you exit the lab, your answers are automatically graded and your results are displayed.

2. Browse the Web and locate a software application that you might like to download. Use information supplied by the Web site to answer the following questions:

   a. What is the name of the program and the URL of the download site?

   b. What is the size of the download file?

   c. According to the instructions, does the download file appear to require manual installation, is it a self-executing zip file, or is it a self-installing executable file?

3. On the computer that you typically use, look through the list of programs (click Start, then select Programs to see a list). List the names of any programs that include their own uninstall routine.

4. On the computer that you typically use, open the Control Panel and then open the Add/Remove Programs dialog box. List the first 10 programs that are currently installed on the computer.

Exercises

▼ VISUAL WORKSHOP

Operating systems are not unique to the PC and mainframe markets. Apple Computer has been developing operating systems for its computers since the early days of the Apple II computer. While the PC market has its share of versions from MS DOS to Windows XP, Apple Computer has developed its share of operating systems. Apple Computer has been using open-source projects to allow developers to enhance and customize Apple software. MAC OS X v. 10.1 is based on Darwin, which is the core of the MAC OS X. The source code for Darwin is freely available through Apple's public source project. Figure C-31 shows the Web page for Apple's latest offering of Mac OS.

FIGURE C-31

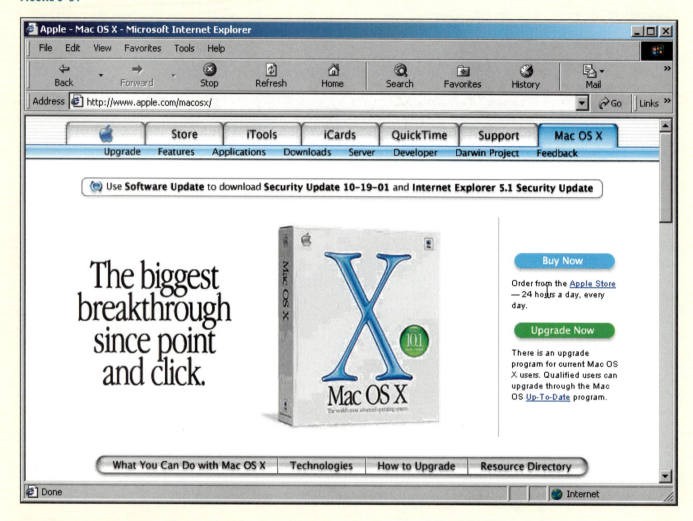

1. Log onto the Internet, then use your favorite search engine to research MAC OS. You might start by going to the Apple Computer Web site.

2. Research the various features that MAC OS supports. Write a brief list of the features and explain each one.

3. Research Darwin. List three new open-source projects that are currently in development.

4. Research the history of MAC OS. What new features does it have over the previous version?

UNIT D

Digital Electronics and File Management

OBJECTIVES

Introduce digital data representation

Introduce integrated circuits

Explore microprocessor performance factors

Understand computer memory: RAM

Explore computer memory

Introduce computer file basics

Understand file locations

Explore file management

Understand logical file storage

Use files

Understand physical file storage

Tech Talk: How a Microprocessor Executes Instructions

In this unit, you will learn how data representation and digital electronics work together to make computers tick. You will learn about two of the most important components in a computer—the microprocessor and memory. You will learn how they work and how they affect computer performance. You will learn about the different types of memory and how memory works to store and process data. You will get a general introduction to computer files and learn some very practical information about filenames. You will learn techniques for organizing computer files so that they are easy to access and update. You will also learn how an operating system stores, deletes, and tracks files. The Tech Talk section explains the details of how a microprocessor executes instructions.

Introducing digital data representation

FYI

If you need to brush up on binary numbers, refer to the Working with Binary Numbers lab in Unit B.

Data representation refers to the form in which information is conceived, manipulated, and recorded. Because a computer is an electronic digital device, it uses electrical signals to represent data. A **digital device** works with discrete data or digits, such as 1 and 0, "on" and "off," or "yes" and "no." Data exists in the computer as a series of electronic signals represented as 1s and 0s, each of which is referred to as a **bit**. Most computer coding schemes use eight bits to represent each number, letter, or symbol. A series of eight bits is referred to as a **byte**. This lesson looks more closely at the coding schemes used in digital representation.

DETAILS

- Just as Morse code uses dashes and dots to represent the letters of the alphabet, computers use sequences of bits to represent numbers, letters, punctuation marks, music, pictures, and videos. **Digital electronics** makes it possible for a computer to manipulate simple "on" and "off" signals to perform complex tasks. The **binary number system** allows computers to represent virtually any number simply by using 0s and 1s, which translate into electrical "on" and "off" signals.

- Digital computers use many different coding schemes to represent data. The coding scheme used by a computer depends on whether the data is numeric data or character data.

- **Numeric data** consists of numbers representing quantities that might be used in arithmetic operations. For example, your annual income is numeric data, as is your age. Computers represent numeric data using the binary number system, also called "base 2." The binary number system has only two digits: 0 and 1. These digits can be converted to electrical "ons" or "offs" inside a computer. The number 2 cannot be used in the binary number system; so instead of writing *2* you would write *10*, which you would pronounce as *one zero*. See Figure D-1.

- **Character data** is composed of letters, symbols, and numerals that will not be used in arithmetic operations. Examples of character data include your name, address, and hair color. Character data is also represented by a series of 1s and 0s.

- Several types of codes are used to represent character data, including ASCII, EBCDIC, and Unicode. **ASCII** (American Standard Code for Information Interchange) requires only seven bits for each character. For example, the ASCII code for an uppercase "A" is

1000001. ASCII provides codes for 128 characters, including uppercase letters, lowercase letters, punctuation symbols, and numerals. A superset of ASCII, called **Extended ASCII**, uses eight bits to represent each character. See Figure D-2. The eighth bit provides codes for 128 additional characters, which are usually boxes, circles, and other graphical symbols. **EBCDIC** (Extended Binary-Coded Decimal Interchange Code) is an alternative 8-bit code, usually used by older IBM mainframe computers. **Unicode** uses 16 bits and provides codes for 65,000 characters, a real bonus for representing the alphabets of multiple languages. Most personal computers use Extended ASCII code, although Unicode is becoming increasingly popular.

- Because computers represent numeric data with binary equivalents, ASCII codes that represent numbers might seem unnecessary. Computers, however, sometimes distinguish between numeric data and numerals. For example, you don't use your social security number in calculations, so a computer considers it character data composed of numerals, not numbers.

- To work with pictures and sounds, a computer must digitize the information that makes up the picture (such as the colors) and the information that makes up the sound (such as the notes) into 1s and 0s. Computers convert colors and notes into numbers, which can be represented by bits and stored in files as a long series of 1s and 0s.

- Your computer needs to know whether to interpret those 1s and 0s as ASCII code, binary numbers, or the code for a picture or sound. Most computer files contain a file header with information on the code that was used to represent the file data. A file header is stored along with the file and can be read by the computer, but never appears on the screen.

FIGURE D-1: Comparing decimal and binary numbers

▶ The decimal system uses ten symbols to represent numbers: 0, 1, 2, 3, 4, 5, 6, 7, 8, and 9; the binary number system uses only two symbols: 0 and 1

Decimal (Base 10)	Binary (Base 2)
0	0
1	1
2	10
3	11
4	100
5	101
6	110
7	111
8	1000
9	1001
10	1010
11	1011
1000	1111101000

FIGURE D-2: Extended ASCII code

▶ The extended ASCII code uses a series of eight 1s and 0s to represent 256 characters, including lowercase letters, upper-case letters, symbols, and numerals. The first 63 ASCII characters are not shown in this table because they represent special control sequences that cannot be printed.

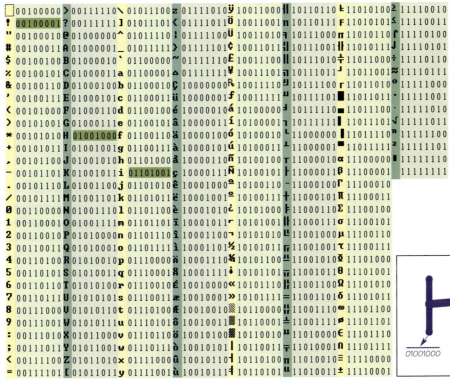

Quantifying bits and bytes

A bit is one binary digit and a byte is eight bits. Halfway between a "bit" and a "byte" is a nibble (four bits). The word "bit" can be abbreviated as a lowercase "b" and byte can be abbreviated as an uppercase "B."

Bits and bytes are used in different ways. Transmission speeds are usually expressed in bits, whereas storage space is usually expressed in bytes. The speed 56 Kbps means 56 kilobits per second; the capacity 8 GB means 8 gigabytes. "Kilo" is usually a prefix that means 1,000. For example, $50 K means $50,000. However, when it refers to bits or bytes, a "kilo"

is 1,024 because computer engineers measure everything in base 2, and 2^{10} in base 2 is 1,024, not 1,000. So a **kilobit** (abbreviated Kb or Kbit) is 1,024 bits and a **kilobyte** (abbreviated KB or Kbyte) is 1,024 bytes. The prefix "mega" refers to a million, or in the context of bits and bytes, precisely 1,048,576 (the equivalent of 2^{20}). Mb or Mbit is the abbreviation for **megabit**. MB or Mbyte is the abbreviation for **megabyte**. The prefixes giga- (billion), tera- (trillion), and exa- (quintillion) can be used to quantify bits and bytes.

Introducing integrated circuits

UNIT D

Computers are electronic devices that use electrical signals and circuits to represent, process, and move data. Bits take the form of electrical pulses that can travel over circuits. An **integrated circuit (IC)** is a super-thin slice of semi-conducting material packed with microscopic circuit elements such as wires, transistors, capacitors, logic gates, and resistors. This lesson takes a closer look at integrated circuits and the important role they play in computers.

DETAILS

- If it weren't for the miniaturization made possible by digital electronics, computers would be huge, and the inside of a computer's system unit would contain a complex jumble of wires and other electronic components. Instead, today's computers contain relatively few parts. A computer's system unit contains circuit boards, storage devices, and a power supply that converts current from an AC wall outlet into the DC current used by computer circuitry. See Figure D-3.

- Integrated circuits can be used for microprocessors, memory, and support circuitry. The terms computer chip, microchip, and chip originated as jargon for integrated circuit.

- The microprocessor, memory modules, and support circuitry chips are packaged in a protective carrier or "chip package." Chip carriers vary in shape and size including small rectangular **DIPs (dual in-line packages)** with caterpillar-like legs protruding from a black, rectangular body; long, slim **DIMMs (dual in-line memory modules)**; pin-cushion-like **PGAs (pin-grid arrays)**; and cassette-like **SEC (single-edge contact) cartridges**, such as those pictured in Figure D-4. The pins on each chip package provides the electronic connection between the integrated circuit and other computer components.

- The computer's main circuit board, called a **motherboard** or main board, houses all essential chips and provides the connecting circuitry between them. See Figure D-5. If you look carefully at a motherboard, you'll see that some chips are permanently soldered in place. Other chips are plugged into special sockets and connectors, which allow chips to be removed for repairs or upgrades. When multiple chips are required for a single function, such as generating stereo-quality sound, the chips might be gathered together on a separate small circuit board, such as a sound card, which can be plugged into a special slot-like connector on the motherboard.

- A **microprocessor** (sometimes referred to as a processor) is an integrated circuit designed to process instructions. It is the most important component of a computer, and usually the most expensive single component. Looking inside a computer, you can usually identify the microprocessor because it is the largest chip on the motherboard. Depending on the brand and model, a microprocessor might be housed in a cartridge-like SEC cartridge or in a square PGA. Inside the chip carrier, a microprocessor is a very complex integrated circuit, containing as many as 50 million miniaturized electronic components. Some of these components are only 30 nanometers thick—a nanometer is 10^{-9} meter, or one-billionth of a meter. An atom is 10 nanometers thick.

Comparing today's microprocessors

A typical computer ad contains a long list of specifications describing a computer's components and capabilities. Most computer specifications begin with the microprocessor brand, type, and speed. Intel is the world's largest chipmaker and supplies a sizeable percentage of the microprocessors that power PCs. In 1971, Intel introduced the world's first microprocessor, the 4004. The company has continued to produce a steady stream of new processor models, beginning with the 8088 processor.

AMD (Advanced Micro Devices) is Intel's chief rival in the PC chip market. It produces microprocessors that work just like Intel's chips, but at a lower price. AMD's

Athlon processors are direct competitors to Intel's Pentium line and have a slight performance advantage according to some benchmarks. The Duron processor is AMD's "budget" model to compete with Intel's Celeron processors.

The microprocessors that are marketed with today's computers will handle most business, educational, and entertainment applications. While it is technically possible to upgrade your computer's microprocessor, the cost and technical factors discourage microprocessor upgrades.

FIGURE D-3: Inside a typical desktop computer

Power supply and fan

Microprocessor with built-in fan

Expansion cards

CD-ROM drive

Floppy disk drive

Hard disk drive

Cables that transfer data from storage devices to motherboard

Main circuit board (motherboard)

FIGURE D-4: Integrated circuits

▲ A DIP has two rows of pins that connect the IC circuitry to a circuit board

▲ A DIMM is a small circuit board containing several chips, typically used for memory

▲ A PGA is a square chip package with pins arranged in concentric squares, typically used for microprocessors

▲ An SEC cartridge is a popular chip package for microprocessors

FIGURE D-5: The motherboard

▶ A computer motherboard provides sockets for chips, slots for small circuit boards, and the circuitry that connects all these components

DIMM module containing memory chips

SEC-style microprocessor

Connectors for storage device cables

Battery that powers the computer's real-time clock

Expansion slots hold additional expansion cards, such as a modem or sound card

Expansion card

DIP holding a ROM chip

Circuitry that transports data from one component to another

Connector for power supply

Exploring microprocessor performance factors

All microprocessors have two main parts: the **arithmetic logic unit (ALU)** and the **control unit**. To process data, each of these units performs specific tasks. The performance of a microprocessor is affected by several factors, including clock speed, word size, cache size, instruction set, and processing techniques. This lesson looks at the two main parts of a microprocessor and the factors that affect microprocessor performance.

DETAILS

● The ALU is the circuitry that performs arithmetic operations, such as addition and subtraction. It also performs logical operations, such as comparing two numbers using the logical operators such as less than (<), greater than (>), or equal to (=). Logical operations also allow for comparing characters and sorting and grouping information. The ALU uses **registers** to hold data that is being processed. Figure D-6 illustrates how the ALU works.

● The microprocessor's **control unit** fetches each instruction, as illustrated in Figure D-7. A microprocessor executes instructions that are provided by a computer program. The list of instructions that a microprocessor can perform is called its **instruction set**. These instructions are hard-wired into the processor's circuitry and include basic arithmetic and logical operations, fetching data, and clearing registers. A computer can perform very complex tasks, but it does so by performing a combination of simple tasks from its instruction set.

● How efficiently the ALU and the control unit work are determined by different performance factors. Processor speed is one of the most important indicators in determining the power of a computer system. The **microprocessor clock** is a timing device that sets the pace (the clock speed) for executing instructions. The clock speed of a microprocessor is specified in megahertz (MHz) or gigahertz (GHz) cycles per second. A cycle is the smallest unit of time in a microprocessor's universe. Every action that a processor performs is measured by these cycles. The clock speed is not equal to the number of instructions that a processor can execute in one second. In many computers, some instructions occur within one cycle, but other instructions might require multiple cycles. Some processors can even execute several instructions in a single clock cycle. A specification such as 1.3 GHz means that the microprocessor's clock operates at a speed of 1.3 billion cycles per second.

● **Word size**, another performance factor, refers to the number of bits that a microprocessor can manipulate at one time. Word size is based on the size of the registers in the ALU and the capacity of circuits that lead to those registers. A microprocessor with an 8-bit word size, for example, has 8-bit registers, processes eight bits at a time, and is referred to as an 8-bit processor. Processors with a larger word size can process more data during each processor cycle, a factor that leads to improved computer performance. Today's personal computers typically contain 32-bit or 64-bit processors.

● **Cache**, sometimes called RAM cache or cache memory, is special high-speed memory that a microprocessor can access more rapidly than memory elsewhere on the motherboard. Because it is another measure of performance, some computer ads specify cache type and capacity. Cache capacity is usually measured in kilobytes.

● Another performance factor is the type of instruction set a microprocessor uses. As chip designers developed various instruction sets for microprocessors, they tended to add increasingly more complex instructions, each of which required several clock cycles for execution. A microprocessor with such an instruction set uses **CISC (complex instruction set computer)** technology. A microprocessor with a limited set of simple instructions uses **RISC (reduced instruction set computer)** technology.

● The processing technique a microprocessor uses also affects performance. With **serial processing**, the processor must complete all of the steps in the instruction cycle before it begins to execute the next instruction. However, using a technology called **pipelining**, a processor can begin executing an instruction before it completes the previous instruction. Many of today's microprocessors also perform **parallel processing**, in which multiple instructions are executed at the same time.

FIGURE D-6: How the ALU works

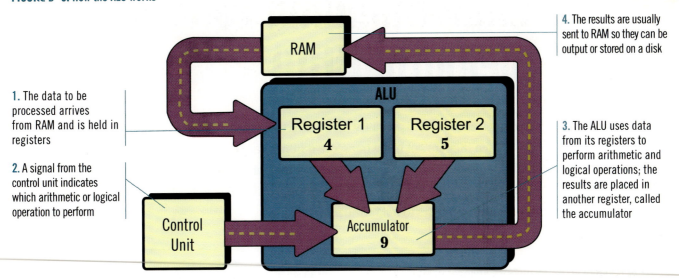

1. The data to be processed arrives from RAM and is held in registers

2. A signal from the control unit indicates which arithmetic or logical operation to perform

4. The results are usually sent to RAM so they can be output or stored on a disk

3. The ALU uses data from its registers to perform arithmetic and logical operations; the results are placed in another register, called the accumulator

RAM

ALU

Register 1
4

Register 2
5

Control Unit

Accumulator
9

FIGURE D-7: How the control unit works

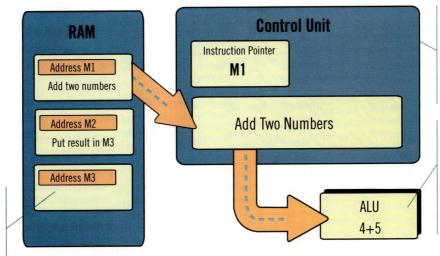

The RAM address of the instruction is kept in the instruction pointer; when the instruction has been executed, the address in the instruction pointer changes to indicate the RAM address of the next instruction to be executed

RAM

Address M1
Add two numbers

Address M2
Put result in M3

Address M3

Control Unit

Instruction Pointer
M1

Add Two Numbers

ALU
4+5

The control unit retrieves an instruction from RAM and puts it in the instruction register; the control unit interprets the instruction in its instruction register

Depending on the instruction, the control unit will get data from RAM, tell the ALU to perform an operation, or change the memory address of the instruction pointer

Benchmarking

All things being equal, a computer with a 1.3 GHz processor is faster than a computer with a 1 GHz processor and a computer with a processor that has a larger word size can process more data during each processor cycle than a computer with a processor that has a smaller word size. Furthermore, all things being equal, a computer with more Level 1 cache (L1), which is built into the processor chip, is faster than a computer with the same amount of Level 2 cache (L2), which is located on a separate chip and takes a little more time to get data to the processor.

But all things aren't equal. So how do you tell the overall performance of a computer and its microprocessor? Various testing laboratories run a series of tests called benchmarks to gauge the overall speed of a microprocessor. These results can be used to compare the results for other microprocessors. The results of benchmark tests are usually available on the Web and are published in computer magazine articles.

Understanding computer memory: RAM

Memory is the electronic circuitry linked directly to the processor that holds data and instructions when they are not being transported from one place to another. Computers use four categories of memory: random access memory (RAM), virtual memory, read-only memory (ROM), and CMOS memory. Each type of memory is characterized by the type of data it contains and the technology it uses to hold the data.

DETAILS

- **RAM** (random access memory) is a temporary holding area for data, application program instructions, and the operating system. In a personal computer, RAM is usually several chips or small circuit boards that plug into the motherboard within the computer's system unit. Next to the microprocessor, RAM is one of the most expensive computer components. The amount of RAM in a computer can, therefore, affect the overall price of a computer system. Along with processor speed, RAM capacity is the other most important factor in determining and comparing the power of a computer system.

- RAM is the "waiting room" for the computer's processor. Refer to Figure D-8. It holds raw data that is waiting to be processed and the program instructions for processing that data. In addition, RAM holds the results of processing until they can be stored more permanently on disk or tape.

- RAM also holds operating system instructions that control the basic functions of a computer system. These instructions are loaded into RAM every time you start your computer, and they remain there until you turn off your computer.

- People who are new to computers sometimes confuse RAM and disk storage, perhaps because both of these components hold data. To distinguish between RAM and disk storage, remember that RAM holds data in circuitry, whereas disk storage places data on storage media such as floppy disks, hard disks, or CDs. RAM is temporary storage; disk storage is more permanent. In addition, RAM usually has less storage capacity than disk storage.

- In RAM, microscopic electronic parts called **capacitors** hold the bits that represent data. You can visualize the capacitors as microscopic lights that can be turned on or off. Refer to Figure D-9. A charged capacitor is "turned on" and represents a "1" bit. A discharged capacitor is "turned off" and represents a "0" bit. You

can visualize the capacitors as being arranged in banks of eight. Each bank holds eight bits, or one byte, of data.

- Each RAM location has an address and holds one byte of data. A RAM address on each bank helps the computer locate data as needed for processing.

- In some respects, RAM is similar to a chalkboard. You can use a chalkboard to write mathematical formulas, erase them, and then write an outline for a report. In a similar way, RAM can hold numbers and formulas when you balance your checkbook, then hold the text of your English essay when you use word processing software. The contents of RAM can be changed just by changing the charge of the capacitors. Unlike a chalkboard, however, RAM is volatile, which means that it requires electrical power to hold data. If the computer is turned off, or if the power goes out, all data stored in RAM instantly and permanently disappears.

- The capacity of RAM is usually expressed in megabytes (MB). Today's personal computers typically feature between 64 and 512 MB of RAM. The amount of RAM needed by your computer depends on the software that you use. RAM requirements are routinely specified on the outside of a software package. If it turns out that you need more RAM, you can purchase and install additional memory up to the limit set by the computer manufacturer.

- RAM components vary in speed. RAM speed is often expressed in **nanoseconds**, or billionths of a second. Lower numbers mean faster transmission, processing, and storage of data. For example, 8 ns RAM is faster than 10 ns RAM. RAM speed can also be expressed in MHz (millions of cycles per second). Just the opposite of nanoseconds, higher MHz ratings mean faster speeds. For example, 100 MHz RAM is faster than 80 MHz RAM.

FIGURE D-8: Contents of RAM

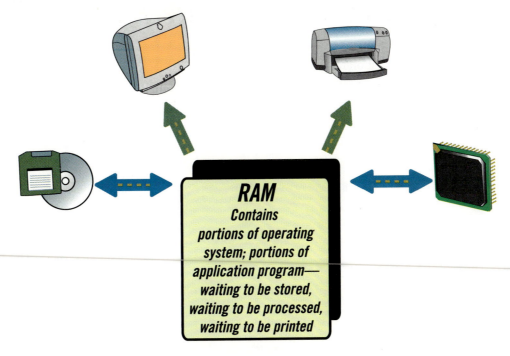

FIGURE D-9: How RAM works

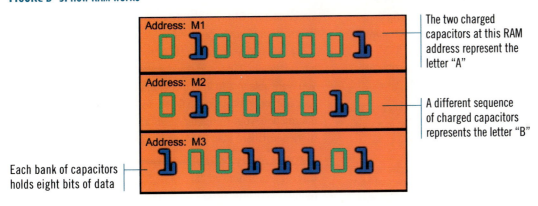

Address: M1
The two charged capacitors at this RAM address represent the letter "A"

Address: M2
A different sequence of charged capacitors represents the letter "B"

Address: M3
Each bank of capacitors holds eight bits of data

Different types of RAM

Most of today's personal computers use **SDRAM** (Figure D-10) or RDRAM. SDRAM (synchronous dynamic RAM) is fast and relatively inexpensive. **RDRAM** (Rambus dynamic RAM) was first developed for the popular Nintendo 64® game system, and was adapted for use in personal computers in 1999. Although more expensive than SDRAM, RDRAM is usually paired with microprocessors that run at speeds faster than 1 GHz because it can somewhat increase overall system performance. RAM is usually configured as a series of DIPs soldered onto a small circuit board called a **DIMM** (dual in-line memory module), **RIMM** (Rambus in-line memory module), or **SO-RIMM** (small outline Rambus in-line memory module). DIMMs contain SDRAM, whereas RIMMs and SO-RIMMs contain RDRAM.

FIGURE D-10

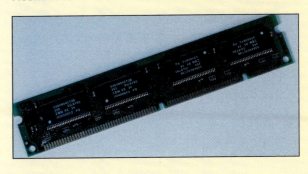

Exploring computer memory

In addition to RAM, a computer uses three other types of memory: virtual memory, ROM, and CMOS. This lesson looks at these types of computer memory and how all computer memory types work together.

DETAILS

- It might seem logical that the more you do with your computer, the more memory it needs. However, if you want to work with several programs and large graphics at the same time, personal computer operating systems are quite adept at allocating RAM space to multiple programs. If a program exceeds the allocated space, the operating system uses an area of the hard disk called **virtual memory** to store parts of a program or data file until they are needed. By selectively exchanging the data in RAM with the data in virtual memory, your computer effectively gains almost unlimited memory capacity.

  One disadvantage of virtual memory is reduced performance. Too much dependence on virtual memory can have a negative affect on your computer's performance because getting data from a mechanical device, such as a hard disk, is much slower than getting data from an electronic device, such as RAM. Loading up your computer with as much RAM as possible will help your computer speed through all of its tasks.

- **ROM (read-only memory)** is a type of memory circuitry that holds the computer's startup routine. ROM is housed in a single integrated circuit, usually a fairly large, caterpillar-like DIP package that is plugged into the motherboard.

  While RAM is temporary and volatile, ROM is permanent and non-volatile. ROM circuitry holds "hard-wired" instructions that remain in place even when the computer power is turned off. This is a familiar concept to anyone who has used a hand calculator, which includes various "hard-wired" routines for calculating square roots, cosines, and other functions. The instructions in ROM are permanent, and the only way to change them is to replace the ROM chip.

  PROM (programmable read-only memory) is read-only memory that can be created by a user with a special machine through a process called "burning." ROM chips that can be erased and reused using another technique are **EPROM (erasable programmable read-only memory)**.

- When you turn on your computer, the microprocessor receives electrical power and is ready to begin executing instructions. But, because the power had been off, RAM is empty and contains no instructions for the microprocessor to execute. Now ROM plays its part. ROM contains a small set of instructions called the **ROM BIOS (basic input/output system)**. See Figure D-11. These instructions tell the computer how to access the hard disk, find the operating system, and load it into RAM. Once the operating system is loaded, the computer can understand your input, display output, run software, and access your data. While ROM BIOS instructions are accomplished mainly without user intervention or knowledge, the computer will not function without the ROM chip and the BIOS instructions.

- In order to operate correctly, a computer must have some basic information about storage, memory, and display configurations. For example, your computer needs to know how much memory is available so that it can allocate space for all of the programs that you want to run. RAM goes blank when the computer power is turned off, so configuration information cannot be stored there. ROM would not be a good place for this information either because it holds data on a permanent basis. If, for example, your computer stored memory specification information in ROM, you could never add more memory; or if you were able to add it, you couldn't change the memory specification information in ROM. To store some basic system information, your computer needs a type of memory that's more permanent than RAM but less permanent than ROM.

- **CMOS memory (complementary metal oxide semiconductor)**, pronounced "SEE moss," is a type of memory that requires very little power to hold data. CMOS memory is stored on a chip that can be powered by a small, rechargeable battery integrated into the motherboard. The battery trickles power to the CMOS chip so that it can retain vital data about your computer system configuration even when your computer is turned off.

  When you change the configuration of your computer system by adding RAM, for example, the data in CMOS must be updated. Some operating systems recognize such changes and automatically perform the update; or you can manually change CMOS settings by running the CMOS setup program. See Figure D-12.

- Even though virtual memory, ROM, and CMOS have important roles in the operation of a computer, it is really RAM capacity that makes a difference you can notice. The more data and programs that can fit into RAM, the less time your computer will spend moving data to and from virtual memory. With lots of RAM, you'll find that documents scroll faster, and many graphics operations take less time than with a computer that has less RAM capacity.

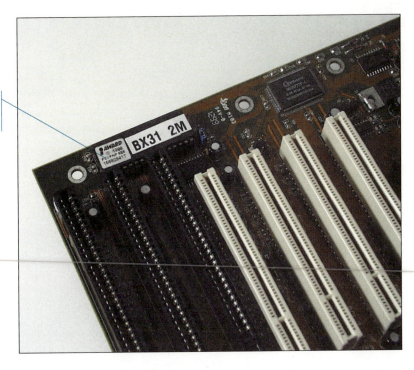

ROM BIOS is housed in one
or more ROM chips on the
motherboard

FIGURE D-12: CMOS setup program

▶ CMOS holds computer
configuration settings,
such as the date and
time, hard disk capacity,
number of floppy disk drives, and RAM capacity

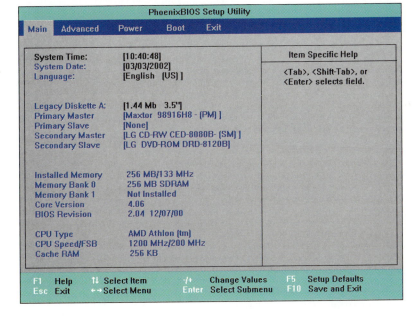

The difference between
memory types: RAM is
temporary; virtual
memory is disk-based;
ROM is permanent;
CMOS is battery-
powered and more
permanent than RAM
but less permanent
than ROM.

Introducing computer file basics

The term "file" was used for filing cabinets and collections of papers long before it became part of the personal computer lexicon. Today, a **computer file** or simply "file" is defined as a named collection of data that exists on a storage medium, such as a hard disk, floppy disk, CD, DVD, or tape. A file can contain a group of records, a document, a photo, music, a video, an e-mail message, or a computer program. This lesson looks at several common characteristics of computer files—type, filename, and format.

DETAILS

● There are several categories of files, such as data files, executable files, configuration files, drivers, and modules. A computer file is classified according to the data it contains, the software that was used to create it, and the way you should use it. See Table D-1.

● Every file has a filename. The filename has two parts—the filename itself and the filename extension.

● A **filename** is a unique set of characters and numbers that identifies a file and should describe its contents. When you save a file, you must provide it with a valid filename that adheres to specific rules, referred to as **file-naming conventions**. Each operating system has a unique set of file-naming conventions. See Figure D-13.

If an operating system attaches special significance to a symbol, you might not be able to use it in a filename. For example, Windows uses the colon (:) and the backslash (\) to separate the device letter from a filename or folder, as in C:\Music. A filename such as Report:\2002 is not valid because the operating system would become confused about how to interpret the colon and backslash.

Some operating systems also contain a list of **reserved words** that are used as commands or special identifiers. You cannot use these words alone as a filename. You can, however, use these words as part of a longer filename. For example, under Windows XP, the filename Nul would not be valid, but you could name a file something like Nul Committee Notes.doc.

● A **filename extension** (or file extension) is separated from the main filename by a period, as in Paint.exe. A filename extension further describes the file contents. Generally, the software application you are using automatically assigns the filename extension when you save a file. If you don't see a filename extension

when you use the Save or Save as dialog box to save a file, the option to show filename extensions has been deactivated. When using Windows, you can choose to hide (but not erase) or display the filename extensions through the Folder Options setting in the Control Panel.

Knowledge of filename extensions comes in handy when you receive a file on a disk or over the Internet but you don't know much about its contents. If you are familiar with filename extensions, you will know the file format and, therefore, which application to use when you want to open the file.

● A filename extension is usually related to the **file format**, which is defined as the arrangement of data in a file and the coding scheme that is used to represent the data. Files that contain graphics are usually stored using a different file format than files containing text. Hundreds of file formats exist, and you'll encounter many of them as you use a variety of software. As you work with a variety of files, you will begin to recognize that some filename extensions, such as .txt (text file) or .jpg (graphics file), indicate a file type and are not specific to application software.

You will also recognize that other filename extensions, such as .doc (Word), .xls (Excel), and .zip (Winzip), can help you identify which application was used to create the file. These filename extensions indicate the **native file format**, which is the file format used to store files created with that software program. For example, Microsoft Word stores files in doc format, whereas Adobe Illustrator stores graphics files in ai format. When using a software application such as Microsoft Word to open a file, the program displays any files that have the filename extension for its native file format, as shown in Figure D-14.

FIGURE D-13: File-naming conventions

	DOS AND WINDOWS 3.1	WINDOWS 95/98/ME/XP/NT/2000	MAC OS	UNIX/LINUX
Maximum length of filename	8-character filename plus an extension of 3 characters or less	255-character filename including an extension of up to 3 characters	31 characters (no extensions)	14–256 characters (depending on UNIX/Linux version) including an extension of any length
Spaces allowed	No	Yes	Yes	No
Numbers allowed	Yes	Yes	Yes	Yes
Characters not allowed	* / [ ] ; " = \ : , | ?	* \ : < > | " / ?	None	* ! @ # $ % ^ & ( ) { } [ ] " \ ? ; < >
Filenames not allowed	Aux, Com1, Com2, Com3, Com4, Con, Lpt1, Lpt2, Lpt3, Prn, Nul	Aux, Com1, Com2, Com3, Com4, Con, Lpt1, Lpt2, Lpt3, Prn, Nul	None	Depends on the version of UNIX or Linux
Case sensitive	No	No	Yes	Yes (use lowercase)

FIGURE D-14: Filename extensions

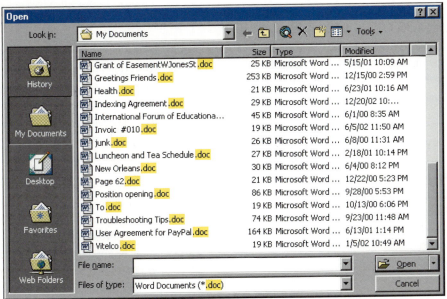

TABLE D-1: Types of files

TYPE OF FILE	DESCRIPTION	EXTENSION
Batch file	A sequence of operating system commands that is executed automatically when the computer boots	.bat
Configuration file	Information about programs that the computer uses to allocate the resources necessary to run them	.cfg .sys .mif .bin .ini
Help	The information that is displayed by online Help	.hlp
Temporary file	Contains data while a file is open, but that is discarded when you close the file	.tmp
Program modules	The main executable files for a computer program	.exe .com
Support modules	Program instructions that are executed in conjunction with the main .exe file for a program	.ocx .vbx .vbs .dll

Understanding file locations

Programs and data files have unique names and locations to ensure that the computer can find them. To designate a file's location, you must specify where the file is stored on the storage media. This lesson looks more closely at file locations—how to assign them and the information about each file that is available at the file's location.

DETAILS

- Each storage device on a PC is identified by a device letter. The floppy disk drive is usually assigned device letter A and is referred to as "drive A." A device letter is usually followed by a colon, so drive A could be designated as A: or as 3½" Floppy (A:). The main hard disk drive is usually referred to as "drive C." Additional storage devices can be assigned letters from D through Z. Although most PCs stick to the standard of drive A for the floppy disk drive and drive C for the hard disk drive, the device letters for CD, Zip, and DVD drives are not standardized. For example, the CD-writer on your computer might be assigned device letter E, whereas the CD-writer on another computer might be assigned device letter R.

- An operating system maintains a list of files called a **directory** for each storage disk, tape, CD, or DVD. The main directory of a disk is referred to as the **root directory**. On a PC, the root directory is typically identified by the device letter followed by a backslash. For example, the root directory of the hard disk drive would be C:\. You should try to avoid storing your data files in the root directory of your hard disk, and instead store them in a subdirectory.

- A root directory is often subdivided into smaller lists called **subdirectories**. When you use Windows, Mac OS, or a Linux graphical file manager, these subdirectories are depicted as **folders** because they work like the folders in a filing cabinet to store an assortment of related items. Each folder has a name, so you can easily create a folder called Documents to hold reports, letters, and so on. You can create another folder called Music to hold your MP3 files. Folders can be created within other folders. You might, for example, create a folder within your Music folder to hold your jazz collection and another to hold your reggae collection.

   A folder name is separated from a drive letter and other folder names by a special symbol.

In Microsoft Windows, this symbol is the backslash (\). For example, the folder for your reggae music (within the Music folder on drive C) would be written as C:\Music\Reggae.

   Imagine how hard it would be to find a specific piece of paper in a filing cabinet that was stuffed with a random assortment of reports, letters, and newspaper clippings. By storing a file in a folder, you assign it a place in an organized hierarchy of folders and files.

- A computer file's location is defined by a **file specification** (sometimes called a **path**), which begins with the drive letter and is followed by the folder(s), filename, and filename extension. Suppose that you have stored an MP3 file called Marley One Love in the Reggae folder on your hard disk drive. Its file specification would be as shown in Figure D-15.

- A file contains data, stored as a group of bits. The more bits, the larger the file. **File size** is usually measured in bytes, kilobytes, or megabytes. Knowing the size of a file can be important especially when you are sending a file as an e-mail attachment. Your computer's operating system keeps track of file sizes.

- Your computer keeps track of the date on which a file was created or last modified. The **file date** is useful if you have created several versions of a file and want to make sure that you know which version is the most recent. It can also come in handy if you have downloaded several updates of player software, such as an MP3 player, and you want to make sure that you install the latest version.

- The operating system keeps track of file locations, filenames, filename extensions, file size, and file dates. See Figure D-16. This information is always available to you through a file management utility, which will be discussed in the next lesson.

C:\Music\Reggae\Marley One Love.mp3

| Drive letter | Primary folder | Secondary folder | Filename | Filename extension |

FIGURE D-16: File sizes and dates

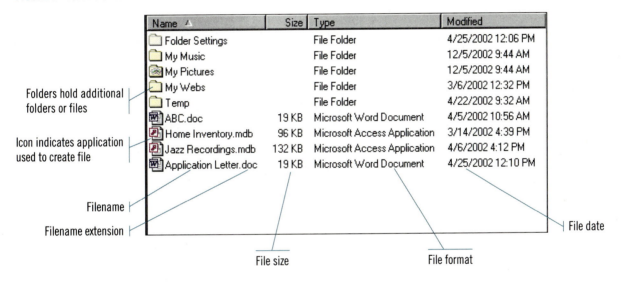

Folders hold additional folders or files

Icon indicates application used to create file

Filename

Filename extension

Name △	Size	Type	Modified
Folder Settings		File Folder	4/25/2002 12:06 PM
My Music		File Folder	12/5/2002 9:44 AM
My Pictures		File Folder	12/5/2002 9:44 AM
My Webs		File Folder	3/6/2002 12:32 PM
Temp		File Folder	4/22/2002 9:32 AM
ABC.doc	19 KB	Microsoft Word Document	4/5/2002 10:56 AM
Home Inventory.mdb	96 KB	Microsoft Access Application	3/14/2002 4:39 PM
Jazz Recordings.mdb	132 KB	Microsoft Access Application	4/6/2002 4:12 PM
Application Letter.doc	19 KB	Microsoft Word Document	4/25/2002 12:10 PM

File date

File size

File format

Deleting files

You may have noticed when using Windows that when you delete a file it is moved to the Recycle Bin. The Windows Recycle Bin and similar utilities in other operating systems are designed to protect you from accidentally deleting hard disk files that you actually need. The operating system moves the file to the Recycle Bin folder. The "deleted" file still takes up space on the disk, but does not appear in the usual directory listing. The file does, however, appear in the directory listing for the Recycle Bin folder, and you can undelete any files in this listing.

To delete data from a disk in such a way that no one can ever read it, you can use special file shredder software that overwrites "empty" sectors with random 1s and 0s. You might find this software handy if you plan to donate your computer to an organization, and you want to make sure that your personal data no longer remains on the hard disk. It is important to remember that only files you delete from your hard disk drive are sent to the Recycle Bin; files you delete from a floppy disk drive are not sent to the Recycle Bin.

Exploring file management

File management encompasses any procedure that helps you organize your computer-based files so that you can find and use them more efficiently. Depending on your computer's operating system, you may be able to organize and manipulate your files from within an application program, or by using a special file management utility provided by the operating system.

DETAILS

● Applications, such as word processing software or graphics software, typically provide file management capabilities for files created within the application. For example, most applications provide a way to open files and save them in a specific folder on a designated storage device. An application might also provide additional file management capabilities, such as deleting and renaming files.

● Most application software provides access to file management tasks through the Save and Open dialog boxes. The Save As dialog box that is displayed by Windows applications allows you to do more than just save a file. You can use it to perform other file management tasks such as rename a file, delete a file, or create a folder, as shown in Figure D-18. At times, however, you might want to work with groups of files, or perform other file operations that are inconvenient within the Save or Open dialog boxes. Most operating systems

provide **file management utilities** that give you the "big picture" of the files you have stored on your disks and help you work with them. For example, Windows provides **Windows Explorer**, which is a file management utility that is bundled with the Windows operating system. On computers with Mac OS, the file management utility is called Finder. These utilities, shown in Figure D-19, help you view a list of files, find files, move files from one place to another, make copies of files, delete files, and rename files.

● File management utilities are designed to help you organize and manipulate the files that are stored on your computer. Most file management operations begin with locating a particular file or folder. A file management utility should make it easy to find what you're looking for by drilling down through your computer's hierarchy of folders and files.

The Save v. Save As dialog box

Knowing how to save a file is a crucial file management skill. The Save As command is generally an option on the File menu. In addition to the Save As option, the menu also contains a Save option. The difference between the two options is subtle, but useful. The Save As option allows you to select a name and storage device for a file, whereas the Save option simply saves the latest version of a file under its current name and at its current location. When you try to use the Save option for a file that doesn't yet have a name, your application will display the Save As dialog box, even though you selected the Save option. The flow chart in Figure D-17 will help you decide whether to use the Save or Save As command.

FIGURE D-17: Save or Save As

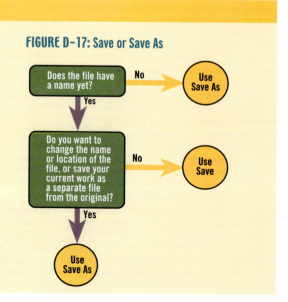

FIGURE D-18: The Save As dialog box

Click this button to create a new folder

To rename or delete a folder, right-click it and then use one of the options on the shortcut menu

To rename or delete a file, right-click the file-name, then select a command from the short-cut menu that appears; in addition to the Rename and Delete options, this menu might also include options to print the file, e-mail it, or scan it for viruses

FIGURE D-19: Operating system file managers

► The Windows File Manager utility can be tailored to show files as icons or as a list

▼ Mac OS provides a file management utility called the Finder

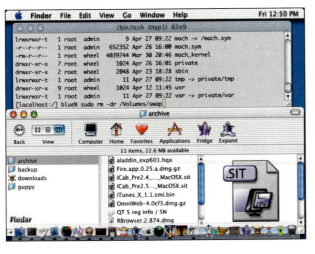

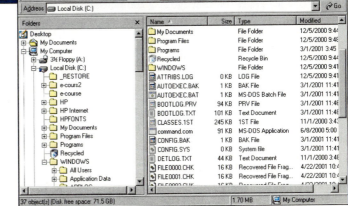

Understanding logical file storage

File management utilities often use some sort of metaphor to help you visualize and mentally organize the files on your disks and other storage devices. These metaphors are sometimes referred to as **logical storage models** because they help you form a mental (logical) picture of the way in which your files are stored. Windows Explorer is based on logical file storage. This lesson looks at a logical file storage metaphor and how Windows Explorer implements that model.

LAB
WORKING WITH
WINDOWS EXPLORER

DETAILS

● After hearing so much about files and folders, you might have guessed that the filing cabinet is a popular metaphor for computer storage. In this metaphor, each storage device of a computer corresponds to one of the drawers in a filing cabinet. The drawers hold folders and the folders hold files, as illustrated in Figure D-20.

You might also find it helpful to think of the logical storage model as an outline. In the hierarchy of an outline, the highest or top level is the general level (root directory). As you move down to lower levels in the outline you have greater detail (primary subfolders and then secondary subfolders and so on). When you expand a higher level (a folder), you can see all the subordinate (subfolder) levels for that folder.

● Figure D-21 shows how Microsoft programmers used the filing cabinet metaphor within the file management utility called Windows Explorer.

The Windows Explorer window is divided into two "window panes." The pane on the left side of the window lists each of the storage devices connected to your computer, plus several important system objects, such as My Computer, Network Neighborhood, and the Desktop. Each storage device is synonymous with a file drawer in the file cabinet metaphor.

An icon for a storage device or other system object can be "expanded" by clicking its corresponding plus-sign icon. Once an icon is opened, its contents appear in the pane on the right side of the Windows Explorer window. Opening an icon displays the next level of the storage hierarchy, usually a collection of folders. Each folder is synonymous with the folders in the file cabinet metaphor.

Any of these folders can contain files or subfolders. Files are synonymous with papers in the file cabinet metaphor. Subfolders can be further expanded by clicking their plus-sign icons. You continue expanding folders in this manner until you reach the file you need.

The minus-sign icon can be used to collapse a device or folder to hide the levels of the hierarchy.

● To work with either a single or a group of files or folders, you must first select them. Windows Explorer displays all of the items that you select by highlighting them. Once a folder or file or a group of folders or files are highlighted, you can use the same copy, move, or delete procedure that you would use for a single item.

● In addition to locating files and folders, Windows Explorer provides a set of file management tools that will help you manipulate files and folders in the following ways:

* Rename. You might want to change the name of a file or folder to better describe its contents. When renaming a file, you should be careful to keep the same filename extension so that you can open it with the correct application software.

* Copy. You can copy a file or folder. For example, you can copy a file from your hard disk to a floppy disk if you want to send it to a friend or colleague. You might also want to make a copy of a document so that you can revise the copy and leave the original intact. When you copy a file, the file remains in the original location and a duplicate file is added to a different location—two copies of the same file now exist but with different paths.

* Move. You can move a file from one folder to another, or from one storage device to another. When you move a file, it is erased from its original location, so make sure that you remember the new location of the file. You can also move folders from one storage device to another, or from one folder to another.

* Delete. You can delete a file when you no longer need it. You can also delete a folder. Be careful when you delete a folder because most file management utilities also delete all the files (and subfolders) that a folder contains.

FIGURE D-20: A filing cabinet as a metaphor

The file cabinet represents all of the storage devices connected to a computer

Each drawer represents one storage device

A drawer can contain folders that hold documents and other folders

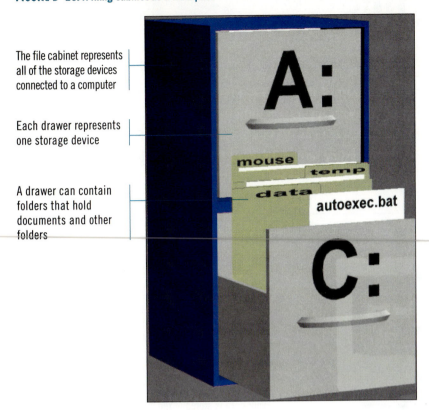

FIGURE D-21: Windows Explorer

▶ Windows Explorer borrows the folders from the filing cabinet metaphor and places them in a hierarchical structure, which makes it easy to drill down through the levels of the directory hierarchy to locate a folder or file

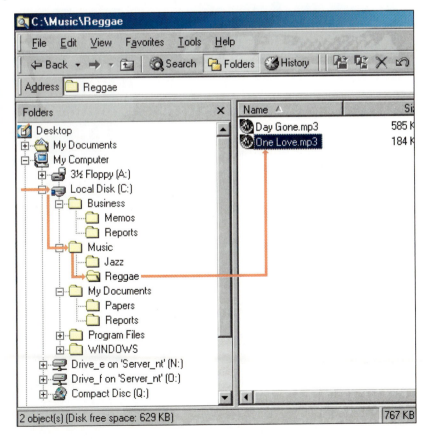

Using files

As you will recall, most users create, open, or save data files using application software. You are now ready to apply what you've learned about files and file management to see how you would typically use files when you work with application software. Using word processing software to produce a document is a common way to use files on a computer, so we'll take a look at the file operations for a typical word processing session. Examine Figure D-22 to get an overview of the file activities of a typical word processing session.

FIGURE D-22

Word.exe is loaded into memory from the hard disk

Your data is stored in memory while you type

A:Vacation.doc is copied from memory to the floppy disk

1. Running an Application

Suppose you want to create a document about the summer vacation packages your company offers. You decide to create the document using the word processing software, Microsoft Word. Your first step is to start the Word program. When you run Word, the program file is copied from the hard drive to the memory of the computer.

2. Creating a File

You begin to type the text of the document. As you type, your data is stored in the memory of the computer. Your data will not be stored on disk until you initiate the Save command.

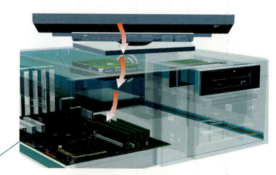

3. Saving a Data File

When you create a file and save it on disk for the first time, you must name the file so that you can later retrieve it by name. Earlier in this unit, you learned that the name you give to a file must follow the file-naming conventions for the operating system. You name the file *A:Vacation.doc*. By typing *A:* you direct the computer to save the file on the floppy disk in drive A. The computer looks for empty clusters on the disk where it can store the file. It then adds the filename to the directory, along with the number of the cluster that contains the beginning of the file. Once you have saved your file, you can continue to work on the document, exit the Word program, or work on another document.

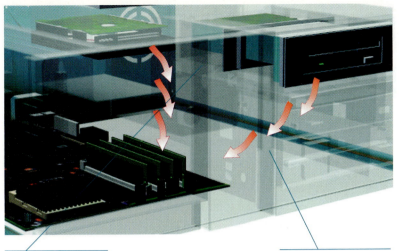

Word.exe is loaded into memory

A:Vacation.doc is copied from disk into memory

4. Retrieving a Data File

Suppose that a few days later, you decide that you want to re-read *Vacation.doc*. You need to start Microsoft Word. Once the Word program is running, you can retrieve the *Vacation.doc* file from the disk on which it is stored.

When you want to use a data file that already exists on disk storage, you must tell the application to open the file. In Microsoft Word, you either type the name of the file, *A:Vacation.doc*, or select the filename from a list of files stored on the disk. The application communicates the filename to the operating system.

The operating system looks at the directory and FAT to find which clusters contain the file, then moves the read-write head to the appropriate disk location to read the file. The electronics on the disk drive transfer the file data into the main memory of the computer, where your application software can manipulate it. Once the operating system has retrieved the file, the word processing software displays it on the screen.

5. Revising a Data File

When you see the *Vacation.doc* file on the screen, you can modify it. Each character that you type and each change that you make are stored temporarily in the main memory of the computer, but not on the disk.

The *Vacation.doc* file is already on the disk, so when you are done with the modifications you have two options. Option 1 is to store the revised version in place of the old version. Option 2 is to create a new file for your revision and give it a different name, such as *Holiday.doc*.

If you decide to go with option 1—store the revised version in place of the old version—the operating system copies your revised data from the computer memory to the same clusters that contained the old file. You do not have to take a separate step to delete the old file—the operating system automatically records the new file over it.

If you decide to go with option 2—create a new file for the revision—the application prompts you for a filename. Your revisions will be stored under the new filename. The original file, *Vacation.doc*, will remain on the disk in its unrevised form.

The changes you make to the document are stored in memory; when you save your revisions, they overwrite the previous version of *Vacation.doc*

Understanding physical file storage

So far, you've seen how an operating system like Windows can help you visualize computer storage as files and folders. The structure of files and folders that you see in Windows Explorer is called a "logical" model, because it helps you create a mental picture. You have also seen how files are created, saved, retrieved, and revised during a typical word processing session. What actually happens to a file when you save it is called physical file storage.

DETAILS

● Before a computer can store data, the storage medium must be formatted so that it contains the equivalent of electronic storage bins. This is accomplished by dividing a disk into **tracks**, and dividing each track into wedge-shaped **sectors**, both of which are created when a disk or disk drive is formatted. See Figure D-23. Tracks and sectors are numbered to provide addresses for each data storage bin. The numbering scheme depends on the storage device and the operating system. On CDs and DVDs, one or more tracks spiral out from the center of the disk; on floppy, Zip, and hard disks, tracks are arranged as concentric circles.

Today, most floppy, Zip, and hard disks are preformatted at the factory to meet the specifications of a particular operating system; however, computer operating systems provide formatting utilities that you can use to reformat some storage devices such as floppy and hard disks. The companies that manufacture hard disk drives, writable CD drives, and writable DVD drives also supply formatting utilities. Windows includes a floppy disk formatting utility. When you use a formatting utility, it erases any data that happens to be on the disk, then prepares the tracks and sectors necessary to hold data.

● The operating system uses a **file system** to keep track of the names and locations of files that reside on a storage medium, such as a hard disk. Different operating systems use different file systems. Most versions of Mac OS use the Macintosh Hierarchical File System (HFS). Ext2fs (extended 2 file system) is the native file system for Linux. Windows NT, Windows 2000, and Windows XP use a file system called New Technology FileSystem (NTFS). Windows versions 95, 98, and ME use a file system called FAT32.

● To speed up the process of storing and retrieving data, a disk drive usually works with a group of sectors called a **cluster** or a "block." The number of sectors that form a cluster varies depending on the capacity of the disk and how the operating system works with files. A file system's primary task is to maintain a list of clusters and keep track of which ones are empty and which ones hold data. This information is stored in a special file.

● If your computer uses the FAT32 file system, for example, this special file is called the **File Allocation Table** (FAT). Each of your disks contains its own FAT, so that information about its contents is always available when the disk is in use. Unfortunately, storing this crucial file on disk presents a risk; if the FAT is damaged by a hard disk head crash, a computer virus, or scratch, you'll generally lose access to all of the data that is stored on the disk.

● When you save a file, your PC's operating system looks at the FAT to see which clusters are empty. It will select one of these clusters, record the file data there, and then revise the FAT to include the filename and its location. A file that does not fit into a single cluster spills over into the next contiguous (meaning adjacent) cluster unless that cluster already contains data. When contiguous clusters are not available, the operating system stores parts of a file in noncontiguous (nonadjacent) clusters. Figure D-24 helps you visualize how the FAT keeps track of filenames and locations.

● When you want to retrieve a file, the OS looks through the FAT for the filename and its location. It directs the disk drive's read-write head to move to the first cluster that contains the file data. Using additional data from the FAT, the operating system can move the read-write head to each of the clusters that contain the remaining parts of the file.

● When you click a file's icon and then select the delete option, the operating system simply changes the status of the file's clusters to "empty" and removes the filename from the FAT. The filename no longer appears in a directory listing, but the file's data remains in the clusters until a new file is stored there. You might think that this data is erased, but it is possible to purchase utilities that recover a lot of this "deleted" data. Law enforcement agents, for example, use these utilities to gather evidence from "deleted" files on the computer disks of suspected criminals.

● As a computer writes files on a disk, parts of files tend to become scattered all over the disk. These **fragmented files** are stored in noncontiguous clusters. Drive performance generally declines as the read-write heads move back and forth to locate the clusters that contain the parts of a file. To regain peak performance, you can use a **defragmentation utility** to rearrange the files on a disk so that they are stored in contiguous clusters. See Figure D-25.

FIGURE D-23: Formatting a disk

► Formatting prepares the surface of a disk to hold data
► Disks are divided into tracks and wedge-shaped sectors—each side of a floppy disk typically has 80 tracks divided into 18 sectors; each sector holds 512 bytes of data
► On a typical CD, a single track is about three miles long and is divided into 336,000 sectors; each sector holds 2,048 bytes of data

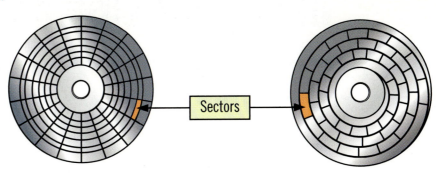

Sectors

FIGURE D-24: How the FAT works

► Each colored cluster on the disk contains part of a file; clusters 3 and 4 (blue) contain the *Bio.txt* file
► Cluster 9 (aqua) contains the *Pick.wps* file; clusters 7, 8, and 10 contain the *Jordan.wks* file
► A computer locates and displays the *Jordan.wks* file, by looking for its name in the File Allocation Table; by following the pointers listed in the Status column, the computer can then see that the file is continued in clusters 8 and 10

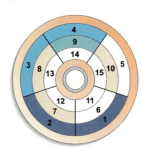

File Allocation Table

CLUSTER	STATUS	COMMENT
1	1	Reserved for operating system
2	1	Reserved for operating system
3	4	First cluster of Bio.txt. Points to cluster 4, which holds more data for Bio.txt
4	999	Last cluster for Bio.txt
5	0	Empty
6	0	Empty
7	8	First cluster for Jordan.wks. Points to cluster 8, which holds more data for the Jordan.wks file
8	10	Second cluster for Jordan.wks. Points to cluster 10, which holds more data for the Jordan.wks file
9	999	First and last cluster containing Pick.wps
10	999	Last cluster of Jordan.wks

FIGURE D-25: Defragmenting a disk

Defragmenting a disk helps your computer operate more efficiently; consider using a defragmentation utility a couple of times per year to keep your computer running in top form

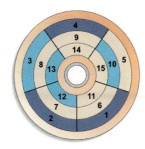

▲ On this fragmented disk, the purple, yellow, and blue files are stored in non-contiguous clusters

▲ When the disk is defragmented, the sectors of data for each file are moved to contiguous clusters

How a Microprocessor Executes Instructions

Remarkable advances in microprocessor technology have produced exponential increases in computer speed and power. In 1965, Gordon Moore, co-founder of chip-production giant Intel Corporation, predicted that the number of transistors on a chip would double every 18 to 24 months. Much to the surprise of engineers and Moore himself, "Moore's law" accurately predicted 30 years of chip development. In 1958, the first integrated circuit contained two transistors. The Pentium III Xeon processor, introduced in 1999, had 9.5 million transistors. The Pentium 4 processor, introduced only a year later, featured 42 million transistors.

What's really fascinating, though, is how these chips perform complex tasks simply by manipulating bits. How can pushing around 1s and 0s result in professional-quality documents, exciting action games, animated graphics, cool music, street maps, and e-commerce Web sites? To satisfy your curiosity about what happens deep in the heart of a microprocessor, you'll need to venture into the realm of instruction sets, fetch cycles, accumulators, and pointers.

A computer accomplishes a complex task by performing a series of very simple steps, referred to as instructions. An instruction tells the computer to perform a specific arithmetic, logical, or control operation. To be executed by a computer, an instruction must be in the form of electrical signals, those now-familiar 1s and 0s that represent "ons" and "offs." In this form, instructions are referred to as machine code. They are, of course, very difficult for people to read, so typically when discussing them, we use more understandable mnemonics, such as JMP, MI, and REG1.

An instruction has two parts: the op code and the operands. An op code, which is short for "operation code," is a command word for an operation such as add, compare, or jump. The operands for an instruction specify the data, or the address of the data, for the operation.

In the instruction JMP M1, the op code is JMP and the operand is M1. The op code JMP means jump or go to a different instruction. The operand M1 stands for the RAM address of the instruction to which the computer is supposed to go. The instruction JMP M1 has only one operand, but some instructions have more than one operand. For example, the instruction ADD REG1 REG2 has two operands: REG1 and REG2.

The list of instructions that a microprocessor is able to execute is known as its instruction set. This instruction set is built into the microprocessor when it is manufactured. Every task that a computer performs is determined by the list of instructions in its instruction set.

FIGURE D–26: The instruction cycle

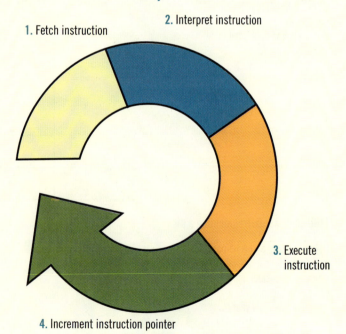

1. Fetch instruction
2. Interpret instruction
3. Execute instruction
4. Increment instruction pointer

The term **instruction cycle** refers to the process in which a computer executes a single instruction. Some parts of the instruction cycle are performed by the microprocessor's control unit; other parts of the cycle are performed by the ALU. The steps in this cycle are summarized in Figure D-26. Figure D-27 explains how the ALU, control unit, and RAM work together to process instructions.

FIGURE D-27: The ALU, the control unit, and RAM work to process instructions

1. The instruction pointer indicates the memory location that holds the first instruction (M1).
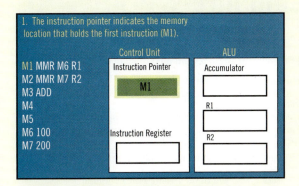

2. The computer fetches the instruction and puts it into the instruction register.
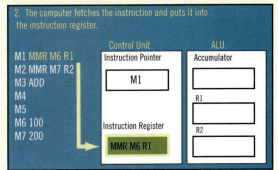

3. The computer executes the instruction that is in the instruction register; it moves the contents of M6 into register 1 of the ALU.
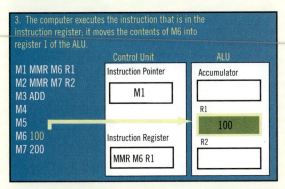

4. The instruction pointer changes to point to the memory location that holds the next instruction.
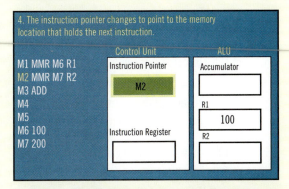

5. The computer fetches the instruction and puts it in the instruction register.
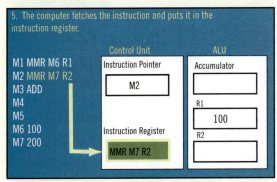

6. The computer executes the instruction; it moves the contents of M7 into register 2 of the ALU.

7. The computer fetches the instruction and puts it in the instruction register.
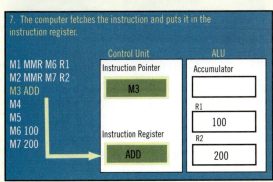

8. The computer executes the instruction. The result is put in the accumulator.

Who Invented the Computer?

Just think how wealthy you would be if you had invented the computer, held a patent for its technology, and could collect even $1 in royalties for every computer ever sold. In 1973, a company called Sperry-Rand claimed to hold a patent on the technology for electronic digital computers. If the courts had upheld this claim, then no company would have been able to manufacture computers without obtaining a license from and paying royalties to Sperry-Rand. As you might expect, other computer companies, such as IBM, took issue with Sperry-Rand's claim. During the ensuing court battle, opposition lawyers suggested a surprising number of candidates as the "inventor" of the computer. You can read the brief sketches of these candidates and their machines, and then do some supplementary research on the Web, before deciding who you think invented the computer.

During the period 1821-1832, Charles Babbage drew up plans for a machine that he called the Analytical Engine. Like modern computers, this device was designed to be programmable. It would accept input from a set of punched cards that contained the instructions for performing calculations. The plans for the Analytical Engine called for it to store the results of intermediary calculations in a sort of memory. Results would be printed on paper. Babbage intended to power his device using a steam engine, which was the cutting-edge technology of his day. Unfortunately, Babbage worked on this machine for 11 years but never completed it.

In 1939, John Atanasoff began to construct a machine that came to be known as the Atanasoff-Berry Computer (ABC). Like today's computers, the ABC was powered by electricity, but it used vacuum tubes instead of integrated circuits. This machine was designed to accept input, store the intermediary results of calculations, and produce output. Unlike today's computers, the ABC was not a multipurpose machine. Instead, it was designed for a single purpose—finding solutions to systems of linear equations.

Atanasoff never completed the ABC, but he shared his ideas and technology with John Mauchly and J. Presper Eckert, who were working on plans for the ENIAC (Electronic Numerical Integrator and Computer). Like the ABC, the ENIAC was powered by electricity and used vacuum tubes for its computational circuitry. The machine could be "programmed" by rewiring its circuitry and it produced printed output. ENIAC went online in 1946. Eckert and Mauchly filed for a patent on their technology and formed a company that became Sperry-Rand.

The ENIAC was not originally designed to store a program in memory, along with data. The stored program concept—a key feature of today's computers—was proposed by John von Neumann, who visited the ENIAC project and then collaborated with Eckert and Mauchly on the EDVAC computer, which was completed in 1949. The EDVAC was an electronic, digital computer that could accept input, process data, store data and programs, and produce output. Like the ENIAC, the EDVAC used vacuum tubes for its computational circuitry. Whereas the ENIAC worked with decimal numbers, however, the EDVAC worked with binary numbers much like today's computers.

In 1938, German scientist Conrad Zuse developed a binary, digital computer called the Z-1. Zuse had designed his machine as a programmable, general-purpose device with input, storage, processing, and output capabilities. Unlike the ABC and ENIAC, the Z-1 was not a fully electronic device. Instead of using electrical signals to represent data, it used mechanical relays.

Zuse's work was cloaked in secrecy during World War II, and scientists in Allied countries had little or no knowledge of his technology. It is somewhat surprising, therefore, that a similar machine was constructed in the United States by Howard Aiken, who was working with funding from IBM. The Harvard Mark I, completed in 1944, was powered by electricity, but used mechanical relays for its computational circuitry.

No list of computer inventors would be complete without Alan Turing, who worked with a group of British scientists, mathematicians, and engineers to create a completely electronic computing device in 1943. Called the Colossus, Turing's machine was essentially a huge version of Atanasoff's ABC—a special-purpose device (designed to break Nazi codes) powered by electricity, with vacuum tubes for its computing circuitry.

The roster of possible computer "inventors" includes Babbage, Atanasoff, Eckert and Mauchly, von Neumann, Zuse, Aiken, and Turing. Patents were filed only by IBM for Aiken's Mark I and by Eckert and Mauchly for the ENIAC. Should any of these inventors be collecting royalties on computer technology?

▼ INTERACTIVE QUESTIONS

○ Yes ○ No ○ Not sure   **1.** The Sperry-Rand lawsuit ended with a ruling that the Eckert and Mauckly patent was not valid because the ENIAC inventors derived their ideas from Atanasoff. Do you think that this decision was correct?

○ Yes ○ No ○ Not sure   **2.** To be credited with an invention, do you think that an inventor should be required to complete a working model?

○ Yes ○ No ○ Not sure   **3.** There are similarities between the development and invention of the automobile and the invention of the computer. Do you believe that inventions developed as a result of teamwork have contributed more to our society than inventions created by individuals?

○ Yes ○ No ○ Not sure   **4.** Do you think the rules specified by a patent encourage future related or similar inventions by others?

▼ EXPAND THE IDEAS

1. The Sperry-Rand lawsuit ended with a ruling that the Eckert and Mauchly patent was not valid because the ENIAC inventors derived their ideas from Atanasoff. Do you think that this decision was correct? Write a one-page paper supporting your answer.

2. To be credited with the invention of the computer, do you think that the inventor should have been required to have completed a working model? Why or why not? Research patent information to provide background information on what is required.

3. What key components do you believe define a computer? Detail the specific characteristics that made the "computer" different from any other machine.

4. Research the development and invention of the automobile. What are the similarities between the invention of the automobile and the invention of the computer? Find several examples of articles, documentaries, or news stories. Write a summary of each article or media piece. Analyze your findings. Was the media voice consistent? Why or why not?

5. Do you know anyone who holds a patent and gets a royalty for an invention? If you don't know anyone personally, research a recent invention. What made it a unique invention and eligible for patent and royalty rights? Compile your findings into a poster presentation.

End of Unit Exercises

▼ KEY TERMS

ALU
ASCII
Benchmark
Binary number system
Bit
Byte
Cache
Capacitor
Character data
CISC
Cluster
CMOS memory
Computer file
Control unit
Data representation
Defragmentation utility
Digital device
Digital electronics
DIMM
DIP

Directory
EBCDIC
EPROM
Extended ASCII
File Allocation Table (FAT)
File date
File format
File management
File management utility
File size
File specification
File system
Filename
Filename extension
File-naming conventions
Folder
Fragmented file
Gigahertz (GHz)
Instruction cycle
Instruction set

Integrated circuit (IC)
Kilobit
Kilobyte
Logical storage model
Megabit
Megabyte
Megahertz (MHz)
Microprocessor
Microprocessor clock
Motherboard
Nanosecond
Native file format
Numeric data
Parallel processing
Path
PGA
Pipelining
PROM
RAM
RDRAM

Register
Reserved word
RIMM
RISC
ROM
ROM BIOS
Root directory
SDRAM
SEC cartridge
Sectors
Serial processing
SO-RIMM
Subdirectory
Tracks
Unicode
Virtual memory
Windows Explorer
Word size

▼ UNIT REVIEW

1. Review the bold terms in this unit. Then pick 10 terms that are most unfamiliar to you. Be sure that you can use your own words to define the terms you have selected.

2. Describe how the binary number system and binary coded decimals can use only 1s and 0s to represent numbers.

3. Describe the difference between numeric data, character data, and numerals. Then, list and briefly describe the four codes that computers typically use for character data.

4. Make sure that you understand the meaning of the following measurement terms; indicate what aspects of a computer system they are used to measure: KB, Kb, MB, Mb, GB, Kbps, MHz, GHz, ns.

5. List four types of memory and briefly describe how each one works.

6. Describe how the ALU and the control unit interact to process data.

7. Describe the difference between the Save and the Save As options provided by an application.

8. Explain the kinds of file management tasks that might best be accomplished using a file management utility such as Windows Explorer.

9. In your own words, describe the difference between a logical storage model and a physical storage model.

10. Make sure that you can describe what happens in the FAT when a file is stored or deleted.

▼ FILL IN THE BEST ANSWER

1. The _____ number system represents numeric data as a series of 0s and 1s.

2. ASCII is used primarily to represent _____ data.

3. Most personal computers use the _____ code to represent character data.

4. Digital _____ makes it possible for a computer to manipulate simple "on" and "off" signals to perform complex tasks.

5. An integrated _____ contains microscopic circuit elements, such as wires, transistors, and capacitors that are packed onto a very small square of semiconducting material.

6. The _____ in the microprocessor performs arithmetic and logical operations.

7. The _____ in the CPU directs and coordinates the operation of the entire computer system.

8. The timing in a computer system is established by the _____.

9. In RAM, microscopic electronic parts called _____ hold the electrical signals that represent data.

10. The instructions for the operations your computer performs when it is first turned on are permanently stored in _____.

11. System configuration information about the hard disk, date, and RAM capacity is stored in battery-powered _____ memory.

12. An operating system's file-naming _____ provide a set of rules for naming files.

13. A file _____ refers to the arrangement of data in a file and the coding scheme that is used to represent the data.

14. The main directory of a disk is sometimes referred to as the _____ directory.

15. A file's location is defined by a file _____, which includes the drive letter, folder(s), filename, and extension.

16. The file _____ can be important information when you've created several versions of a file and you want to know which version is the most recent.

17. The _____ option on an application's File menu allows you to name a file and specify its storage location.

18. A(n) _____ storage model helps you form a mental picture of how your files are arranged on a disk.

19. On a floppy disk or hard disk, data is stored in concentric circles called _____, which are divided into wedge-shaped _____.

20. Windows Explorer is an example of a file _____ utility.

▼ PRACTICE TESTS

When you use the Interactive CD, you can take Practice Tests that consist of 10 multiple-choice, true/false, and fill-in-the blank questions. The questions are selected at random from a large test bank, so each time you take a test, you'll receive a different set of questions. Your tests are scored immediately, and you can print study guides to determine which questions you answered incorrectly. If you are using a Tracking Disk, insert in the floppy disk drive to save your test scores.

▼ INDEPENDENT CHALLENGE 1

The three leading manufacturers of processors are Intel, AMD, and Transmeta. These companies manufacture processors for personal computers as well as other devices.

1. Based on what you read in this unit, list and describe the factors that affect microprocessor performance. Create a table using the performance factors as column heads.

2. Use your favorite search engine on the Internet to research any two companies that produce microprocessors.

3. List their Web sites and any other pertinent contact information for the companies that you chose.

4. List three of the models that each company produces as row labels in the table you created in Step 1. Complete the table to show how these models rate, that is, their specifications for each performance factor.

5. Write a brief statement describing any new research or new products that each company is developing.

▼ INDEPENDENT CHALLENGE 2

How quickly could you code a sentence using the Extended ASCII code? What is the history of coding and coding schemes? You can find a wealth of information about coding schemes that have been developed throughout the history of computing as well as coding used to transmit information.

1. Use your favorite search engine to research the history of Morse code. Write a brief paragraph outlining your findings.

2. Use the International Morse Code alphabet to write your full name.

3. Research the history of the ASCII code. Write a one-page summary of your findings.

4. Use the extended ASCII code to write your full name.

5. Research the history of the EBCDIC code. Write a one-page summary of your findings.

6. Use the extended EBCDIC code to write your full name.

▼ INDEPENDENT CHALLENGE 3

How will you organize the information that you store on your hard drive? Your hard disk will be your electronic filing cabinet for all your work and papers. You can create many different filing systems. The way you set up your folders will guide your work and help you keep your ideas and projects organized so you can work efficiently with your computer. Take some time to think about the work that you do, the types of documents or files you will be creating, and then decide how you will create files and folders.

1. Read each of the following plans for organizing files and folders on a hard disk and comment on the advantages and disadvantages of each plan.

    a. Create a folder for each file you create.

    b. Store all the files in the root directory.

    c. Store all files in the My Documents folder.

    d. Create a folder for each application you plan to use and store only documents you generate with that application in each folder.

    e. Create folders for broad topics such as memos, letters, budget, art, personal, and then store all related documents and files within those folders.

    f. Create folders based on specific topics such as tax, applications, household, school, then store all related documents and files within those folders.

    g. Create a new folder for each month and store all files or documents created in that month in that appropriate folder.

2. Write up a summary of how you plan to organize your hard disk and explain why you chose the method you did.

▼ INDEPENDENT CHALLENGE 4

You can use Windows Explorer or any file management program on your computer to explore and find specific files and folders on your hard disk.

1. Start Windows Explorer then expand the My Computer icon. List the devices under My Computer.

2. Open the My Documents folder on the Local Disk C: (if not available, find the folder that has your documents). List how many folders are in the My Documents folder on your hard disk.

3. Open one of the folders in the My Documents folder, then display the Details View. Are filename extensions showing? If so, list them and identify which programs would open those files.

4. How many different types of files can you find on your hard disk? List up to 10.

5. Make a list of five filenames that are valid under the file-naming conventions for your operating system. Create a list of five filenames that are not valid and explain the problem with each one.

6. Create five filenames that meet the file-naming conventions for Windows and for MAC OS. Then create five filenames that do not meet the file-naming conventions for Windows or for MAC OS, and explain why these filenames do not meet the file-naming conventions.

7. Pick any five files on the computer that you typically use, and write out the full path for each one. If you can, identify the programs that were used to create each of the files you found.

▼ LAB: BENCHMARKING

1. Start the interactive part of the lab. Insert your Tracking Disk if you want to save your QuickCheck results. Perform each of the lab steps as directed and answer all of the lab QuickCheck questions. When you exit the lab, your answers are automatically graded and your results are displayed.

2. Use the System Info button that's available in Microsoft Word to analyze the computer that you typically use. Provide the results of the analysis along with a brief description of the computer that you tested and its location (at home, at work, in a computer lab, etc.).

3. From the Processor Benchmarks table above, which processor appears to be faster at graphics processing? Which processor appears to be better at overall processing tasks?

4. Explain why you might perform a benchmark test on your own computer but get different results from those that you read about in a computer magazine that tested the same computer with the same benchmark test.

5. Use a search engine on the Web to find benchmark ratings for Intel's Pentium 4 processors. What do these ratings show about the relative performance for 1.36 GHz, 1.5 GHz, and 1.7 GHz Pentium 4s?

▼ LAB: WORKING WITH WINDOWS EXPLORER

1. Start the interactive part of the lab. Insert your Tracking Disk if you want to save your QuickCheck results. Perform each of the lab steps as directed and answer all of the lab QuickCheck questions. When you exit the lab, your answers are automatically graded and your results are displayed.

2. Use Windows Explorer to look at the directory of the hard disk or floppy disk that currently contains most of your files. Draw a diagram showing the hierarchy of folders. Write a paragraph explaining how you could improve this hierarchy and draw a diagram to illustrate your plan.

3. Use a new floppy disk or format an old disk that doesn't contain important data. Create three folders on the disk: Music, Web Graphics, and Articles. Within the Music folder, create four additional folders: Jazz, Reggae, Rock, and Classical. Within the Classical folder, create two more folders: Classical MIDI and Classical MP3.

4. Use your browser software to connect to the Internet, then go to a Web site, such as www.zdnet.com or www.cnet.com. Look for a small graphic (remember, you only have 1.44 MB of space on your floppy disk!) and download it to your Web Graphics folder. Next, use a search engine like www.google.com or www.yahoo.com to search for "classical MIDI music." Download one of the compositions to the Music\Classical\Classical MIDI folder. Open Windows Explorer and expand all of the directories for drive A. Open the Music\Classical\Classical MIDI folder and make sure that your music download appears. Capture a screenshot. Follow your instructor's directions to submit this screenshot as a printout or e-mail attachment.

▼ VISUAL WORKSHOP

Your computer probably came with a specific amount of RAM. What if you wanted to upgrade to more RAM? How would you go about finding the RAM to purchase? How much RAM is enough? Is there too much RAM? Figure D-28 shows the Web page for Kingston Technology, a leading distributor and manufacturer of computer memory. You can use the Internet for researching and buying RAM. You will research RAM and determine the best buy for your system.

FIGURE D-28

1. Use a search engine to search on RAM. What kinds of Web sites did you find? Did you need to be more specific in your search to find the RAM for your computer?

2. Complete a search on DRAM. Was this more successful in finding Web sites that would sell you chips to update the memory capacity on your computer?

3. Go to www.kingston.com, the page shown in Figure D-28, and click the link for the Memory Configurator. See if you can find the best memory for upgrading your system.

4. Write a brief summary of your findings.

5. Click the links for Desktop, Notebook, and then Server memory. Read the pages and write a brief summary of what you read for two of the links.

UNIT
E

Network Technology and the Internet

Although network technology continues to evolve, it is based on a set of fairly stable concepts. This unit discusses network building blocks and evolving network technologies. The unit begins with the concepts of coding, data transmission, and other basic building blocks. The unit discusses not only the technology of simple local area networks (LANs) but also the technology behind a complex network—the Internet. You will learn about the devices, connections, and protocols that make it possible to communicate over networks. The unit compares and contrasts various options for accessing the Internet and concludes with a lesson on installing a LAN.

Introducing coding and data transmission

A **communications network** is the combination of hardware, software, and connecting links that transport data. In 1948, Claude Shannon, an engineer at the prestigious Bell Labs, published an article that described a communications system model. In this model, data from a source is "encoded," or changed from one form to another, and sent over a communications channel to its destination, where it is decoded. According to Shannon, effective communication depends on the efficiency of the coding process and the channel's resistance to interference, called noise. Figure E-1 illustrates Shannon's communications system model.

DETAILS

- As you'll recall from Unit D, the use of bits can form the basis of very efficient coding schemes, such as ASCII and UNICODE. Figure E-2 helps you visualize how a bit, like a lantern, has two states: on (1) and off (0). A single bit represents one of two possible messages, each called a unit of information. Increasing the number of bits increases the units of information that can be conveyed.

- The number of units of information that you can convey is simply the number of different combinations that you can make with a given number of bits. With one bit, you can convey two units of information; with two bits, you can convey four units; with three bits, you can convey eight units; with eight bits you can convey 256 units. The maximum number of different units of information possible with n bits is 2^n; 2 represents the states "on" and "off," and n represents the number of bits.

- Computers use several coding schemes that are based on binary digits, including ASCII, EBCDIC, UNICODE, and binary numbers. The extended ASCII code uses eight bits, which can represent 256 unique units of information: enough for uppercase letters, lowercase letters, punctuation symbols, numerals, and assorted other symbols and control characters. The underlying principle is that computer data is digital—a series of 0s and 1s.

- When data is transmitted, it usually takes the form of an electromagnetic signal. On a communications network, your data might be converted into several different types of waves before reaching its destination. It might originate in your computer as electrical voltages, get converted into analog tones by a modem, and then undergo another conversion into bursts of laser light, radio waves, or infrared light.

- Electromagnetic signals are characterized by their frequency, wavelength, and amplitude. **Frequency** is the number of times that a wave oscillates (moves back and forth between two points) per second. Short wave lengths have high frequencies; many are packed into a one-second interval. Signals with shorter wavelengths tend to travel farther. **Wavelength** is the distance between the peaks; **amplitude** is the height of the wave.

- Although you usually see a wave depicted as a smooth curve, waves can have different shapes, referred to as "waveforms" or "wave patterns." Analog signals have an unlimited range of values and therefore have a smooth, curved waveform. Digital signals, on the other hand, represent discrete values within a limited range and therefore have a square or "stepped" waveform. Compare the analog and digital waveforms shown in Figure E-3.

- Digital signals require simple circuitry and are easy to "clean up" after being affected by noise. Digital equipment must be sensitive to only two frequencies: that representing 1s and that representing 0s. In contrast, analog equipment—a telephone or a microphone, for example—must be sensitive to a wide range of audible frequencies.

FIGURE E-1: Shannon's communications system model

▶ A communications system sends information from a source to a destination; the path between the source and destination might appear to be straight as in the diagram, but the data may pass through several devices, which convert it to electrical, sound, light, or radio signals; beam it up to satellites; route it along the least congested links; or clean up parts of the signal that have been distorted by noise

Noise
Encoded Data
Decoded Data
Signal
Source
Transmitter
Communications Channel
Receiver
Destination

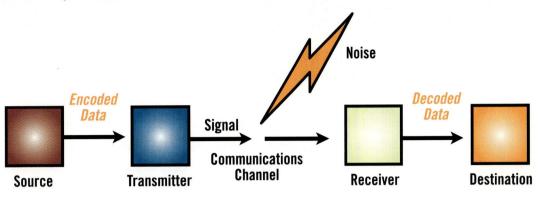

FIGURE E-2: Using lanterns to illustrate a coding scheme

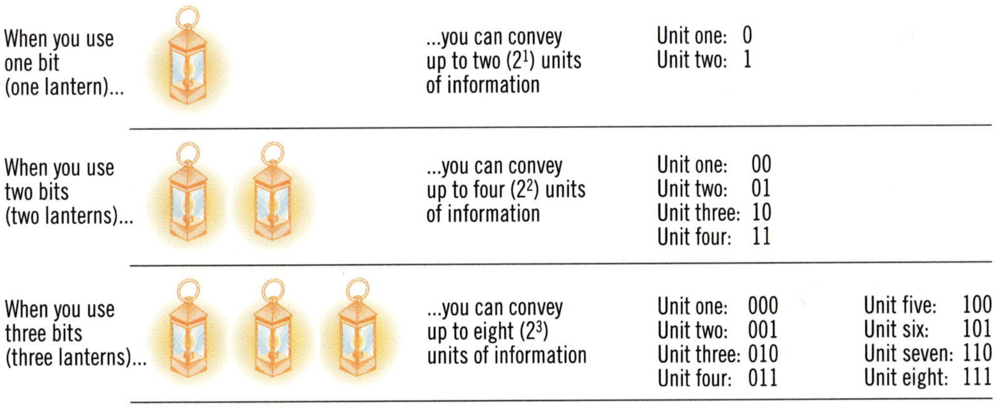

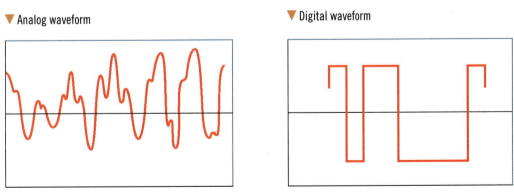

When you use one bit (one lantern)...
...you can convey up to two (2¹) units of information
Unit one: 0
Unit two: 1
When you use two bits (two lanterns)...
...you can convey up to four (2²) units of information
Unit one: 00
Unit two: 01
Unit three: 10
Unit four: 11
When you use three bits (three lanterns)...
...you can convey up to eight (2³) units of information
Unit one: 000
Unit two: 001
Unit three: 010
Unit four: 011
Unit five: 100
Unit six: 101
Unit seven: 110
Unit eight: 111

FIGURE E-3: Analog v. digital waveforms

▼ Analog waveform

▼ Digital waveform

Exploring communications channels

Each device that is connected to a network is referred to as a **node**. Data travels from one node to another through a communications channel. A **communications channel**, or "link," is a physical path (such as a cable) or a frequency (such as a radio wave) for signal transmission. Computer networks use a variety of links to carry data between nodes; the most common being wired communications channels: twisted-pair cable, coaxial cable, and fiber-optic cable. Wireless communications channels include radio waves, microwaves, satellites, infrared light, and laser beams.

Info Web
FIBER OPTICS

DETAILS

● Computer data can travel over wired communications channels. Many networks use **twisted-pair cables** for data communications. See Figure E-4. Twisted-pair cables are similar to the telephone wiring that runs throughout a house and can be shielded or unshielded. **STP** (shielded twisted pair) encases its twisted pairs with a foil shield, which reduces signal noise that might interfere with data transmission. **UTP** (unshielded twisted pair) contains no shielding and is less expensive than shielded cable but it is more susceptible to noise. UTP is probably the most commonly used transmission medium for small networks.

Coaxial cable, shown in Figure E-5, is often called coax cable or co-ax. It is the cable of choice for cable television because its high capacity allows it to carry signals for more than 100 television channels and cable modem signals simultaneously.

Fiber-optic cable, shown in Figure E-6, is a bundle of extremely thin tubes of glass. Each tube, called an optical fiber, is much thinner than a human hair. Fiber-optic cables do not conduct or transmit electrical signals; instead, miniature lasers convert data into pulses of light that flash through the cables. Fiber-optic cables are an essential part of the Internet backbone.

● In addition to wired communication channels, computer data can also travel the airwaves via wireless communications channels. **RF signals** (radio frequency signals), commonly called radio waves, are sent and received by a **transceiver** (a combined transmitter and receiver), which is equipped with an antenna. RF signals provide data transport for small home networks, campus networks, and business networks.

Microwaves provide another option for transporting data over wireless communications channels. Microwaves can be aimed in a single direction, have more carrying capacity than radio waves, and work best when a clear path exists between the transmitter and receiver. Microwaves cannot penetrate metal objects. Microwave installations typically provide data transport for large corporate networks and form part of the Internet backbone.

Radio and microwave transmissions cannot bend around the surface of the earth, so earth-orbiting **communications satellites** play an important role in long-distance communications. A signal can be relayed from a ground station to a communications satellite. A **transponder** on the satellite receives, amplifies, and retransmits the signal to a ground station on earth. Satellite transmissions are a key technology for the Internet backbone and provide a way for individuals to connect personal computers to the Internet.

Other wireless communications channels include infrared light, laser light, and airborne data transmission. **Infrared light** can carry data signals, but only for short distances and with a clear line of sight. Its most practical use seems to be transmission of data between a notebook computer and a printer or between a PDA and a desktop computer, and in remote controls to change television channels. **Laser light** can stay focused over a larger distance but requires a clear line of sight; no trees, snow, fog, or rain. Airborne data transmission is currently in the experimental stage, but may eventually prove useful for transmitting data between buildings.

Defining broadband and narrowband

Bandwidth is the transmission capacity of a communications channel. A high-bandwidth communications channel can carry more data than a low-bandwidth channel. For example, the coaxial cable that provides you with more than 100 channels of cable TV has a higher bandwidth than your home telephone line.

High-bandwidth communications systems, such as cable TV or DSL lines, are sometimes referred to as **broadband**; systems with less capacity, such as the telephone system, are referred to as **narrowband**. The bandwidth of a digital channel is usually measured in bits per second (bps).

FIGURE E-4: Twisted-pair cable

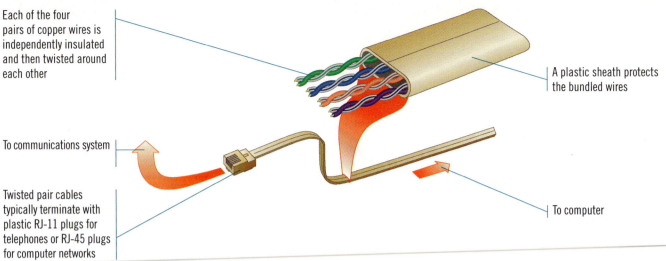

Each of the four pairs of copper wires is independently insulated and then twisted around each other

A plastic sheath protects the bundled wires

To communications system

To computer

Twisted pair cables typically terminate with plastic RJ-11 plugs for telephones or RJ-45 plugs for computer networks

FIGURE E-5: Coaxial cable

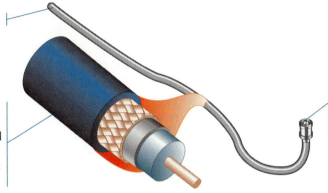

To communication system

Consists of a copper wire core encased in a non-conducting insulator, a foil shield, a woven metal outer shield, and a plastic outer coating

To computer; a metal BNC connector links the cable to a T-shaped connector on the back of the computer

FIGURE E-6: Fiber-optic cable

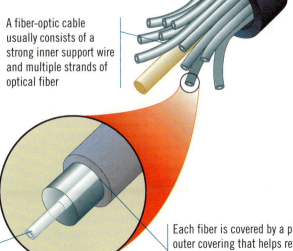

A plastic coating protects the bundle of fibers

A fiber-optic cable usually consists of a strong inner support wire and multiple strands of optical fiber

The core of each fiber is a perfectly formed glass tube with a diameter less than that of a human hair

Each fiber is covered by a plastic insulator and a tough outer covering that helps reflect the light that travels through the fiber

Introducing network hardware

Many network nodes are computers; some of them busily serve out information, and others simply request information. Behind the scenes, other nodes, which are a variety of network devices, handle specialized network tasks. Even though networks come in many sizes and configurations, they all require some basic network hardware components. Figure E-7 provides an overview of network hardware.

DETAILS

● Computers perform different functions on a network. For example, a computer might be a network server, a host computer, a workstation, or a client. The term **server** refers to a computer connected to a network that "serves" or distributes resources to network users. A server contains the software to manage and process files for other network nodes. E-mail servers, communications servers, file servers, and Web servers are some of the most common servers on today's networks. The term **host computer**, or "host," usually refers to any computer that provides services to network users. The terms "host" and "server" are often used interchangeably, but "host" is more commonly used in the context of the Internet. "Server" is used both in the context of the Internet and LANs.

The term **workstation** usually refers to a personal computer connected to a local area network (LAN). The term **client** usually refers to software on a computer that allows a user to access the services of a server. The terms client and workstation are sometimes used interchangeably, but client is more commonly used in the context of a personal computer that is connected to the Internet.

● A **network interface card (NIC)** is a small circuit board that converts the digital signals from a computer into signals that can travel over a network. Figure E-8 shows a NIC for a desktop computer that plugs into an expansion slot on the motherboard and a NIC for a notebook computer that fits into the PCMCIA slot of the notebook. NICs send data to and from network devices such as workstations or printers over the network.

● A variety of devices connect computers over a network, either individually or in combination. These devices include modems, hubs, routers, gateways, and repeaters. A **modem** is a network device connected to a computer that converts the digital signals from a computer into signals that can travel over a network, such as the telephone system or the Internet.

A **hub** is a network device that connects several nodes of a local area network. All of the devices that attach to a hub are part of the same local area network. Multiple hubs can be linked to expand a local area network. To connect more than one local area network or to connect a local area network to the Internet, an additional device, such as a router or a gateway, is necessary.

A **router** is a network device that is connected to at least two networks. Routers make decisions about the best route for data based on the data's destination and the state of the available network links. A **gateway** is a network device that serves as an entrance to another network. Both routers and gateways can be used as part of local area networks or the Internet.

A **repeater** is a network device that amplifies and regenerates signals so that they can retain the necessary strength to reach their destinations.

● Every node on a network, whether it is a computer or a network device, has an address. Every packet of data that travels over a network also has an address, which helps to route a packet to its destination, much like the address on a letter. A **physical address** is built into the circuitry of most network devices at the time they are manufactured. A device's physical address, however, is not always in a format that can be used by a particular network. If that is the case, a network device is assigned a **logical address**. Network software keeps track of which physical address corresponds to each logical address.

Software on a network

Special network operating systems (NOS), such as Novell NetWare, were quite popular at one time and are still used on some networks. The need for a special NOS has declined, however, because today's popular desktop and server operating systems include the software necessary to establish communication with the other computers and devices on a network.

Most application software designed for stand-alone computers can also be used on a network. Setting up such access is easy under some operating systems,

but difficult in others. For example, in order to run a Windows program from a server, you or your network administrator must complete a workstation installation of the software. A workstation installation copies the required program files to your local hard disk, then updates the Windows Registry and the Windows Start menu to include a listing for the new program. When you use the program, your computer is able to access program files from both your workstation and the server.

FIGURE E-7: Network hardware

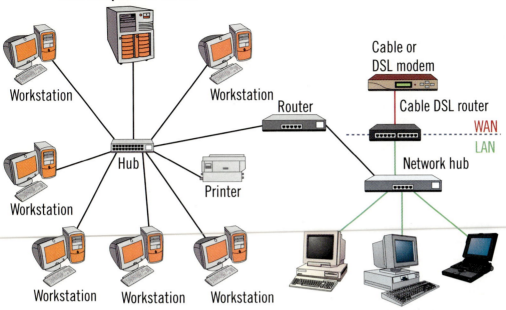

host computer or server

Workstation

Workstation

Router

Hub

Printer

Workstation

Cable or DSL modem

Cable DSL router

WAN

LAN

Network hub

Workstation   Workstation   Workstation

Figure E-8: Network interface cards

▶ Desktop (left) and notebook (below) network interface cards are expansion cards that can be used to connect a computer to a network

10/100M Fast Ethernet PC Card

Licensing software for use on a network

Even though an application might run on a LAN, it is still subject to copyright law and the terms of the license agreement. A **single-user license** agreement typically allows one copy of the software to be in use at a time. A **multiple-user license** allows more than one person to use a particular software package. Multiple-user licenses are generally priced per user, but the price for each user is typically less than the price of a single-user license. A **concurrent-user** license allows a certain number of copies of the software to be used at the same time. This type of license is popular for application software that might be accessed through the day by 100 or more different people, but when no more than, for instance, 20 copies would be in use at any one time. A **site license** generally allows software to be used on any and all computers at a specific location, such as within a corporate office or on a university campus.

Transporting data

The way data is transported over a network depends on the network topology, the packet switching technology, and protocols. **Topology** is the configuration of a network. **Packet switching** technology determines how data is broken up so that it can be transported over a network. **Protocols** are rules that ensure the orderly and accurate transmission and reception of data. Protocols start and end transmission, recognize errors, send data at the appropriate speed, and identify the correct senders and recipients.

DETAILS

- Networks have a **logical topology** (the way messages flow) and a **physical topology** (the layout of devices, wires, and cables on a network). Logical topologies fall into the same three categories as physical topologies: star, bus, and ring. Figure E-9 illustrates these three most common network topologies. A real-world network can make use of more than one topology. A network's physical topology and its logical topology don't have to match.

- When you send a file or an e-mail message over a network, the file is actually broken up into small pieces called packets. A **packet** is a "parcel" of data that is sent across a computer network. Each packet contains the address of its sender, the destination address, a sequence number, and some data. Dividing messages into equal-size packets makes them easier to handle than an assortment of different-sized files.

- **Packet switching**, see Figure E-10, divides a message into several packets that can be routed independently to their destination to avoid out-of-service or congested links. Packet switching uses available bandwidth efficiently because packets from many different messages can share a single communications channel, or "circuit." Packets are shipped over the circuit on a "first come, first served" basis. If some packets from a message are not available, the system does not need to wait for them. Instead, the system moves on to send packets from other messages, resulting in a steady stream of data.

  When a packet reaches an intersection in the network's communications channels, a router examines the packet's address. The router checks the address in a routing table and then sends the packet along the appropriate link toward its destination. As packets arrive at their destination, they are reassembled into a replica of the original file. Today, packet switching is the technology used for virtually every computer network.

- In general, a "protocol" is a set of rules for interacting and negotiating. In the context of networks, the term "protocol," or **communications protocol**, refers to a set of rules for efficiently transmitting data from one network node to another. Protocols allow two devices to negotiate and agree on how data will be transmitted. The most commonly used network protocol is TCP/IP (Transport Control Protocol/Internet Protocol). **TCP/IP**

is a suite of protocols that includes TCP, IP, and others. **TCP** (Transmission Control Protocol) breaks a message or file into packets. **IP** (Internet Protocol) is responsible for addressing packets so that they can be routed to their destination.

  There are several characteristics of communications protocols that decide the direction of the flow of data: **Simplex**, in which a signal travels in only one direction (for example, a TV set or a clock radio); **Half duplex**, in which it is possible to send and receive data, but not at the same time (for example, a walkie-talkie or a CB radio); and **Full duplex**, in which it is possible to send and receive at the same time over the same channel (for example, a telephone conversation).

- Protocols help two network devices negotiate and establish communications through a process called **handshaking**. The transmitting device sends a signal and waits for an acknowledgment signal from the receiving device. The two devices then "negotiate" a transmission speed that both can handle.

- Protocols also decide on how to coordinate the transmission. Using a **synchronous protocol**, the sender's signals and the receiver's signals are synchronized by a signal called a clock. The transmitting computer sends data at a fixed clock rate, and the receiving computer expects the incoming data at the same fixed rate. The rules for **asynchronous protocol** require the transmitting computer to send a start bit that indicates the beginning of a packet. Data is then transmitted as a series of bytes; the number of bytes that can be sent in each series is specified by the protocol. A stop bit marks the end of the data. Most data communications systems implement asynchronous protocol.

- Computers use error-checking protocols to ensure accurate delivery of data. As an example, one error-checking protocol adds a **parity bit** to a sequence of bits in order to keep track of the number of 1s and 0s it should contain. **Even parity** protocol requires the number of 1 bits, including the parity bit, to be an even number. When a device receives the data that you sent, it counts the number of 1s. If the count reveals an even number of 1s, the device assumes the data is correct. If it finds an odd number of 1s, it assumes that some type of interference changed one of the bits during transmission. See Figure E-11.

FIGURE E-9: Typical physical topologies: star, bus, and ring

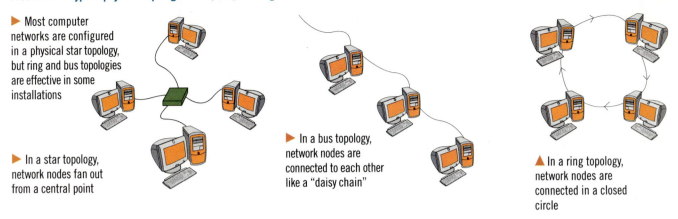

▶ Most computer networks are configured in a physical star topology, but ring and bus topologies are effective in some installations

▶ In a star topology, network nodes fan out from a central point

▶ In a bus topology, network nodes are connected to each other like a "daisy chain"

▲ In a ring topology, network nodes are connected in a closed circle

FIGURE E-10: Sending data as packets

A message is divided into packets

Each packet is addressed to the destination

If a route is congested, a packet can be rerouted

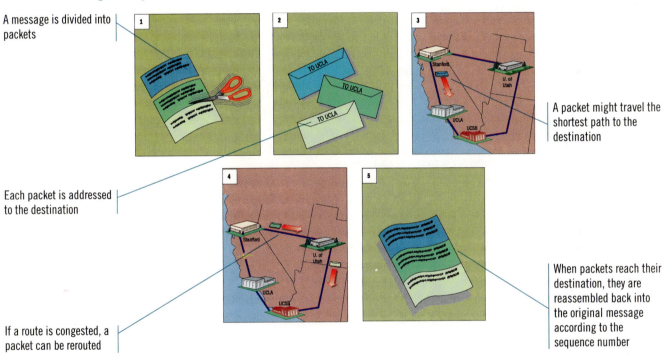

A packet might travel the shortest path to the destination

When packets reach their destination, they are reassembled back into the original message according to the sequence number

FIGURE E-11: Error detection using parity

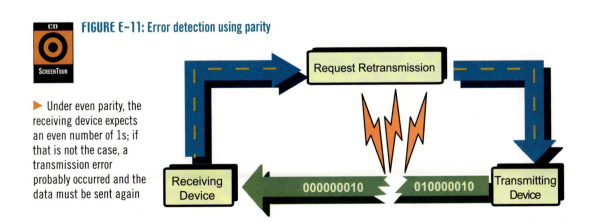

▶ Under even parity, the receiving device expects an even number of 1s; if that is not the case, a transmission error probably occurred and the data must be sent again

Request Retransmission

Receiving Device

000000010   010000010

Transmitting Device

Classifying networks

Networks can be categorized by distinguishing characteristics, such as their geographical coverage, wiring technology, protocols, or operating systems. This lesson contains brief definitions of terms used when classifying networks.

Info Web — HOME NETWORK · Info Web — ETHERNET

DETAILS

● Networks can be classified by their geographic coverage:

An **internetwork**, or "internet" (with a lowercase "i"), is a network that is composed of many smaller networks. When spelled with an uppercase "I," the **Internet** refers to a global, public network that uses TCP/IP protocol and includes servers that handle e-mail, Web sites, file downloads, and so on.

An **intranet** is a network that uses TCP/IP protocols and provides many of the same services as the Internet, but has two differences. First, an intranet is usually owned by a private business and its use is limited to the business's employees. Second, as a protection against hackers, an intranet typically does not provide remote access.

An **extranet** is similar to an intranet, except that it allows password-protected access by authorized outside users. A business or organization might use an extranet to provide remote access for branch offices, for example, or for employees who are working at home.

A **WAN** (wide area network) covers a large geographical area and may consist of several smaller networks. WANs can use any protocol, but today TCP/IP is the norm for wide area computer networks. The Internet is the largest example of a WAN.

A **MAN** (metropolitan area network) is a public high-speed network capable of voice and data transmission within a range of about 50 miles (80 km). A local ISP is a good example of a MAN.

A **LAN** (local area network) is a network that typically connects personal computers within a very limited geographical area, usually a single building.

● Networks can be classified by their use of wireless technology:

A **wireless network** uses radio frequencies instead of cables to send data from one network node to another. A **HomeRF** network is a low-power, wireless network designed for home use.

● Networks can be classified by their use of existing wiring technology:

A **HomePLC** network uses a building's existing power line cables (PLCs) to connect network nodes. A **HomePNA** network makes use of a building's existing telephone cables to connect network nodes.

● Networks can be classified by their architecture:

An **Ethernet** network can be configured as a physical star or bus. Each packet sent over an Ethernet network is broadcast over the entire network, but it is accepted only by the workstation to which it was addressed. Occasionally, two network devices on an Ethernet network attempt to send packets at the same time and a collision occurs. Ethernets use a standard called **CSMA/CD** (carrier sense multiple access with collision detection) to deal with these collisions. See Figure E-12. 10BaseT and 100BaseT refer to two of the most popular standards for Ethernet networks. A **10BaseT network** uses a type of twisted-pair cable called 10BaseT and transmits data at 10 Mbps. A **100BaseT network**, often referred to as Fast Ethernet, supports transfer rates up to 100 Mbps.

A **Token Ring network** connects nodes in a physical star configuration, but passes data around a logical ring using a technology called a "token." Tokens move in a circular path in a Token Ring network, which prevents collisions. See Figure E-13.

FDDI (Fiber Distributed Data Interconnect) is a specification for a type of high-speed network that uses fiber-optic cable to link workstations.

ATM (asynchronous transfer mode) is a network technology that can transmit all of the packets in a message over the same channel, providing smooth transmission of high-bandwidth files, such as those containing music and video.

A **client/server network** contains one or more computers configured with server software, and other computers, configured with client software, that access the servers.

Nicknamed "P2P," a **peer-to-peer network** treats every computer as an "equal" so that workstations can run local applications and also provide network resources, such as file access. P2P technology forms the basis for networks that share files. Figure E-14 compares the client/server model to the peer-to-peer model.

● Networks can be classified by their operating system:

The term **Novell network** refers to a local area network that uses Novell NetWare as its operating system.

FIGURE E-12: How Ethernets work

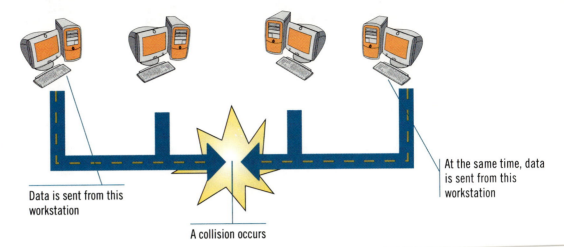

▶ On an Ethernet network, data travels on a first come first served basis; if two workstations attempt to send data at the same time, a collision occurs and that data must be resent

Data is sent from this workstation

At the same time, data is sent from this workstation

A collision occurs

FIGURE E-13: How Token Ring networks work

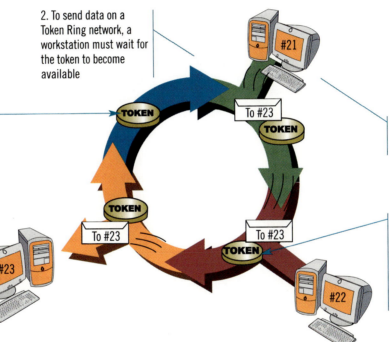

2. To send data on a Token Ring network, a workstation must wait for the token to become available

1. A signal called a token speeds over the network; the token is available when not escorting a packet

5. This workstation sees its address on the packet and detaches the data from the token

3. This workstation attached a packet to the token

4. The token and packet circles around the network, if the packet is not addressed to the workstation, it continues to circle until it reaches its destination

FIGURE E-14: Comparing the client/server model to the peer-to-peer model

▶ A client/server network provides more centralized services than a peer-to-peer network

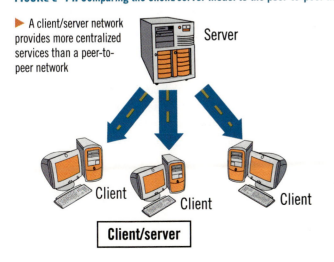

Server

Client

Client

Client

Client/server

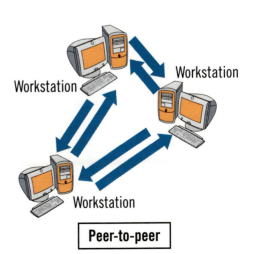

Workstation

Workstation

Workstation

Peer-to-peer

Understanding Internet connections

Even people who haven't used the Internet know a lot about it from watching the news, reading magazines, and watching movies. With more than 100 million nodes and 350 million users, the Internet is huge. The Internet lets you browse Web sites, shop at the Net mall, send e-mail, and chat online. But how does this one network provide so much information to so many people? This lesson discusses Internet connections and Internet protocols.

Info Web — TRACEROUTE UTILITIES

LAB — TRACKING PACKETS

DETAILS

- To access the Internet, you do not typically connect your computer directly to the Internet backbone. Instead, you connect to an ISP that in turn connects to the backbone. An **ISP** (Internet Service Provider) operates network devices that handle the physical aspects of transmitting and receiving data from your computer.

- An ISP is a point of access to the Internet. Figure E-15 is a simplified diagram that reflects how your own computer fits into the sprawling global Internet communications network.

- An ISP typically maintains the devices that provide subscribers with e-mail and access to the Web. Figure E-16 illustrates the equipment at a typical ISP. Customers arrange for service for which they pay a monthly fee. In addition, an ISP might charge an installation fee.

  The ISP you select should provide services in the places you typically use your computer. If your work takes you on the road a lot, you'll want to consider a national ISP that provides local access numbers in the cities you visit.

- An ISP links to other ISPs in a sort of ISP network, which makes it easy to route data among subscribers. **Network service providers** (NSPs), such as MCI, Sprint, UUNET, or AT&T, supply ISPs with access to high-speed transmission lines that form the backbone of the Internet. NSPs provide routers at network connection points.

- The Internet and many other networks use the TCP/IP suite of protocols, which is responsible for addressing packets so that they can be routed to their destination. TCP/IP provides a standard that is free, public, and fairly easy to implement. TCP/IP defines data transport on the Internet.

- In addition to TCP/IP, several other protocols are used on the Internet. Table E-1 briefly describes some of them.

- Internet pathways can be checked to be sure that they are open to Internet traffic. A software utility called **Ping** (Packet Internet Groper) sends a signal to a specific Internet address and waits for a reply. If a reply arrives, Ping reports that the computer is online and displays the elapsed time, or latency delay, for the round-trip message. Ping is useful for finding out if a site is up and running. Ping is also useful for determining whether the connection is adequate for online computer games or videoconferencing.

  Data traveling over the Internet can be traced. A software utility called **Traceroute** records a packet's path, including intermediate routers, from your computer to its destination.

  Using Ping or Traceroute, you can discover how long data is in transit from point A to point B. On average, data within the continental U.S. arrives at its destination 110-120 ms (milliseconds) after it is sent. Overseas transmissions usually require a little more time.

- With the right software and a valid password, the Internet can allow one computer to control another. An example of remote control is when a technical support person located in a manufacturer's service center takes control of your computer to fix a problem. Commands entered on one computer are actually executed on the other computer. One version of this process is referred to as **Telnet**.

  P2P makes it possible for one person's computer to access the content of another person's hard drive directly over the Internet—with permission, of course. This technology is the basis for Gnutella and the controversial Napster, which uses the Internet to give individuals access to each other's music files. It is also the model for distributed computing, which breaks down large projects into small processing tasks and then distributes these tasks to individual computers connected to the network.

FIGURE E-15: Connecting your computer to the Internet

▶ Typically you connect your computer to an ISP over a telephone line, cable TV line, or personal satellite link

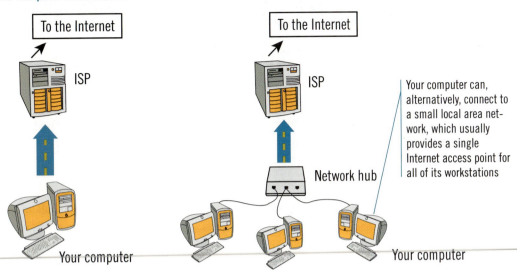

Your computer can, alternatively, connect to a small local area network, which usually provides a single Internet access point for all of its workstations

FIGURE E-16: Devices maintained by an ISP

▶ A router sends your data to the next "hop" toward its destination

▶ A domain name server that translates an address, such as www.nike.com, into a valid, numeric Internet address, such as 208.50.141.12

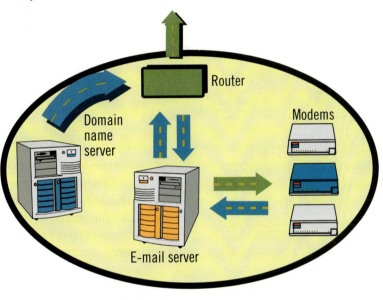

◀ A bank of modems that answer when your computer dials the ISP's access number

◀ An e-mail server to handle incoming and out-going mail for its subscribers

TABLE E-1: Protocols used on the Internet

PROTOCOL	NAME	FUNCTION
HTTP	Hypertext Transfer Protocol	Exchanges information over the Web
FTP	File Transfer Protocol	Transfers files between local and remote host computers
POP	Post Office Protocol	Transfers mail from an e-mail server to a client Inbox
SMTP	Simple Mail Transfer Protocol	Transfers e-mail messages from client computers to an e-mail server
IMAP	Internet Mail Access Protocol	An alternative to POP
TELNET	Telecommunication Network	Allows users who are logged on to one host to access another host
SSL	Secure Sockets Layer	Provides secure data transfer over the Internet

Introducing IP addresses and domain names

Computers on the Internet are identified using **IP addresses**. The "IP" part of TCP/IP defines the format for the IP addresses.

DETAILS

- Every ISP controls a unique pool of IP addresses, which can be assigned to subscribers as needed.

- An IP address is a series of numbers, such as 204.127.129.001. When written, an IP address is separated into four sections by periods for the convenience of readers. The number in a section cannot exceed 255. In binary representation, each section of an IP address requires 8 bits, so the entire address requires 32 bits. The four sections are used to create classes of IP addresses where each part is assigned based on the size, type of network, and other Internet functions.

- A permanently assigned IP address is called a **static IP address**. As a rule of thumb, computers that need a permanent IP address are servers or "hosts" on the Internet, for example, ISPs, Web sites, Web hosting services, or e-mail servers. Computers with static IP addresses usually are connected to the Internet all the time. For example, the computer that hosts the Course Technology Web site has a permanent address so that Internet users can always find it.

- A temporarily assigned IP address is called a **dynamic IP address**. Dynamic IP addresses are typically assigned by ISPs for most dial-up connections, and some DSL, ISDN, or cable modem connections. When you use a dial-up connection, for example, your ISP assigns a temporary IP address to your computer for use as long as your computer remains connected to the Internet. When you end a session, that IP address goes back into a pool of addresses that can be distributed to other subscribers when they log in. Your computer will rarely be assigned the same IP address it had during a previous dial-up session.

  Dynamic IP addresses are generally assigned to computers for client activities such as surfing the Web, sending and receiving e-mail, listening to Internet radio, or participating in chat groups.

- The IP address situation for ISP subscribers varies. Depending on the ISP, your computer might be assigned a static IP address, it might be assigned a dynamic address each time you connect, or it might be assigned a semi-permanent address that lasts for several months. If you want your computer to function as an Internet server, ask your ISP about its method of IP address allocation and its policies on allowing server activities.

- Because your ISP assigns IP addresses, you usually do not need to know the IP address assigned to your computer. However, if you need to identify how your computer is connected to the Internet or troubleshoot your connection, you can see your computer's IP address by reviewing the Internet configuration settings.

- IP addresses work well for communication between computers, but people often have difficulty remembering a series of numbers. As a result, many host computers have an easy-to-remember name that translates directly to the computer's IP address. See Figure E-17. This name is the "fully qualified domain name" (FQDN), but most people just refer to it as a **domain name**.

- A domain name is a key component of URLs and e-mail addresses. It is the Web server name in a URL and the e-mail server name in an e-mail address. For example, in the URL www.course.com, the domain name is course.com. In the e-mail addresses jsmith@rutgers.edu and emilyh@course.com the domain names are rutgers.edu and course.com, respectively.

- A domain name ends with an extension that indicates its **top-level domain**. For example, in the domain name course.com, "com" indicates that the host computer is maintained by a commercial business, in this case, Course Technology. Top-level domains and their uses are listed in Table E-2. Other domains are also in use. For example, country codes also serve as top-level domains. Canada's top-level domain is ca; the United Kingdom's is uk; Australia's is au. Another domain with growing popularity is .tv. Originally assigned to the small Polynesian island of Tuvalu, the .tv domain has been obtained by a professional management team and is available for a fee to media-related Web sites.

- Every domain name corresponds to a unique IP address that has been entered into a database called the **domain name system**. Computers that host this database are referred to as **domain name servers**. A domain name must be converted into an IP address before any packets can be routed to it.

FIGURE E-17: How domain names convert to IP addresses

▶ When you type a domain name into your browser, a domain name request is routed through your ISP to your designated domain name server, which then searches through its database to find a corresponding IP address; the IP address can then be attached to packets, such as requests for Web pages

TABLE E-2: Top-level domains

DOMAIN	DESCRIPTION	DOMAIN	DESCRIPTION
com	Unrestricted use; usually for commercial businesses	int	Restricted to organizations established by international treaties
edu	Restricted to North American four-year colleges and universities	mil	Restricted to U.S. military agencies
gov	Restricted to U.S. Government agencies	net	Unrestricted use; traditionally for Internet administrative organizations
info	Unrestricted use	org	Unrestricted use; traditionally for professional and nonprofit organizations

How your computer connects with a domain name server

An organization called ICANN (Internet Corporation for Assigned Names and Numbers) is recognized by the U.S. and other governments as the global organization that coordinates the technical management of the Internet's domain name system, the allocation of IP addresses, and the assignment of protocol parameters.

The domain name system is based on a distributed database. This database is not stored as a whole in any single location; it exists in parts all over the Internet. Your Internet connection is set up to access one of the many domain name servers that reside on the Internet. When you enter a domain name or URL, it is sent to your designated domain server, which can either send back the IP address that corresponds to the domain name, or if your domain name server does not have a record of the domain name, it can contact another domain name server and request the IP address. The servers in the domain name system supply IP addresses in a matter of milliseconds. Organizations or individuals can select a domain name and register it by using an online registration service, as shown in Figure E-18.

FIGURE E-18: Registering a domain name

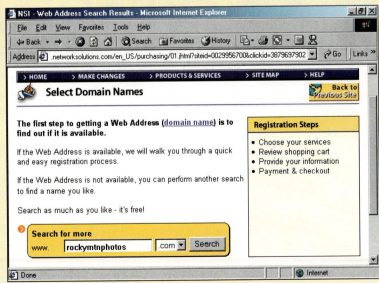

Connecting to the Internet using POTS

The most difficult aspect of the Internet is getting connected. Although many high-speed Internet access options, such as cable modems, DSL, personal satellite dishes, and ISDN are available, most people's first experience connecting to the Internet begins with a dial-up connection. A dial-up connection uses **POTS** (plain old telephone service) to transport data between your computer and your ISP. This lesson explores dial-up connections.

DETAILS

- The telephone communications system uses a tiered network to transport calls locally, cross-country, and internationally. At each level of the network, a switch creates a connection so that a call eventually has a continuous circuit to its destination. The first tier of this network uses a star topology to physically connect each telephone in a city to a switch in a "switching station," "local switch," or "central office." The second tier of the telephone network links several local switching stations. Connections then fan out to switches that are maintained by many different local and long-distance telephone companies.

- The telephone network uses a technology called **circuit switching**, which essentially establishes a continuous private link between two telephones for the duration of a call. This type of switching provides callers with a direct pipeline over which streams of voice data can flow. Because a circuit-switching network devotes an entire circuit to each call when someone is "on hold," no communication is taking place; yet the circuit is reserved and cannot be used for other communications.

- When you use a dial-up connection, your computer's modem places a regular telephone call to your ISP. Your call is routed through the telephone company's local switch and out to the ISP. When the ISP's computer answers your call, a dedicated circuit is established between you and your ISP, just as if you had made a voice call and someone at the ISP had picked up the phone. The circuit remains connected for the duration of your call and provides a communications link that carries data between your computer and the ISP. As your data arrives at the ISP, a router sends it out over the Internet. See Figure E-19.

- The signals that represent data bits exist in your computer as digital signals. The telephone system, however, expects to work with human voices, so the data that it carries must be in the format of analog audio tones. A **voice band modem**, usually referred to as a modem, converts the digital signals from your computer into signals that can travel over telephone lines.

- The term modem is derived from the words "modulate" and "demodulate." In communications terminology, **modulation** means changing the characteristics of a signal, as when a modem changes a digital signal into an analog audio signal. **Demodulation** means changing a signal back to its original state, as when a modem changes an audio signal back to a digital signal. See Figure E-20.

- Although telephone companies "went digital" long ago, their digital switches kick into action only after your call arrives at the local switching station. The technology between your telephone and your local switch is designed to carry analog voice signals. To transport data over this loop, the digital signals from your computer must be converted into analog signals that can travel over the telephone lines to your local switch. When these signals arrive at the local switch, they are converted into digital signals.

- When your computer is connected to your ISP using a standard dial-up connection, data is transmitted over the same frequencies that are normally used for voice conversations. If you have only one telephone line, you cannot pick up your telephone receiver, dial your friend, and carry on a voice conversation while you are connected to your ISP. You can, however, use the Internet to carry voice signals from your computer's microphone through the dial-up connection to the sound card of another computer. This technology, called **voice over IP (VoIP)**, allows you to play games over the Internet and chat about your moves, all while you are online.

FIGURE E-19: Dialing into the Internet

▶ When you use an ISP to access the Internet, your data travels through the local telephone switch to your ISP, which sends it onto the Internet

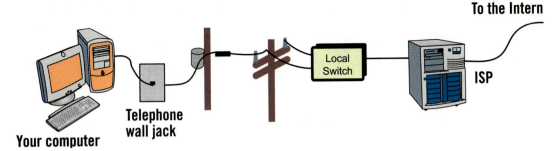

To the Intern

Local Switch

ISP

Telephone wall jack

Your computer

FIGURE E-20: How a modem works

▶ When you send data, your modem modulates the signal that carries your data; a modem at the other end of the transmission demodulates the signal

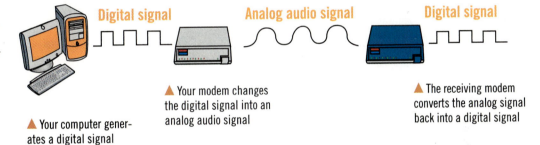

Digital signal　　Analog audio signal　　Digital signal

▲ Your computer generates a digital signal

▲ Your modem changes the digital signal into an analog audio signal

▲ The receiving modem converts the analog signal back into a digital signal

---

How fast is a modem?

When modems were a new technology, their speed was measured as **baud rate**, the number of times per second that a signal in a communications channel varies, or makes a transition between states. An example of such a transition is the change from a signal representing a 1 bit to a signal representing a 0 bit. A 300-baud modem's signal changes state 300 times each second; however, each baud doesn't necessarily carry one bit. So, a 300-baud modem might be able to transmit more than 300 bits per second.

To help consumers make sense of modem speeds, they are now measured in bits per second. This is actually a measure of capacity, but everyone calls it "speed." Actual data transfer speeds are affected by factors such as the quality of your local loop connection to the telephone switch. Even with a "perfect" connection, a 56 Kbps modem tops out at about 44 Kbps. Many Internet connection methods provide faster downstream (data received) transmission rates than upstream (data sent) rates. Dial-up connections are no exception: 44 Kbps is a typical downstream speed for a 56 Kbps modem; upstream, the data rate drops to about 33 Kbps, or less.

Connecting to the Internet using broadband

Although the standard equipment provided by telephone companies limits the amount of data that you can transmit and receive over a voice band modem, the copper wire that runs from your wall jacks to the switching station actually has a fair amount of capacity. This lesson discusses other Internet connection options, such as DSL, ISDN, T1, and T3, all of which offer high-speed digital communications links for voice and data.

DETAILS

- **DSL** (Digital Subscriber Line) is a high-speed, digital, always-on Internet access technology that uses standard phone lines to transport data. It is one of the fastest Internet connections affordable to the individual consumer.

- Several variations of DSL technology exist, including ADSL (asymmetric DSL with downstream speed faster than upstream speed), SDSL (symmetric DSL with the same upstream and downstream speed), HDSL (high-rate DSL), and DSL lite. This entire group of DSL technologies is sometimes called xDSL, but xDSL is not a variation of DSL.

  DSL is digital, so data doesn't need to be changed into analog form and then back to digital, resulting in fast data transmission over standard copper telephone cable. If permitted by your DSL provider, you can use your DSL line instead of your POTS line for voice calls. Figure E-21 illustrates how voice and data signals travel over DSL to a special device at the local telephone switching station, where they are divided and routed either to an ISP or to the regular telephone network.

  In many areas, DSL is a joint venture between the telephone company and the DSL provider. The telephone company is responsible for the physical cabling and voice transmission. The DSL provider is responsible for data traffic.

  The speed of a DSL connection varies according to the characteristics of your telephone line, the equipment at your local switch, and your DSL provider. Most **DSL modems** are rated for 1.5 Mbps downstream, compared to standard 56 Kbps for a dial-up connection. When shopping for a DSL connection, you should inquire about actual speed and find out if the upstream rate differs from the downstream rate.

  Currently, most DSL installations require trained service technicians. You can obtain service from a special DSL provider. A typical DSL installation begins when your local telephone company designates a telephone line for the DSL connection.

This line might utilize unused twisted-pair cables in your current telephone line, if they are available, or it might require a new line from the nearest telephone pole to the telephone box outside of your house. This line is connected to a special type of DSL switch. A technician from the DSL provider has to run cables, install a DSL wall jack if necessary, and then connect a DSL modem to your computer's Ethernet card. See Figure E-22.

- **ISDN** (Integrated Services Digital Network) connections move data at speeds of 64 Kbps or 128 Kbps—not as fast as DSL or cable modems, but faster than a dial-up connection. ISDN is an all-digital service with the potential to carry voice and data. A device called an **ISDN terminal adapter** connects a computer to a telephone wall jack and translates the computer's digital signals into a different kind of digital signal that can travel over the ISDN connection. ISDN service is typically regarded as a high-speed Internet connection option for businesses that maintain small local area networks. The service is usually obtained from a local telephone company or a dedicated ISDN service provider.

- **T1** is a high-speed (1.544 Mbps) digital network developed by AT&T in the early 1960s to support long-haul voice transmission in North America. Similar service is available in Europe under **CEPT** (Conference of European Postal and Telecommunications) standards. A T1 line consists of 24 individual channels. Each channel has a capacity of 64 Kbps, and can be configured to carry voice or data. T1 lines provide a dedicated link between two points, so they are popular for businesses and ISPs that want a high-speed connection to the Internet, regardless of cost. A **T3** connection consists of 672 channels and supports data rates of about 43 Mbps. Sometimes referred to as DS3 (Digital Service-3) lines, T3 lines provide many of the links on the Internet backbone. Both T1 and T3 services are considered dedicated leased lines, which means that they are essentially rented from the telephone company and are not typically shared by other customers. T1 and T3 services are usually too expensive for individuals.

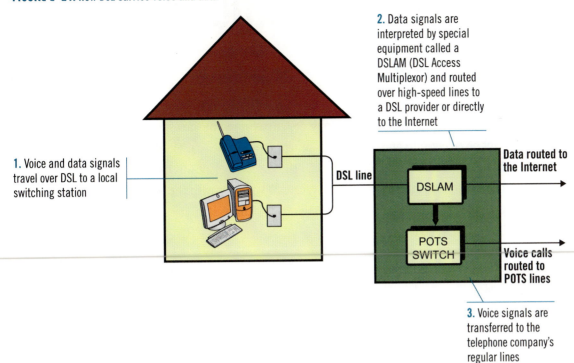

2. Data signals are interpreted by special equipment called a DSLAM (DSL Access Multiplexor) and routed over high-speed lines to a DSL provider or directly to the Internet

1. Voice and data signals travel over DSL to a local switching station

DSL line

DSLAM

Data routed to the Internet

POTS SWITCH

Voice calls routed to POTS lines

3. Voice signals are transferred to the telephone company's regular lines

FIGURE E-22: Connecting your computer to DSL

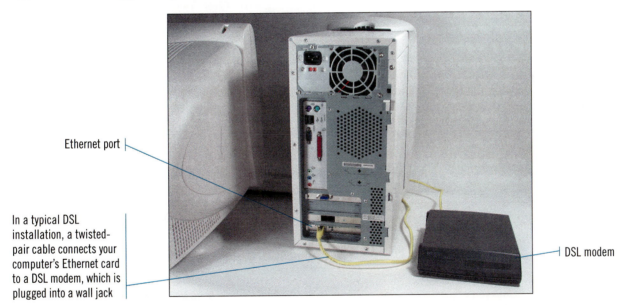

Ethernet port

In a typical DSL installation, a twisted-pair cable connects your computer's Ethernet card to a DSL modem, which is plugged into a wall jack

DSL modem

Security and always-on connections

Unlike a dial-up connection, which is only connected for the duration of your "call" or connection, an **always-on connection** is always connected, and it is "on" whenever your computer is powered up. With an always-on connection, you might have the same IP address for days, or even months, depending on your ISP. A hacker who discovers that your computer is always on can easily find your computer again, and its high-speed access makes it a very desirable target.

When your computer is turned off, it is not vulnerable to attack. Therefore, it is a good idea to shut down your computer when you are not using it. Putting your computer into sleep mode or activating a screen saver is not sufficient protection. Your computer must be shut down and turned off. Additional steps you can take to protect yourself from security breaches through your cable connection to the Internet are discussed in Unit F.

Connecting to the Internet using cable

The cable television system was originally designed for remote areas where TV broadcast signals could not be received in an acceptable manner with an antenna. These systems were called "community antenna television," or CATV. The CATV concept was to install one or more large, expensive satellite dishes in a community, catch TV signals with these dishes, and then send the signals over a system of cables to individual homes. This system has been adapted and now provides Internet service to many homes.

Info Web
CABLE MODEM

DETAILS

- The satellite dish "farm" where television broadcasts are received and retransmitted is referred to as the head-end. From the head-end, a cabling system branches out and eventually reaches consumers' homes. The topology of a CATV system has the physical topology of a computer network.

- When your cable TV company becomes your Internet service provider, your computer becomes part of a neighborhood local area network, as shown in Figure E-23. A router and high-speed connection from the head-end to the Internet provide the potential for Internet connectivity over every cable in the system.

- To offer both television and Internet access, the cable's bandwidth is divided among three activities. As shown in Figure E-24, a CATV cable must provide bandwidth for television signals, incoming data signals, and outgoing data signals. Even dividing the bandwidth among these activities, the lowest-capacity coaxial cable used by the CATV system has a far greater carrying capacity than a POTS line.

- What do you need to configure your computer to access the Internet over a CATV system? First, your computer needs an Ethernet card, a network interface card designed for Ethernet. If your computer is "network ready," it is likely equipped with the necessary Ethernet card. The second piece of equipment for a CATV Internet connection is a **cable modem**, a device that converts your computer's signal into one that can travel over the CATV cable. Your cable ISP usually provides the cable modem when you sign up for service.

  If you have only one CATV cable, you will need to use a splitter to connect both your cable modem and your television to that one CATV cable. If you have multiple CATV cables, you can connect your cable modem directly to any one of them. See Figure E-25.

- When your CATV connection is up and running, your computer becomes part of a neighborhood network because the cable from your computer and the cables from your neighbors' computers essentially connect at a centralized point.

- A communications channel like your CATV cable carries packets at a constant speed. The CATV cable also has a certain amount of bandwidth. As more and more neighbors use the service, data transport might seem to get slower.

FIGURE E-23: The topology of CATV

▶ Cables from the CATV head-end extend out as a series of "trunks;" the trunks are then connected to "feeders" that serve neighborhoods; the connection from a feeder to a consumer's home is referred to as a "drop"

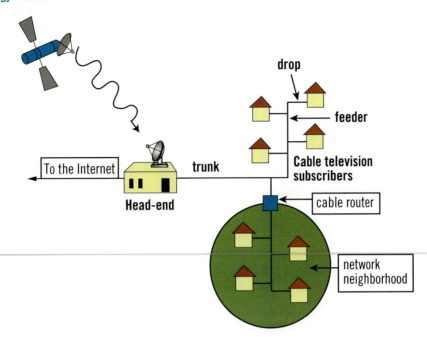

FIGURE E-24: CATV Cable

▶ CATV cable has enough bandwidth to support TV channels and data flowing downstream, as well as data flowing upstream

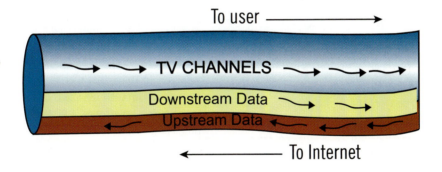

FIGURE E-25: Connecting your computer to a CATV cable

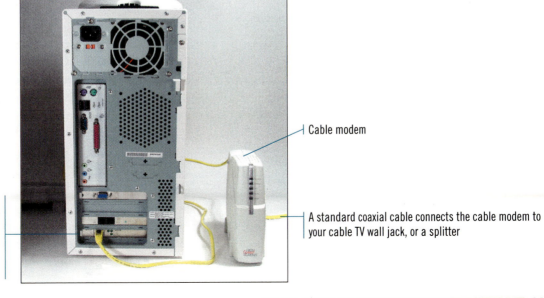

An Ethernet card is installed in a slot on your computer's motherboard; a cable connects the Ethernet card to the cable modem

Cable modem

A standard coaxial cable connects the cable modem to your cable TV wall jack, or a splitter

Connecting to the Internet without wires

You don't need wires anymore to connect to the Internet. You can connect a computer to the Internet using several wireless options, including personal satellites and cellular telephones. Most people are familiar with services that provide access to "pay TV" over a personal satellite dish. Many of the companies that provide satellite TV also provide satellite Internet access.

DETAILS

● Satellite connections include direct satellite service and two-way satellite service. Both of these services are relatively expensive; but in some areas, particularly remote rural areas, they might be the only high-speed option available.

● **Direct satellite service** (DSS) uses a low-earth satellite to send television (such as DirectTV) or computer data (such as DirectTV DSL) directly to a satellite dish owned by an individual. Some direct satellite services provide only downstream data transport. If so, then upstream data transport, such as Web page requests, must be sent using a dial-up or DSL modem. See Figure E-26.

● Two-way satellite service sends both upstream and downstream data through the satellite. Two-way satellite service typically offers 500 Kbps downstream, but only 40–60 Kbps upstream. Satellite data transport is subject to delays of one second or more, which occur as your data is routed between your computer and a satellite that orbits 22,200 miles above the earth. Delays may not pose much of a problem for general Web surfing and downloading MP3 files, but they can become a showstopper for interactive gaming that requires quick reactions.

As with cable modem service, satellite data transport speeds may decline when other users subscribe to the service because the bandwidth provided by the satellite is shared among all users.

● If you require mobile Internet access, the cellular telephone infrastructure has the advantage of providing mobile Internet access from a notebook computer or PDA. Currently it is the slowest Internet access option, even slower than a dial-up connection. Even so, many "road warriors" opt to install a cellular-ready PC card modem in their notebook computers, as represented in Figure E-27. As an alternative to the PC modem card, some cellular telephones can become modems when connected by a special cable to a notebook computer.

Whatever mobile technology you select, your Internet connection will be slow. The fastest cellular connections top out at a mere 14.4 Kbps, as opposed to a 56 Kbps dial-up connection, which tops out at 44 Kbps. Moreover, the static

that you usually tolerate on a voice call can terminate an Internet connection, making it difficult to maintain a connection in an area where the signal is weak or where there is lots of interference. Maintaining a connection while you move—when you are in a taxi, for example—often becomes difficult near the edges of the area covered by a cell tower.

Some PDAs go mobile with the addition of snap-on wireless hardware, which essentially converts your PDA into a wireless phone. Other PDAs, like the one pictured in Figure E-28, have built-in wireless communications circuitry. A selection of third-party software can be installed on a PDA to provide client services for Web access and e-mail. PDA owners typically must subscribe to an ISP that specializes in wireless communications. Information on such services is usually packaged with PDAs and their wireless accessories. A PDA's limited screen size poses a problem for Web browsing because you can't really see enough of a standard Web page to make much sense of it. Special PDA-enabled Web sites overcome this problem by using small, text-based design elements.

● Wireless connections are typically slower than other networks; signals can be disrupted by interference from large metal objects, metal wall studs, cell phones, pagers, and other wireless devices. The most popular wireless network standard is the IEEE 802.11b, which operates at 11 Mbps, and can be used in conjunction with standard Ethernet networks. An alternative standard, called **Bluetooth technology**, is a standard for low-cost personal area network connections among mobile users. Bluetooth uses a globally available frequency range and operates at speeds between 200 and 400 Kbps.

● The best Internet connection depends on your budget and what's available in your area. Most people begin with a dial-up connection and eventually look for a connection that provides faster access speeds. Cable modem service is usually the first choice, when available. If cable modem service is not available, or proves to be slower or less dependable than expected, the next choice would be DSL or satellite service.

▶ Some satellite services only provide a data down-link; if you use this type of satellite service, you need a conventional modem to send data to the Internet

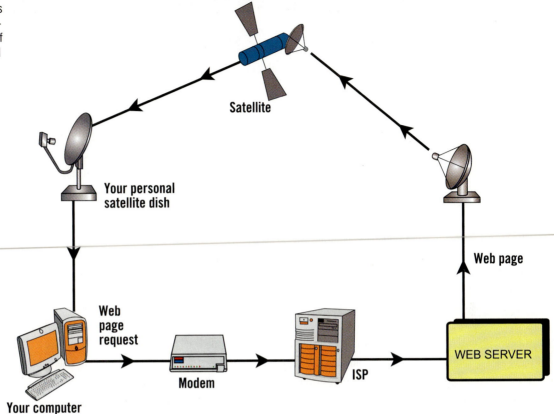

Satellite

Your personal satellite dish

Web page

Web page request

Your computer

Modem

ISP

WEB SERVER

FIGURE E-27: A cellular modem

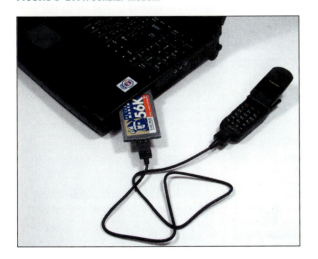

FIGURE E-28: Using a PDA to connect to the Internet

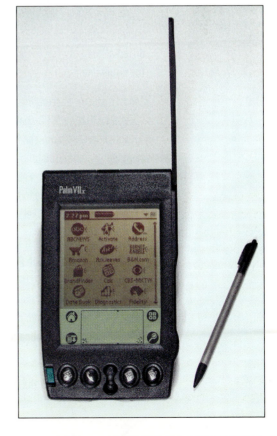

A LAN (local area network) allows several computers to share a high-speed (and expensive) Internet connection. A LAN may connect as few as two computers, or it may encompass hundreds of devices, including computers, hubs, routers, printers, and modems.

The main advantage of a LAN is that multiple users can share a limited number of resources. Instead of providing individual high-speed Internet connections for many stand-alone computers, for example, a network can allow all of its workstations to access a single high-speed connection. Some computers on a network might have high-speed laser printers or specialized photo printers; a network can make these printers accessible to all of the LAN's workstations. On a network, you can directly access the shared disk drives of other computers that are connected to the LAN.

When you boot your computer, the operating system typically checks to see if it can access a LAN. Your computer's operating system keeps track of the network resources that you can automatically access. Some network resources, such as an Internet connection, may become available as soon as your computer completes the boot process. For access to other network resources, you might have to set up connections using networking utilities provided by your computer's operating system, such as Windows Network Neighborhood.

On a typical network, each computer or peripheral device requires a network interface card, which provides a connection port for a cable. When connecting only two computers, you can simply use a single "cross-connect" cable. A hub or a hub/router is usually used to connect more than two computers. LAN hubs provide several connection ports. A small hub might provide four ports, whereas a larger hub would provide 64 ports. Each network device requires one of the hub's ports. To expand a network beyond the capacity of a single hub, you can add other hubs. These hubs connect to each other via an **uplink port**.

Most LANs use Category 5 ("cat 5") UTP (unshielded twisted pair) cables with plastic RJ-45 connections at both ends. These cables, sometimes referred to as "patch cables," are sold in various lengths up to 100 feet. Category 5 cables are suitable for networks that transmit data at speeds up to 100 Mbps. An enhanced version Category 5e is suitable for 1 Gbps speeds. "Cat 5" and "Cat 5e" cables look very similar. To differentiate between them, you can read the specifications that appear on the package or are stamped on the cable itself.

FIGURE E-29

The first step in assembling your own LAN is to make sure that each PC contains an Ethernet network interface card. The NIC for a desktop computer is usually installed in a slot on the motherboard. See Figure E-29. A NIC for a notebook computer takes the form of a PC card. Both types feature a port (socket) for a network cable.

After the NICs are installed in all of the PCs, the next step is to attach each PC to a hub. To do so, simply connect a cable to the NIC's port, then connect the other end of the cable to one of the ports in the hub. If the hub requires power, plug it in. With all of the PCs connected, you can turn them on. Windows should automatically detect the NICs and establish a connection to the network. The PCs are now workstations on the network.

For each workstation on the network, the workstation's owner or the network administrator can specify whether its files will be accessible to other workstations. If you want the files on a workstation to be available to everyone on a network, you must activate file sharing. Once file sharing is activated, you can map connections to that workstation from other workstations on the network.

Drive mapping is Windows terminology for assigning a drive letter to a storage device located on a different workstation. You use Windows Network Neighborhood to map the hard disk drives on the network. Once drives have been mapped, you can access any drive on the LAN as if it were attached to your own workstation.

One of the main reasons for creating a small LAN is to provide all the workstations with shared access to a single high-speed Internet connection, such as a cable modem or DSL line. The value of this distributed Internet access is so high that many non-technical computer owners are venturing into this somewhat "tricky" aspect of network installation. To add high-speed Internet access to a LAN, you need a cable modem or DSL modem, a corresponding ISP, and a router.

While this TechTalk discusses setting up a LAN using Windows and Network Neighborhood, there are a variety of home network technologies. Table E-3 provides a quick comparison of other home network technologies.

TABLE E-3: Home network technology comparisons

NETWORK TYPE	ADVANTAGES	DISADVANTAGES	SPEED
HomePNA	Uses existing telephone wiring; can use the phone and send data at the same time; NIC eliminates need for hub	Requires telephone jacks near computers; slow transmission speed; uses a special NIC and cable	10 Mbps
HomePLC	Uses standard electrical outlet	Requires special NIC; susceptible to electrical interference; very slow	2 Mbps
Ethernet	Inexpensive; reliable; standard technology; fast	Unsightly cables; may require running cables through walls, ceilings, and floors	10 Mbps, 100 Mbps, or 1 Gbps
Wireless	No cables required	Each device requires a transceiver, which adds cost; susceptible to interference from large metal objects and other wireless devices	11 Mbps (802.11b) 100-700 Kbps (Bluetooth)

P2P Philanthropy?

Info Web

DISTRIBUTED COMPUTING

"Volunteer your PC. Don't just make a donation. Make a difference." It's an appealing slogan, and the trade-marked tag line for a company that uses donated CPU cycles to look for a cure for cancer. Similar projects are tackling AIDS research, searching for extraterrestrial life, and cracking codes.

Should you and your computer volunteer to participate in these projects? Are they legitimate? Can your computer really make a difference in solving such large and complex problems? Would participation open your computer to viruses and other intrusions? To answer these questions, you'll need some background information about this philanthropic "twist" to peer-to-peer networks, known as distributed computing.

Distributed computing breaks down large projects into many small processing tasks, and then distributes those tasks to individual computers connected to the network. Distributed computing is a variation of peer-to-peer network technology. It works by tapping into the idle computing resources of thousands of individual PCs connected to a local area network or the Internet.

As one analyst explained, "By combining thousands of ordinary PCs to work on extremely large computational projects, problems can be solved more quickly and less expensively than by conventional methods. Now regular people can help fuel research and projects that previously may have required a bank of supercomputers or a hundred years to complete."

To participate in a distributed computing project, you download special client software that provides your computer with instructions for processing the problem and submitting your results. Distributed computing tasks are typically processed during idle CPU cycles when your computer is not being used for other tasks, so it is not supposed to interfere with the speed or reliability of your own computer work.

The idea for distributing processing tasks among many personal computers is not a new one. Beowulf clusters, a technology developed by two NASA engineers Thomas Sterling and Don Becker, have been used in universities and research labs to connect groups of low-powered computers into a low-cost surrogate for a supercomputer. Many of today's distributed computing projects use the Internet to harness computer-processing power in the homes and dorm rooms of thousands of individual volunteers.

One of the first Internet-based distributed computing projects, SETI@home, was designed to search for extraterrestrial intelligence. Since the project started in 1999, more than 3 million people have donated the equivalent of 700,000+ years of CPU time to analyzing radio telescope data for any signals that could have come from an alien civilization.

The potential of distributed computing is astounding. As one project manager explained, "What we're talking about is the possibility of getting something like 50 teraflops of computer capacity for almost free." Of course, you've heard the old adage that "nothing in life is free," and so it is with distributed computing. Although the processor cycles might be "free," distributed computing requires software and a computer to consolidate the results sent in by thousands of volunteers. Projects require advertising and managers, and none of this over-head is free. Some projects may be financed by donations, corporations, and organizations. A leukemia research project, for example, is jointly sponsored by Intel, the American Cancer Society, and the National Foundation for Cancer Research. Other projects, however, might rely on financial support from commercial sources.

One distributed computing venture runs several nonprofit and for-profit projects. Although it uses nonprofit projects to recruit volunteers, donated CPU cycles are sometimes used, without their owners' knowledge, to run commercial tasks. As a result, you might volunteer your computer's CPU cycles for a humanitarian nonprofit project, but your computer might also be used to process an inventory management job for a commercial business. The company that runs the distributed computing venture gets paid for this service, but you don't.

Financial issues aside, some computer owners find it a bit disturbing for their computers to be processing data from unknown sources and for unknown purposes.

Distributed computing also poses a potential security issue. SETI@home has already been attacked by hackers trying to simulate alien signals! A harmless prank? Perhaps. But the software for a distributed computing project downloaded by thousands or millions of volunteers is a highly attractive target for hackers.

The jury is still out on the effectiveness of distributed computing projects. Distributed computing works best for problems that can be broken down into many small independent calculations. It is less effective when individual calculations affect each other. It fails at weather forecasting, for example, where a disturbance in one part of the atmosphere affects neighboring weather systems. Potential volunteers might have difficulty assessing the likelihood that a particular problem can be solved using distributed computing. Therefore, a certain degree of trust is required, and that can only be established after this technology acquires a more substantial track record.

▼ INTERACTIVE QUESTIONS

◯ Yes   ◯ No   ◯ Not sure

1. Have you ever participated in a distributed computing project?

◯ Yes   ◯ No   ◯ Not sure

2. Would you participate in a purely nonprofit project that appeared to be legitimate?

◯ Yes   ◯ No   ◯ Not sure

3. Would you participate in a distributed computing project without asking for compensation, if you knew that some of your CPU cycles were being sold to profit-based businesses?

▼ EXPAND THE IDEAS

1. Have you ever participated in a distributed computing project? If so, what were the goals and what was your involvement? Write a short paper explaining the experience. If not, write a short paper describing a project that you might like to be involved in. Describe your expectations for the project and any ideas you may have.

2. Would you participate in a purely nonprofit project that appeared to be legitimate? Why or why not? Research a current distributed computing project. Write a summary of the project and then include a concluding statement explaining your position on whether or not you would want to participate in the project. Support your position with facts about the project.

3. Would you participate in a distributed computing project without asking for compensation, if you knew that some of your CPU cycles were being sold to profit-based businesses? Research the current trends. Document any projects that may be underway in which distributed computing cycles are being sold. Compile your findings in a short report. Include your opinion in the conclusion.

End of Unit Exercises

▼ KEY TERMS

10 BaseT network	Drive mapping	LAN	Server
100 BaseT network	DSL modem	Laser light	Simplex
Always-on connection	DSL	Logical address	Single-user license
Amplitude	Dynamic IP address	Logical topology	Site license
Asynchronous protocol	Ethernet	MAN	Static IP address
ATM	Even parity	Microwaves	STP (shielded twisted pair)
Bandwidth	Extranet	Modem	Synchronous protocol
Baud rate	FDDI	Modulation	T1
Bluetooth technology	Fiber-optic cable	Multiple-user license	T3
Broadband	Frequency	Narrowband	TCP/IP
Cable modem	Full duplex	Network interface card (NIC)	Telnet
CEPT	Gateway	Network service provider (NSP)	Token Ring network
Circuit switching	Half duplex	Node	Top-level domain
Client	Handshaking	Novell network	Topology
Client/server network	HomePIC	Packet	Traceroute
Coaxial cable	HomePNA	Packet switching	Transceiver
Communications channel	HomeRF	Parity bit	Transponder
Communications network	Host computer	Peer-to-peer network	Twisted-pair cable
Communications protocol	Hub	Physical address	Uplink port
Communications satellite	ICANN	Physical topology	UTP (unshielded twisted pair)
Concurrent-user license	Infrared light	Ping	Voice band modem
CSMA/CD	Internet service provider (ISP)	POTS	Voice over IP
Demodulation	Internetwork	Private IP address	WAN
Direct satellite service	Intranet	Protocols	Wavelength
Domain name	IP address	Repeater	Wireless network
Domain name server	ISDN	RF signals	Workstation
Domain name system	ISDN terminal adapter	Router	

▼ UNIT REVIEW

1. Use your own words to define bold terms that appear throughout the unit. List the 10 terms that are least familiar to you and write a sentence for each of them.

2. Draw a diagram of Shannon's communications model. Apply this model to an Internet dial-up connection by indicating which real-world devices would exist at various points in the model to originate data, encode it, transmit signals, and so on.

3. Create a table listing communications channels. Include advantages, disadvantages, relative speed/capacity, and quality of connection for each channel.

4. Draw a simple model that explains the idea that you can use four bits to convey 16 different messages.

5. Make a list of the networks discussed in this unit, and then briefly describe each.

6. Create a list of network devices mentioned in this unit. Write a brief description of each one.

7. Draw diagrams of star, ring, and bus network topologies. Make sure that you can trace the route of data over a Token Ring network and an Ethernet network.

8. Make a list of protocols mentioned throughout this unit and briefly describe each.

9. Make a list of Internet access methods. Briefly describe each, and include a comment about upstream transmission rates and downstream transmission rates.

10. Draw a diagram of the Internet that includes the following devices connected in a technically correct configuration so that data can flow from the personal computer to the Web server: a personal computer, voice band modem, ISP modem, e-mail server, ISP router, domain name server, two backbone routers, backbone repeater, and Web server.

▼ FILL IN THE BEST ANSWER

1. A communications _____ is the combination of hardware, software, and connecting links that transport data.

2. With one bit, you can convey two units of information; with _____ bits, you can convey four units; with _____ bits, you can convey eight units; with _____ bits you can convey 256 units.

3. _____ is the number of times that a wave oscillates.

4. The _____, or capacity, of a digital channel is usually measured in bps.

5. The _____ topology of a network refers to the layout of cables, devices, and connections; the _____ topology refers to the path of data over the network.

6. A technology called _____ switching divides messages into small parcels and handles them on a first come, first served basis.

7. _____ is one of the most widely used network technologies, and it uses a protocol called CSMA/CD to deal with collisions.

8. The communications protocol used by devices such as CB radio called _____ duplex, makes it possible to send and receive data, but not at the same time.

9. Protocols help two network devices negotiate and establish communications through a process called _____.

10. When you use a dial-up connection, your ISP gives you a temporary address, called a(n) _____ IP address, for use as long as you remain connected.

11. The database that keeps track of the names that correspond to IP addresses is called the _____ name system.

12. In communications terminology, _____ means changing the characteristics of a signal, whereas _____ means changing a signal back to its original state.

13. Although the speed of a modem was once measured by _____ rate, today's modem transmission speeds are measured in bps.

14. A software utility called _____ sends a signal to a specific Internet address and waits for a reply.

15. DSL, ISDN, _____, and T3 connections provide digital service over the telephone system's "local loop."

16. DSS service uses a low-earth _____ to send television, voice, or computer data directly to a dish owned by an individual.

17. A(n) _____ network uses radio frequencies instead of cables to send data from one network node to another.

18. A(n) _____ is a low-power, wireless network designed for home use.

19. _____ technology is a standard for low-cost personal area network connections among mobile users that uses a globally available frequency range.

20. Single-user software might be installed on a LAN server, but would require a multi-user, concurrent-user, or _____ license if more than one copy is to be used at a time.

▼ PRACTICE TEST TEXT

When you use the Interactive CD, you can take Practice Tests that consist of 10 multiple-choice, true/false, and fill-in-the-blank questions. The questions are selected at random from a large test bank, so each time you take a test, you'll receive a different set of questions. Your tests are scored immediately, and you can print study guides to determine which questions you answered incorrectly. If you are using a Tracking Disk, insert it in the floppy disk drive to save your test scores.

▼ INDEPENDENT CHALLENGE 1

You can connect to the Internet in a variety of ways, including dial-up connections, cable modem connections, DSL service, ISDN service, and direct satellite service. The Internet connection service you chose may be based more on availability than on what is the best and fastest technologically.

1. Write a brief statement explaining your Internet needs. Be sure to include whether you are planning to use the Internet for research, shopping, business, how often you need to log on, and if you need mobile access or high-speed access.

2. Research Internet connection options available in your area.

3. Create a table that lists the vendors for each available option and compares the options in terms of their setup cost, monthly fees, maximum speed upstream, and maximum speed downstream. Provide a summary of which Internet access options would be your first and second choices and why.

▼ INDEPENDENT CHALLENGE 2

You've decided to network a few computers in your home. This is the first time you have been put to this task, so you have to research and develop a plan for the project.

1. Describe the number, type, and location of the computers that will form your network.

2. Decide what type of network technology you want to use: Ethernet, HomePNA, wireless, or HomePLC.

3. Create a diagram showing the location of each computer, the wiring path (for Ethernet), the location of electrical outlets (for HomePLC), the location of telephone outlets (for HomePNA), or potential signal interference (for wireless).

4. Create a shopping list of the network components that you will need to purchase; research prices for each item on your list.

5. Indicate any software that you would have to purchase for the network.

▼ INDEPENDENT CHALLENGE 3

 The domain name system contains a vast array of names for businesses, organizations and institutions. When you see a URL in an advertisement or a book, you often know immediately what the company or organization is and what the site will be about when you get to the page.

1. Use your favorite search engine to research top-level domains; or you might start by visiting the ICANN Web site.

2. Find out the latest information about the new top-level domains (TLD)

3. Think about a URL that you might want to register, for example, yourname.com or something else that is important to you personally. Also think about a business venture that you might want to begin. What URL would you want for that business?

4. Find out if these URLS are available. Track your research. If the first choice was not available, list how you went about finding a URL that you could use. For example, if your name is Jennifer Dumont, would you want jenniferdumont.com? If that isn't available, would you go for jdumont.com? or Jenniferdumont.org?

5. Submit a paper detailing your quest and the results you achieved.

▼ INDEPENDENT CHALLENGE 4

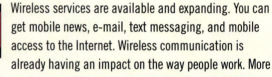 Wireless services are available and expanding. You can get mobile news, e-mail, text messaging, and mobile access to the Internet. Wireless communication is already having an impact on the way people work. More and more people are working at least part-time from a remote location such as a satellite office or a home office. As this becomes the emerging business model, employees are finding that being connected is a necessity, not just a nicety.

1. Write a brief statement explaining your position and opinions on each of the following:

    a. how you think wireless e-mail is changing the way business is conducted;

    b. how it is changing the relationship between employer and employee; and

    c. how it is affecting personal relationships.

2. Wireless e-mail raises societal questions such as privacy issues, employer expectations vs. employee responsibilities, and impact on family life. Choose one societal issue impacted by wireless e-mail. Research the issue and write a paper presenting your findings.

3. Write a short summary of your findings. In your conclusion, compare your research findings with the opinions you expressed when you answered STEP 1.

4. Be sure to include references and resources for your research.

LAB: TRACKING PACKETS

1. Start the interactive part of the lab. Insert your Tracking Disk if you want to save your QuickCheck results. Perform each of the lab steps as directed and answer all of the lab QuickCheck questions. When you exit the lab, your answers are automatically graded and your results are displayed.

2. Use the Ping utility that is supplied by Windows to ping www.abcnews.com. Record the IP address for the ABC News site, plus the minimum, maximum, and average times. For each time, indicate whether it would be considered poor, average, or good.

3. Use the Tracert utility that's supplied by Windows to trace a packet between your computer and the Web. Print the Traceroute report. Circle any pings on the report that indicate high latency.

4. Locate a Web-based Ping utility and use it to ping www.gobledegok.com. Include the URL for the Web site where you found the Ping utility. Explain the results of the ping.

5. Connect to the Internet Traffic Report Web site, make a note of the date and time, and then answer the following questions:

    a. What is the traffic index for Asia?

    b. How does the index for Asia compare with the traffic index for North America?

    c. During the previous 24 hours in Europe, what was the period with the worst response time?

LAB: SECURING YOUR CONNECTION

1. Start the interactive part of the lab. Insert your Tracking Disk if you want to save your QuickCheck results. Perform each of the lab steps as directed, and answer all of the lab QuickCheck questions. When you exit the lab, your answers are automatically graded and your results are displayed.

2. Use the Netstat utility to scan any computer that you typically use. Write out the Netstat report or print it. To print the report, copy it to Paint or Word, and then print. Explain what the Netstat report tells you about the security of that computer.

3. Connect to the grc.com site and access the Shields Up! tests. Test the shields and probe the ports for the same computer that you used for Assignment 2. Explain the similarities and differences between the Shields Up! report and the Netstat report for this computer. Which report indicates more security risks? Why?

4. In the lab, you learned which dialog boxes to use for disabling Windows file and print sharing, plus a technique for unbinding TCP from file and print sharing. Without actually changing the settings, use the dialog boxes to determine whether file and print sharing is active or disabled on your computer. Also, discover if file and print sharing is bound to TCP on your computer. Report your findings and indicate if these settings are appropriate in terms of network access and security.

▼ VISUAL WORKSHOP

The Bluetooth wireless technology, see Figure E-30, is a standard for low-cost, personal area network connection among mobile computers, mobile phones and other devices. Using a globally available frequency range, Bluetooth eliminates the need for cables and provides secure, radio-based transmission of data and voice.

Figure E-30: Bluetooth Technology

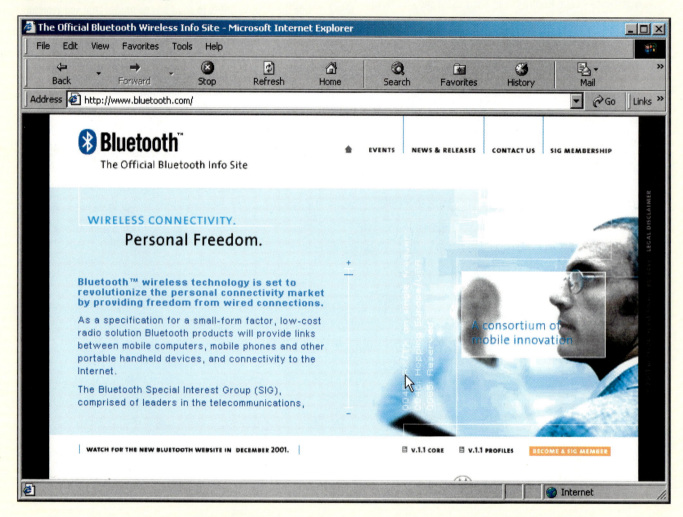

1. Log onto the Internet and go to the Bluetooth SIG (special interest group) Web site. Find the answers to the following questions: Who developed the Bluetooth wireless technology? When was it developed? What were the goals or reasons for developing the technology?

2. Bluetooth technology is being included in many new applications. List two applications that are discussed on the Web site.

3. Find the Web site of one of the companies using Bluetooth technology in their products. Describe one of the applications. Be sure to cite your sources.

UNIT F

Data Security

Understanding how to create, organize, and interpret your data is very important. However, if your data is not secure, it could be lost. Unit F discusses factors that may work against you to destroy your data and ways to secure your computer and computer data. The unit begins with an introduction and discussion on what can go wrong and then discusses computer viruses and the potential attacks that affect files and disrupt computer operations. You will learn how to restrict user access and how to use antivirus software to protect or recover your computer data. You will also learn one of the most important aspects of computing—how to back up your data.

Knowing what can go wrong

Data stored on computers is vulnerable to human error, deliberate vandalism, and power problems. As a result of this vulnerability, data can be lost, stolen, and inaccurate. Lost data, also referred to as missing data, is inaccessible usually because it was accidentally removed. Stolen data is not necessarily missing, but has been accessed or copied without authorization. Inaccurate data is data that was entered incorrectly, deliberately or accidentally altered, or not edited to reflect current facts. This lesson looks at factors that contribute to data vulnerability.

DETAILS

- Operator error: Despite the sometimes sensational press coverage of computer criminals and viruses, the most common cause of lost and/or inaccurate data is a mistake made by a computer user; this problem is known as operator error. **Operator error** refers to mistakes such as entering the wrong data or deleting a file that is still needed. Some companies establish usage procedures, which, if followed, can reduce operator error. Many organizations have reduced the incidence of operator error by using a **direct source input device**, such as a bar code reader, to collect data directly from a document or object.

  Computer software designers can also help prevent operator error by designing products that anticipate mistakes users are likely to make and that provide features to help users avoid those mistakes.

- Computer software problems: Software is complex and, therefore, is sometimes released with program errors that can affect the integrity of your data. Although catastrophic loss of data due to programming errors is rare, it is important to monitor your data closely for inaccuracies that may be caused by the program itself.

- Power problems: Because computers are powered by electricity, they are susceptible to power failures, spikes, and surges. A **power failure** is a complete loss of power to the computer system, usually caused by something over which you have no control. Even a brief interruption in power can force your computer to reboot and lose all of the data in RAM. Although a power failure results in lost data from RAM, it is unlikely to cause data loss from disks.

  Two other common power-related problems are spikes and surges. Both of these can damage sensitive computer components. A **power spike** is an increase in power that lasts only a short time—less than one millionth of a second. A **power surge** lasts a little longer—a few millionths of a second. Spikes and surges can be caused by malfunctions in the local generating plant or the power distribution network, and they are potentially more damaging than a power failure. Both can destroy the circuitry that operates your hard disk drive or damage your computer's motherboard.

- There are several devices that can help protect computer systems from power problems. A **UPS (uninterruptible power supply)** represents the best protection against power problems. A UPS is a device containing a battery that provides a continuous supply of power and other circuitry to prevent spikes and surges from reaching your computer. It is designed to provide enough power to keep your computer working through momentary power interruptions. A UPS gives you enough time to save your files and exit your programs in the event of a longer power outage. Figure F-1 shows a typical UPS. A UPS is essential equipment for Internet and LAN servers but is also recommended for individual computer users.

  As a low-cost alternative, you can plug your computer into a **surge strip** (also called a surge protector or surge suppressor) to protect it and your modem from power spikes and surges. Just remember that a surge strip does not contain a battery to keep the computer running and protect the data in RAM if the power fails. Figure F-2 shows a surge strip. When you shop for a surge strip, do not mistakenly purchase a **power strip** such as the one shown in Figure F-3.

  While the UPS and surge strip can help protect your computer systems, there are some situations (for example, an electrical storm) when it is best to simply unplug your computer equipment, including your modem.

FIGURE F-1: A UPS

To connect to a UPS, plug it into a wall outlet, then plug your computer and monitor cables into the outlets on the UPS

A light on the case lets you know that the UPS is charged and ready

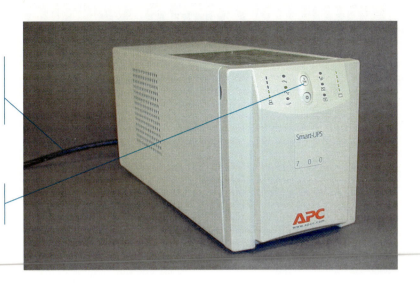

FIGURE F-2: A surge strip

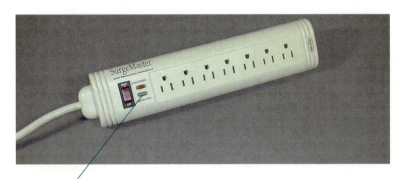

A surge strip contains the electronics to prevent power spikes and surges from damaging your computer

FIGURE F-3: A power strip

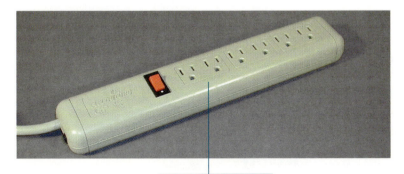

Although a power strip contains multiple outlets for power plugs, it does not contain the electronics necessary to filter out power spikes and surges

Exploring data security issues

In addition to falling prey to operator error, software problems, and power problems, data is also vulnerable to hardware failure, natural disasters, and vandalism. This lesson looks at more factors that can result in data security problems.

DETAILS

● Hardware failure: Much of the computer hardware that fails does so within the first hours or days of operation. If this period passes without problems, hardware can be expected to work fairly reliably until it nears the end of its useful life. The effect of a hardware failure depends on which component fails. Most hardware failures are simply an inconvenience. For example, if your monitor fails, you can obtain a replacement monitor, plug it in, and get back to work. A hard disk drive failure, however, can be a disaster because you might lose all stored data. Although an experienced computer technician might be able to recover some of the files on the damaged hard disk drive, it is more often the case that all programs and data files stored on the hard disk are permanently lost.

The reliability of computer components is expressed as mean time between failures, or MTBF. The **MTBF** is calculated by observing test equipment in a laboratory, then dividing the number of failures by the total number of hours of observation. This statistic is an estimate based on laboratory tests of a few sample components. The measurement is somewhat misleading, however, because the tests are conducted in a regulated laboratory environment where power problems, failure of other components, and regular wear and tear do not exist. For example, a 300,000-hour MTBF means that, on average, a hard disk drive is likely to function for 300,000 hours or 14 years without failing.

However, because devices aren't tested using real-word conditions, it is important to plan for hardware failures, rather than hope they won't happen. The effects of a hard disk drive failure are considerably reduced if you have complete, up-to-date backups of the programs and data files on your hard disk. Data backup is discussed later in this unit.

● Physical damage: Computers are not immune to unexpected damage from smoke, fire, water, and breakage. See Figure F-4. They are also not immune to theft, burglary, or other forms of vandalism. To minimize your losses due to physical damage, it is a good practice to carry insurance to cover your equipment. Under the terms of many standard household and business insurance policies, a computer is treated like any other appliance. You should make sure, however, that your insurance policy covers the full cost of purchasing a new computer at current market prices.

Replacing your damaged computer equipment will not replace your data. Some insurance companies provide extra coverage for the data on your computer. With this type of coverage, you would receive a sum of money to compensate you for the time it takes to reload your data on a replacement computer. A good insurance policy provides funds to replace computer equipment, but the only insurance for your data is an up-to-date backup tape or disk.

● Data vandalism: Your data can also be destroyed by vandalism. Computer vandals are people who, acting for thrills or illegal gain, attack the data of other computer users. Computer viruses can destroy data. Understanding how programs such as viruses work is the first line of defense against attacks and pranks.

● **Data security** consists of techniques that provide protection for data. **Risk management** is the process of weighing threats to computer data against the amount of expendable data and the cost of protecting crucial data. Table F-1 shows steps for formulating a risk management strategy. Once you have completed your risk management analysis, you can establish policies and procedures to help you maintain data security.

Why viruses are a threat to data security

The number of computer viruses is increasing at an unprecedented rate. In 1986, there was one known computer virus. By 1990, the total had jumped to 80. Today, the count exceeds 50,000, and between 10 and 15 new viruses appear every day. In addition, they are also spreading more rapidly than ever. The Michelangelo virus took seven months to reach 75,000 people; Melissa took 10 hours to reach 3.5 million people; and I-love-you took only three hours to reach 72 million. This rapid distribution of viruses greatly threatens your data security.

FIGURE F-4: A disaster can destroy computers

▶ After a severe thunderstorm, a worker pokes a hole in a ceiling tile to let out water in the computer information systems department; employees covered most of the computers before too much damage was done

TABLE F-1: Planning a risk management strategy

STEP	FOR THIS STEP
1. Consider the likely threats to your computer data.	You must evaluate the likely threat of hardware failure, human error, and vandalism.
2. Assess the amount of data that is expendable.	You must ask yourself, "How much data will I have to reenter if my hard drive is erased?" and "How much of my data will be lost forever because it cannot be reconstructed?"
3. Determine the cost of protecting all of your data versus protecting some of your data.	You must include time as well as money in your cost analysis.
4. Select the protective measures that meet your needs.	You must take into account which protective measures are affordable to you, effective against the threats you identified, and easy for you to implement.

What are disaster recovery centers?

Disaster recovery centers provide emergency computing facilities to businesses. A business can build its own disaster recovery center or contract with a third party for this service. When disaster strikes, businesses cannot afford to disrupt their operations. Disaster recovery facilities stand ready to take over operations until the main systems can be restored. This type of facility might be a remote location that stores a complete backup of the hardware, software, and data for a company, or it might provide a building where computers can be brought in quickly.

Introducing computer viruses

Computer viruses invade all types of computers, including mainframes, servers, personal computers, and even handheld computers. Spreading a virus is a crime in the U.S. and in many other countries. Although the term virus technically refers to a type of program that behaves in a specific way, it has become a generic term that refers to a variety of destructive programs. To defend your computer against viruses, you should understand what they are, how they work, and how to use antivirus software.

DETAILS

- A **computer virus** is a set of program instructions that attaches itself to a file, reproduces itself, and spreads to other files. It can corrupt files, destroy data, display an irritating message, or otherwise disrupt computer operations. In addition to replicating itself, a virus might perform a **trigger event**, sometimes referred to as a payload, which could be as harmless as displaying an annoying message or as devastating as corrupting the data on your computer's hard disk. Trigger events are often keyed to a specific date. For example, the Michelangelo virus is designed to damage hard disk files on March 6, the artist's birthday.

- Viruses have the ability to lurk in a computer for days or months, quietly replicating themselves. While this is taking place, you might not even know that your computer has a virus, which makes it easy to spread infected files to other people's computers inadvertently.

- Viruses can be classified by the types of files they infect. A virus that attaches to an application program, such as a game, is known as a **file virus**. Chernobyl, a notorious file virus, is designed to lurk in a computer until April 26th, the anniversary of the Chernobyl nuclear disaster, and then overwrite a section of the hard disk, making it impossible to access data.

  A **boot sector virus** infects the system files that your computer uses every time you turn it on. These viruses can cause widespread damage and recurring problems. The Stoned virus infects the boot sector, which means every time you start your computer, you activate the virus.

  A **macro virus** infects a set of instructions called a "macro." A **macro** is essentially a miniature program that usually contains legitimate instructions to automate document and worksheet tasks. A hacker can create a destructive macro, attach it to a document or worksheet, and then distribute it. When anyone views the document, the macro virus duplicates itself into the general macro pool, where it is picked up by other documents. The two most common macro viruses are the Melissa virus, which attaches itself to Microsoft Word documents, and the Codemas virus, which attaches itself to Microsoft Excel spreadsheets.

- A **Trojan horse** is a computer program that seems to perform one function while actually doing something else. See Figure F-5. Technically, it is different from a virus because it is not designed to make copies of itself. Trojan horses are notorious for stealing passwords. Some Trojan horses delete files and cause other trouble. Even handheld computers are susceptible. A Trojan horse called Ardiri is disguised as a program that pretends to provide free access to a Game Boy emulator, but it actually deletes all programs from PDAs. Although a Trojan horse is not defined as self-replicating, some Trojan horses can replicate and spread.

- With the proliferation of network traffic and e-mail, worms have become a major concern in the computing community. Unlike a virus, which is designed to spread from file to file, a **worm** is designed to spread from computer to computer. See Figure F-6. Most worms take advantage of communications networks (especially the Internet) to travel within e-mail and TCP/IP packets, jumping from one computer to another. Some worms spread throughout a network. Others also deliver payloads that vary from harmless messages to malicious file deletions.

  One notorious worm known as "Love Bug" arrives as an e-mail attachment called LOVE-LETTER-FOR-YOU.TXT.vbs. (Variations of this worm might also use attachments called mothersday.vbs, protect.vbs, or IMPORTANT.TXT.vbs.) Once you open the attachment, the worm overwrites most of the music, graphics, documents, spreadsheets, and Web files on your disk. After trashing your files, the worm automatically mails itself to everyone in your e-mail address book, looking for other victims.

  Some worms are designed to generate a lot of activity on a network by flooding it with useless traffic—enough to overwhelm the network's processing capability and essentially bring all communications to a halt. These **Denial of Service attacks** have the effect of cutting network users off from e-mail and Web browsing.

FIGURE F-5: A Trojan horse

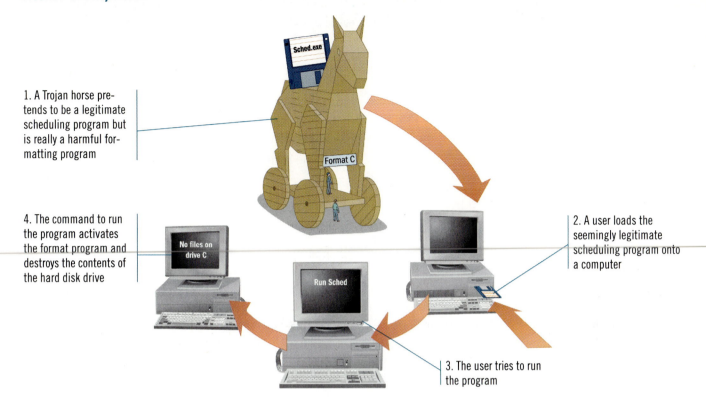

1. A Trojan horse pretends to be a legitimate scheduling program but is really a harmful formatting program

4. The command to run the program activates the format program and destroys the contents of the hard disk drive

2. A user loads the seemingly legitimate scheduling program onto a computer

3. The user tries to run the program

FIGURE F-6: A worm attacks

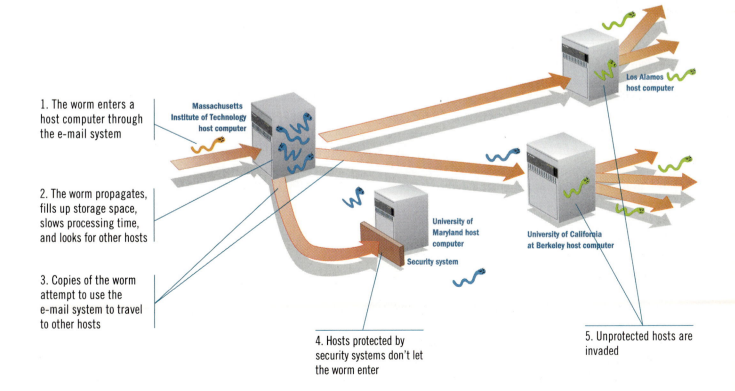

1. The worm enters a host computer through the e-mail system

2. The worm propagates, fills up storage space, slows processing time, and looks for other hosts

3. Copies of the worm attempt to use the e-mail system to travel to other hosts

4. Hosts protected by security systems don't let the worm enter

5. Unprotected hosts are invaded

Massachusetts Institute of Technology host computer

Los Alamos host computer

University of Maryland host computer

Security system

University of California at Berkeley host computer

Understanding how viruses spread

Viruses spread because people distribute infected files by exchanging disks and CDs, sending e-mail attachments, and downloading software from the Web. A virus infects the files with .exe, .com, or .vbs filename extensions by attaching itself to them. When you open an infected file, the attached virus instructions also open. These instructions then remain in RAM, waiting to infect the next program that your computer runs or the next disk that it accesses.

DETAILS

- Shared files are a common source of viruses. Figure F-7 illustrates how a single disk can easily infect many computers. Floppy disks, homemade CDs, and Web sites that contain games and other fun stuff are the most common sources of viruses.

- E-mail attachments are another common source of viruses. A seemingly innocent attachment can harbor a file virus or a boot sector virus. Typically, infected attachments look like executable files, usually with .exe filename extensions, although in some cases they can have .sys, .drv, .com, .bin, .vbs, .scr, or .ovl extensions. These files cannot infect your computer unless you open them, which executes the virus code that they contain.

  If you get an e-mail message that appears to have two filename extensions, such as LOVE-LETTER-FOR-YOU.TXT.vbs, your suspicions should be aroused; filenames have only one extension. In the example, the second extension, .vbs, is the real filename extension, and it means that the file contains an executable program—potentially a virus, such as a worm.

  Remember that you can set Windows to hide filename extensions. If you do, the worm-harboring attachment appears simply as LOVE-LETTER-FOR-YOU.TXT. It looks like the attachment has an innocent .txt extension. You might increase your chances of identifying "bad" e-mail attachments if you make sure that Windows is set to display all filename extensions. You should follow the experts' advice about e-mail attachments: never open a suspicious attachment without first checking it with antivirus software. If you don't want the attachment, simply delete the e-mail message to which it was attached.

- In addition to problems with e-mail attachments, e-mail messages themselves can carry viruses to unsuspecting recipients. This is particularly true if you receive your e-mail in HTML format, which allows you to use different fonts and different font formatting features (such as colors and sizes) for your messages. E-mail in HTML format can harbor viruses and worms hidden in program-like scripts that are embedded in the HTML tags. These viruses are difficult to detect even for antivirus software. To avoid the threat to data security, many people stick with plain text, non-HTML e-mail format for sending and receiving e-mail messages.

- Web sites that contain games and music are also a common source of viruses. When you download files from these sites, the downloaded files often contain scripts that harbor viruses. You should scan all files with up-to-date antivirus software before downloading files. Antivirus software is discussed in a later lesson.

- Documents created with Microsoft Word and spreadsheets created with Microsoft Excel are a common source of a specific virus known as a **macro virus**. You might receive files infected with macro viruses on a disk, as a Web download, or as an e-mail attachment. Since the infected files display the usual .doc or .xls extensions, there are no outward clues that the file contains a macro virus. Whenever you try to open a file that contains a macro (regardless of whether it is infected), you will see a message on your screen asking if you want to open the macro. Unless you are certain that the file contains a legitimate macro, respond to this message with "No."

What are the symptoms of a virus?

The symptoms depend on the virus. The following symptoms might indicate that your computer has contracted a virus, though some of these symptoms can have other causes: Your computer displays vulgar, embarrassing, or annoying messages; your computer develops unusual visual or sound effects; you have difficulty saving files, or files mysteriously disappear; your computer suddenly seems to work very slowly; your computer reboots unexpectedly; your executable files unaccountably increase in size; or your computer starts sending out lots of e-mail messages on its own.

It is important to remember, however, that some viruses, worms, and Trojan horses have no recognizable symptoms. Your computer can contract a worm, for example, that never displays an irritating message or attempts to delete your files, but which replicates itself through your e-mail until it eventually arrives at a server where it can do some real damage to a network communications system. You should use antivirus software to evict any viruses, worms, or Trojan horses that try to take up residence in your computer.

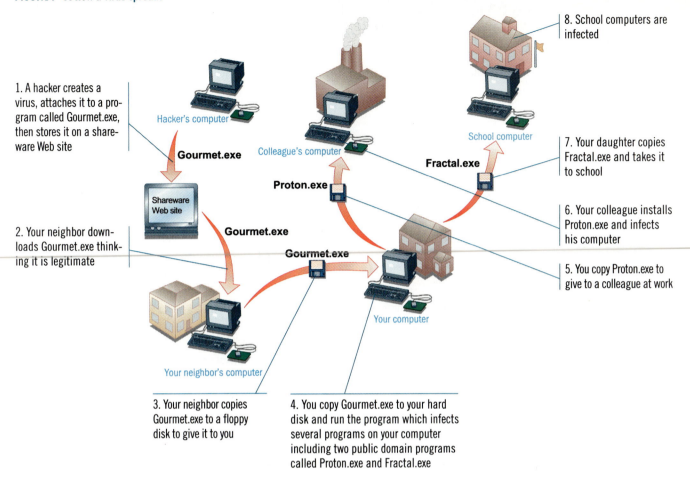

1. A hacker creates a virus, attaches it to a program called Gourmet.exe, then stores it on a shareware Web site

Hacker's computer

Gourmet.exe

Shareware Web site

2. Your neighbor downloads Gourmet.exe thinking it is legitimate

Gourmet.exe

Gourmet.exe

Your neighbor's computer

Colleague's computer

Proton.exe

Fractal.exe

School computer

8. School computers are infected

7. Your daughter copies Fractal.exe and takes it to school

6. Your colleague installs Proton.exe and infects his computer

5. You copy Proton.exe to give to a colleague at work

Your computer

3. Your neighbor copies Gourmet.exe to a floppy disk to give it to you

4. You copy Gourmet.exe to your hard disk and run the program which infects several programs on your computer including two public domain programs called Proton.exe and Fractal.exe

Write-protecting floppies will not help stop viruses

Floppy disks have a write-protect window. See Figure F-8. With the write-protect window open, all you can do is look at the files on a disk. But typically when you use a disk, you want to save a new file or modify the data in an existing file. To do so, you must close the write-protect window, and the disk is no longer protected. Therefore, when you use a disk, you're not likely to have the write-protect feature activated. Although a virus cannot jump onto your disk when it is write-protected, you must remove the write protection each time you save a file on the disk. With the write protection removed, your disk is open to a virus attack. So, while it is true that write protect does effectively protect data, a write-protected disk is not very useful because you cannot save data to it.

FIGURE F-8: A write-protect window

Write-protect window

Restricting access

The preceding lessons presented ways in which computers and computer data are vulnerable. The next few lessons look at ways to approach data security. This lesson looks at restricting user access—both physically and through user rights restrictions.

DETAILS

● One of the best ways to prevent people from damaging a computer system's equipment is to restrict physical access. If potential criminals cannot get to a computer or a terminal, stealing or damaging data becomes more difficult. See Figure F-9 for suggested ways to restrict physical access. Keep in mind, however, that restricting physical access will not prevent a determined criminal from stealing data.

● Three methods of personal identification are used to restrict access: something a person carries, something a person knows, or some unique physical characteristic. Any one of these methods has the potential to positively identify a person, and each has a unique set of advantages and disadvantages.

  • Something a person carries: An identity badge or pass card featuring a photo, or perhaps a magnetic strip or bar code with unique coded information, remains a popular form of personal identification. Designers have created high-tech identity card readers, like the one shown in Figure F-10. Because an identity badge can be lost, stolen, or duplicated, however, it works best when used on site where a security guard verifies that the face on the badge is the face of the person wearing the badge. Without visual verification, the use of identity badges from a remote site is not secure, unless combined with a password or PIN (personal identification number) that is coded on the badge.

  • Something a person knows: User IDs and passwords fall into this category of personal identification. When you work on a multiuser system or network, you generally must have a user ID and password. Data security on a computer system that is guarded by user IDs and passwords depends on password secrecy. If users give out their passwords, choose obvious passwords, or write them down in obvious places, hackers can break in. The method of trying every word in an electronic dictionary to steal a password decreases in effectiveness if a password is based on two words, a word and number, or a nonsense word that does not appear in a dictionary.

  • Some unique physical characteristic: This third method of personal identification, called **biometrics**, bases identification on some physical trait, such as a fingerprint or the pattern of blood vessels in the retina of the eye. Unlike passwords, biometric data can't be forgotten, lost, or borrowed. Once the technological fiction of spy thrillers, biometric devices are becoming affordable technologies. Such technologies include hand-geometry scanners, voice recognition, face recognition, fingerprint scanners (see Figure F-11), and retinal scanners (see Figure F-12).

● In today's web of interlaced computer technologies, however, it has also become critical to restrict not only physical access but also user access. Data access can be restricted to authorized users. Restricting the access of users—especially those who are logging in from sites thousands of miles away—is a critical step in data security.

Passwords are critical to user access and are a first line of defense against unauthorized access. What if a hacker breaks in anyway? One way to limit the amount of damage from a break-in is to assign user rights. **User rights** are rules that limit the directories and files that each user can access. They can restrict your ability to erase, create, write, read, and find files. When you receive a user ID and password for a password-protected system, the system administrator gives you rights that allow you to access and perform specified tasks only on particular directories and files on the host computer or file server. Assigning user rights helps prevent both accidental and deliberate damage to data. If users are granted limited rights, a hacker who steals someone's password has only the same access as the person from whom the password was stolen.

FIGURE F-9: Ways to restrict physical access

- ⊘ Restrict access to the area surrounding the computer to prevent physical damage to the equipment.

- ⊘ Keep floppy disks and data backups in a locked vault to prevent theft and to protect against fire or water damage.

- ⊘ Keep offices containing computers locked to prevent theft and to deter unauthorized users.

- ⊘ Lock the computer case to prevent theft of components such as RAM and processors.

FIGURE F-10: Identity card reader

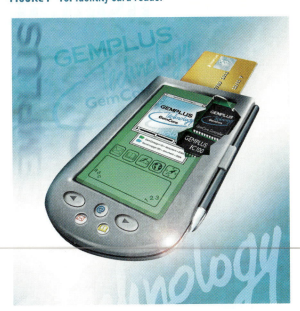

FIGURE F-11: Fingerprint scanner

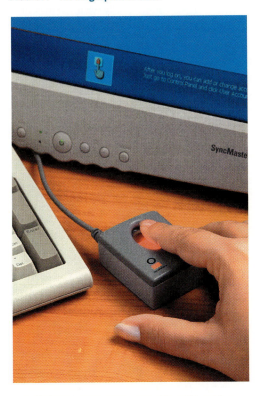

FIGURE F-12: Retinal scanner

Using antivirus software

In addition to restricting user access, data security involves the use of antivirus software. **Antivirus software** is a set of utility programs that looks for and eradicates a wide spectrum of problems, such as viruses, Trojan horses, and worms. Versions of antivirus software are available for handheld computers, personal computers, and servers. Figure F-13 shows a popular antivirus package. Considering the sheer number of existing viruses and the number of new viruses that debut every week, antivirus software is a must as part of your data security plan.

Info Web — ANTIVIRUS SOFTWARE
Info Web — HOAX

DETAILS

- Antivirus software uses several techniques to find viruses. The earliest antivirus software simply examined the programs on a computer and recorded their length. A change in the length of a program from one computing session to the next indicated the possible presence of a virus. This method of virus detection requires that you start with a virus-free copy of the program.

- In response to early antivirus software, hackers became more cunning. They created viruses that insert themselves into unused portions of a program file without changing its length. Of course, the people who designed antivirus software fought back. They designed software that examines the bytes in an uninfected application program and calculates a checksum. A **checksum** is a number that is calculated by combining the binary values of all bytes in a file. Each time you run an application program, the antivirus software calculates the checksum and compares it with the previous checksum. If any byte in the application program has changed, the checksum will be different, and the antivirus software assumes that a virus is present. The checksum approach also requires that you start with a copy of the program that is not infected with a virus. If the original copy is infected, the virus is included in the original checksum, and the antivirus software never detects it.

- Antivirus software also identifies viruses by searching your files for a **virus signature**, a unique series of bytes that can be used to identify a known virus, much as a fingerprint is used to identify an individual. Most of today's antivirus software scans for virus signatures. The signature search technique is fairly quick, but it identifies only those viruses with a known signature. To detect new viruses—and new viruses appear at an alarming rate—virus detection software must be updated regularly.

- Viruses try to escape detection in many ways. **Multi-partite viruses** are able to infect multiple types of targets. For example, a multi-partite virus might combine the characteristics of a file virus (which hides in .exe files) and a boot sector virus (which

hides in the boot sector). If your antivirus software looks for that particular virus only in .exe files, the virus could escape detection by hiding in the boot sector as well. **Polymorphic viruses** mutate to escape detection by changing their signatures. **Stealth viruses** remove their signatures from a disk-based file and temporarily conceal themselves in memory. Antivirus software can find stealth viruses only by scanning memory. Some viruses called **retro viruses** are designed to attack antivirus software by deleting the files that contain virus descriptions or by corrupting the main executable virus program.

- Most antivirus software allows you to specify what to check and when to check it. You can, for example, start the program when you receive a suspicious e-mail attachment. Or, you can set it to look through all of the files on your computer once a week. The best practice, however, is to keep your antivirus software running full-time in the background so that it scans all files the moment they are accessed, and checks every e-mail message as it arrives.

- Keeping a virus out of your computer and files is preferable to trying to eradicate a virus that has taken up residence. Once a virus infiltrates your computer, it can be difficult to eradicate, even with antivirus software. Certain viruses are particularly tenacious; just the process of booting up your computer can trigger their replication sequence or send them into hiding.

- To keep up with newly identified viruses and variations of old viruses, antivirus software publishers provide periodic updates, which are usually available as Web downloads. You should check your antivirus publisher's Web site for the latest updates every few weeks, or if you hear of a new virus.

- Antivirus software is not 100% reliable. On occasions, it might not identify a virus, or it might think that your computer has a virus when one does not actually exist. Despite these mistakes, the protection you get using antivirus software is worth the required investment of time and money.

FIGURE F-13: Antivirus software

▶ You can buy the CD or download the program from the Internet; some antivirus vendors provide an electronic update service that automatically contacts your computer when a new version is available, and then downloads the updated files; this controversial service may save you the trouble of periodically checking for automatic updates; however, it does supply your computer with unknown files; many people prefer to know exactly what is installed on their computers and when such files are added

Virus hoaxes

Some viruses are very real, but you're likely to get e-mail about "viruses" that don't really exist. A virus hoax usually arrives as an e-mail message containing dire warnings about a supposedly new virus that is on the loose. The message typically suggests some strategy for avoiding the virus, and recommends that you forward the e-mail warning to all of your friends and colleagues. In most cases, however, the alleged virus does not exist, and the e-mail message is a prank designed to send people into a panic.

Bogus virus e-mail messages usually contain a long list of people in the To: and Cc: boxes; they have been forwarded many times. Most hoaxes include a recommended procedure for eradicating the virus, such as reformatting your computer's hard disk drive—a process that could cause more damage than the virus itself! Fake viruses are often characterized as being capable of bizarre acts. For example, check out the message about a phony virus in Figure F-14.

When you receive an e-mail message about a virus, don't panic. Virtually all of them are hoaxes. If you are uncertain, check one of the many antivirus Web sites and look up the alleged virus by name to see if it is a hoax or if it is a real threat. If the virus is a real threat, the antivirus Web site will provide the information that you need to check your computer and download an update to your antivirus software.

FIGURE F-14: Message announcing a virus hoax

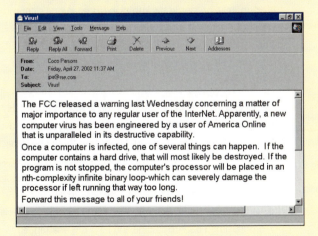

Introducing data backup

Data disasters are not rare; they happen to everyone. Since you can't always prevent disasters from happening, you need a backup plan that helps you recover data that's been wiped out by operator error, viruses, or hardware failures. Computer experts universally recommend that you make back-ups of your data.

DETAILS

● A **backup** is a copy of one or more files that has been made in case the original files become damaged. A backup is usually stored on a different storage medium from the original files. For example, you can back up files from your hard disk to a different hard disk, a writable CD or DVD, tape, floppy disk, or Web site. The exact steps that you follow to make a backup depend on your backup equipment, your backup software, and your personal backup plan. Figure F-15 gives you a general idea of the steps that are involved in a typical backup session.

● You **restore** data from a backup to the original storage medium or its replacement. As with the procedures for backing up data, the process that you use to restore data to your hard disk varies, depending on your backup equipment, backup software, and exactly what you need to restore. After a hard disk crash, for example, you'll probably need to restore all of your backup data to a new hard disk. On the other hand, if you inadvertently delete a file, or mistakenly copy one file over another, you might need to restore only a single file from the backup. Most backup software allows you to select which files you want to restore.

● A good backup plan allows you to restore your computing environment to its pre-disaster state with a minimum of fuss. Unfortunately, no single backup plan fits everyone's computing style or budget. You must tailor your own backup plan to your particular computing needs. The checklist in Figure F-16 outlines the factors you should consider as you formulate your own backup plan.

● What files should you back up? The short answer is all files, but the reality is that, depending on time and resources, you may have to select which files to back up. Your first option should be to back up all files on your hard disk. The advantage of backing up your com-puter's entire hard disk is that you can restore everything to its pre-disaster state simply by copying the backup files to a new hard disk. Under ideal circumstances, you would be able to start a pre-programmed backup routine and let it run unattended. However, this strategy is possible only if you have a large-capacity backup device and special backup software.

An alternative is to back up your most important data files. By doing so, you make sure that your computer-based documents and projects are protected from data disasters. You can back up these files on floppy disks, Zip disks, removable hard disks, CDs, or DVDs. The disadvantage of this backup strategy is that because you backed up only data files, you must manually reinstall all of your software, in addition to restoring your data files.

● Some applications, such as financial software, create files and update them without your direct intervention. If you have the option during setup, make sure that these files end up in a folder you always backup, such as My Documents. Otherwise, you must discover the location of the files and make sure that they are backed up with the rest of your data.

● In addition to data files that you create, consider making back-ups of the following files:

- Internet connection information. Your ISP's phone number and TCP/IP address, your user ID, and your password are often stored in an encrypted file somewhere in the Windows\System folder. Your ISP can usually help you find this file.

- E-mail folders. If you're using POP e-mail software, your e-mail folder contains all of the e-mail messages that you've sent and received, but not deleted. Check the Help menu on your e-mail program to discover the location of these files.

- E-mail address book. Your e-mail address book might be stored separately from your e-mail messages. If it is not located at C:\Windows\Application\Data\Microsoft\Address book, the documentation for your e-mail software should tell you where it is stored.

- Favorite URLs. If you're attached to the URLs that you've collected in your Favorites or Bookmarks list, you might want to back up the file that contains this list.

- Downloads. If you paid to download any files, you might want to back them up so that you don't have to pay for them again. These files include software, which usually arrives in the form of a compressed .exe file that expands into several separate files as you install it. For backup purposes, the compressed .exe file should be all that you need.

FIGURE F-15: Steps in a typical backup session

1. Insert the disk, CD, or tape on which you'll store the backup.

2. Start your backup software.

3. Select the folders and files that you want to back up.

4. Give the go ahead to start copying data.

5. Feed in additional disks, CDs, or tapes if prompted to do so.

6. Clearly label each disk, CD, or tape that you use.

7. Test your backup.

FIGURE F-16: Backup tips

☑ Decide how much of your data you want, need, and can afford to back up.

☑ Create a realistic schedule for making backups.

☑ Make sure that you have a way to avoid backing up files that contain viruses.

☑ Find out what kind of boot disks you might need to get your computer up and running after a hard disk failure or boot sector virus attack.

☑ Make sure that you have a procedure for testing your restore procedure so that you can successfully retrieve the data that you've backed up.

☑ Find a safe place to store your backups.

☑ Decide what kind of storage device you'll use to make backups.

☑ Select backup software.

Backing up the Windows Registry

The Windows Registry is an important file that is used by the Windows operating system to store configuration information about all of the devices and software installed on a computer system. If the Registry becomes damaged, your computer might not be able to boot up, launch programs, or communicate with peripheral devices. It is a good idea to have an extra copy of the Registry in case the original file is damaged.

Backing up the Registry can present a problem because the Registry file is always open while your computer is on. Some backup software will not copy open files, and if this is the type of backup software that you are using, the Registry will never make its way onto a backup. Windows users whose backup plans encompass all of the files on the hard disk must make sure that their backup software provides an option for including the Windows Registry. Even if a full-system backup is not planned, many experts recommend that you at least copy the Registry file to a separate folder on the hard disk or to a floppy disk. If you do so, it is necessary to update this copy whenever you install new software or hardware.

Examining backup procedures

One of the most distressing computing experiences is to lose all of your data. This problem might be the result of a hardware failure or a virus. Whatever its cause, most users experience only a moment of surprise and disbelief before the depressing realization sinks in that they might have to recreate all of their data and reinstall all of their programs. A backup can pull you through such trying times, making the data loss a minor inconvenience rather than a major disaster. This lesson looks at the three main backup procedures.

DETAILS

- A **full backup** (Figure F-17) makes a copy of every file that exists in the folders that you've specified for the backup. Because a full backup includes a copy of every file on a disk, it can take a long time to make one for a hard disk. Some users consider it worth the extra time, however, because this type of backup is easy to restore. You simply have the computer copy the files from your backup to the hard disk. It might, however, not be necessary to make a full backup on every backup date, especially if most of your files don't change from one backup session to another.

- A **differential backup** (Figure F-18) makes a backup of only those files that were added or changed since your last full backup session. After making a full backup of your important files, you will make differential backups at regular intervals. You maintain two sets of backups: a full backup that you make infrequently (once a week); and a differential backup that you make more frequently (once a day). It takes less time to make a differential backup than to make a full backup, but it is a little more complex to restore data from a differential backup than from a full backup. If you need to restore all of your files after a hard disk crash, first restore the files from your full backup, then restore the files from your latest differential backup.

- An **incremental backup** (Figure F-19) makes a backup of the files that were added or changed since the last backup, which might have been a full backup or an incremental backup. First you make a full backup, then when you make your first incremental backup, it will contain the files that have changed since the full backup. When you make your second incremental backup, it will contain only the files that changed since the first incremental backup. Incremental backups take the least time to make, and they provide a little better protection from viruses than other backup methods because your backup contains a series of copies of your files. They are, however, the most complex type of backup to restore. If you need to restore all of your files after a hard disk crash, first restore the files from the full backup, then restore the files from each incremental backup, starting with the oldest and working your way to the most recent.

- Any data backup plan represents a compromise between the level of protection and the amount of time and resources you can devote to backup. To be safe, you would need to backup your data every time you change the contents of a file, which would reduce the amount of work you could complete in a day. Realistically you should perform backups at regular intervals (including copies of the Registry). The interval between backups will depend on the value of your data—what that data is worth to you.

FIGURE F-17: A full backup

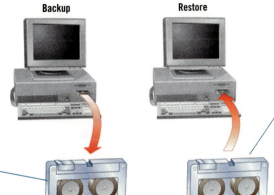

► A full backup is simply a copy of all files on your hard disk

Backup

Restore

2. If the hard drive fails, you can restore all of the files from the backup to the hard disk drive

1. Back up all files from the hard disk drive to a backup tape

FIGURE F-18: A differential backup

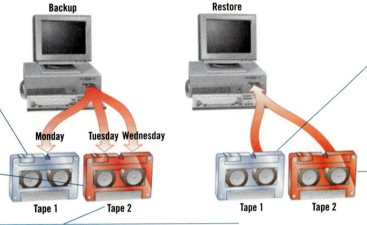

► A differential backup copies any files that have changed since your last backup

Backup

Restore

1. Make a full backup on Monday evening

2. On Tuesday evening, use a different tape to back up only the files that have been changed since the full backup

Monday **Tuesday** **Wednesday**

Tape 1 **Tape 2**

Tape 1 **Tape 2**

4. Now, suppose the hard disk fails; to restore your data, first load the full backup onto the hard disk; this step restores the files as they existed on Monday evening

5. Next, load the data from the differential backup tape; this step restores the files you changed on Tuesday and Wednesday

3. On Wednesday evening, back up only the files that have changed since the full backup; these files are the ones you changed or created on Tuesday and Wednesday; put these files on the same tape you used for Tuesday's backup.

FIGURE F-19: An incremental backup

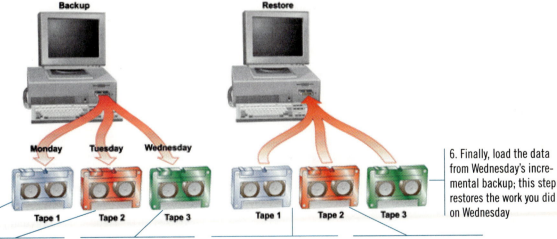

► Of the three backup techniques, an incremental backup takes the least time, but is the most complex to restore

Backup

Restore

1. Make a full backup on Monday evening

Monday **Tuesday** **Wednesday**

Tape 1 **Tape 2** **Tape 3**

Tape 1 **Tape 2** **Tape 3**

2. On Tuesday evening, back up only the files that have been changed or created on Tuesday

3. On Wednesday evening, back up only the files that have been changed or created on Wednesday

4. Now, suppose the hard disk fails; to begin the restoration process, first load the data from the full backup

5. Next, load the data from Tuesday's incremental backup; this step restores the work you did on Tuesday

6. Finally, load the data from Wednesday's incremental backup; this step restores the work you did on Wednesday

Exploring backup hardware and media

The hardware and media you use to backup your data is very important in determining the reliability and success of the procedure. The backup device that you select depends on the value of your data, your current computer configuration, equipment, and budget. If you can afford a tape drive, buy one, install it, and use it. Otherwise, use what you have: your CD-R drive, Zip drive, or floppy disk drive.

DETAILS

● Tape drives remain the best backup device for personal computers. They can be installed in an open drive bay of a desktop computer, or connected to a notebook computer by an external cable. Tape drives are inexpensive. Make sure that you purchase a tape drive with the capacity to hold the entire contents of your hard disk so you can leave the tape unattended during backup.

The most popular types of tape drives for personal computers use tape cartridges, but there are several tape specifications and cartridge sizes, including ADR (advanced digital recording), Ditto, Travan, and DDS (digital data storage). See Figure F-20. Check the tape drive manual to make sure that you purchase the correct type of tape for your tape drive. Tape is a storage medium similar in reliability to floppy disks and Zip disks but not as durable as writable CDs and DVDs. Even though tape is simply too slow to be practical as your computer's main storage device, it is effective as a backup device. When you make a backup, you're simply copying lots of data onto the tape. You don't need to locate specific data or jump back and forth between different files. For a backup device, access time is less important than the time it takes to copy data from your hard disk to tape. Manufacturers do not always supply such performance specifications, but most users can expect a tape drive to back up 1 GB in 15-20 minutes.

● While floppy disks are inexpensive and just about every computer has a floppy disk drive, they are not an effective medium for a backup procedure. The 1.44 MB capacity of a floppy disk is suitable for storing several documents, but it does not provide enough capacity for digital photos or most MP3 music files. It would take an unreasonable number of disks if you tried to use floppies for one of the three main backup procedures. If you have no other means to back up your data, however, floppies provide an acceptable means of copying your must critical files, such as your e-mail address book and important data files.

● A Zip disk's 100 MB or 250 MB capacity is sufficient for documents and digital graphics. A few of these disks might be sufficient for backing up all of your data files. A backup of your entire hard disk would probably require too many disks to be feasible, however.

● Writable CDs and DVDs provide good storage capacity and blank disks are fairly inexpensive. You can typically use them to back up all of your data files. It might also be feasible to back up your entire system on a series of CDs or DVDs. You would, however, have to monitor the backup process and switch disks occasionally. The major disadvantage of writable CDs and DVDs is that the writing process is slower than writing data to tape or a removable hard disk.

● A second hard disk drive is a good backup option. If it has equivalent capacity to your main hard disk, the backup process can proceed unattended because you won't have to swap disks. Unfortunately, your backup hard disk is susceptible to head crashes, just like your main hard disk, making it one of the least reliable storage options. Another disadvantage: unless your second hard disk drive uses removable storage cartridges that you can store in a safe place, your backups will also be susceptible to electrical damage and any other catastrophe that happens to your computer.

● Remote storage is also an option for your backup. If your computer is connected to a local area network, you might be able to use the network server as a backup device. Before backing up your data to a network server, you want to check with the network administrator to make sure that you are allowed to store a large amount of data on the server. If you want to limit access to your data, ask the network administrator to let you store your data in a password-protected area. Also make sure that the server is backed up on a regular basis and that you have access to the backups in case you need to restore data to your local computer.

Storing data on the Web

Another possibility for remote storage is the Internet. Several Web sites, such as the one in Figure F-21, offer fee-based backup storage space. When needed, you can simply download backup files from the Web site to your hard disk. These sites are an excellent idea for backups of your data files. When used in conjunction with a recovery CD, you can usually get your computer into functional condition after a data disaster. For most personal computer owners, however, a Web site might not be feasible for storing a backup image of an entire hard disk. First, it would be necessary to recover enough of your system files to get your computer connected to the Internet before the restoration files could be downloaded. In addition, the transfer time for several gigabytes of files could be days.

FIGURE F-21: Web-based storage for backup

Exploring backup strategies

Once you have established which backup procedure and hardware to use, you should develop a backup plan that includes additional backup practices. This lesson discusses backup practices to consider including in your backup plan.

DETAILS

● Run up-to-date antivirus software before creating a backup. Viruses can damage files to the point that your computer can't access any data on its hard disk. In such a case, it is really frustrating when you restore data from a backup only to discover that the restored files contain the same virus that wiped out your data. If your antivirus software is not set to scan for viruses on your computer system constantly, you should run an up-to-date virus check as the first step in your backup routine.

● Create a boot disk. If your computer's hard disk is out of commission, you might wonder how it can access the operating system files that are needed to carry out the boot process. If your hard disk failed, or a virus wiped out the boot sector files on your hard disk, you will not be able to use your normal procedures to boot your computer. A **boot disk** is a floppy disk or CD that contains the operating system files needed to boot your computer without accessing the hard disk.

Several types of boot disks exist, including recovery CDs, Windows Startup Disks, and rescue disks. It is a good idea to have one of each. Most of today's computer manufacturers supply a type of boot disk with new computer systems called a **recovery CD**. It contains the operating system files needed to boot the computer, plus all of the Windows and application software files needed to restore your computer to the state it was in when you bought it. A recovery CD is a valuable part of your backup arsenal when used in conjunction with a backup of your data files.

Another type of boot disk, called the **Windows Startup Disk**, is valuable to Windows users because it loads not only the operating system, but also the CD-ROM drivers necessary for your computer to access files on the CD-ROM. You can create this disk by following the steps in Figure F-22.

Your antivirus software company probably advises you to create another version of a boot disk, called a **rescue disk**, which contains operating system files, plus a special version of the antivirus software that can perform the first wave of virus cleanup in RAM and on the hard disk.

● Decide on a storage medium. Once you have determined what procedure you will follow, researched various storage media, and created your boot disk, you need to determine what storage media you will use. Table F-2 provides information about various media that can be used for backup storage.

● Make rotating sets of backups. One backup is good, but in case your backup gets corrupted, you should maintain a rotating set of backups. For example, if you are backing up to tape, you can use one tape for your first backup, then use a different tape for your next backup. Use even another tape for your third backup. For your fourth backup, you can overwrite the data on your first backup; for your fifth backup, you can overwrite the data on the second tape, and so on. Make sure that you write the date of the backup on the tape label so that you know which backup is the most recent.

● Test your backups. As soon as you make a backup, test your backup to be sure you can restore your data.

● Store your backups in a safe place. Don't keep them at your computer desk because a fire or flood that damages your computer could also wipe out your backups. In addition, a thief who steals your computer might also scoop up nearby equipment and media. Storing your backups at a different location is the best idea, but at least store them in a room apart from your computer.

FIGURE F-22: Creating a Windows Startup disk

1. Click Start, point to Settings, and then click Control Panel

2. Double-click Add/Remove Programs

3. Click the Startup Disk tab

4. Make sure that you have a blank, formatted floppy disk in drive A, click Create Disk, and then follow the on-screen instructions

TABLE F-2: Comparison of storage media

	DEVICE COST	MEDIA COST	CAPACITY	COMMENTS
Floppy disk	$40-99	30¢	1.44 MB	Low capacity means that you have to wait around to feed in disks
Zip disk	$139 (average)	$11.00	250 MB	Holds much more than a floppy but a backup still requires multiple disks
Fixed hard disk	$150 (average)	-NA-	40 GB (average)	Fast and convenient, but risky because it is susceptible to damage or theft of your computer
Removable hard disk	$150 (average)	-NA-	2.2 GB (average)	Fast, limited capacity, but disks can be removed and locked in a secure location
CD-R	$130-200	50¢	680 MB	Limited capacity, can't be reused, long shelf life
CD-RW	$130-200	$1.50	680 MB	Limited capacity, reusable, very slow
Writable DVD	$500 (average)	$25.00	5.2 GB	Good capacity, not yet standardized
Tape	$199 (average)	$50.00	30 GB (average)	Great capacity, convenient—you can let backups run overnight
Web site		$5.95 per month		Transfer rate depends on your Internet connection; security and privacy of your data may be a concern

Exploring backup software

Choosing the software you use to create your backups depends on your backup plan. If you are simply copying one or more data files to a floppy or Zip disk, you can use the Copy command that is provided by your operating system or a file management utility, such as Windows Explorer. However, many types of backup software are available if you want to go beyond a simple file backup.

DETAILS

● Many personal computer operating systems provide a **Copy Disk utility** that makes an exact copy of one floppy disk onto another disk of the same size and capacity. See Figure F-23. This utility is useful for students working in school computer labs, who often save and transport their files on floppy disks. This utility does not typically make copies of hard disks or CDs—only floppy disks—so its use for backups is limited to those occasions when you need a backup of a floppy disk.

● Backup software gives you great flexibility in selecting the series of files and folders that you want to back up. It might even allow you to schedule automated backups. Your operating system is likely to include backup software. For example, some versions of Windows include Microsoft Backup software, which you can usually find by using the Start button, then selecting Accessories and System Tools.

● Backup software is supplied with many backup devices, particularly tape drives. You can also download and purchase backup software from companies that specialize in data protection software. Useful features include the following:

- The ability to restore all of your programs and data files without manually re-installing Windows or any other applications

- An option to schedule unattended backups

- Support for a variety of backup devices, including tape drives, CD-R and CD-RW, DVD-RAM, Zip, Jaz, SuperDisk, and floppy disks

● Whatever backup software you use, remember that it needs to be accessible when it comes time to restore your data. If the only copy of your backup software exists on your backup disks, you will be in a "Catch-22" situation. You won't be able to access your backup software until you restore the files from your backup, but you won't be able to restore your files until your backup software is running! Make sure that you keep the original distribution CD for your backup software or that you have a separate backup that contains any backup software that you downloaded from the Web. Also be sure to make the required recovery disks so that you can restore Windows and get your backup program running.

FIGURE F-23: The Copy Disk utility

1. Place the disk that you want to copy in the floppy disk drive; make sure that you also have a blank disk handy

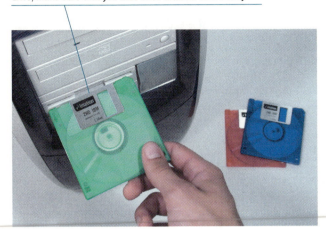

2. Double-click the My Computer icon

3. Right-click the 3½ Floppy (A:) icon

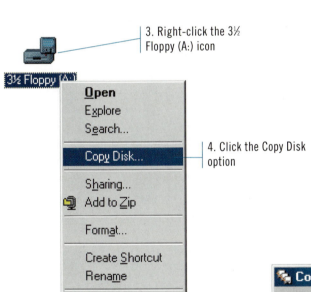

4. Click the Copy Disk option

5. Click the Start button; the contents of the disk are copied into RAM; when prompted, insert a blank disk in drive A so that the data can be copied from RAM to the blank disk

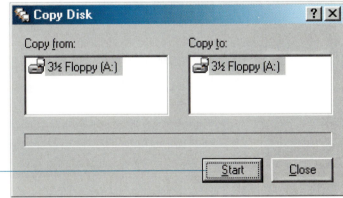

Local area networks are susceptible to internal security breaches, such as when a person at one workstation gains unauthorized access to the files on another workstation. If a LAN is equipped with an always-on Internet connection, it also becomes vulnerable to external attacks. Security is an issue you must address if you are on a LAN or if you are using an ISP or a cable modem to connect to the Internet.

Any home network that is connected to an always-on Internet connection is vulnerable to intrusions. You should make sure that password protection is enabled on every workstation.

For added protection, you might also want to purchase and install **personal firewall software**, which is designed to analyze and control incoming and outgoing packets. This software helps to keep your computer secure in several ways. It makes sure that incoming information was actually requested and is not an unauthorized intrusion. It blocks activity from suspicious IP addresses and, best of all, it reports intrusion attempts so that you can discover if any hackers are trying to break into your computer. Most firewall software allows you to set up various filters to control the type of packets that your workstation accepts. Most packages allow you simply to select a level of security, such as high, medium, or low.

You can also use **network address translation (NAT)** as a line of defense. Your ISP typically assigns an IP address to your high-speed connection; that is the address that's visible to the rest of the Internet. Within your LAN, however, the workstations should use private Internet addresses. When the IP addressing scheme was devised, three ranges of addresses were reserved for internal or "private" use: 10.0.0.010.255.255.255, 172.16.0.0172.31.255.255, and 192.168.0.0192.168.255.255. These private IP addresses cannot be routed over the Internet. If you've assigned private IP addresses to your workstations, they are essentially hidden from hackers, who only see the IP address for your router.

You might wonder how you can transmit and receive data from a workstation with a non-routable address. Your router maintains a network address translation table that keeps track of the private IP addresses assigned to each workstation. For outgoing packets, the router substitutes its own address for the address of the workstation. When a response to a packet arrives, the router forwards it to the appropriate workstation. In that way, only the router's address is publicly visible.

If you are connected to the Internet using a cable modem, and if you have an Ethernet card in your PC, Windows automatically takes inventory of the local area network during boot-up. It looks for any computers on the network that have file and print sharing activated, and then lists them in the Network Places window. If your PC is part of a network and has print and file sharing activated, other network users might be able to access your files by opening the My Network Places window, as shown in Figure F-24.

Today, many cable companies use DOCSIS-compliant cable modems to block this "crossover" access among computers owned by their cable modem subscribers. **DOCSIS** (Data Over Cable Service Interface Specification) is a security technology that filters packets to certain ports, including the port that Windows uses for networking. DOCSIS secures your computer from your neighbors, but it does not close up all of the security holes that are opened when you use an always-on connection, such as a cable modem or DSL.

Unlike a dial-up connection that's only connected for the duration of your call, an always-on connection is always connected, and it is "on" whenever your computer is powered up. With an always-on connection, you might have the same IP address for days, or even months, depending on your ISP. A hacker who discovers that your computer has a security weakness can easily find it again, and its high-speed access makes it a very desirable target.

Therefore, if your PC is connected to a cable modem, you should take steps to protect it from hackers. The first step is to disable file and print sharing. When you turn off file and print sharing, your files and printer cannot be accessed by other network users. The Networking icon in the Windows Control Panel provides the setting that you need for this step. See Figure F-25.

When your computer is turned off, it is not vulnerable to attack. It is a good idea to shut down your computer when you are not using it. Putting your computer into sleep mode or activating a screen saver is not sufficient protection. Your computer must be shut down and turned off.

FIGURE F-24: My Network Places window

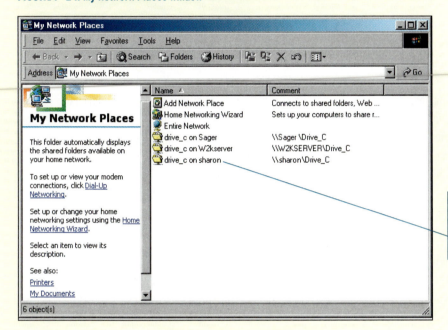

Sharon left file and print sharing on, so her drive C shows up when other users open their Network Places windows

FIGURE F-25: Turning off file sharing

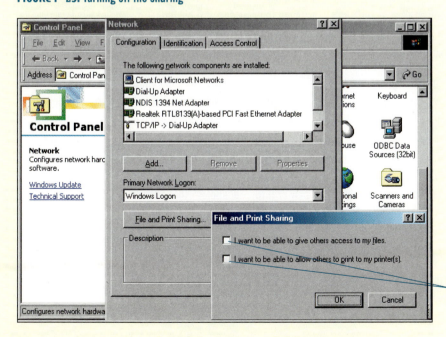

When these two boxes are not checked, file and print sharing is deactivated

It doesn't take any special digital expertise to mastermind every computer crime. Setting fire to a computer doesn't require the same finesse as writing a stealthy virus, but both can have the same disastrous effect on data. "Old-fashioned" crimes, like arson, that take a high-tech twist because they involve a computer, can be prosecuted using traditional laws. Traditional laws do not, however, cover the range of possibilities for computer crimes. Suppose a person unlawfully enters a computer facility and steals backup tapes. That person might be prosecuted for breaking and entering. But would breaking and entering laws apply to a person who uses an off-site terminal to "enter" a computer system without authorization? And what if a person copies a data file without authorization? Has that file really been "stolen" if the original remains on the computer?

Many countries have computer crime laws that specifically define computer data and software as personal property. These laws also define as crimes the unauthorized access, use, modification, or disabling of a computer system or data. But laws don't necessarily stop criminals. If they did, hackers, such as Mafiaboy and Kevin Mitnick, would not make the evening news. In a 1995 case that still echoes in the halls of justice, a computer hacker named Kevin Mitnick was accused of breaking into dozens of corporate, university, government, and personal computers. Before being arrested, Mitnick reportedly stole thousands of data files and more than 20,000 credit card numbers. U.S. attorney Kent Walker commented, "He was clearly the most wanted computer hacker in the world." Mitnick's unauthorized access and use of computer data are explicitly defined as criminal acts by computer crime laws in most countries.

Denying many, but not all, of the accusations against him, Mitnick claimed, "No way, no how, did I break into NORAD. That's a complete myth. And I never attempted to access anything considered to be classified government systems." Although vilified in the media, Mitnick had the support of many hackers and other people who believed that the prosecution grossly exaggerated the extent of his crimes. Nonetheless, Mitnick was sentenced to 46 months in prison, and ordered to pay restitution in the amount of $4,125 during his three-year period of supervised release. The prosecution was horrified by such a paltry sum, an amount that was much less than its request for $1.5 million in restitution.

Forbes reporter Adam L. Penenberg took issue with the 46-month sentence imposed by Judge Marianne Pfaelzer, and wrote, "This in a country where the average prison term for manslaughter is three years. Mitnick's crimes were curiously innocuous. He broke into corporate computers, but no evidence indicates that he destroyed data. Or sold anything he copied. Yes, he pilfered software but in doing so left it behind. This world of bits is a strange one, in which you can take something and still leave it for its rightful owner. The theft laws designed for payroll sacks and motor vehicles just don't apply to a hacker."

Unfortunately for Mitnick, the jail term and $4,125 fine were, perhaps, the most lenient part of his sentence. Mitnick, who had served most of his jail term while awaiting trial, was scheduled for a supervised release soon after sentencing. The additional conditions of Mitnick's supervised release included a ban on access to computer hardware, software, and any form of wireless communication. He was prohibited from possessing any kind of passwords, cellular phone codes, or data encryption devices. And just to make sure that he didn't get into any trouble with technologies that are not specifically mentioned in the terms of his supervised release, Mitnick was prohibited from using any new or future technology that performs as a computer or provides access to one. Perhaps worst of all, he could not work for a company with computers or computer access on its premises.

The Mitnick case illustrates our culture's ambivalent attitude toward hackers. On the one hand, they are viewed as evil cyberterrorists who are set on destroying the glue that binds together the Information Age. From this perspective, hackers are criminals who must be hunted down, forced to make restitution for damages, and prevented from creating further havoc. From another perspective, hackers are viewed more as

Casper, the friendly ghost, in our complex cyber machines; moderately bothersome entities whose pranks are tolerated by the computer community, along with software bugs and hardware glitches. Seen from this perspective, a hacker's pranks are part of the normal course of study that leads to the highest echelons of computer expertise. "Everyone has done it," claim devotees, "even Bill Gates (founder of Microsoft) and Steve Jobs (founder of Apple Computer)."

Which perspective is right? Are hackers dangerous cyberterrorists or harmless pranksters? Before you make up your mind about computer hacking and cracking, you might want to further investigate the Mitnick case and similar cases by following the Computer Crime InfoWeb links.

▼ INTERACTIVE QUESTIONS

⭕ Yes   ⭕ No   ⭕ Not sure

1. Should it be a crime to steal a copy of computer data while leaving the original data in place and unaltered?

⭕ Yes   ⭕ No   ⭕ Not sure

2. Was Mitnick's sentence fair?

⭕ Yes   ⭕ No   ⭕ Not sure

3. Should hackers be sent to jail if they cannot pay restitution to companies and individuals who lost money as the result of a prank?

⭕ Yes   ⭕ No   ⭕ Not sure

4. Do you think that a hacker would make a good consultant on computer security?

▼ EXPAND THE IDEAS

1. Should it be a crime to steal a copy of computer data while leaving the original data in place and unaltered? Why or why not? Write a short paper on detailing your opinion and supporting your position.

2. Who's in cybercrime news these days? Are there any new techniques being used to catch cybercriminals? Research the current news items and past stories. Who is Mafiaboy and what has happened to him? Where is Kevin Mitnick today? Compile your findings in a short report. Include your resources as part of the report.

3. Should hackers be sent to jail if they cannot pay restitution to companies and individuals who lost money as the result of a prank? Do you think that a hacker would make a good consultant on computer security? Why or why not? Based on what you read, do you think Mitnick's sentence was fair? Write a short paper on detailing your opinion and supporting your positions.

End of Unit Exercises

▼ KEY TERMS

Antivirus software	DOCSIS	Personal firewall	Stealth virus
Backup	File virus	Polymorphic virus	Surge strip
Biometrics	Full backup	Power failure	Trigger event
Boot disk	Incremental backup	Power spike	Trojan horse
Boot sector virus	Macro	Power strip	UPS (uninterruptible power
Checksum	Macro virus	Power surge	supply)
Computer virus	MTBF	Recovery CD	User rights
Copy Disk utility	Multi-partite virus	Rescue disk	Virus hoax
Data security	Network address translation	Restore	Virus signature
Denial of Service attack	(NAT)	Retro virus	Windows Startup Disk
Differential backup	Operator error	Risk management	Worm
Direct source input device			

▼ UNIT REVIEW

1. Use your own words to define bold terms that appear throughout the unit. List 10 of the terms that are least familiar to you and write a sentence for each of them.

2. Create a chart to review the factors that cause data loss or misuse. List the factors you learned about in this unit in the first column. Then place an X in the appropriate column to indicate whether that factor leads to data loss, inaccurate data, stolen data, or intentionally damaged data. Some factors might have more than one X.

3. Summarize what you have learned about viruses, Trojan horses, and software worms.

4. Make a checklist of steps to follow if you suspect that your computer is infected with a virus.

5. You receive three e-mail messages as follows:

   a. an e-mail attachment called Read this.txt.vbs. Because it appears to have two filename extensions, should you assume that this file harbors a virus?

   b. an e-mail message from a friend that says, "My antivirus software says that an attachment I received from you contains the QAZ virus." Would you assume that this message from your friend is a hoax?

   c. a message from an address you can't recognize with several lines of forwarded text that states that "If you receive an e-mail entitled "Badtimes", delete it IMMEDIATELY. Do not open it. Apparently this one is pretty nasty. It will not only erase everything on your hard drive, but it will also delete anything on disks within 20 feet of your computer." Do you believe it? Would you assume that this message is a hoax?

6. List the filename extensions of files that might typically harbor a virus.

7. Explain how multi-partite, stealth, polymorphic, and retro viruses work.

8. Explain how antivirus software works and how it is able to catch new viruses that are created after the software is installed on your computer.

9. Describe the various types of boot disks that might help you recover from a hard disk crash.

10. Devise a backup plan for the computer you use regularly. Explain how you would implement your plan.

▼ FILL IN THE BEST ANSWER

1. A(n) _____ is a device containing a battery that provides a continuous supply of power and other circuitry to prevent spikes and surges from reaching your computer.

2. Although a(n) _____ contains multiple outlets for power plugs, it does not contain the electronics necessary to filter out power spikes and surges.

3. The _____ is calculated by observing test equipment in a laboratory, then dividing the number of failures by the total number of hours of observation.

4. Three methods of personal identification used to restrict access: something a person knows, something a person carries, or some unique _____ characteristics.

5. A method of personal identification called _____ bases identification on some physical trait, such as a fingerprint or the pattern of blood vessels in the retina of the eye.

6. User _____ are rules that limit the directories and files that each user can access.

7. A computer _____ is a program that attaches itself to a file and reproduces itself so as to spread from one file to another.

8. A boot _____ virus infects the system files that your computer uses every time you turn it on.

9. A Trojan _____ is a computer program that seems to perform one function while actually doing something else.

10. Viruses often attach themselves to a program file with a(n) _____ extension so that when you run the program, you also run the virus code.

11. Unlike a virus, which is designed to spread from file to file, a(n) _____ is designed to spread from computer to computer.

12. A virus can enter a computer as an e-mail attachment or as a script in an e-mail message formatted as _____.

13. Antivirus software calculates a(n) _____ to make sure that the bytes in an executable file have not changed from one computing session to another.

14. _____ viruses remove their signatures from a disk in order to conceal themselves in memory temporarily, and avoid detection by antivirus software.

15. A virus that doesn't really exist is referred to as a virus _____.

16. Some full-system backups miss the Windows _____ because that file is always open while the computer is on.

17. The three types of backup plans are full, _____, and differential.

18. A(n) _____ disk is a floppy disk or CD that contains the operating system files needed to start your computer without accessing the hard disk.

19. It is important to test your _____ and restore procedures to make sure that you can successfully recover your data.

20. Many personal computer operating systems provide a(n) _____ utility that makes an exact copy of a floppy disk.

▼ PRACTICE TESTS

When you use the Interactive CD, you can take Practice Tests that consist of 10 multiple-choice, true/false, and fill-in-the-blank questions. The questions are selected at random from a large test bank, so each time you take a test, you'll receive a different set of questions. Your tests are scored immediately, and you can print study guides to determine which questions you answered incorrectly. If you are using a Tracking Disk, insert it in the floppy disk drive to save your test scores.

▼ INDEPENDENT CHALLENGE 1

Losing data can be devastating to a business and certainly upsetting to an individual. We have all experienced that moment of panic when we go to retrieve a file only to receive some error message when we try to open it or find that it isn't where we thought we saved it. Describe a situation in which you or someone you know lost data stored on a computer.

Write a brief essay that answers the following questions:

1. Was the data lost, stolen, or just inaccessible? What caused the data loss?

2. What steps could have been taken to prevent the loss?

3. What steps could you or this other person have taken to recover the lost data?

▼ INDEPENDENT CHALLENGE 2

Do you have a plan for data recovery in place for your computer data? Are you working at a company that practices data backup and recovery on a regular basis? Is there antivirus software in place on the computer you use regularly? Assess the risk to the programs and data files stored on the hard disk drive of your computer.

Write a brief essay that answers the following questions:

1. What threats are likely to cause your data to be lost, stolen, or damaged?

2. How many data files do you have?

3. If you add up the size of all your files, how many megabytes of data do you have?

4. How many of these files are critical and would need to be replaced if you lost all of your data?

5. What would you need to do to reconstruct the critical files if the hard disk drive failed and you did not have any backups?

6. What measures could you use to protect your data from the threats you identified in Question 1? What is the cost of each of these measures?

7. Taking into account the threats to your data, the importance of your data, and the cost of possible protective measures, what do you think is the best plan for the security of your own data?

▼ INDEPENDENT CHALLENGE 3

If you suspect your computer has become infected with a virus, it is prudent to activate virus detection software to scan your files immediately. With the continued spread of viruses, virus detection software has become an essential utility in today's computing environment. Many virus detection software packages are available in computer stores, on computer bulletin boards, and on the Internet.

1. Find information about three virus detection software packages. Write a brief report on each one, and compare and contrast the features and benefits of each.

2. Microsoft Word documents can harbor macro viruses. This type of virus is documented in many sources. Using library or Internet resources, find a list of symptoms for the Word macro virus that is currently circulating. Write a one-page report describing what you learned about the Word macro virus and its presence on, or absence from, the documents you have on your disks.

3. Use the latest version of your virus protection software to check your disks to see whether you have the Word macro virus and to check the list of signatures in your virus software to see whether the virus is listed there.

▼ INDEPENDENT CHALLENGE 4

An Internet worm created concern about the security of data on military and research computer systems, and it raised ethical questions about the rights and responsibilities of computer users. Select one of the following statements and write a two-page paper that argues for or against it. Use the Internet or library resources to learn more about each viewpoint. Be sure to include the resources you used in a bibliography. Whatever viewpoint you decide to present, make sure that you back it up with facts and references to authoritative articles and Web pages. You can place citations to these pages (include the author's name, article title, date of publication, and URL) at the end of your paper as endnotes, on each page as footnotes, or along with the appropriate paragraphs using parentheses.

1. People have the right to hone their computing skills by breaking into computers. As a computer scientist once said, "The right to hack is held higher than the right of someone to tell you not to. It's an inalienable right."

2. If problems exist, it is acceptable to use any means to point them out. The computer science student who created the Internet worm was perfectly justified in claiming that he should not be prosecuted because he was just trying to point out that security holes exist in large computer networks.

3. Computer crimes are no different from other crimes, and computer criminals should be held responsible for the damage they cause by paying for the time and cost of replacing or restoring data.

▼ INDEPENDENT CHALLENGE 5

Obtain a copy of your school or work place's student/employee code or computer use policy. If your school or work place does not have a student/employee code or a computer use policy, use your favorite search engine to find one on the Internet. Use the document you select to write a brief paper that answers the following questions:

1. To whom does the policy apply: students, faculty, staff, community members, others?

2. What types of activities does the policy specifically prohibit?

3. If a computer crime is committed, would the crime be dealt with by campus authorities or by state law enforcement agents?

4. Does the policy state the penalties for computer crimes? If so, what are they?

▼ INDEPENDENT CHALLENGE 6

Suppose that you work as a reporter for a local television station. Your boss wants the station to run a 90-second story about virus hoaxes and gives you the responsibility for writing the script. The basic objectives of the story are: (1) to remind people not to panic when they receive e-mail about viruses and (2) to provide a set of concrete steps that a person could take to discover whether a virus threat is real or a hoax. Of course, your boss wants the story to be interesting, so you have to include a human-interest angle.

1. Write the script for the story, including notes about the visuals that will appear.

2. Create a storyboard that outlines the first few scenes of the story.

3. There are several Web sites that list virus hoaxes. Use your favorite search engine to research recent hoaxes. You can use the www.urbanlegends.com Web page to find recent virus hoaxes.

4. Write a summary of two hoaxes to include in the script.

▼ INDEPENDENT CHALLENGE 7

Is it a good idea to use the Web to backup your data? Is this something that individuals as well as businesses should consider? At what point would a small business choose this option? What are the benefits and risks?

1. Log onto the Internet and then investigate a Web site that provides storage for data backups.

2. Find out the cost of using the site and investigate the site's terms and conditions for use. Try to discover if data stored at the site would be secure and private. Also try to determine whether the backup and restore procedures seem feasible. Try to determine whether a plan exists for notifying customers if the site is about to go out of business. You might also look for a review of the backup provider at sites such as www.zdnet.com or www.cnet.com.

3. After completing your research, organize your notes into a two-page paper that explains whether or not you would use the site for storing your backups.

▼ LAB: BACKING UP YOUR COMPUTER

1. Start the interactive part of the lab. Insert your Tracking Disk if you want to save your QuickCheck results. Perform each of the lab steps as directed and answer all of the lab QuickCheck questions. When you exit the lab, your answers are automatically graded and your results are displayed.

2. Describe where most of your data files are stored and estimate how many megabytes of data (not programs) you have in all of these files. Next, take a close look at these files and estimate how much data (in megabytes) you cannot afford to lose. Finally, explain what you think would be the best hardware device for backing up this amount of data.

3. Draw a sketch or capture a screenshot of the Microsoft Backup window's toolbar. Use ToolTips or the window's status bar to find the name of each toolbar button. Use this information to label the buttons on your sketch or screenshot.

4. Assume that you will use Microsoft Backup to make a backup of your data files. Describe the backup procedure you would use to specify the folders that you must include. It is not necessary to list individual files unless they are not within one of the folders that you would back up. Make sure that you indicate whether or not you would use password protection, the type of compression that you would select, and how you would handle the Windows Registry.

▼ VISUAL WORKSHOP

As network technologies continue to emerge, security will always be a factor, and businesses and consumers will find themselves asking, "How vulnerable is our business data?" Virtual private networks (VPNs) are an advancement in network systems that are used to provide secure private network access over an otherwise insecure public access network, typically the Internet. VPNs are generally less expensive than establishing and maintaining a private network over private lines. VPNs allow businesses to provide secure communications and connections over the Internet. Figure F-26 shows a Web page from a company that provides VPN services.

FIGURE F-26

Log onto the Internet and use a favorite search engine to find businesses that offer VPN service.

1. Review three Web sites.

2. Use the information on the Web site and other resources to define VPN and briefly describe how it works.

3. Create a table that compares the VPN services offered by the three companies you researched.

4. Summarize by stating why you would or would not use a VPN as a backup resource.

UNIT G

The Web and E-commerce

OBJECTIVES

Explore Web technology

Explore HTML

Use Web browsers

Understand HTTP and Web servers

Introduce Web page authoring

Enhance Web pages

Explore navigation elements

Organize information on Web pages

Introduce cookies

Introduce e-commerce

Execute e-commerce transactions

Tech Talk: Encryption

Unit G focuses on the Web and the variety of key technologies that make the Web what it is today. The unit begins with an introduction to the technologies that bring the Web to your computer screen. The unit continues by exploring the tools that make it possible to create and enhance Web pages while providing a consistent look across all pages in a Web site. You will also explore e-commerce topics and learn about buying and selling merchandise and services over the Web. The unit wraps up with a Tech Talk section on encryption.

Exploring Web technology

Although many people use the terms interchangeably, there is a difference between the Web and the Internet. The Internet is basically a collection of computers and cables that forms a communications network. The Internet carries a variety of data, including e-mail, videoconferences, and instant messages. The Web is a collection of documents that can be accessed over the Internet and can be related by using links. This lesson discusses technologies (HTTP, HTML, Web servers, URLs, and browsers) behind the Web.

DETAILS

- Two of the most important elements of the Web are Hypertext Transfer Protocol (HTTP) and Hypertext Markup Language (HTML). **HTTP** is the communications protocol used to transport data over the Web. HTML is the set of specifications used to create Web pages. Notice that both of these Web elements contain hypertext in their names. **Hypertext** is a key concept for understanding the Web.

  The idea of hypertext originated much earlier than the Web, or even the Internet, when in 1945, an engineer named Vannevar Bush described a machine that could link associated information or ideas through trails. The idea resurfaced in the mid-1960s, when Harvard graduate Ted Nelson coined the term hypertext to describe a computer system that could store literary documents, link them according to logical relationships, and allow readers to comment and annotate what they read. Nelson sketched the diagram shown in Figure G-1 to explain his idea. This early sketch of project Xanadu, a distant relative of the Web, used the terms links and web.

  In 1990, a British scientist named Tim Berners-Lee developed specifications for HTML, HTTP, and URLs. He hoped that these technologies would help researchers share information by creating access to a sort of web of electronic documents. In the words of Berners-Lee, "The Web is an abstract (imaginary) space of information. On the Net, you find computers; on the Web, you find documents, sounds, videos, and information. On the Net, the connections are cables between computers; on the Web, connections are hypertext links."

- A **Web server** stores one or more Web pages that form a Web site. Each page is stored as a file called an **HTML document**—a text, or ASCII, document with embedded HTML tags. Some of these tags specify how the document is to be displayed when viewed in a browser. Other tags contain **hyper-text links** (or simply links) to related documents, graphics, and sound files that are also stored on Web servers. You can click a hypertext link—an underlined word or phrase—to access related documents. In addition to storing these files, a Web server runs software that handles requests for specific Web pages.

- Every Web page is a document stored on a Web server and identified by a unique address called a **URL (Uniform Resource Locator)**.

- You use Web client software called a **browser** to view Web pages. When you type a URL into the browser's address box, you are requesting the HTML document for the Web page that you want to view. Your browser creates a request for the specified file using a command provided by the HTTP communications protocol. The request is sent to a Web server, which has been listening for HTTP requests. When your request arrives, the Web server examines it, locates the HTML document that you requested, and sends it back to your computer. If additional elements are needed to view the Web page correctly—a graphic, for example—your browser must issue a new request to the server for that element. The cycle continues until the Web page appears in your browser window. Figure G-2 illustrates the entire process.

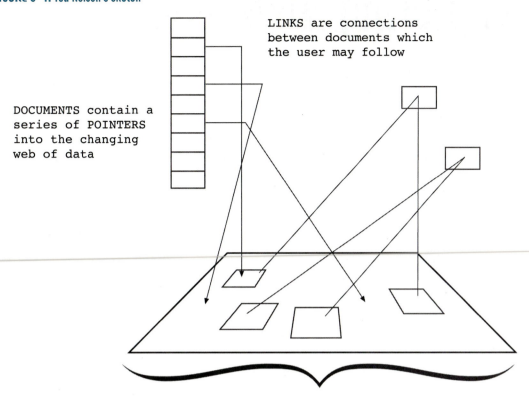

LINKS are connections
between documents which
the user may follow

DOCUMENTS contain a
series of POINTERS
into the changing
web of data

Expanding Tissue of Text,
Data, and Graphics

FIGURE G-2: How browsers and Web servers exchange HTTP messages

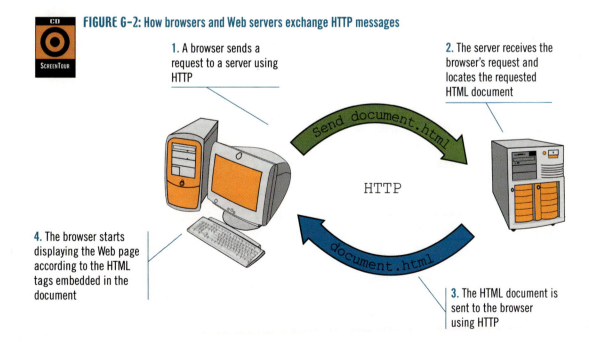

1. A browser sends a
request to a server using
HTTP

2. The server receives the
browser's request and
locates the requested
HTML document

Send document.html

HTTP

document.html

4. The browser starts
displaying the Web page
according to the HTML
tags embedded in the
document

3. The HTML document is
sent to the browser
using HTTP

Exploring HTML

HTML (Hypertext Markup Language) is a set of specifications for creating HTML documents that a browser can display as a Web page. HTML is called a **markup language** because authors mark up their documents by inserting special instructions called **HTML tags** that specify how the document should appear when displayed on a computer screen or printed. The original HTML specifications that were developed by Tim Berners-Lee in 1990 have been revised several times by an organization called the **World Wide Web Consortium (W3C)**. This lesson discusses how the current HTML specifications work to display the lines of text on your computer screen in the right color and size and to position graphics in your browser.

DETAILS

- In an HTML document, HTML tags, such as <HR> and <B>, are enclosed in angle brackets. These tags are treated as instructions to the browser. When your browser displays a Web page on your computer screen, it does not show the tags or angle brackets. Instead, it follows the instructions specified by the tags.

  Most HTML tags work in pairs. An opening tag begins an instruction, which stays in effect until a closing tag appears. Closing tags always contain a slash. For example, the following sentence contains opening and closing bold tags:

  <B>Caterpillars</B> love sugar.
  When displayed by a browser, the word "Caterpillars" will be bold, but the other words in the sentence will not. HTML is not a case-sensitive language, so tags may be entered as uppercase, lowercase, or a mixture of both.

- HTML documents contain no graphics. So, in addition to specifying how text should be formatted, HTML tags can be used to specify how to incorporate graphics on a page. The <IMG SRC> tag is used to specify the name and location of a graphic file that is to be displayed as part of a Web page. Figure G-3 illustrates how browsers use HTML tags to display content.

- HTML tags also produce the links that connect you to other Web documents. The <A HREF> tag

specifies the information necessary to display the links that allow you to jump to related Web pages. Each link carries the URL for the page that is the destination for the link.

- HTML includes hundreds of tags. For convenience, tags are classified into four groups. See Table G-1. **Operational tags** specify the basic setup for a Web page, provide ways for users to interact with a page, and offer ways for Web pages to incorporate information derived from databases. **Formatting tags** change the appearance of text and work much like the formatting options in a word processor to create bold and italic text, adjust the size of text, change the color of text and backgrounds, arrange text in table format, or align text on a page. **Link tags** specify where and how to display links to other Web pages and e-mail addresses. **Media tags** specify how to display media elements, such as graphics, sound clips, or videos.

- The term Web page refers to both the HTML document and the corresponding Web page that is displayed by your browser. The term source is used to refer to the document that has the HTML tags. Most browsers include a menu option that allows you to view the source HTML document with its HTML tags. For example, when using the Internet Explorer browser, you can click View on the menu bar, then click Source. See Figure G-4.

FIGURE G-3: How browsers interpret HTML tags

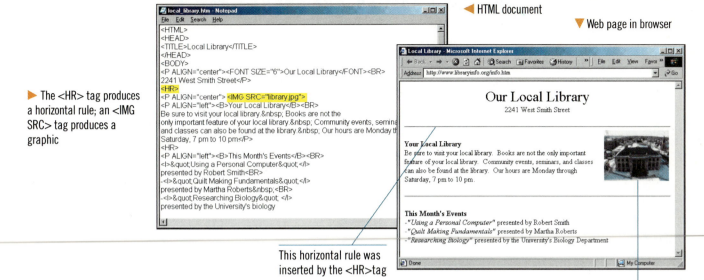

◀ HTML document

▼ Web page in browser

▶ The <HR> tag produces a horizontal rule; an <IMG SRC> tag produces a graphic

This horizontal rule was inserted by the <HR>tag

This graphic was inserted by the <IMG SRC> tag

TABLE G-1: Examples of basic HTML tags

TAG	DESCRIPTION AND USE	CATEGORY
<HTML> </HTML>	Place the <HTML> tag at the beginning of a document and place the </HTML> tag at the end of the document.	Operational
<TITLE> </TITLE>	Place immediately after the <HTML> tag. The text between the TITLE tags will appear on the browser's title bar.	Operational
<FONT SIZE=+3> ... </FONT>	To specify a font size, use a positive or negative number in place of +3.	Formatting
 	The BR tag creates a line break.	Formatting
<A HREF = " "> ... </A>	To create an underlined link, place the URL for the link between the quotation marks, then type the link name between the tags.	Link
<IMG SRC=" ">	To display a graphic, place its filename between the quotation marks.	Media

FIGURE G-4: Viewing the source HTML document

Using Web browsers

A **Web browser**, usually referred to simply as a browser, is a software program that runs on your computer and helps you access Web pages. Technically, a browser is the client half of the client/server software that facilitates communication between a personal computer and Web server. The software on the Web server is the 'server' side of the system. The browser is installed on your computer, and the Web server software is installed on a host computer on the Internet. This lesson discusses the roles your browser plays, gives an overview of the various browsers that are available, and explains how helper applications, plug-ins, and players work with your browser to display Web pages.

Info Web

BROWSER PLAYERS

DETAILS

- Your browser plays two roles in accessing and displaying Web pages. First, a browser uses HTTP to send messages to a Web server—usually a request for a specific HTML document. Second, when it receives an HTML document from a Web server, your browser interprets the HTML tags in order to display the requested Web page.

- Popular browsers include Internet Explorer (IE), Netscape Navigator, and Opera. Internet Explorer and Netscape Navigator share similar features—perhaps because they evolved from the earliest graphical browser, Mosaic. Opera is an alternative that offers unique features such as multi-page display, which IE and Navigator do not offer. Table G-2 provides a brief history of popular Web browsers.

- All browsers are designed to interpret HTML documents. Modern browsers also handle additional file formats, such as GIF and JPEG graphic formats. However, if you click a link that leads to a file that your browser cannot handle, you will see a message that directs you to download the software necessary to read the file format. For example, you might be directed to the Adobe Web site to download the Acrobat Reader software, which handles PDF (Portable Document Format) files and lets you view documents created from a variety of desktop publishing applications uniformly on any system.

- The software that your browser uses to read file formats other than HTML is referred to as a helper application, a plug-in, or a player. A **helper application** is a program that understands how to work with a specific file format. When a helper application is installed, it updates your computer system so that your browser knows which file formats it can accept. Whenever your browser encounters a non-HTML file format,

it automatically runs the corresponding helper application, which in turn opens the file. A helper application opens a new window for displaying the file. A **plug-in** is similar to a helper application, but it displays files within the browser window.

In today's computing environment, the distinction between helper applications and plug-ins is disappearing because Web development tools provide so much flexibility for specifying how auxiliary programs will handle files. The current trend is to use the term player to refer to any helper application or plug-in that helps a browser display a particular file format. When you're using the Netscape Navigator browser, you can see a list of installed players. See Figure G-5. Although IE does not provide a list of installed players, they are included in the list of applications maintained by the Control Panel's Add/Remove Programs icon.

- It is a good idea to upgrade when a new version of your browser appears. You can get up-to-date browser functionality and often increased security simply by spending a few minutes downloading and installing an update. Because Web pages may depend on new HTML features that are supported only by the latest browser versions, you might encounter errors as your browser tries to display a page, but cannot interpret some of the HTML without the latest upgrade. In other cases, your browser might display the Web page without errors, but you will not see all of the intended effects.

Another important reason to upgrade is increased security. As hackers discover and take advantage of security holes, browser publishers try to patch them. Upgrades typically contain patches for known security holes, though new features in the upgrade may open new ones.

TABLE G-2: A brief history of browsers

BROWSER	IMPORTANT DATES	AVAILABLE FOR	DESCRIPTION
Mosaic	Introduced November 1993, NCSA discontinued Mosaic support in 1997	Macintosh, PC, and UNIX operating systems	The earliest graphical browsers, developed at the University of Illinois National Center for Supercomputing Applications (NCSA), also licensed and sold as Spyglass
Netscape Navigator	Version 1.0 published in December 1994; in 1998 became available as open source software through an organization called Mozilla; version 6.0 appeared in 2001	Mac and PC platforms, Linux and several versions of UNIX	Developed by a group of programmers who worked on Mosaic; quickly became the most popular browser, numerous revisions added pioneering features such as frames, plug-ins, and JavaScript support
Internet Explorer (IE)	Version 1.0 was published by Microsoft in August 1995; version 4.0 appeared in 1997; version 6.0 appeared in 2001	Mac and PC platforms, Linux and several versions of UNIX	Original IE 1.0 browser code was licensed from Spyglass; not until 1997 did it match and then surpass Navigator's popularity
Opera	Published in December 1996	Windows, Linux, UNIX, and Mac OS	Opera began as a Telenor (Norwegian phone company) project to develop a small and fast browser for computers with meager memory and processing resources; Opera was written from scratch, and as a result, it has some unique features, such as page zoom and a multi-document display

FIGURE G-5: Viewing installed players in Netscape Navigator

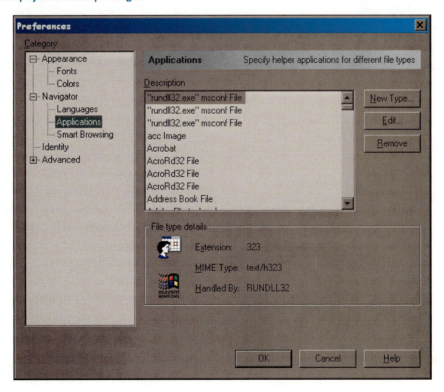

Understanding HTTP and Web servers

HTTP is a communications protocol that works in conjunction with the TCP/IP communications protocol to get Web resources to your desktop. A **Web resource** is any data file that has a URL, such as an HTML document, a graphic, or a sound file. This lesson explains how HTTP works with Web servers to send and receive Web resources.

DETAILS

● HTTP includes commands called methods that help browsers communicate with Web servers. GET is the most frequently used HTTP method and is typically used to retrieve the text and graphics files necessary for displaying a Web page. HTTP transports a request for a Web resource to a Web server, then transports the Web server's response back to a browser.

● An HTTP communications transaction takes place over a pair of sockets. A **socket** is an abstract concept that represents one end of a connection. In an HTTP communications transaction, your browser opens a socket, connects to a similar open socket at the Web server, and issues a command like "send me an HTML document." The server receives the command, executes it, and sends a response back through the socket. The sockets are then closed until the browser is ready to issue another command. Figure G-6 illustrates how the messages flow between your browser and a Web server in order to retrieve an HTML document.

● HTTP is classified as a **stateless protocol**, which generally allows one request and one response per session. As a result, your browser can request an HTML document during a session, but as soon as the document is sent, the session is closed, and the Web server will forget that your browser ever made a request. To make additional requests, your browser must make another HTTP request. This is why assembling a complex Web page with several graphics, buttons, and sounds requires your browser to make many HTTP requests to the Web server.

● A Web server's response to a browser's request includes an **HTTP status code** that indicates whether or not the browser's request can be fulfilled. You may have encountered the "404 Not Found" message that a browser displays when a Web server sends a 404 status code to indicate that the requested resource does not exist. HTTP status codes are summarized in Table G-3.

● A Web server is configured to include HTTP software, which is always running when the server is up and ready to fulfill requests. One of the server's ports is dedicated to listening for

HTTP requests. When a request arrives, the server software analyzes the request and takes whatever action is necessary to fulfill it. The computer that runs Web server software might have other software running on it as well. For example, a computer might operate as a Web server, as an e-mail server, and as an FTP (File Transfer Protocol) server all at the same time! To handle these diverse duties efficiently, a computer devotes one port to HTTP requests (usually Port 80), another to handling e-mail (usually Port 25), and a third to FTP requests (usually Port 21).

In the context of TCP/IP networks, the term port is a logical, not physical, connection point between two network nodes. A **logical port**, such as Port 80, is created by communications software and uses whatever network interface cards and cables provide the standard Internet connection. See Figure G-7.

● The way that a computer allocates one port to each service helps explain how it is possible for a Web service to be down when the Web server is still up and running. A Web server runs separate software for each service it offers. As long as the right software is running, the service is available.

● A single port on a Web server can connect to many sockets carrying requests from browsers. The number of socket connections a port can handle depends on the server's memory and operating system, but at minimum, hundreds of requests can be handled at the same time. Some large-volume sites, such as yahoo.com and amazon.com, have more traffic than any single Web server can handle. These sites tend to use a group of multiple servers, also known as a **server farm**, to handle the thousands of requests that come in each second.

● Most Web server software can be configured so that the server responds to requests addressed to more than one IP address or domain name. In such a case, one computer running one Web server program can act like multiple Web sites. This type of shared hosting is typically supplied to small Web sites that don't have enough traffic to justify the cost of a dedicated server.

FIGURE G-6: How HTTP messages flow between a browser and a Web server

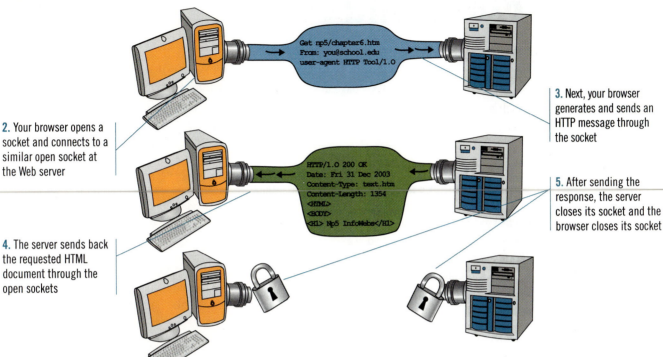

1. The URL in the browser's Address bar contains the domain name of the Web server that your browser contacts

Address www.infoweblinks.com/np5/chapter6.html

Get np5/chapter6.htm
From: you@school.edu
user-agent HTTP Tool/1.0

3. Next, your browser generates and sends an HTTP message through the socket

2. Your browser opens a socket and connects to a similar open socket at the Web server

HTTP/1.0 200 OK
Date: Fri 31 Dec 2003
Content-Type: text.htm
Content-Length: 1354
<HTML>
<BODY>
<H1> Np5 InfoWebs</H1>

5. After sending the response, the server closes its socket and the browser closes its socket

4. The server sends back the requested HTML document through the open sockets

TABLE G-3: HTTP Status Codes

CODE	MESSAGE	DESCRIPTION
200	OK	The request succeeded, and the resulting resource, such as a file or script output, was sent.
301	Moved Permanently	The resource was moved.
302	Moved Temporarily	The resource is temporarily unavailable.
303	See Other	The resource moved to another URL and should be automatically retrieved by the client.
404	Not Found	The requested resource doesn't exist.
500	Server Error	An unexpected server error, such as encountering a scripting error, occurred.

FIGURE G-7: The difference between logical and physical ports

A logical port is a software-based connection

A physical port is a connection point dedicated to a cable or wireless connection; for example, a server's Ethernet port is a physical port—it exists as a real socket for a cable

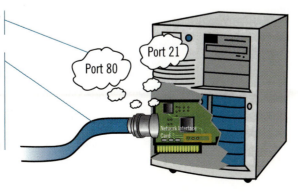

Port 80

Port 21

Network Interface Card

Introducing Web page authoring

With today's Web page authoring tools, it is easy to create your own Web pages. You have several choices when it comes to Web page authoring tools. In this lesson, you'll explore these different tools and get an overview of the basic components of a Web page.

DETAILS

- At the most basic level, you can use a text editor such as NotePad to create Web pages. A **text editor** is similar to word processing software. Unlike word processing software, however, a text editor creates a plain text ASCII document with no hidden formatting codes. See Figure G-8. The only codes included in a document created with a text editor are the HTML tags you type along with the text that you want your browser to display.

  When you save the document you create with a text editor, you must specify an .html or .htm filename extension, so that browsers will recognize it as an HTML document. If you want to create Web pages using a text editor, you will need a good HTML reference book.

- A second way to create Web pages is to use the HTML conversion option included with many software applications. Microsoft Word, for example, allows you to create a standard DOC file and then use the File menu's Save As Web Page option to convert the document into HTML format. Most recent versions of spreadsheet, presentation, or desktop publishing software include HTML capabilities. To discover whether an application has an HTML option, click File on the menu bar, then click Save As or click Export. Converting a document into HTML format sometimes produces an unexpected result because some of the features and formatting in your original document might not translate well into HTML.

- A third option for creating Web pages is to use the online Web page authoring tools provided by some ISPs and other companies that host Web pages. Working with these tools is typically quite simple. You type, select, drag, and drop elements onto a Web page. These simple tools are great for beginners, but they sometimes omit features that are included with more sophisticated authoring tools.

- A fourth way to create Web pages is to use a special category of software called **Web authoring software**, which provides tools specifically designed to enter and format Web page text, graphics, and links. See Figure G-9. Most Web authoring software includes features that help you manage an entire Web site, as opposed to simply creating Web pages. Web site management tools include the capability to link the pages within a site automatically and easily change those links. They are also capable of checking all of the external links at a site to make sure that they still link to valid Web pages.

- Whether you create Web pages using a very basic text editor or a very sophisticated Web authoring program, all Web pages have common characteristics. Figure G-10 illustrates the basic components of a typical Web page.

  The HTML document for a Web page is divided into two sections: the head and the body. If you create an HTML document using a text editor, you must manually enter the tags that begin and end these two sections. If you use Web authoring software, these tags are automatically entered for you. The **head section** begins with the <HEAD> HTML tag and contains information that defines some global properties for the document, but it is not displayed by your browser. Information in the head section of an HTML document can include the following: the title of your page as it will appear in the title bar of your browser window, global formatting information, information about your page that can be used by search engines, and scripts that add interactivity to your page.

  The **body section** of an HTML document begins with the <BODY> HTML tag. It contains the text that you want the browser to display, the HTML tags that format the text, plus a variety of links, including links to graphics. Most Web pages use headers to break up the text into organized sections. A **Web page header** or header is simply a subtitle that appears in a font that is a different size or color than the normal text on the page. HTML supports six pre-defined levels of headers, with H1 using the largest font and H6 using the smallest font.

  Other common characteristics of Web pages include navigation tools such as scroll bars and navigation bars, hyperlinks such as hypertext or graphics, Web page components such as search features, visual elements such as graphics, and multimedia elements such as video, audio, and animation.

FIGURE G-8: Notepad as a Web page authoring tool

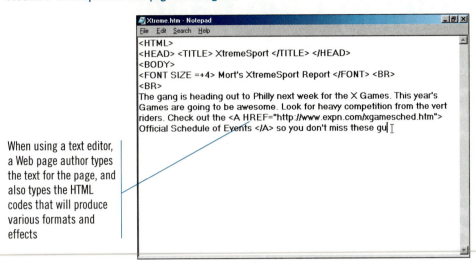

When using a text editor, a Web page author types the text for the page, and also types the HTML codes that will produce various formats and effects

FIGURE G-9: Web authoring software

When creating a Web page, you can type the text without worrying about HTML tags; to format words, phrases, or paragraphs, simply use the formatting buttons on the toolbars

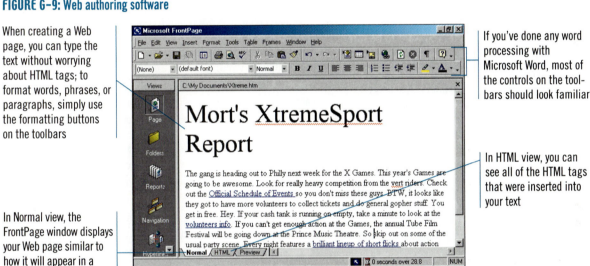

If you've done any word processing with Microsoft Word, most of the controls on the toolbars should look familiar

In HTML view, you can see all of the HTML tags that were inserted into your text

In Normal view, the FrontPage window displays your Web page similar to how it will appear in a browser window

FIGURE G-10: Elements in a typical Web page

Web page title

Theme elements

Header

Graphical link

Non-scrolling frame

Scrolling frame

Graphic

Navigation links

Text link

Enhancing Web pages

Web pages consist of visual elements that enhance the way the information is conveyed. Whether you are creating a Web page or a Web site, it is important that these visual elements have a consistent look and feel. This lesson discusses styles, style sheets, themes, and graphics, which enhance Web pages and create visual consistency.

DETAILS

- A **style** is a combination of attributes—colors, sizes, and fonts—that specify the way text is displayed. When working with Web page authoring software, you can simply highlight the text that you want to format and select the formatting attributes from a list. When you create Web pages with a text editor, you can format text by inserting the appropriate HTML tags. Table G-4 provides a list of basic HTML formatting tags.

- When creating a Web page or a Web site, you want to be sure that your styles are consistent. Manually inserting styles can be time-consuming and can also result in inconsistencies, because styles you apply to one element must be applied to all occurrences of that element on all pages in the Web site. If you have more than a few styles in a Web page, you must apply those styles consistently to the other pages in the Web site. You can use a style sheet to ensure this consistency.

  A **style sheet**, also called a **cascading style sheet (CSS)**, acts as a template to control the layout and design of Web pages. Style sheets work in conjunction with HTML tags to make it easy to change the format of elements in a Web page globally and consistently. They allow Web page authors to separate the format specifications for an element from the element itself. A style sheet allows you simply to define the style for an element, such as a price list, once at the beginning of the HTML document, then apply it by using a single HTML tag (if you are using a text editor), or by selecting the format from a list (if you are using Web page authoring software). You can also set up an **external style sheet** that contains formatting specifications for a group of Web pages. All Web pages in a Web site can use the external style sheet by means of a link placed in their head sections.

  Style sheets make it easy to apply styles and change them consistently. For example, if you define the style for prices in a price list as centered, italic, and red, then every time this style is applied to the prices in a price list they will be centered, italic, and red. If later you decide to change the style associated with prices to different specifications, such as right-aligned, bold, and blue, you change the specification for the prices style once in the style sheet, not each time the prices style is used.

Changing the style causes the change to cascade through the entire Web page or Web site.

The main disadvantage of style sheets is that some features are not uniformly supported by all browsers. An HTML document that uses style sheets might be displayed differently by Netscape than by IE. If you decide to use style sheets for the Web pages that you create, it is important to preview your pages using the browsers that might be used by visitors to your Web site.

- In addition to styles, themes are often used to enhance Web pages. A **theme** is a collection of coordinated graphics, colors, and fonts applied to individual pages or all pages in a Web site. Themes are generally available as part of Web authoring software.

- Another way to enhance Web pages is through the use of graphics. The HTML document that your browser receives does not contain any graphics but does contain an HTML tag that references a graphic. If you use a text editor to create a Web page, you must enter the complete tag manually. For example, <IMG SRC = "truck.gif"> includes the filename for the truck.gif graphic. When using Web page authoring software, you typically use a menu option to select the graphic from a list of files that are stored on your computer. Figure G-11 illustrates how you insert a graphic when creating a Web page using FrontPage.

  Most of the graphics used for Web pages are stored in **GIF (Graphics Interchange Format)**, **JPEG (Joint Photographics Experts Group)**, or **PNG (Portable Network Graphics)** format. Keeping graphics files small helps Web pages download and appear quickly in the browser window.

  An **animated GIF** is a graphic file that consists of a sequence of frames or related images. When an animated GIF is displayed, your browser cycles through the frames, resulting in a simple, repeating animation. Animated GIFs, like the one presented in the ScreenTour associated with Figure G-12, have become quite popular—perhaps because they are one of the easiest ways to add simple animation to a Web page.

TABLE G-4: HTML formatting tags

TAG	USE
<FONT COLOR = "xxx">	Change the color of text by inserting a color name between the quotes
<FONT SIZE = xxx>	Specify a text size by inserting a number after the equal sign
<B>	Bold text
<I>	Italicize text
<U>	Underline text
<ALIGN = direction>	Align paragraphs by substituting right, center, or left for direction
<BGCOLOR = color>	Specify a background color for the entire page

FIGURE G-11: Inserting a graphic

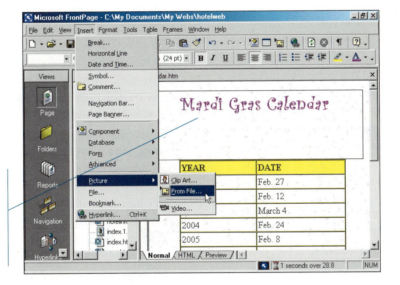

Adding a graphic to this space is simple; use the From File menu option to view a list of graphics stored on your hard disk, and select the one you want to use

FIGURE G-12: Simple animation on a Web page

► An animated GIF adds simple animation to a Web page; in this example, the spacecraft spins to illustrate its operation in space

Exploring navigation elements

For a Web page or Web site to be effective, visitors must be able to move intuitively to the information they want. Web pages should include clear and consistent navigation elements. This lesson looks at navigation elements, such as hypertext links, graphics links, hot spots, and navigation bars, used to make navigating a Web page or Web site easy.

DETAILS

- **Links** (also called hyperlinks) open a location in the same Web page, a different Web page, or a different Web site. Links, whether they are text or graphics, provide the fundamental tools for navigating Web pages. An **internal link** (also called a local link or page link) links to other pages at the same Web site, providing navigation capability. An **external link** (also called a remote link) links to pages outside of the Web site. You can create links to any Web site in the world, but it is a good idea to check the site's policies on external links. An **interpage link** is a type of link usually used to jump to a different location within the current Web page. These links are handy for a long page divided into sections. For example, user group FAQs are often structured as a long page of questions and answers. The page begins with a list of questions, each of which is linked to its answer, which appears farther down the page. A **mailto link** automatically opens a pre-addressed e-mail form that can be filled in and sent. These links are typically used to provide a method for contacting the Webmaster, the Web site's author, or a customer service representative.

- Typically, a link appears on a Web page as underlined, blue text, but a link can also be a graphic such as a picture or a button. The arrow-shaped pointer changes, usually to a pointing hand, when it moves over any text or graphics link in the browser window.

- The HTML that specifies a link typically has two parts: a destination and a label. See Figure G-13. The <A HREF> link tag also allows a Web page author to specify whether the linked page will appear in the current browser window or in a new browser window. You've probably encountered Web page links that create a new window. When used effectively, new windows help you easily return to previous pages. However, too many new windows can clutter your screen.

- Instead of a text label, you can use an image as a clickable link. These graphical links can connect to other Web pages or graphics. You might have encountered graphical links called **thumbnails** that expand in size when clicked. Graphical links can even look like buttons, complete with labels and icons. Figure G-14 shows

the HTML tag you might use to create a clickable image in a Web page.

- While browsing the Web, you've probably encountered graphics that are divided into several clickable areas. These images might be maps that allow you to click a geographic region to view a list of local attractions, businesses, or dealers. You also might encounter technical diagrams that link to information about the part that you click. You might even come across a Web site with a photo on the main page that is divided into areas representing different parts of the Web site.

  A clickable map, photo, or diagram is referred to as an **image map**, and each of the links within the image map is sometimes referred to as a **hot spot**. To create an image map with a text editor, a Web page author uses a set of HTML tags that specify the coordinates and destination page for each clickable hot spot. A Web page authoring tool typically makes it easy to drag over an area of an image, then use menus and dialog boxes to specify the destination page for each hot spot.

- Most Web pages include link bars. A **link bar** contains links to other pages in a Web site based on the hierarchy—the relationship—of the pages. Themes often include link bars, which appear as the same graphic links and in the same location on each page. Figure G-15 shows a link bar in a Web page.

- A Web page link only works as long as a file with the corresponding URL exists on the server. A non-functioning link is called a **broken link**. If a Webmaster moves, deletes, or changes the name of the requested file, the link will not function properly. If a broken link points to a non-existent HTML document, your browser typically produces a 404 Page Not Found error. When a broken link points to a non-existent graphic or other non-HTML format file, your browser typically displays a broken link icon.

- It is the responsibility of Web page authors to check the links on their Web pages periodically to make sure they work. To test links, an author can click through them manually or use the link-checking feature of Web authoring software. Bad links must be removed or edited to reflect the correct URL for a destination page.

FIGURE G-13: A link to display another Web page

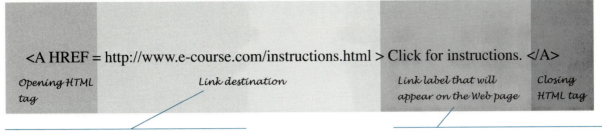

<A HREF = http://www.e-course.com/instructions.html > Click for instructions. </A>

Opening HTML tag   *Link destination*   *Link label that will appear on the Web page*   *Closing HTML tag*

The destination specifies a URL, usually the Web page that will appear as a result of clicking the link

The label is the wording for the underlined text that appears on the Web page as the clickable link

FIGURE G-14: A link to display a graphic

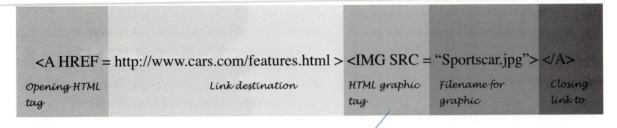

<A HREF = http://www.cars.com/features.html > <IMG SRC = "Sportscar.jpg"> </A>

Opening HTML tag   *Link destination*   *HTML graphic tag*   *Filename for graphic*   *Closing link to*

The <IMG SRC> tag contains the name of the graphics file; the graphic appears on the Web page as a clickable link; when a visitor clicks the image of the sports car, a list of its features appears on the screen

FIGURE G-15: A link bar

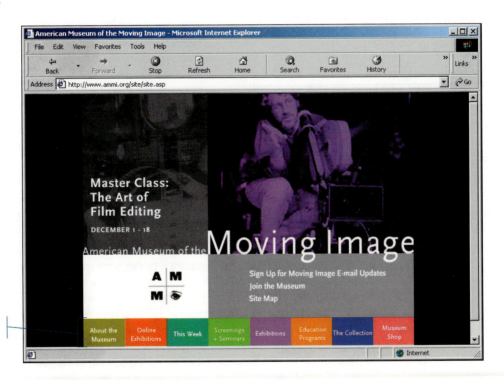

Link bar to pages in this Web site

Organizing information on Web pages

If the information in your Web page is not organized into logical areas, it will not be usable by visitors. Tables and frames are tools you can use to help organize areas of text or graphics on a page. This lesson explains how to use tables and frames to layout the content on a Web page. Once you have finished your pages, you must test and publish them. Table G-5 gives you tips for testing and publishing your completed HTML documents.

DETAILS

- A **Web page table** (usually referred to simply as a "table") is a grid of cells that can be used as a layout tool for specifying the placement of text and graphics on a Web page. Tables are an important part of Web page design because HTML does not include a formatting feature for multiple columns. Without tables, authors have less control over the position of text and graphics displayed in the browser window. The effectiveness of tables is illustrated in Figure G-16, where one Web page uses tables and the other page does not.

- Web tables provide Web page designers with flexibility. For example, the cells of a table can contain text or graphics; columns and rows in a table can be different sizes. Individual cells can be sized according to the material they contain and their contents can be formatted individually. Many Web page designers put the entire contents of a Web page into a single table. These features make Web tables a flexible layout tool.

- Tables are very easy to use, whether you create them with Web authoring software or with word processing software that converts documents into HTML format. You simply define the number of columns and rows for a table, then specify the size for

each row and each column. You can merge two or more cells to create a larger cell, or you can split a cell to make smaller cells.

Creating tables with a text editor is more of a challenge. You use a variety of HTML tags to specify the beginning of the table, each row, and each cell in the row. What makes this task particularly difficult is that you cannot see the table as you construct it. To view the table, you must preview your Web page using your browser.

- In addition to Web tables, designers often use frames to create Web pages. An **HTML frame** (or simply frame) is a part of a Web page that scrolls independently of other parts of the Web page. The main advantage of frames is the ability to display multiple documents at once. Frames can also be used to provide navigation elements, such as a link bar. A typical use of frames, shown in Figure G-17, is to display a stationary banner at the top of a page and a set of links on the left side of the screen that do not move as you scroll through the main text on the Web page.

Until HTML version 4.0 was introduced in 1997, some browsers did not support frames. You might still find Web sites that include no frames versions of their Web pages, but today, all of the popular browsers support frames.

TABLE G-5: Testing and publishing Web pages

STEPS	DESCRIPTION
Test each page locally	You must test your Web page locally to verify that every element is displayed correctly by any browsers that might be used by visitors to your Web page. You can accomplish this task without connecting to the Web. Simply open a browser, then enter the local filename for the HTML document that you created for your Web page. Because your hard disk drive is much faster than a dial-up connection, the text and graphics for your Web page will appear faster during your local test than when viewed over the Internet.
Transfer pages to a Web server	Whether you're publishing a single page, a series of pages, or an entire Web site, you must put your pages on a Web server. Although Web server software is available for your home computer, you probably will not want to leave your computer continually linked to the Internet. Instead, you should look for a Web hosting site that will host your pages, usually for a monthly fee.
Review all content and test all links	After you publish your pages on a Web server, make sure that all content appears as expected. Be sure to test the links between your pages, as well as the links to pages on other sites.
Update your site to keep it current	Periodically, you should review the information on your Web pages and verify that the links still connect to existing Web pages. You can easily change your pages and then test them offline before reposting them.

FIGURE G-16: Using tables

▶ The Web page that's displayed at the top uses a table to position graphics and text; without a table, the Web page below simply displays text and graphics in a single column

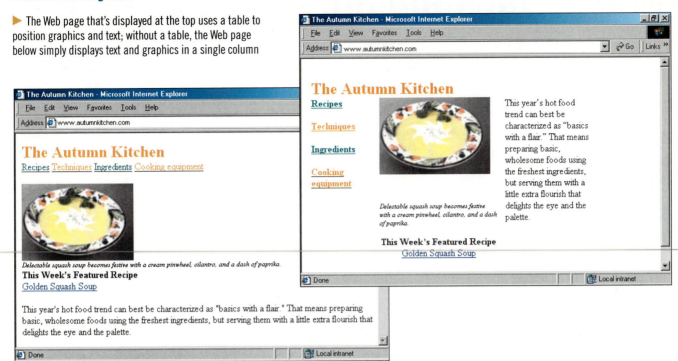

FIGURE G-17: Using frames

▶ A frame can be stationary, or it can scroll independently of the text and graphics in other frames

The left frame remains stationary

The upper frame remains stationary

The main frame scrolls

Introducing cookies

While browsing the Web, you might encounter a message like "Do you want to accept a cookie?" This message is not a joke or a malicious virus preparing to attack your computer. This message is a polite way of asking if you'll permit a Web site to collect and store some information about you. Not all sites ask your permission before creating cookies; in fact, most sites proceed on the assumption that you'll have no objection to the use of cookies. This lesson explains what cookies are and how they work on the Web.

DETAILS

- A **cookie** is data generated by a Web server and stored in a text file on your computer. Cookies allow a Web site to store information on a client computer for later retrieval. Cookies are used to remind a Web server who you are each time your browser makes a request. Cookies can also be used to store information necessary to keep track of your preferences and activities while visiting a Web site.

- Web sites use cookies to track your path through a site—to help the site remember the pages you viewed or the items you purchased. Cookies provide information that allows the Web site to present you with ad banners targeted to products you previously purchased at that Web site. Cookies retain personal information that you type into a Web page form.

- When your browser connects to a Web site that uses cookies, it receives an HTTP Set-cookie message from the Web server. This cookie message contains some information that your browser stores on your computer's hard disk. The cookie information can include a customer number, a shopping cart number, a part number, or any other data. In addition, the cookie usually contains the date the cookie expires and the domain name of the Web server that created the cookie. Any server that creates a cookie can request it the next time you connect to one of its Web pages.

- Cookies provide a way to store information as you link from one page to another page on a Web site. Because the data is stored on your computer rather than on the Web server, it doesn't require server space, it requires very little server processing time, and the Web server is not responsible for the security of the cookie data.

- Cookies don't use your name for identification purposes. Instead, a Web server provides your browser with a randomly generated number, which is saved in the cookie and used to identify you and keep track of your activity on the site. Your name is not associated with your cookies unless you entered it into a form, which is then transferred to the cookie.

- Cookies are a relatively safe technology and have several important privacy features. A cookie is data, not a computer program or script; so while a cookie is sent to your computer and stored

there, it cannot be executed to activate a virus or worm. In addition, only the site that created the cookie can access it. Finally, a cookie can contain only as much information as you disclose while using the Web site that sets the cookie. For example, a cookie cannot rummage through your hard disk to find the password for your e-mail account, the number for your checking account, or the PIN number for your credit card. However, if you enter your credit card number in the process of making an online purchase, it is possible for the cookie to store that number. Most reputable Web sites do not store such sensitive information; you can read a Web site's privacy policy for more information on this important privacy and security topic.

- Most browsers allow you to set your security level to block cookies. See Figure G-18. On many Web sites, cookies are the only mechanism available for tracking your activity or remembering your purchases. If you set the security level to block cookies, then you will not be able to access all the activities when you visit these Web sites.

  A more sophisticated approach to cookie security is provided by **P3P (Platform for Privacy Preferences Project)**, which defined a standard set of security tags that become part of the HTTP header for every cookie. This header, called a **Compact Privacy Policy**, describes how cookie data is used by a Web site. Based on your security preferences, your browser can use this header data to decide whether or not to accept the cookie. Compact Privacy Policy headers are supported by recent versions of browsers.

- Cookies can be deleted from your hard drive automatically or you can delete them manually. To delete cookies automatically, you let the cookie expire. When a cookie reaches the end of its pre-defined lifetime, your browser simply erases it. A cookie is programmed to time out by the site's Web developer. To delete cookies manually, you must know where the cookies are stored on your hard drive. Netscape Navigator stores the cookie files in the Netscape folder in one large file called Cookies.txt on the PC or in Magic cookie on the Macintosh. IE stores each cookie in a separate file, usually in the Windows/Cookies folder. See Figure G-19.

FIGURE G-18: Blocking cookies

Click to disable cookies on your computer

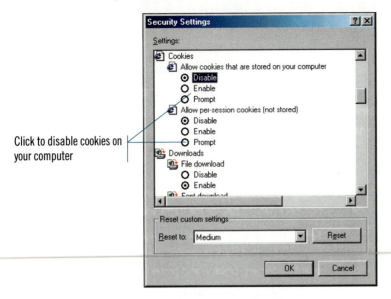

FIGURE G-19: Cookies stored on a hard disk

IE typically stores cookies as small individual files on your computer's hard disk in a folder called Cookies

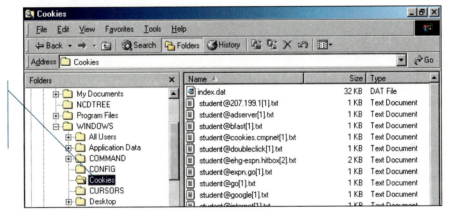

Why you would want to use cookies

When Web users first hear about cookies, they often wonder: Why use cookies at all? To answer that question, pretend that you use your browser to visit a popular online music store. You search for your favorite groups, listen to some sample tracks, and select a few CDs that you want to purchase. After browsing through 20 or 30 pages, you eventually go to the checkout counter, where you see a list of the CDs that you selected. You fill out a form that requests your name, shipping address, and payment information.

Because HTTP is a stateless protocol, each time that you connect to a different page, the server regards it as a new visit. So, while it seems to you that you're connected to the music site for the length of your visit, from the perspective of the Web site's server, it seems like 20 or more people have

made 20 or more successive visits. In order to keep track of you and your purchases, the Web site's server uses cookies to distinguish your requests from those of other people visiting the site. The cookies track your activity so that the Web server can compile a list of your purchases.

If you set your security level to turn off cookies, you probably won't be able to make online purchases, you'll have to enter your user IDs and passwords manually, and you won't be able to take advantage of targeted marketing (for example, when a music Web site keeps track of your favorite bands and shows you their new CDs). In the end, an individual must weigh privacy issues against convenience when deciding whether to use cookies or not use cookies.

Introducing e-commerce

The Internet was first opened to commercial use in 1991. Since that date, thousands of businesses have taken up residence at Web sites, making online shopping a popular Web activity. The economics of the Web go beyond retail catalogs; even small businesses, individual artists, and isolated craftsmen can post Web pages that display their wares.

DETAILS

- **E-commerce** is used to describe financial transactions conducted over a computer network. E-commerce activities include online shopping, electronic auctions, and online stock trading.

- E-commerce includes many kinds of physical products, digital products, and services. Physical products offered at e-commerce sites include clothing, shoes, skateboards, and cars. Most of these products can be shipped to buyers using the U.S. Postal Service or a parcel delivery service or can be picked up by buyers at a designated spot, generally a storefront.

  Increasingly, e-commerce goods include digital products such as news, music, video, databases, software, and all types of knowledge-based items. The unique feature of these products is that they can be transformed into bits and delivered over the Web. Consumers can get them immediately upon completing their orders, and no one must pay shipping costs.

  E-commerce merchants also sell services, such as arranging trips, medical consultation, and remote education. These services can be handled through the transfer of information between computers. E-commerce services can be delivered electronically; for example, an e-ticket, which is confirmation that an airline reservation is being held in your name. You print the e-ticket and use it instead of a ticket issued by an airline.

- E-commerce offers unique advantages over brick and mortar stores for both customers and merchants. Customers can search through large catalogs, compare prices of multiple vendors, configure products online, see prices, and build an order over days. The Web and its search engines provide merchants with a way to attract customers without expensive national advertising. Web technology also allows merchants to track customer preferences and produce marketing tailored to the individual.

- E-commerce seems simple from the perspective of a shopper who simply connects to an online store, browses the electronic catalog, selects merchandise, and then pays for it. The screen tour associated with Figure G-20 illustrates a typical shopping session. As you browse, you can drop items into your electronic shopping cart. At the checkout counter, you enter the information necessary to pay for the items you selected.

- Behind the scenes, e-commerce is based on a Web site and technologies that track shoppers' selections, collect payment data, guard customers' privacy, and protect credit card numbers.

  A merchant establishes a Web site on a Web server. Depending on the volume of expected transactions, a merchant may decide to operate its own Web server or outsource the site to a Web hosting service. Some ISPs provide starter kits for entrepreneurs who want to establish a small e-commerce site.

- An e-commerce Web site is based on a domain name, such as www.amazon.com, which is the entry to the online store. A Web page at this location welcomes customers and provides links to various parts of the site, such as the goods and services for sale, privacy policy, company background, customer service, and special promotions. For small e-commerce businesses, this online catalog might exist as a series of HTML documents. For large businesses, however, the online catalog is based on the information stored in a conventional database.

- An e-commerce site also typically includes some mechanism for customers to select merchandise and then pay for it. Most e-commerce businesses use automation; their order-processing systems automatically update inventories and then print the packing slips and mailing labels. These printouts are used by employees to pack orders and ship them to customers.

- An **online shopping cart** is a cyberspace version of the cart that you wheel around a store and fill up with merchandise. Most shopping carts work by using cookies to store information about your activities on a Web site. An e-commerce site might use cookies as a storage bin for all of the items that you load into your shopping cart, as shown in Figure G-21. Some e-commerce sites use cookies simply to identify each shopper uniquely. These sites use your unique number to store your item selections in a server-side database.

FIGURE G-20: Shopping on the Web

A shopping cart keeps track of the merchandise you want to purchase

You can find items by browsing through the catalog, or by searching for specific items

FIGURE G-21: Storing shopping cart items in a cookie

ADD TO CART

1. When you click the Add to Cart button, the merchant's server sends a message to your browser to add that item number to the cookie, which is stored on your computer

ITEM #B7655

VIEW CART

2. When you check out, the server asks your browser for all of the cookie data that pertains to your shopping cart items

3. Your browser sends those cookies along with a request for an order summary

Your order:
1 Blender   29.95
1 Wok   38.49

4. The Web server uses the cookies to produce a Web page that lists the items you want to purchase

E-commerce categories

E-commerce activities fall into different categories depending on the seller and buyer. Most of the e-commerce activities that the typical Web surfer enjoys are classified as **B2C (business-to-consumer)** e-commerce. In the B2C model, businesses supply goods and services to individual consumers. In another popular e-commerce model, consumers sell to each other. This **C2C (consumer-to-consumer)** model includes wildly popular online auctions and rummage sales. **B2B (business-to-business)** e-commerce involves one enterprise buying goods or services from another enterprise. **B2G (business-to-government)** e-commerce aims to help businesses sell to governments.

Executing e-commerce transactions

After you wheel your cyber shopping cart over to the checkout line, you must verify the items you plan to purchase and you must pay for the merchandise online before your transaction can be completed. This lesson explores order forms, secure transactions, and the ways you pay for merchandise and services you purchase on the Web.

DETAILS

- An **HTML form** (usually referred to simply as a form) is used to collect payment and shipping information at the checkout counter of e-commerce Web sites. See Figure G-22. The information you enter into an HTML form is held in the memory of your computer, where your browser creates temporary storage bins that correspond to the input field names designated by the form's HTML tags. After you enter the information, you click a Submit button to send the form. Then your browser gathers the data held in memory and sends it to a specially designated program on an HTTP server. This server could be the one that sent the original HTML form to you or it could be a different server that's set up exclusively to process form data.

- Customers often worry about the security of their online transactions. They want to be sure their credit card and other personal information is secure. Several encryption technologies are used to secure online transactions. **Encryption** is the science of coding data. You will learn more about encryption in the Tech Talk in this unit.

  SSL (Secure Sockets Layer) protocol encrypts the data that travels between a client computer and an HTTP server. This encryption protocol creates what's called an SSL connection using a specially designated port, typically Port 443 rather than Port 80, which is used for unsecured HTTP communication. You will notice https: instead of http: in the URL of Web pages that provide an SSL connection.

  S-HTTP (secure HTTP) is an extension of HTTP that encrypts the text of an HTTP message before it is sent. Although SSL and S-HTTP both use encryption techniques to transmit data securely, they are technically different. Whereas SSL creates a secure connection between a client and a server over which any amount of data can be sent securely, S-HTTP is designed simply to encrypt and transmit an individual message. From the consumer's perspective, however, either one of these security measures can do an excellent job of protecting the data you send over the Internet.

- Securing your credit card number as it travels over the Internet solves only half of the security problem. Both parties in an e-commerce transaction must make sure that they are dealing with authorized and reputable entities. Consumers want to make sure that a merchant is legitimate. Merchants want to make sure that the credit card charges are authorized by the card's rightful owner.

  SET (Secure Electronic Transaction) is a security method that relies on cryptography and digital certificates to ensure that transactions are legitimate and secure. A **digital certificate** is a specially coded electronic attachment to a file that verifies the identity of its source. SET uses digital certificates and secure connections to transfer consumers' credit card numbers directly to a credit card processing service for verification.

- An **electronic wallet** (also called a digital wallet) is software that stores and handles the information a customer typically submits when finalizing an e-commerce purchase. It typically holds your name, shipping address, and the number, expiration date, and billing address for one or more credit cards. It might also hold a digital certificate that verifies your identity. You can create an electronic wallet by subscribing at the wallet provider's site. The ScreenTour associated with Figure G-23 illustrates a typical electronic wallet.

- A **person-to-person payment** (sometimes called an on-line payment) offers an alternative to credit cards. It can be used to pay for auction items and wire money over the Internet. A service called PayPal pioneered person-to-person payments and has since been copied by several other service providers. The process begins when you open an account at a person-to-person payment service. As with a checking account, you deposit some money in your account by using your credit card. You receive a user ID and password that allows you to access your account to make purchases and deposit additional funds. Money can be sent to anyone who has an e-mail account, as shown in Figure G-24.

FIGURE G-22: An HTML form

▶ HTML forms are easy to create and are typically used to collect payment and shipping information at the "checkout counter" of e-commerce Web sites

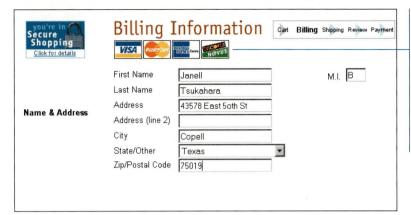

Many online merchants accept payment using a major credit card; you can reduce the probability of online credit card fraud by making sure that you deal with legitimate merchants, use secure connections, and employ common sense when using your card

FIGURE G-23: An electronic wallet

▶ When you proceed to an online checkout, software on the merchant's server sends an HTTP message to your PC that looks for and activates compatible wallet software; by clicking a Submit button, your payment data is transferred from your electric wallet to the server

FIGURE G-24: Sending and receiving payment

1. To use a person-to-person payment service, simply log into your account, enter the recipient's e-mail address, and indicate the payment amount

2. The recipient immediately receives an e-mail notification of your payment

3. The recipient connects to the payment site to pick up the money by transferring the funds to a checking account, requesting a check, or sending the funds to someone else

Encryption is one of the most important technologies for maintaining your privacy and the security of important information, such as your credit card number. Encryption makes a message illegible to unauthorized users, and is designed to keep messages secret. Its purpose, therefore, is quite different from simple coding schemes, such as ASCII and EBCDIC, which are designed to transform data into formats that are publicly known and shared.

An original message that has not yet been encrypted is referred to as **plaintext** or cleartext. An encrypted message is referred to as **ciphertext**. The process of converting plaintext into ciphertext is called **encryption**. Reconverting ciphertext to plaintext is called **decryption**. In an e-commerce transaction, for example, your credit card number exists as plaintext, which is encrypted into ciphertext for its journey over a secure connection to the merchant. When the ciphertext arrives at its destination, it is decrypted back into the original plaintext credit card number.

Messages are encrypted using a cryptographic algorithm and key. A **cryptographic algorithm** is a specific procedure for encrypting or decrypting a message. A **cryptographic key** (usually just called a key) is a word, number, or phrase that must be known in order to encrypt or decrypt a message. An encryption method called simple substitution uses a transformation table like the one in Figure G-25 to encrypt or decrypt messages.

The simple substitution key is an example of **weak encryption**, because it is easy to decrypt even without the algorithm and key. Unauthorized decryption is sometimes referred to as breaking or cracking a code. **Strong encryption** is loosely defined as very difficult to break. Of course, with continuous advances in technology, strong encryption is a moving target. For example, several encryption methods that were considered impossible to break 10 years ago have recently been cracked using networks of personal computers. The encryption methods that are used for most e-commerce transactions are considered strong but not unbreakable.

Encryption methods can be broken by the use of expensive, specialized, code-breaking computers. The cost of these machines is substantial, but not beyond the reach of government agencies, major corporations, and organized crime. Encryption methods can also be broken by standard computer hardware—supercomputers, mainframes, workstations, and even personal computers. These computers typically break codes using a **brute force method**, which consists of trying all possible keys.

The simple substitution encryption method is an example of **symmetric key encryption**, which is also called secret key or conventional encryption. With symmetric key encryption, the same key used to encrypt a message is also used to decrypt a message. Symmetric key encryption is often used to encrypt stationary data, such as corporate financial records. It is not, however, a very desirable encryption method for data that's on the move. The person who encrypts the data must get the key to the person who decrypts the data, without the key falling into the wrong hands. On a computer network, key distribution is a major security problem because of the potential for interception.

To eliminate the key-distribution problem, Whitfield Diffie and Martin Helman introduced a concept called **public key encryption (PKE)** in 1975. It uses asymmetric key encryption, in which one key is used to encrypt a message, but another key is used to decrypt the message. Figure G-26 illustrates how public key encryption works. Public key encryption is a crucial technology for the Web and e-commerce. When you use an SSL (secure socket layer) connection to transmit your credit card number, the server sends a public key to your browser, which uses this public key to encrypt the credit card number. Once encrypted, no one can use this public key to decrypt the message. The encrypted message is sent to the Web server, where the private key is used to decrypt it.

When you engage in an e-commerce transaction, the e-commerce site provides secure connections that encrypt your data. In most cases, this is all the encryption necessary for the transaction. If you were to encrypt your data further, it is unlikely that the e-commerce server would be equipped to handle the decryption. You might, however, want to encrypt other data, such as your e-mail messages or your data files.

When personal computer users want to encrypt e-mail or other documents, they turn to Phillip Zimmerman's **PGP** (Pretty Good Privacy) software. In addition to encrypting data files, this software lets you digitally sign a message, which verifies to the recipient that you are the sender and that no tampering is involved. PGP is a type of public key encryption. When you first use PGP, the software generates a private key and a public key. You must keep your private key hidden. You typically e-mail the public key to the people you authorize to send encrypted messages to you. The people who receive your public key can store it in their PGP programs, which they will then use to encrypt messages. They will send these messages to you, and you will be able to decrypt them using your private key. PGP software is available as a free download from several Web sites.

FIGURE G-25: Simple substitution

The algorithm for a simple encryption technique was to offset the letters of the alphabet; a simple transformation table helped to encrypt or decrypt a message; for example, if a "G" appears in the encrypted message, it would be a "D" in the original, unencrypted message

Cyphertext letters:
D E F G H I J K L M N O P Q R S T U V W X Y Z A B C

Equivalent plaintext letters:
A B C D E F G H I J K L M N O P Q R S T U V W X Y Z

FIGURE G-26: Public key encryption uses two keys

A public key is used to encrypt a message

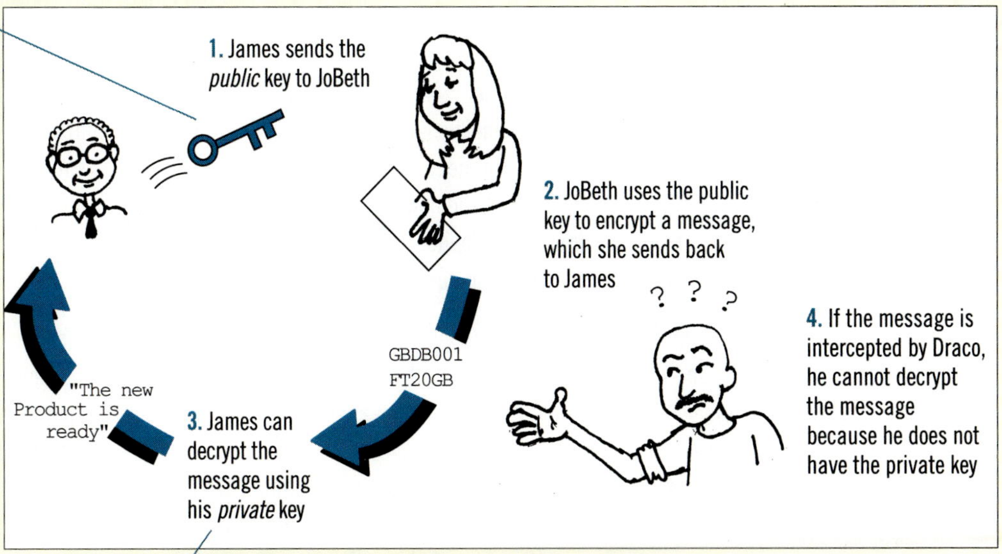

1. James sends the *public* key to JoBeth

2. JoBeth uses the public key to encrypt a message, which she sends back to James

GBDB001 FT20GB

"The new Product is ready"

3. James can decrypt the message using his *private* key

4. If the message is intercepted by Draco, he cannot decrypt the message because he does not have the private key

A private key is used to decrypt the message

Is The Truth Out There?

In an episode of the X-Files, Agent Scully warns Mulder about his search into the unexplored realm of extra-terrestrial and paranormal phenomena: "The truth is out there, but so are lies." And so it is on the Internet, where truth mingles with lies, rumors, myths, and urban legends. The Internet is uncensored and unregulated. Anyone with a Web page or an e-mail account can rapidly and widely distribute information, which is often redistributed and forwarded like a chain letter. As an example, one e-mail message, circulated in the summer of 1999, contained this alarming first-person account: "When Zack was 2 years old, I put on the waterproof sunscreen. I don't know how, but he got some in his eyes. I called the poison control center and they told me to rush Zack to the ER now. I found out for the first time that many kids each year lose their sight to waterproof sunscreen. Zack did go blind for two days. It was horrible."

Worried parents forwarded this e-mail message to their friends, and many of them threw their sunscreen in the trash. In August of that year, members of an NBC television news team reported that they had researched the story but failed to find evidence of any child becoming blind from sunscreen. They concluded their report by saying, "This is one of those stories that has spun out of control—touted as fact, when in reality, it's nothing more than a modern Internet myth."

The Internet has also been blamed for circulating reports that the U.S. Navy shot down TWA Flight 800. Pierre Salinger, an ex-TV reporter and a former advisor to President John F. Kennedy, made front-page headlines in November 1996 when he displayed documents that described how the Navy was testing missiles off Long Island and accidentally hit Flight 800. Although Salinger would not reveal the source of the documents, it turned out that they had been circulated on the Internet months earlier. The Chicago Tribune described Salinger's error as "merely the latest outbreak of the disturbing new information-age phenomenon of bogus news," and went on to say that "America is awash in a growing and often disruptive avalanche of false information that takes on a life of its own in the electronic ether of the Internet, talk radio, and voice mail until it becomes impervious to denial and debunking."

In a more recent debacle, a seemingly legitimate news wire flashed over the Internet: "A city still mourning the death of punk rock innovator Joey Ramone has endured another tragedy as Velvet Underground leader Lou Reed was found dead in his apartment last night, apparently from an overdose of the painkiller Demerol." The fake wire story fooled several radio stations, which reported it as hard news.

But is it fair to say that the Internet has a monopoly on false information? Probably not. Even well-established newspapers, magazines, and television news shows report stories that are later found to be misleading or untrue. In an article published online in Salon, Scott Rosenberg asks, "Who's more responsible for the spread of misinformation, the Internet or the news media? Well, ask yourself how you first heard of Salinger's memo: was it from the Net or from a TV broadcast? The sad truth is that the old media are far more efficient disseminators of bogus news than the new."

Before the Internet became a ubiquitous part of modern life, certain rules of thumb helped to distinguish truth from lies and fact from fiction. In The Truth About URLs, Robin Raskin writes, "When printed junk mail floods our overcrowded mailboxes we have some antennae for the bogus causes and the fly-by-night foundations. We've come to expect the New York Times to be a credible source of information; we're not as sure about The National Inquirer… It takes years to establish these sorts of cultural cues for knowing whether we're getting good information or a bum steer." Perhaps the Internet has not been around long enough for us to establish the cultural cues we need to distinguish fact from fiction in Web pages, e-mails, online chats, and discussion groups. You can, however, get some help from the Web itself. Several sites keep track of the myths and so-called urban legends that circulate on the Internet. Before you spread dire warnings about sunscreen or call a press conference to report a government coverup, you might want to check one of these sites for the real scoop.

Holding writers accountable for their facts does not seem to work, and governments, already overburdened with other problems, have scant resources available to sift through mountains of information and set the record straight. It seems that the burden of verifying facts is ultimately left to the reader. However, many people do not have the time, motivation, expertise, or resources to verify facts before they pass them through the information mill.

We live in an information age. Ironically, much of what we hear and read just isn't true. False and misleading information is not unique to our time, but now it propagates more rapidly, fed by new technologies and nurtured by "spin doctors." As one commentator suggested, "The danger is that we are reaching a moment when nothing can be said to be objectively true, when consensus about reality disappears. The Information Age could leave us with no information at all, only assertions."

▼ INTERACTIVE QUESTIONS

○ Yes   ○ No   ○ Not sure   **1.** Would you agree that it sometimes seems difficult to determine whether information is true or false?

○ Yes   ○ No   ○ Not sure   **2.** Do older people tend to be more susceptible than younger people to false information that's disseminated over the Internet?

○ Yes   ○ No   ○ Not sure   **3.** Have you ever received an e-mail that provided inaccurate information?

     4. Do you have your own set of rules to help you evaluate the truth of information that's disseminated over the Internet?

○ Yes   ○ No   ○ Not sure

▼ EXPAND THE IDEAS

1. Do older people with less Internet experience tend to be more naïve about Internet information than younger people who have been raised on the Internet? Find several examples of articles, documentaries, or news stories on verifying facts and data on the Internet. Write a summary of each article or media piece. Analyze your findings. Was the media voice consistent? Why or why not?

2. Can you think of another way in which information spreads so quickly? How does society monitor and check the facts for other media, like newspapers and television? Find several examples of articles, documentaries, or news stories on integrity in journalism. Form a discussion group and share your articles. Compile a group presentation on your articles, summarizing them for the class. How are the situations in the articles similar and how are they different? What steps were taken to verify the facts? Were these steps appropriate? Sufficient? What else would you have done to monitor the facts?

3. Do you have your own set of rules to help you evaluate information on the Internet? Write a two-page paper detailing how you evaluate information. Do you follow an existing model? Be sure to include your resources.

End of Unit Exercises

▼ KEY TERMS

Animated GIF	External style sheet	Link bar	SSL
B2B	Formatting tag	Link tag	Stateless protocol
B2C	GIF	Logical port	Strong encryption
B2G	Head section	Mailto link	Style
Body section	Helper application	Markup language	Style sheet
Broken link	Hot spot	Media tag	Symmetric key encryption
Brute force method	HTML	Online shopping cart	Text editor
C2C	HTML document	Operational tag	Theme
Cascading style sheet	HTML form	P3P	Thumbnail
Ciphertext	HTML frame	Person-to-person payment	URL
Compact Privacy Policy	HTML tag	PGP	Weak encryption
Cookie	HTTP	Plaintext	Web authoring software
Cryptographic algorithm	HTTP status code	Plug-in	Web browser
Cryptographic key	Hypertext	PNG	Web page header
Decryption	Hypertext link	Public key encryption	Web page table
Digital certificate	Image map	Server farm	Web resource
E-commerce	Internal link	SET	Web server
Electronic wallet	Interpage link	S-HTTP	World Wide Web Consortium
Encryption	JPEG	Socket	(W3C)
External link			

▼ UNIT REVIEW

1. Use your own words to define bold terms that appear throughout the unit. List 10 of the terms that are least familiar to you and write a sentence for each of them.

2. Draw a multi-panel cartoon that shows how a Web server and browser interact. Include the following terms: Web server, browser, HTTP, HTML, Port 80, socket, HTML document, graphic file, and URL.

3. Create a timeline of the history of HTML and browsers based on the information provided in this unit. Your timeline should begin in 1990 and continue through 2001.

4. Explain the relationship between an HTML document and a Web page in a short paragraph.

5. List and describe in your own words the four classifications of HTML tags as presented in this unit.

6. List the port numbers that are traditionally used for HTTP traffic, SMTP e-mail, and FTP.

7. List the major security and privacy features of cookies.

8. Describe the advantages and disadvantages of each type of Web page development tool that was discussed in this unit.

9. Locate a Web page, print it out, and then identify the following parts of the Web page: title, header, graphic, link, button, menu, and frame.

10. Describe some of the ways that Web page designers use links. Describe external links, mailto links, and internal links.

▼ FILL IN THE BEST ANSWER

1. The _____ is a collection of documents that can be related by links.

2. HTML is called a markup language because authors insert special instructions called HTML _____ that specify how a document should appear when printed or displayed on a computer screen.

3. A(n) _____ is the client half of the client/server software that facilitates communication between a personal computer and Web server.

4. _____ is a protocol that works in conjunction with TCP/IP to get Web resources to your desktop.

5. A Web server usually listens for HTTP requests on _____ 80.

6. If you use a text _____ to create an HTML document, you must manually enter HTML tags.

7. The _____ section of an HTML document contains information that defines global properties but is not displayed by your browser.

8. A(n) _____ style sheet allows you to create an HTML document that contains style specifications for multiple Web pages.

9. A(n) _____ is a collection of coordinated graphics, colors, and fonts applied to individual pages or all pages in a Web site.

10. The <IMG SRC> _____ tag is used to reference an image that will appear on a Web page.

11. The three graphics formats that are most commonly used for Web pages are GIF, JPEG, and _____.

12. A(n) _____ link is used to send an e-mail message to an address specified by the Web page author.

13. A diagram that contains clickable hot spots is referred to as an image _____.

14. Many Web page authors and designers use _____ as a layout tool for positioning the elements of a Web page.

15. On a Web page, a(n) _____ scrolls independently of other parts of the page.

16. A(n) _____ helps a Web server track visitors and overcome some of the limitations of HTTP's "stateless" nature.

17. _____ is typically used to describe financial transactions conducted over a computer network.

18. Most shopping carts work because they use _____ to store information about your activities on a Web site.

19. A(n) _____ wallet stores and handles the information that a customer typically submits when finalizing an e-commerce purchase.

20. _____ e-commerce involves one enterprise buying goods or services from another enterprise, whereas _____ e-commerce aims to help businesses sell to governments.

▼ PRACTICE TESTS

When you use the Interactive CD, you can take Practice Tests that consist of 10 multiple-choice, true/false, and fill-in-the-blank questions. The questions are selected at random from a large test bank, so each time you take a test, you'll receive a different set of questions. Your tests are scored immediately, and you can print study guides to determine which questions you answered incorrectly. If you are using a Tracking Disk, insert it in the floppy disk drive to save your test scores.

▼ INDEPENDENT CHALLENGE 1

 Surfing the Web will take you to many interesting sites. As you visit each one, you will notice differences among Web pages. To some extent, good design is a matter of taste; when it comes to Web page design, there are usually many possible solutions that will provide a pleasing look and efficient navigational tools. On the other hand, some designs just don't seem to work because they make the text difficult to read or navigate.

1. Select a Web page or several pages that have many of the elements described in this unit, including hot spots, image maps, links, images, or other media.

2. Find the page by browsing on the Web; save and print the page or pages.

3. Using colored markers or pens, identify each of the elements and write a brief explanation of how each element enhances or detracts from the message of the page.

4. What tools do you think the Web page designer used to organize the information on the page? Was it done effectively? Identify the sections of content on the printouts.

5. Do you think styles were used in developing the page? Do you see common fonts and colors in the text portions? Identify these elements on the printout.

6. Next, find one Web page that you think could use improvement. Use colored pencils or markers to sketch your plan for improving the page. Annotate your sketch by pointing out the features you would change and explain why you think your makeover will be more effective than the original Web page.

▼ INDEPENDENT CHALLENGE 2

Many people have their own home pages. A home page is a statement of who you are and what your interests may be. You can design your own home page. Depending on the tools you have available, you might be able to create a real page and publish it on the Web. If these tools are not available, you will still be able to complete the initial design work.

1. Write a brief description of the purpose of your home page and your expected audience. For example, you might plan to use your home page to showcase your résumé to prospective employers.

2. List the elements you plan to include on your home page. Briefly describe any graphics or media elements you want to include.

3. Create a document that contains the information you want to include on your home page.

4. Make a sketch of your home page showing the colors you plan to use and the navigation elements you plan to include. Annotate this sketch to describe how these elements follow effective Web page design guidelines.

▼ INDEPENDENT CHALLENGE 3

 Shopping on the Web has benefits for consumers as well as merchants. You will take a quick shopping tour of the Web and compare a few sites to see how they differ. You do not have to make any purchases to complete this independent challenge.

1. Find three retailers on the Internet. If possible find e-commerce retailers that also have "brick and mortar" stores, for example, Bed, Bath, and Beyond, or Barnes & Noble.

2. Besides the name of the Web site, what clues on the Web page help you identify the products or services being offered?

3. For each of the retailers, search for two items and place them in a shopping cart. Do not complete the purchase and do not enter any credit card or personal information.

4. Create a chart with three columns, one for each retailer. Complete the chart by answering the questions that follow:

   a. What procedures did you go through to find the merchandise?

   b. Was there a shopping cart or comparable way of gathering your purchases?

   c. What methods of payment did they offer you?

   d. Were there any warning dialog boxes that opened in your browser during the shopping trip?

   e. Did the retailer make use of cookies? Could you find them on your computer after you exited the retailer?

   f. Select one store that has a brick and mortar counterpart. Would you prefer to shop online or at its brick and mortar counterpart? Write a brief summary supporting your response.

▼ INDEPENDENT CHALLENGE 4

The World Wide Web Consortium is required to maintain standards for working on the Web. New versions of browsers are constantly appearing with new features. Companies develop plug-in and add-in programs that have to be compatible with browsers, and then the media have to be available on the Web sites to make downloading the additional software worthwhile for consumers. Keeping up with all this change can make any Web surfer dizzy. How can you keep up?

1. Go to the World Wide Web Consortium site at www.w3c.org and find two recent news items that relate to updates in programming Web pages and write a brief summary of your findings. Be sure to include the sources.

2. Go to the Microsoft Web site at www.microsoft.com and find one recent news item about the latest release of the Internet Explorer Web browser. Write a brief summary of your findings. Be sure to include the sources.

3. Go to the Netscape Web site at www.netscape.com, click the Download link, and find one recent news item about the latest release of the Netscape Web browser. Write a brief summary of your findings. Be sure to include the sources.

4. Go to the Opera Web site at www.opera.com and find one recent news item about the latest release of the Opera Web browser. Write a brief summary of your findings. Be sure to include the sources.

5. Write a summary of the features that are advertised for each of the three browsers. Which features are similar and which are different.

6. Go to the Adobe Web site at www.adobe.com and find recent news about the latest release of Acrobat reader. Write a brief summary of your findings. Be sure to include the sources.

▼ LAB:WORKING WITH COOKIES

1. Start the interactive part of the lab. Insert your Tracking Disk if you want to save your QuickCheck results. Perform each of the lab steps as directed and answer all of the lab QuickCheck questions. When you exit the lab, your answers are automatically graded and your results are displayed.

2. Use Windows Explorer to look at the cookies stored on your computer. Indicate how many cookies are currently stored. Examine the contents of one cookie and indicate whether or not you think it poses a threat to your privacy.

3. Indicate the name and the version of the browser that you typically use. To find this information, open your browser and select the About option from the Help menu. Next, look at the cookie settings provided by your browser. Describe how you would adjust these settings to produce a level of privacy protection that is right for your needs.

4. Adjust your browser settings so that you are prompted whenever a Web server attempts to send a cookie to your computer. Go to several of your favorite Web sites and watch for third-party cookies. When you receive a message from a third-party Web site, record the name of the third-party site and the contents of the cookie that it is attempting to send. Finally, indicate whether or not you would typically accept such a cookie.

▼ VISUAL WORKSHOP

The presence of visual media enhances any experience. If you are at a news site or a retailer, seeing a video or interacting online helps you understand what the concepts are or just makes it more fun. The Web site shown in Figure G-27 is a music site, and contains links to radio, music, and video. You can go to the site shown in the figure or to another one.

FIGURE G-27

1. What type of media is available at the site you chose? Try to download or listen to at least one music file. Try to view one video file.

2. What players, if any, did you have to use to view or play the media files?

3. What types of images were on the site (what was the file format)? To find out, right-click the image and click Save or Save Picture as. The file format should appear in the Save Picture dialog box.

4. Find two different ways to listen to Internet radio through your computer. What were they and how did they differ?

UNIT H
Digital Media

This unit explores digital media, taking a close look at bitmap graphics—the most popular graphics for photographs and Web use. You will learn about vector graphics, which are often used for clip art and provide the underlying technology for 3-D graphics and 3-D animations. You will explore desktop video technology. You will learn about digital sound, including the different music formats, speech synthesis, and techniques for combining voice recognition with word processing. The Tech Talk explores the topic of compression—you'll find out how it works, and you'll learn how to use a popular compression utility.

Introducing bitmap graphics

Bitmap graphics are images that are composed of a grid of colored dots. Bitmap graphics are often used to create realistic images, such as photographs. You might also encounter bitmaps in the form of cartoons or the images that appear in computer games. There are many sources for bitmaps: photos from a digital camera, images converted by a scanner, photos that you send or receive as e-mail attachments, as well as most Web page graphics.

DETAILS

- A bitmap graphic, also called a raster graphic, or simply a bitmap, is composed of a grid of dots. The color of each dot is stored as a binary number. Think of a grid superimposed on a picture. The grid divides the picture into cells, called pixels. Each pixel is assigned a color, which is stored as a binary number. Figure H-1 illustrates these basic characteristics of a bitmap graphic.

- You can create a bitmap graphic from scratch using the tools provided by graphics software—specifically a category of graphics software referred to as **paint software**. You might be familiar with paint software such as Adobe Photoshop, Jasc Paint Shop Pro, and Microsoft Paint (included with Windows). These programs provide tools for freehand sketching, filling in shapes, adding realistic shading, and creating effects that look like oil paints, charcoal, or watercolors.

- When you already have a printed image, such as a photograph, a page from a magazine, or a picture from a book, you can use a **scanner** to convert the printed image into a bitmap graphic. A scanner essentially divides an image into a fine grid of cells and assigns a digital value for the color of each cell. As the scan progresses, these values are transferred to your computer's RAM. The values can then be saved and stored as a bitmap graphic file on the hard disk. Scanners, such as the one pictured in Figure H-2, are relatively inexpensive and easy to use.

- While a scanner digitizes printed images, a **digital camera** creates digitized images of real objects—that is, converts the images of real objects into bitmap graphics files. Instead of taking a photo with a conventional camera, developing the film, then digitizing it with a scanner, you use a digital camera, such as the one in Figure H-3, to take a photo in digital format. You can then transfer the digital data directly to your computer.

The photos that you take with a digital camera are stored in the camera's memory until you transfer them to your computer.

The type of memory that's used by a digital camera depends on the brand and model. **Flash memory** is a popular technology for digital camera memory, probably because it can be erased and reused. Unlike RAM, flash memory holds data without consuming power, so it doesn't lose data when the camera is turned off. Storage cards for digital camera memory typically include Compact Flash Cards, Memory Sticks®, and SmartMedia.

Digital cameras allow you to preview images and delete those that you don't want from the memory. The photos that you want to keep can be transferred directly to some printers, but typically you'll store the digital photo data on your computer's hard disk as a bitmap graphic file.

- Selecting the best graphics file format for your bitmap graphics files depends on what you intend to do with the images. Many graphics file formats exist, and most graphics software provides you with a choice of popular formats. **BMP** is the native bitmap graphic file format of the Microsoft Windows environment. The BMP format can be used for a wide variety of graphics applications, such as photographs, illustrations, and graphs. BMP files are typically the largest graphics files of any file format. **TIFF**, or **TIF (Tag Image File Format)**, is a highly flexible and platform-independent graphics file format that is supported by most photo-editing software packages. **JPEG (Joint Photographic Experts Group)** is a graphic format that stores bitmap data very efficiently in a small file. **GIF (Graphics Interchange Format)** was specifically designed to create images that can be displayed on multiple platforms, such as PCs and Macs. GIF graphics are a very popular format for Web graphics. **PNG (Portable Network Graphic)** is a graphic format that was designed to improve upon the GIF format. PNG is a public domain format without any restrictions on its use.

FIGURE H-1: A bitmap graphic

▶ A bitmap graphic is divided into a grid of individually colored pixels; the color number for each pixel is stored in binary format

FIGURE H-2: A scanner

To scan an image:
1. Turn on the scanner and start your scanner software
2. Place the image face down on the scanner glass
3. Use the scanner software to initiate the scan
4. The scanned image is stored in RAM
5. Save the image on your computer's hard disk

FIGURE H-3: A digital camera

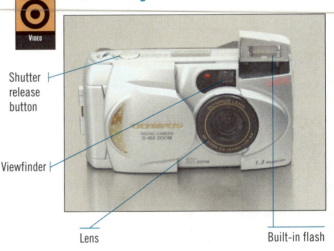

Shutter release button

Viewfinder

Lens

Built-in flash

Transferring digital data from a digital camera to your computer

Transferring the digital data from your digital camera to your computer can be achieved in several ways, depending on your camera. Four common methods are described below:

Direct cable transfer. If your computer and your camera have FireWire ports (also called IEEE-1394 ports), you can connect these two ports with a cable to transfer the photo data. You can use a similar transfer method if your computer and camera have USB ports or serial ports. The camera is connected by cable only during the transfer, then the camera can be disconnected so that you can carry it with you on vacation, or wherever.

Infrared port. Some cameras can beam the photo data to your computer's infrared port. This method eliminates the need for a cable, but is much slower than using your computer's FireWire port, USB, or serial port.

Card reader. A **card reader** is a small device that is connected to your computer's USB or serial port to read the data that's contained in a flash memory card. A card reader acts just like an external disk drive by treating your flash memory card like a floppy disk. To transfer the photo data from a flash memory card, you remove it from the camera and insert it into the card reader.

Floppy disk adapter. A **floppy disk adapter** is a floppy disk-shaped device that contains a slot for a flash memory card. You simply insert the memory card into the floppy disk adapter, then insert the adapter into your computer's floppy disk drive.

Regardless of the technology that you use, transferring photo data from your camera to your computer requires the appropriate software, which allows you to select a file format, specify a filename, and determine the location for each image file. This software may be supplied along with your camera, with your memory card reader, or by a stand-alone graphics software package, such as Adobe Photoshop.

Modifying bitmap graphics

Because bitmap graphics are coded as a series of bits that represent pixels, you can use graphics software to modify or edit this type of graphic by changing individual pixels. You can retouch or repair old photographs to eliminate creases, spots, and discoloration. You can even design new pictures using images that you cut and paste from photos or scanned images. In order to modify bitmap graphics images, you need an understanding of image resolution and density.

DETAILS

- Whether you acquire images from a digital camera or from a scanner, bitmap graphics tend to require a lot of storage space. Each pixel in a bitmap graphic is stored as one or more bits. The more pixels in a bitmap graphic, the more bits needed to store the file. So while a large bitmap graphic file might provide the necessary data for a high-quality printout, these files take up space on your hard disk, can require lengthy e-mail transmission times, and make Web pages seem sluggish.

- Unlike a photograph, a bitmap graphic has no fixed physical size. The size at which a bitmap graphic is displayed or printed depends on the resolution, as well as the density, of the image grid.

- **Resolution**, the dimensions of the grid that forms a bitmap graphic, is usually expressed as the number of horizontal and vertical pixels that it contains. For example, a small graphic for a Web page might have a resolution of 150 × 100 pixels: 150 pixels across and 100 pixels high. High-resolution graphics contain more data and look better at any size than low-resolution graphics. With more data, it is possible to display and print high-quality images that are smoother and cleaner. Bitmap graphics are **resolution-dependent**, which means that the quality of the image depends on its resolution.

  Camera manufacturers sometimes express the resolution of digital cameras as **megapixels** (millions of pixels), the total number of pixels in a graphic. A resolution of 1,600 × 1,200 would be expressed as 1.9 megapixels (1,600 multiplied by 1,200); a bitmap graphic image that has 3.5 megapixels contains more pixels and is a higher quality.

- The data that is contained in a bitmap graphic file retains the same resolution but loses clarity or quality no matter how large it is displayed or printed. See Figure H-4. This concept of stretching and shrinking without changing resolution is important for understanding what happens when bitmap graphics are displayed and printed. The denser the grid, the smaller the image will appear. The **density** of an image grid can be expressed as dots per inch (dpi) for a printer or scanner, or as pixels per inch (ppi) on a monitor.

Most graphics software allows you to specify the size at which an image is printed without changing the resolution of the bitmap graphic. You'll get the highest print quality if the resolution of the graphic meets or exceeds the printer's dpi. An ink jet printer with a resolution of 1,440 × 720 dpi produces a very dense image grid. If each pixel of a 1,600 × 1,200 graphic was printed as a single dot on this printer, the resulting image would be very high quality, but just a bit wider than 1 inch. You can specify a larger size for the printout, in which case the printer must create additional data to fill the print grid. This process can produce a fuzzy and blocky image if the printed image gets very large.

If you attempt to enlarge a bitmap by increasing its resolution, your computer must somehow add pixels because no additional picture data exists. Most graphics software uses a process called **pixel interpolation** to create new pixels by averaging the colors of nearby pixels. See Figure H-5.

- Sometimes the resolution and corresponding file size of a graphic might not be right for your needs. For example, a photo taken with a 3.1 megapixel camera is unsuitable for a Web page or as an e-mail attachment. Not only would it take a long time to download, but it would be larger than most screens. Reducing the resolution of a bitmap can reduce its file size and the size at which it is displayed on a computer screen; however, this also changes the quality of the image. If you reduce the resolution, the computer eliminates pixels from the image, reducing the size of the image grid. The file size is reduced by a similar amount, and image quality is reduced.

  Another way to reduce the size of a bitmap graphic is to crop it. **Cropping** refers to the process of removing part of an image, just like cutting out a section of a photograph. Cropping decreases file size by reducing the number of pixels in a graphic. The visual presentation changes to reflect the cropped changes.

FIGURE H-4: Two views of an image with a 24 × 24 resolution

Imagine that each bitmap image and its grid comes on a surface that you can stretch or shrink, as you shrink the surface, the grid becomes smaller and more dense

24 × 24 resolution

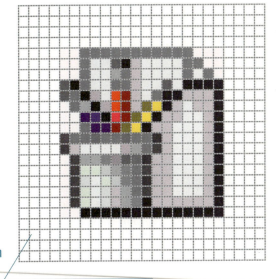

24 × 24 resolution

As you stretch the surface, the grid maintains the same number of horizontal and vertical cells, but each cell becomes larger and the grid becomes less dense

FIGURE H-5: Increasing resolution can reduce image quality

▲ The figure above has a resolution of 130 × 130; the figure at right was enlarged to a resolution of 260 × 260; for some graphics, pixel interpolation results in an image that appears very similar to the original; other images, particularly those that contain strong curved or diagonal lines, develop an undesirable pixelated, or bitmappy, appearance.

Introducing color depth

Color depth refers to the number of colors available for use in an image. As the color depth increases, image quality improves and file size increases. You can adjust color depth in order to decrease the size of the file required for a graphic. This lesson looks at color depth and how it affects your bitmap graphics.

DETAILS

- When monitors were simple monochrome (one-color) devices, each screen pixel was either on or off. A **monochrome bitmap** would be displayed by manipulating the pattern of on and off pixels displayed on the screen. To store the data for a monochrome bitmap, an on pixel is represented by a 1 bit. An off pixel is represented by a 0 bit. Each row of the bitmap grid is stored as a series of 0s and 1s, as shown in Figure H-6.

   Monochrome bitmaps require very little storage space. Each pixel is set to display either a black dot or a white dot, and so requires only one bit for storage. Therefore, the number of bits required to represent a full-screen picture is the same as the number of pixels on the screen.

- Color monitors require a more complex storage scheme. Each screen pixel displays a color based on the intensity of red, green, and blue signals that it receives. A pixel appears white if the red, green, and blue signals are set to maximum intensity. If red, green, and blue signals are equal but at a lower intensity, the pixel displays a shade of gray. If the red signal is set to maximum intensity, but the blue and green signals are off, the pixel appears in brilliant red. A pixel appears purple if it receives red and blue signals, and so on.

   Each red, green, and blue signal is assigned a value ranging from zero to 255, from absence of color to the highest intensity level for that color. These values produce a maximum of 16.7 million colors. A graphic that uses this full range of colors is referred to as a **True Color bitmap** or a **24-bit bitmap**. A **32-bit bitmap** displays 16.7 million colors just like a 24-bit bitmap. The extra bits are used to define special effects, such as the amount of transparency, for a pixel.

   The data for each pixel requires three bytes of storage space: eight bits for red, eight bits for green, and eight bits for blue, for a total of 24 bits per pixel. True Color bitmaps produce photographic-quality images, but they also produce very large files. 32-bit bitmap graphics files are even larger than 24-bit bitmap graphics files.

- To reduce the size of a bitmap file, you can reduce its color depth by using graphics software to work with color palettes. A **color palette** (also called a color lookup table or color map)

holds the selection of colors and allows you to select a group of colors to use for a bitmap graphic. If a palette contains only 256 colors, you can store the data for each pixel in eight bits instead of 24 bits, which reduces the file to a third of the size required for a True Color bitmap.

   A color palette is stored as a table within the header of a graphic file. Each palette contains a list of 256 color numbers. Each of these numbers is mapped to a 24-bit number that corresponds to the actual levels of red, green, and blue required to display the color. Figure H-7 explains how this table works.

- Most graphics software offers a selection of ready-made palettes that you can select using the color palette or color picker tool. Ready-made palettes usually include a grayscale palette, a system palette, and a Web palette. A **grayscale palette** displays an image using shades of gray, which looks similar to a black-and-white photograph. Most grayscale palettes consist of 256 colors. Figure H-8 illustrates a grayscale palette and a grayscale bitmap graphic.

   A **system palette** is the selection of colors used by the operating system for the graphics that represent desktop icons and controls. A **Web palette** contains a standard set of colors used by Internet Web browsers. Because most browsers support this palette, it is typically regarded as a safe choice when preparing graphics for Internet distribution. Additional palettes may be provided by your graphics software.

- A particular 256-color palette sometimes does not contain the right selection of colors for an image. For example, the Windows system palette does not provide a wide enough selection of orange tones for a Halloween or sunset photo. To make up for the lack of colors, your graphics software can dither the image. **Dithering** uses patterns composed of two or more colors to produce the illusion of additional colors and shading, relying on the human eye to blend colors and shapes. Most graphics software provides options that let you control the dithering.

- As a rule of thumb, bitmap graphics that you want to print should remain in True Color format. Any graphics that will be sent as e-mail attachments, posted on a Web site, or viewed only on screen should be reduced to a 256-color palette.

FIGURE H-6: Monochrome bitmap graphic

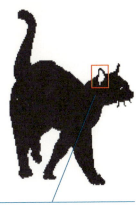

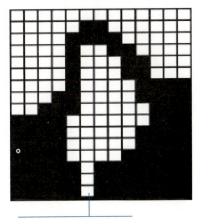

1. The image can originate as a black-and-white silhouette, as a black-and-white photograph, or even as a color photo

2. The computer divides the picture into a matrix

3. If a cell is white, it is coded as a 1; if the cell is black, it is coded as a 0

FIGURE H-7: The color palette

▶ A color palette is a subset of all possible colors; each color in the palette is numbered and its number points to the full 24-bit RGB value that is stored in the graphic file header

0	2	2
1	1	3
2	4	4
3	3	253

Pixels in the upper-left corner of an image

Color Palette	
Index #	RGB Value
0	000 000 000
1	060 000 255
2	020 167 167
3	120 060 060
4	180 060 060
5	255 000 000
.	
.	
.	
253	255 060 060
254	255 000 255
255	255 255 255

FIGURE H-8: Grayscale bitmap graphic

Introducing vector graphics

A **vector graphic** consists of a set of instructions for creating a picture. Unlike a bitmap graphic file, which superimposes a grid of pixels over an image and stores the color value for each pixel, a vector graphic file contains the instructions that the computer needs to create the shape, size, position, and color for each object in an image. This lesson explains the basics of two-dimensional vector graphics and how they differ from bitmap graphics.

DETAILS

- The parts of a vector graphic are created as separate objects. For example, the Stonehenge image in Figure H-9 was created with a series of roughly rectangular objects for the stones and a circular object for the sun.

- It is difficult to identify a vector graphic just by looking at an on-screen image. One clue that an image might be a vector graphic is a flat, cartoon-like quality. Think of clip art images, which are typically stored as vector graphics. For a more definitive identification, however, you should check the filename extension. Vector graphics files have filename extensions such as .wmf, .dxt, .mgx, .eps, .pict, and .cgm.

- Vector graphics are suitable for most line art, logos, simple illustrations, and diagrams that might be displayed and printed at various sizes. When compared to bitmaps, vector graphics have several advantages and disadvantages. You should take the following distinctions into account when deciding which type of graphic to use for a specific project.

  - Vectors resize better than bitmaps. When you change the physical size of a vector graphic, the objects change proportionally and maintain their smooth edges. While a circle in a bitmap graphic might appear to have jagged edges after it is enlarged, a circle in a vector graphic appears as a smooth curve at any size, as shown in Figure H-10.

  - Vector images usually require less storage space than bitmaps, depending on the complexity of the image. Each instruction requires storage space, so the more lines, shapes, and fill patterns in the graphic, the more storage space it requires.

  - It is easier to edit an object in a vector graphic than in a bitmap graphic. In some ways, a vector graphic is like a collage of objects. Each object can be layered over other objects but moved and edited independently. You can individually stretch, shrink, distort, color, move, or delete any object in a vector graphic. For example, if you delete the sun from the Stonehenge vector image, the background and cloud layers remain. In contrast, most bitmap graphics are constructed as a single layer of pixels. If you erase the pixels for some of the stones in the Stonehenge photograph, you'll create a hole of white pixels. See Figure H-11.

  - Vector graphics tend not to produce images that are as realistic as bitmap images. Most vector images tend to be more cartoon-like than the realistic appearance of a photograph. The cartoon-like characteristic of vector images results from the use of objects filled with blocks of color. Because your options for shading and texturing vector graphics are limited, vector graphics tend to have a flat appearance.

Vector graphics on the Web

Web browsers were originally designed to support a limited number of exclusively bitmap graphics formats. Built-in browser support for vector graphics has been slow, but plug-ins and players are currently available for several of the most popular Web-based vector graphics formats.

A graphics format called **SVG**, or Scalable Vector Graphics, is designed specifically for the Web. Graphics in SVG format are automatically resized when displayed on different screens or when printed. SVG supports gradients, drop shadows, multiple levels of transparency, and other effects, along with transportability to other platforms like handheld computers and cellular phones. SVG graphics objects can include regular and irregular shapes, images, and text, and they can be animated.

Macromedia's Flash software, which requires a browser plug-in to be viewed, creates a popular vector graphics format that is stored in SWF files.

Flash graphics can be static or animated, and typically require less storage space than SVG graphics.

Vector graphics files require little storage space and can be transmitted swiftly from a Web server to your browser. On Web pages, vector graphics appear with the same consistent quality on all computer screens, making it possible for browsers to adjust the size of an image instantaneously to fit correctly on a screen, regardless of its size or resolution. Any text contained in a vector image is stored as actual text, not just a series of colored dots. This text can be indexed by search engines so that it can be included in keyword searches, and the image can turn up in the list of search results.

FIGURE H-9: A vector graphic

▶ A vector graphic is formed from lines and shapes, which can be colored or shaded

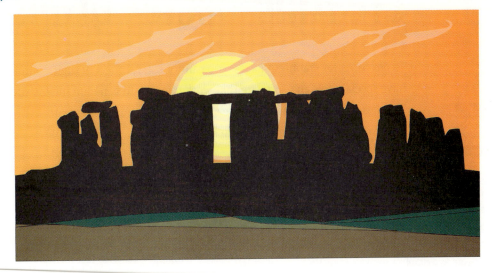

FIGURE H-10: Resizing vector graphic image v. resizing bitmap graphic image

Vector graphic   Bitmap graphic

FIGURE H-11: Vector graphics are layered

Vector graphic objects are layered, so it is easy to move and delete objects without disrupting the rest of the image

Deleting a shape from a bitmap image leaves a hole because the image is only one layer of pixels

Creating vector graphics

To create vector graphics images, you cannot use scanners or digital cameras. Instead, you must have special tools and software that work together to generate the instructions for the image. This lesson discusses the hardware and software you need to create and edit vector graphics and how to create vector graphics from bitmap graphics.

DETAILS

● Usually, vector graphics are created from scratch using vector graphics software, referred to as **drawing software**. Drawing software is sometimes packaged separately from the paint software used to produce bitmap graphics. In other cases, it is included with bitmap software as a graphics software suite. Vector graphics software provides an array of drawing tools that you can use to create objects, position them, and fill them with colors or patterns. For example, you can use the filled circle tool to draw a circle that is filled with a solid color. You can create an irregular shape by connecting points to outline the shape. Figure H-12 illustrates how to use drawing tools to create a vector graphic.

● Vector graphics software helps you edit individual objects easily within a graphic by changing their sizes, shapes, positions, or colors. For example, the data for creating the circle is recorded as an instruction, such as CIRCLE 40 Y 200 150, which means: create a circle with a 40-pixel radius, color it yellow, and place the center of the circle 200 pixels from the left of the screen and 150 pixels from the top of the screen. If you move the circle to the right, the instruction that the computer stores for the circle changes to something like CIRCLE 40 Y 500 150, which means the circle is now 500 pixels from the left instead of 200 pixels.

● When filling in a shape with color, your vector graphics software might provide tools for creating a gradient. A **gradient** is a smooth blending of shades from one color to another or from light to dark. Gradients can be used to create shading and three-dimensional effects.

● Some vector graphics software provides tools that apply bitmapped textures to vector graphics objects, giving them a more realistic appearance. For example, you can create a vector drawing of a house and then apply a brick-like texture that's derived from a bitmap photograph of real bricks. These graphics that contain both bitmap and vector data are called **metafiles**.

● Sometimes a special input device, called a digitizing tablet, is used to create vector graphics. A **digitizing tablet** provides a flat surface for a paper-based drawing, and a pen or puck is used to click the endpoints of each line on the drawing. The endpoints are converted into vectors and stored. Architects and engineers sometimes use a digitizing tablet, like the one in Figure H-13, to turn a paper-based line drawing into a vector graphic.

● To change a bitmap graphic into a vector graphic, you must use special tracing software. **Tracing software** locates the edges of objects in a bitmap graphic image and converts the resulting shapes into vector graphic objects. This software works best on simple images and line drawings, but does not typically provide acceptable results when used on photos.

Using rasterization to create bitmap graphics from vector graphics

You can create a bitmap graphic from a vector graphic through a process called ras-terization. **Rasterization** works by superimposing a grid over a vector graphic and determining the color for each pixel. This process is typically carried out by graphics software, which allows you to specify the output size for the final bitmap image.

It is important to output your rasterized images at the size you will ultimately need. If you rasterize a vector image at a small size and then try to enlarge the resulting bitmap image, you will likely get a poor-quality pixelated image. It is also important to know that once a vector graphic is converted to a bitmap, the resulting graphic no longer has the qualities of a vector graphic; you cannot edit the resulting bitmap graphic as you would the original vector graphic. For exam-ple, if you convert the Stonehenge vector graphic into a bitmap, you cannot grab the entire sun object and move it or change its color.

FIGURE H-12: Drawing vector graphics images

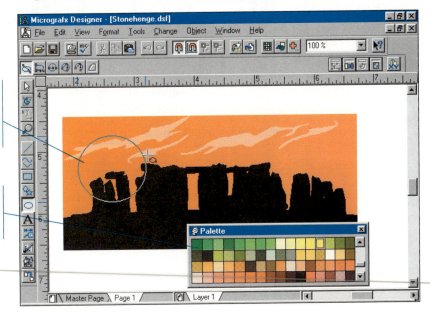

To draw a circle, select the filled circle tool; drag the mouse pointer to indicate the location and size of the circle

A color palette at the bottom of the window allows you to select the circle color

The sun is a circle filled with a gradient

The background is a filled rectangle

The clouds are created as a series of short line segments and filled with color

The stones are created as a series of short line segments and filled with black

FIGURE H-13: A digitizing tablet

▶ A digitizing tablet allows you to trace line drawings to create a vector graphic

Exploring 3-D graphics

Now that you have covered the basics for two-dimensional graphics, this lesson expands what you learned to introduce static 3-D graphics and animated 3-D graphics. If you've played any computer games recently or watched a hit movie like Shrek or Monsters, Inc., you've seen the product of computer-generated 3-D animated graphics. This lesson discusses 3-D graphics in more detail.

Info Web
3-D GRAPHICS

DETAILS

- Like vector graphics, 3-D graphics are stored as a set of instructions. For a 3-D graphic, however, the instructions contain the locations and lengths of lines that form a wireframe for a three-dimensional object. The **wireframe** provides a framework for the 3-D graphic. A 3-D wireframe can be covered with surface texture and color to create a graphic of a 3-D object. The process of covering a wireframe with surface color and texture is called **rendering**. The rendering process outputs a bitmap image. See Figure H-14.

- For added realism, the rendering process can take into account the way that light shines on surfaces and creates shadows. The technique for adding light and shadows to a 3-D image is called **ray tracing**. Ray tracing adds realism to 3-D graphics by adding highlights and shadows that are produced by a light source. Before an image is rendered, the artist selects a location for one or more light sources. The computer applies a complex mathematical algorithm to determine how the light source affects the color of each pixel in the final rendered image. This process can take hours for a complex image, even using today's most powerful personal computers. Figure H-15 shows the image from the previous figure rendered with an additional light source using ray tracing.

- To create 3-D graphics, you need 3-D graphics software, such as AutoCad or Caligari trueSpace. 3-D graphics software provides the tools that you need to draw a wireframe and view it from any angle. See Figure H-16. It provides rendering and ray tracing tools, along with an assortment of surface textures and colors that you can apply to individual objects.

  3-D graphics software runs on most personal computers, though some architects and engineers prefer to use high-end

workstations. A fast processor, lots of RAM, and a fast graphics card with its own video RAM all speed up the rendering process.

- 3-D graphics can be animated to produce special effects for movies or create interactive animated characters and environments for 3-D computer games. Animated special effects are created by rendering a sequence of bitmaps in which one or more objects are moved, or otherwise changed, between each rendering. In traditional hand-drawn animation, a chief artist draws the key frames, and then a team of assistants creates each of the in-between images. There are 24 images for each second of animation. For 3-D computer animation, the computer creates the in-between images by moving the object and rendering each necessary image. All of the images are then combined into a single file, creating essentially a digital movie.

  An important characteristic of special effects and animated films is that the rendering can be accomplished during the production phase of the movie and incorporated into the final footage. In contrast, 3-D computer game animation happens in real time. Each frame that makes the image seem to move must be rendered while you are playing the game—a process that requires an incredible amount of computer power.

- You can create 3-D animations on a desktop computer using commercially available software, but many of the best software packages are expensive and have a steep learning curve. These commercial products used by professionals result in higher quality and require powerful computer hardware. If you want to experiment with 3-D animations before making an expensive software investment, you might try one of the shareware programs.

FIGURE H-14: A 3-D graphic

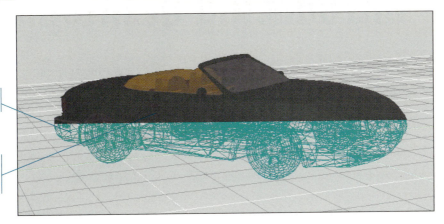

3-D graphics are based on a wireframe...

...which can be rendered into a bitmap image that looks three-dimensional

FIGURE H-15: Ray tracing

Light source

Shadow

Highlight

FIGURE H-16: 3-D graphics software

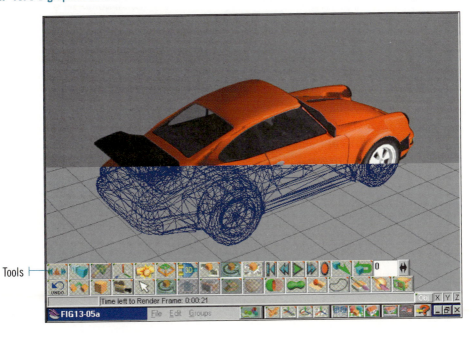

Tools

Introducing desktop video

Desktop videos are constructed and played using a personal computer. These videos can be stored on a hard disk or distributed on CDs, DVDs, videotapes, or the Web. Typically, the footage for a desktop video is captured by a video camera or converted into digital format from video-tape. Although desktop videos do not quite reach the standard of DVD movies, this lesson discusses how you can use a consumer-quality camera and your personal computer to create videos that are suitable for a variety of personal and professional uses.

DETAILS

● A **video** is composed of a series of frames, each of which is essentially a still picture and can be stored as a bitmap graphic. **Frame rate** refers to the number of frames shown per second; the higher the frame rate the better the video image. Feature films are typically projected at a rate of 24 frames per second (fps). Most desktop videos have a frame rate of only 15 fps.

● The basic process of creating desktop videos consists of the following steps: shoot the video footage; transfer the footage to your computer's hard disk; edit the video and soundtrack; output the video in its final format by selecting frame rate, window size, file format, and compression levels.

● Once the video footage is captured and transferred to your computer's memory, you must save the video footage to the hard drive. Several file formats are popular for desktop videos including **AVI**, **QuickTime**, **MPEG**, **RealMedia**, and **ASF**. Table H-1 provides some basic information about each one.

● Although video playback requires no special hardware, it does require a software player that's designed to work with the file format in which the video is stored. Players for most video file formats are available on the Web at no cost. The most popular players are Microsoft Media Player and QuickTime. Microsoft's Media Player is shipped with Windows and is designed to be used on the PC platform. Updates for this player can be obtained from the Microsoft Web site. Apple's QuickTime player is popular for both the PC and Mac platforms. It is available for download at the Apple Web site. Figure H-17 illustrates how to use Media Player to view a video.

● Most of today's personal computers are well-equipped for viewing videos; however, playback quality can vary depending on your computer's microprocessor, RAM capacity, and the capabilities of its graphics card. When viewing Web-based videos, the speed of your Internet connection also affects video quality. Your computer displays video frames as fast as they are received and processed. On a slow computer or using a dial-up Internet connection, videos might appear in a very small window on the screen, images might appear choppy and pixelated, and the sound might get out of sync with the action. The bottom line for digital video viewing is that faster equipment produces better results.

Creating good desktop videos

When desktop videos are processed and stored, some of the image data is eliminated to reduce the video file to a manageable size. Simpler videos tend to maintain better quality as they are edited, processed, and stored. Camera movements, fast actions, patterned clothing, and moving backgrounds all contribute to the complexity of a video, and should be avoided or minimized. The following techniques will help you produce video footage that maintains good quality as it is edited and processed: Use a tripod to maintain a steady image; Move the camera slowly if it is necessary to pan from side to side; Zoom in and out slowly; Direct your subjects to move slowly, when possible; Position your shot to eliminate as much background detail and movement as possible; and Ask the subjects of your video to wear solid-colored clothing, if possible.

TABLE H-1: Popular desktop video file formats

FORMAT	EXTENSION	PLATFORM	PLAYERS	DESCRIPTION
AVI (Audio Video Interleave)	.avi	PC	Microsoft Media Player	Sometimes called "Video for Windows," AVI is the most common format for desktop video on the PC platform
QuickTime Movie	.mov	PC, Mac, UNIX, Linux	QuickTime, Microsoft Media Player	Originally developed for the Mac platform, QuickTime movies are today one of the most popular formats for Web videos
MPEG (Moving Picture Experts Group)	.mpg or .mpeg	PC, Mac, UNIX, Linux	MediaPlayer	MPEG is one of the most sophisticated digital video formats; used both for desktop videos and DVD movies
RealMedia	.rm	PC, Mac, UNIX, Linux	RealPlayer, Microsoft Media Player	RealMedia, produced by RealNetworks, is a popular format for streaming Web videos
ASF	.asf	PC	Microsoft Media Player	ASF is Microsoft's video format for streaming video over the Web

FIGURE H-17: Playing a desktop video

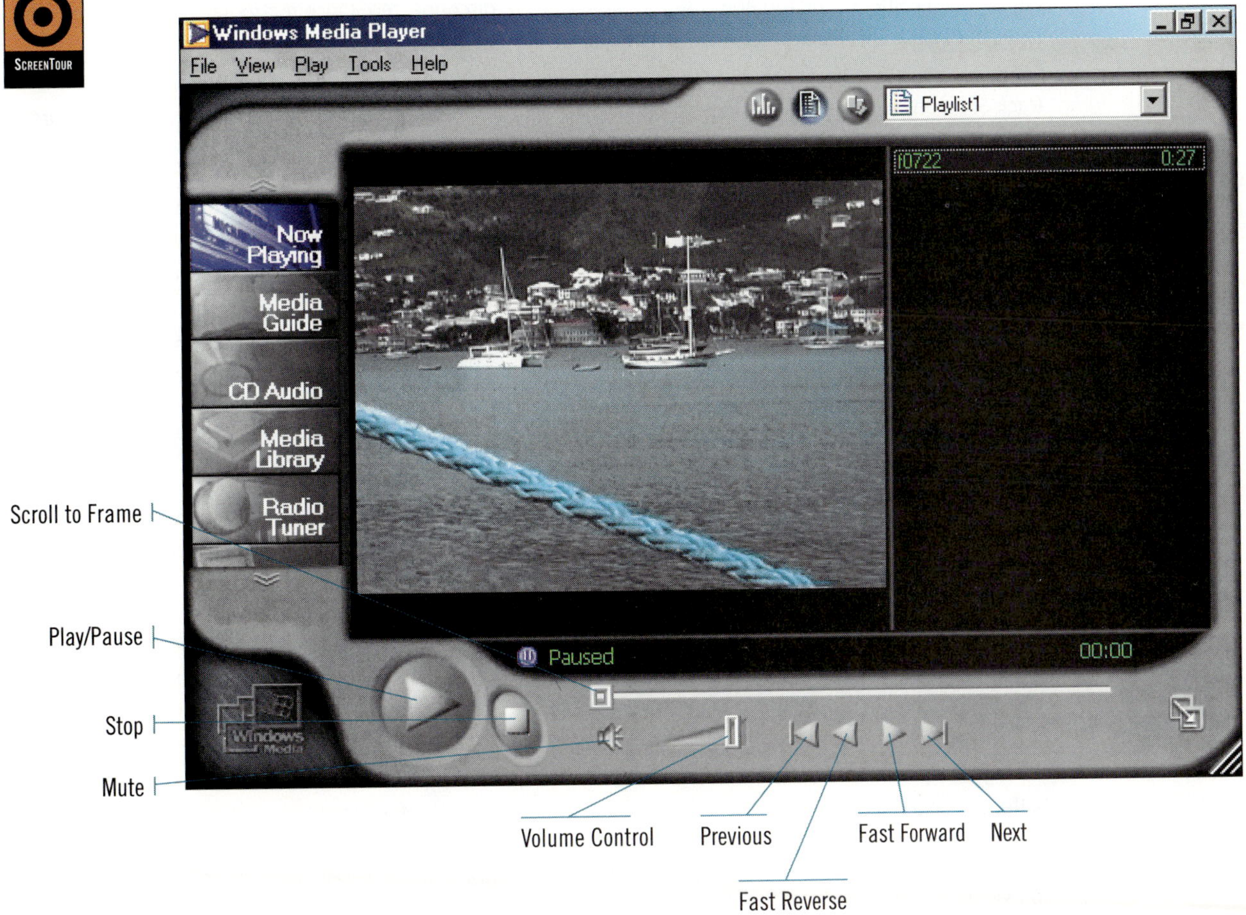

Exploring video equipment

To create a desktop video, you need a video camera. To edit and modify video footage, you transfer the video footage from your video camera to your computer. This lesson explores cameras you can use to capture the video and the equipment that you need for transferring the video footage from your camera to your computer. This lesson also discusses computer devices, such as cards and cables that you will need to transfer the video to a computer for editing.

DETAILS

- You can use either a digital or an analog video camera to shoot the footage for desktop video. A **digital video camera** stores footage as a series of bits. The video data is stored on a tape in much the same way that digital data is stored on a backup tape. Digital video tape formats include miniDV, DVCPro, and DVCam. MiniDV is used by most consumer digital video cameras.

  You can also use an **analog video camera** to shoot the footage for your desktop video. As with digital video cameras, the footage is stored on tape; but instead of storing bits, an analog video camera stores the video signal as a continuous track of magnetic patterns. The three most popular analog video formats are Hi8, S-VHS, and VHS. VHS produces lower quality video than Hi8 or S-VHS, and none of these analog formats produces video that matches the quality of a digital video camera.

- In addition to video cameras, you might also be familiar with the small inexpensive videoconferencing cameras that attach directly to a computer. See Figure H-18. These cameras capture video data in digital format and are designed mainly for talking head applications, such as online video chats and videoconferences. You can use videoconferencing cameras to create digital video, but they produce very low-quality video.

  Digital cameras generally produce higher quality video than analog or videoconferencing cameras. Images produced using digital video cameras tend to be sharper and more colorful. Generally speaking, the higher the quality of the original video, the better the final video will look.

- In order to digitally edit, process, and store a desktop video, you must transfer the video footage from your camera to your computer. A digital video camera captures video data in digital format, which can then be directly transferred to a computer for editing. See Figure H-19. You can transfer video footage from a digital camera to a hard disk by a cable connecting the video camera and computer. Most digital cameras provide a **FireWire port** or **USB port** for this purpose. Your computer needs a corresponding port to accept the cable from the camera. Figure H-20 shows computers with built-in FireWire and USB ports.

  When the transfer is complete, the cable can be disconnected. Once the footage is transferred and stored on a random-access device, such as your computer's hard disk, you can easily cut out unwanted footage, divide the remaining footage into separate clips, and rearrange clips.

- Analog video footage must be converted into digital format before it is stored on your computer's hard disk. This analog-to-digital conversion process is referred to as capturing a video. A **video capture device** converts the camera's analog signal into digital data. If your computer's graphics card does not include video capture capabilities, you can purchase a separate video capture device that connects to your computer's USB port or a video capture card that plugs into one of your computer's PCI slots. A video capture card is shown in Figure H-21.

- Whether you're transferring footage from an analog camera or a digital camera, you must use **video capture software**, which allows you to start and stop the transfer and select the display size, frame rate, filename, and file format for your video footage. Your video will be easier to edit if you divide it into several files, each containing a one-to-two-minute segment of footage.

FIGURE H-18: Video conferencing camera

A video conferencing camera sits on top of a computer monitor

FIGURE H-19: Transferring video from a digital video camera to a computer

Cable connecting a video camera and computer

Digital video camera

FIGURE H-20: FireWire and USB ports

▶ FireWire ports (left) and USB ports (right) can be located on the front or the back of the computer's system unit

FIGURE H-21: A video capture card

Editing and processing desktop video

Before video cameras went digital, editing a video consisted of recording segments from one videotape onto another. This process, called **linear editing**, required at least two VCRs. Today's **non-linear editing** simply requires a computer hard disk and video editing software, and has the advantage of using a random-access device to edit and arrange footage. The disadvantage is that video footage requires a lot of available storage space.

DETAILS

● Once your video footage is transferred to your computer and stored on the hard disk, you can edit it using **video editing software**. Your completed video consists of video tracks containing video segments and transitions, plus audio tracks containing voices and music. You arrange the video tracks and the audio tracks on a timeline. Most video editing software allows you to overlay a video track with several audio tracks. See Figure H-22.

● After you modify your video tracks and audio tracks, your video editing software combines the data from all of the selected tracks into a single file. This file is stored on your computer's hard disk as a desktop video using a video file format, such as AVI.

● The video footage that you capture and transfer to your computer contains more data than can fit on a CD, DVD, or hard disk. For a desktop video to fit on a personal computer storage device, it is necessary to reduce the number of bits used to represent the video data. To shrink videos to a more manageable size, you can do one of the following:

• Decrease the size of the video window. When creating desktop video, you can specify the size of the window in which your video appears. A smaller window contains fewer pixels than a full-screen window and requires fewer bits to represent the data, but some details become difficult to see.

• Reduce the frame rate. The smooth motion that you expect from commercial films is achieved in a desktop video by displaying 24 fps. Reducing the frame rate to 15 fps—a typical rate for desktop video—cuts the file size almost in half. However, reducing the frame rate tends to increase the blurriness of a video, especially for fast-action sequences.

• Compress the video data. Several compression techniques were created specifically to reduce the size of video files. A **codec (compressor/decompressor)** is the software that compresses a file when a desktop video is created and decompresses the file when the video is played. Popular codecs include MPEG, Indeo, Cinepak, DivX, and Video 1. Each of these codecs uses a unique compression algorithm and allows you to specify the level of compression that you desire.

• The three videos associated with Figure H-23 illustrate the differences in image quality and file size that result from using different compression techniques.

● Most video editing software allows you to set the file format, frame rate, color depth, and compression levels as you are saving the video in its final form.

Web-based video

A video for a Web page is stored on a Web server in a file. Usually a link for the video file appears on the Web page. When you click the link, the Web server transmits a copy of the video file to your computer. If you have the correct video player installed on your computer, the video appears on your computer screen. Sometimes your computer has to wait until it receives the entire video file before starting to play it. An alternative method, called **streaming video**, sends a small segment of the video to your computer and begins to play it while your computer continues to receive it. Streaming video is possible with QuickTime, ASF, and RealMedia video formats.

You can add two styles of video to your Web pages. The first style, called **external video**, simply displays a link to a video file; when the link is clicked, the video file is downloaded, the video player is opened, and the video is dis-

played in a separate window. A second style of Web video is called **internal video**, or in-place video. Instead of opening a separate window for the video player, an internal video plays within the Web page.

Although it is possible to play streaming videos over a dial-up connection, it is truly an unsatisfying experience. High-speed Internet connections provide much more bandwidth for streaming video. Videos that are designed to be played over high-speed connections can have a larger video window and less compression, resulting in better quality. Until everyone has a high-speed connection, however, many Web sites provide one video file that's optimized for dial-up connections and a better-quality video file optimized for DSL, cable, and ISDN connections.

FIGURE H-22: Video editing software

Use the video tracks on the timeline to indicate the sequence for your video clips and transitions

Use the audio tracks to add sound clips

The video and sound clips that you import for the project appear in a list

Timeline

Preview your video to see how the video segments, transitions, and sound-track all work together

FIGURE H-23: Comparing compression and frame rates

▶ To achieve the best compression for a particular video, you'll probably have to experiment with different codecs, compression levels, and frame rates; the codec used to compress a video also must be used to decompress the video when it is played; videos intended for a widespread audience should use one of the codecs included in popular video players, such as QuickTime or Windows Media Player; missing codecs account for a high proportion of desktop video glitches

Compression ratio: 35:1
Frame rate: 3
File size: 35 KB

Compression ratio: 14:1
Frame rate: 10
File size: 76 KB

Compression ratio: 3:1
Frame rate: 15
File size: 353 KB

Introducing digital sound

Computers can record, store, and play sounds, such as narrations, sound effects, and music. Swapping music files over the Internet is currently a popular use of digital sound, but digital sound also plays a key role in many other interesting applications. This lesson introduces digital sound concepts and technologies.

DETAILS

● **Waveform audio** is a digital representation of sound. Music, voice, and sound effects can all be recorded as waveforms. To record sound digitally, samples of the sound are collected at periodic intervals and stored as numeric data. Figure H-24 shows how a computer digitally samples a sound wave.

● **Sampling rate** refers to the number of times per second that a sound is collected or measured during the recording process and is expressed in hertz (Hz). One thousand samples per second is 1,000 Hz or 1 KHz (kilohertz). Higher sampling rates increase the quality of the sound recording but require more storage space than lower sampling rates.

● The height of each sample can be saved as an 8-bit number for radio-quality recordings or as a 16-bit number for high-fidelity recordings. Professional audio CDs are recorded at a sampling rate of 44.1 KHz, which means a sample of the sound is taken 44,100 times per second. Sixteen bits are used for each sample. Stereo effects require two of these 16-bit samples. Therefore, each sample requires 32 bits of storage space.

Applications that do not require such high-quality sound use much lower sampling rates. Voice is often recorded with a sampling rate of 11 KHz (11,000 samples per second). This rate results in lower-quality sound, but the file is about one fourth the size of a file for the same sound recorded at 44.1 KHz. The ScreenTours associated with Figure H-25 illustrate how sampling rate affects sound quality.

● Your computer's **sound card** contains a variety of input and output jacks plus audio-processing circuitry. It contains the circuitry responsible for transforming the bits stored in an audio file into music, sound effects, and narrations. You will usually find a desktop computer's sound card plugged into a PCI expansion slot inside the system unit. Sound card circuitry is sometimes built into the motherboard of notebook computers.

A sound card is typically equipped to accept input from a microphone and provide output to speakers or headphones. For processing waveform files, a sound card contains a special type of circuitry called a **digital signal processor**, which transforms digital bits into analog waves when you play back a waveform audio file, transforms analog waves into digital bits

when you make a sound recording, and handles compression and decompression, if necessary.

● Waveform audio can be stored in a variety of file formats. The **Wave** (.wav) audio format was created originally as the native sound format for the Windows platform. Today it is in widespread use on many computer platforms. **Audio Interchange Format** (.aif) was developed by Apple and, like Wave, has become a popular cross-platform audio format. **RealAudio** (.ra) is a proprietary format created especially for the Web by a company called RealNetworks. **MP3** (.mp3) is a type of MPEG format popularized by a free music exchange site called Napster. The extensions of some additional waveform file formats are .au, .mod, .voc, .ram, and .rpm. Table H-2 presents some of the advantages and disadvantages of the most popular waveform audio file formats.

● To play an audio file, you must use an audio player, such as Microsoft Media Player. These players tend to support several audio file formats. Some players, however, might not allow you to record audio data. In the Windows environment, for example, you can use Microsoft Media Player to play Wave, AIF, and MP3 formats, but you cannot use it to record sound. For recording, you must use Microsoft's Sound Recorder software. To play a digitally recorded sound, the bits from an audio file are transferred from disk to the microprocessor, which routes them to your computer's sound card. The digital signal processor handles any necessary decompression and then transforms the data into analog wave signals. These signals are routed to the speakers to create the sound. The software used to play and record various audio file formats might be included with your computer's operating system, packaged with your sound card, or available on the Web.

● Wave format files are supported by most Web browsers, so it is a popular audio file format. RealAudio, AIF, and MP3 can also be delivered over the Web. Web-based waveform audio is often delivered in streaming format over the Internet so it plays as it is downloaded. Streaming audio avoids lengthy delays while the entire audio file is downloaded and provides the technology for real-time Internet radio broadcasts and voice chat sessions.

FIGURE H-24: Sampling a sound wave

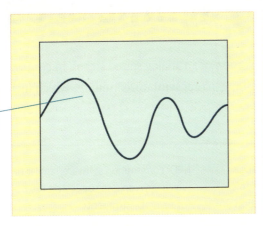

An analog sound wave is a smooth curve of continuous values

Sample	Sample Height (Decimal)	Sample Height (Binary)
1	130	10000010
2	140	10001100
3	160	10100000
4	175	10101111
5	185	10111001

The height of each sample is converted into a binary number and stored; the height of sample 3 is 160 (decimal), so it is stored as its binary equivalent—10100000

To digitize a sound wave, it is sliced into vertical segments, called samples; for purposes of illustration, this one-second sound wave was sliced into 30 samples

FIGURE H-25: Comparing audio clips

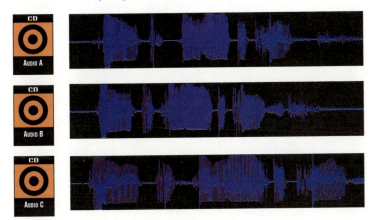

TABLE H-2: Popular waveform audio file formats

AUDIO FORMAT	EXTENSION	ADVANTAGES	DISADVANTAGES
Wave	.wav	Good sound quality; supported in browsers without a plug-in	Audio data is stored in raw, uncompressed format, so files are very large
Audio Interchange Format	.aif	Good sound quality; supported in browsers without a plug-in	Audio data is stored in raw, uncompressed format, so files are very large
MP3 (also called MPEG-1 Layer 3)	.mp3	Good sound quality even though the file is compressed; can be streamed over the Web	Requires a stand-alone player or browser plug-in
RealAudio	.ra	High degree of compression produces small files; data can be streamed over the Web	Sound quality is not up to the standards of other formats; requires a player or plug-in

Exploring synthesized sound

SPEECH SYNTHESIS AND RECOGNITION

Waveform audio is a digital version of an analog sound signal. In contrast, **synthesized sound** is artificially created. This lesson explores synthesized sounds, which include MIDI music and synthesized speech.

DETAILS

● **MIDI (Musical Instrument Digital Interface)** specifies a standard way to store music data for synthesizers, electronic MIDI instruments, and computers. MIDI is a music notation system that allows computers to communicate with music synthesizers. Unlike waveform sound files, which contain digitized recordings of real sound passages, MIDI files contain instructions for creating the pitch, volume, and duration of notes that sound like various musical instruments. MIDI files are much more compact than waveform audio files.

● The computer encodes the music as a **MIDI sequence** and stores it as a file with a .mid, .cmf, or .rol filename extension. A MIDI sequence contains instructions specifying the pitch of a note, the point at which a note begins, the instrument that plays the note, the volume of the note, and the duration of the note.

● Most computer sound cards are equipped to capture music data from a MIDI instrument as well as generate music from MIDI files. A MIDI-capable sound card contains a **wavetable** (sometimes called a patch set), which is a set of pre-recorded musical instrument sounds. The sound card accesses these sounds and plays them as instructed by the MIDI file.

● One of the big disadvantages of MIDI is that it is not suitable for vocals. Another disadvantage is that it does not have the full resonance of waveform audio sound. Most musicians can easily identify MIDI recordings because they simply lack the tonal qualities of symphony-quality sound, as illustrated in the audio clips associated with Figure H-26.

● MIDI is a good choice for adding background music to multimedia projects and Web pages. Using a procedure similar to that for waveform audio files, you can add a link to a MIDI file by inserting a tag within an HTML document. Most browsers include built-in support for MIDI music.

You can use MIDI software to compose your own tunes, or you can get permission to use MIDI files that you find on the Web. For composing your own MIDI music, you can input the notes from a MIDI instrument, such as an electronic keyboard, directly to your computer. The input is typically handled by

MIDI composition software, similar to that shown in Figure H-27, which you can also use to edit the notes and combine the parts for several instruments.

● **Speech synthesis** is the process by which machines, such as computers, produce sound that resembles spoken words. **Speech recognition** (or voice recognition) refers to the ability of a machine to understand spoken words.

● Speech synthesis is a key technology in wireless communication, such as accessing your e-mail via cell phone—a speech synthesizer reads your e-mail messages to you. A speech synthesizer can also read a computer screen aloud, which unlocks access to computers and the Internet for individuals with disabilities. Most speech synthesizers string together basic sound units called **phonemes**. A basic speech synthesizer consists of **text-to-speech software**, which generates sounds that are played through your computer's standard sound card; other speech synthesizers are special-purpose hardware devices.

● On a personal computer, a speech recognition system typically collects words spoken into a microphone that's attached to the sound card. The sound card's digital signal processor transforms the analog sound of your voice into digital data, which is then processed by speech recognition software. **Speech recognition software** analyzes the sounds of your voice and breaks them down into phonemes. Next, the software analyzes the content of your speech and compares the groups of phonemes to the words in a digital dictionary that lists phoneme combinations along with their corresponding English (or French, Spanish, and so on) words. When a match is found, the software displays the correctly spelled word on the screen.

● Speech recognition software can be integrated with word processing software so that you can enter text simply by speaking into a microphone. Besides word processing, speech recognition can also be used instead of a mouse to activate Windows controls. Most speech recognition software also works with your browser, allowing you to use your voice to access the Web.

 **FIGURE H-26: MIDI music**

FIGURE H-27: MIDI composition software

You can also place notes on the staff using your mouse

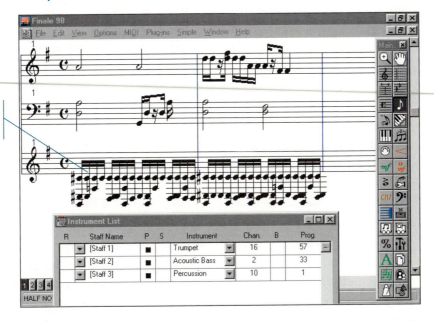

What is MP3?

MP3 is a compressed waveform audio format that stores digitized music, vocals, and narrations in such a way that the sound quality is very good, but the file size remains relatively small—small enough to download from the Web. A CD track that requires 32 MB of storage space shrinks to approximately 3 MB in MP3 format. Famous performing artists and aspiring rock stars use MP3 files to post sample sound tracks from their albums on Web sites.

MP3 files are available from several Web sites, but you can also create your own MP3 files from audio CDs. Software called a CD ripper grabs tracks from an audio CD and stores them in Wave format. After ripping a CD into Wave format, you can use an **MP3 encoder** to convert the Wave file into MP3 format. MP3 files can be stored on your computer's hard disk, transferred to a CD, or relocated to a portable MP3 player. A portable MP3 player (Figure H-28) is a hardware device that plays MP3 files stored in onboard flash memory or on CDs.

FIGURE H-28

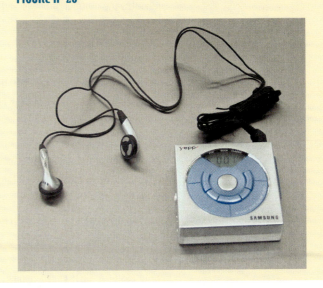

Digital media files can be quite large. They need lots of storage space, require lengthy transmission times, and easily become fragmented, which reduces the efficiency of your computer's hard disk drive. Reducing the size of a file would minimize these problems. **Data compression** is the general term used to describe the process of recoding data so that it requires fewer bytes of storage space; bytes are removed, which reduces the file size. Because data compression is reversible, bytes previously removed from a file can be restored. The process of reversing data compression is sometimes referred to as uncompressing, decompressing, extracting, or expanding a file.

The amount of shrinkage produced by data compression is referred to as the **compression ratio**. A compression ratio of 20:1, for example, means that a compressed file is 20 times smaller than the original file. Data compression is based on a **compression algorithm**—the steps that are required to shrink the data in a file and reconstitute the file to its original state. A compression algorithm is incorporated into a codec, which is used by a computer to compress and decompress file data. Some compression algorithms are designed to shrink text files; other algorithms are for graphics, sound, or video data. Some compression algorithms are generalized and work for any type of data.

Compression that reduces the file size without any data loss, **lossless compression**, provides the means to compress a file and then reconstitute all of the data into its original state. In contrast, **lossy compression** throws away some of the original data during the compression process. Lossy compression can be applied to graphics, videos, and sounds because, in theory, the human eye or ear won't miss the lost information. Most lossy compression techniques provide adjustable compression levels so that you can decide how much data you can afford to lose.

Although most of today's codecs contain sophisticated compression algorithms that are beyond the scope of this book, we can look at some examples of simple compression algorithms to get a general idea of how they work. **Dictionary-based compression** replaces common sequences of characters with a single codeword, or symbol, that points either to a dictionary of the original characters or to the original occurrence of the word. **Statistical compression**, such as the well-known Huffman algorithm, takes advantage of the frequency of characters to reduce file size. Characters that appear frequently are recoded as short bit patterns, while those that appear infrequently are assigned longer bit patterns. **Spatial compression** takes advantage of redundant data within a file by looking for patterns of bytes and replacing them with a message that describes the pattern. **Run-length encoding (RLE)** is an example of a lossless, spatial compression technique that replaces a series of similarly colored pixels with a code that indicates the number of pixels and their colors. **Temporal compression** is a technique that can be applied to video footage or sound clips to eliminate redundant or unnecessary data between video frames or audio samples. In the case of video, for example, if you are working with a video of a talking head, the background image is likely to contain lots of redundant information that doesn't change from one frame to the next. As the temporal compression algorithm begins to analyze the frames, the first frame becomes a **key frame** that contains all of the data. As the compression algorithm analyzes subsequent frames in the video, it stores only the data that is different from the data in the key frame.

Some file formats, such as PCX, GIF, and MP3, always compress data. Other file formats allow you to select not only whether or not you want to compress the file, but also the level of compression. The software that you use to save and open these files contains the codecs necessary to compress and decompress them. Table H-3 lists various file formats and their compression ratios.

To manually compress a file, such as a Word document or a Windows bitmap image, you can work with a **file compression utility**, to shrink one or more files into a single new file. You cannot use this compressed file until it has been decompressed. WinZip, a file compression utility, produces compressed files with .zip extensions. Compressing a file is called **zipping**; decompressing a file is called **unzipping**. Figure H-29 shows files that were zipped using WinZip software.

TABLE H-3: Popular image file formats

FORMAT (EXTENSION)	COMPRESSION	ADVANTAGES	POPULAR USES
Windows Bitmap (.bmp)	Not compressed in any way; creates the largest graphics files of any file format	Native bitmap graphic file format of the Microsoft Windows environment; supports True Color	Wide variety of graphics applications, such as photographs, illustrations, and graphs
PC Paintbrush (.pcx)	Automatic lossless compression	Graphics are usually 8-bit (256-color)	Drawings
Tag Image File Format (.tif or .tiff)	Automatic lossless compression	A flexible and platform-independent format; supported by most photo-editing software; supports True Color; easily converted into other formats	Scanners and digital cameras commonly store images in TIFF format
Joint Photographic Experts Group (.jpeg)	Built-in lossy compression that stores data efficiently in a small file	You control the level of compression and resulting file size; stores True Color bitmap data	Photographs and Web graphics
Graphics Interchange Format (.gif)	Uses lossless compression algorithm patented by UniSys	Limited to 256 colors; images can display on multiple platforms	Format for Web graphics; simple non photographic images
Animated Gig (.gif)	Always compressed	Add animation to Web page	Simple animation on Web
Portable Network Graphics (.png)	Compresses bitmap data without losing any data, images retain same quality as originals	Display up to 48-bit True Color; a public domain format without any restrictions on its use	Web graphics
Vector graphics (.wmf, .dxt, .mgx, .eps, .pict, .cgm)	Consists of instructions to create image	Resizes easily, doesn't become pixilated, easy to edit and move	Line art, logos, simple illustrations, diagrams
Scalable Vector Graphics (.svg)	Designed to produce compact data stream	Supports gradients, drop shadows, transparencies; automatically resized when displayed on different screens or printed	Web, handheld devices, pagers, cell phones
Flash graphics (.swf)	Requires less space than SVG	Animations on the Web	Animation on the Web but require a plug-in

FIGURE H-29: The WinZip window

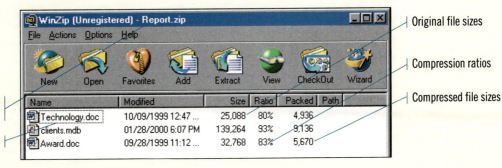

Name of new, compressed file

Names of original files

Original file sizes

Compression ratios

Compressed file sizes

In early 1999, an 18-year-old student named Shawn Fanning developed a Web-based technology for sharing MP3 music files. This technology, dubbed "Napster" after Shawn's nickname, quickly became one of the hottest applications on the Internet. In less than a year, its user base exceeded 25 million. Almost immediately, Napster ran afoul of the Recording Industry Association of America (RIAA), a watchdog organization that represents record companies, such as Columbia Records, Motown Records, and Epic Nashville. The RIAA compiled a list of 12,000 copyrighted songs that Napster technology made available as free downloads. In December of 1999, the RIAA filed suit, accusing Napster of contributing to copyright infringement, which considerably reduced the revenues of record companies and artists. The ensuing court battle stirred up a caldron of issues that relate to the use and abuse of digital media, including music, photos, and videos.

To get a handle on the controversy, it is necessary to understand how Napster works. Napster was created as a peer-to-peer network technology that could run over the Internet. Anyone with an Internet connection could become part of the Napster network simply by registering at the Napster Web site, downloading the Napster client software called MusicShare, and installing it.

Registered users make their MP3 files available over the Napster Network by placing the files in a user library folder on their own computers' hard disks. Whenever a registered Napster user logs in at the Napster Web site, the names of his or her MP3 files are uploaded to the Napster server and incorporated into a master database. These MP3 filenames only remain in the database and accessible while the registered Napster user is logged in.

Any Napster member can search the master database to find the name of a specific music file. Once found, the file is transferred directly between the hard disks of the users. No MP3 files are stored on Napster servers, nor do these files travel through Napster servers as they are transferred from one user to another. No copyrighted material is ever in Napster's possession. So how can Napster be held responsible for copyright violation? The argument went something like the following:

RIAA: Napster is providing technology that is infringing on copyrights held by record companies and recording artists.

Napster: No copyrighted material was ever stored on our servers.

RIAA: But you knew that your registered users were using your technology to illegally exchange copyrighted music files.

Napster: What's illegal about it? The Audio Home Recording Act of 1992 allows people to make recordings and lend them out to people, provided it is not done for commercial purposes. Our members were not getting paid for allowing others to copy their MP3 files, so our network has nothing to do with commercial use.

RIAA: Even though money is not changing hands, Napster-style copying is commercial use for two reasons: First, Napster users are distributing files, not to their friends, but to Napster users they have never met. Second, by getting files for free, Napster users don't buy the music through legitimate channels, and that has tangible commercial repercussions.

Napster: But Napster can't be held responsible for users who break the law. Remember that the courts refused to hold video tape recorder manufacturers and retailers responsible when their machines were used to make tapes of copyrighted television shows. Also, remember that the Digital Millennium Copyright Act protects Internet Service Providers from being liable for illegal actions on the part of their subscribers.

RIAA: Ah, but ISPs are only protected if they have no knowledge of their subscribers' illegal actions. We asked the court to subpoena your e-mail records, and there is clear evidence that you knew what your members were doing! Just look at the names of the files in your database "Yellow Submarine by the Beatles," and "Celebrity - N Sync."

Napster: Even if we knew, how could we stop them? Suppose that instead of calling a file "Yellow Submarine by the Beatles," one of our users named it "Light-Colored Underwater Craft by a Famous British Rock Group?" We would have no way to screen that file out of our database.

RIAA: If you can't find a way to police your network, we'll ask for damages to the tune of $5 million.

The Napster controversy deterred, but did not stop similar file-sharing sites. Some of these sites operate legally by making sure that the files, especially MP3 files, are in the public domain, or posted with permission from the artist and record company. Other music-sharing networks, such as LimeWire and BearShare, provide access to copyrighted material, but use a slightly different technology called Gnutella. Unlike Napster, Gnutella networks require no central database. In true peer-to-peer fashion, client software installed on one user's computer searches for other similar clients. For example, as soon as a Gnutella client comes online, it sends a signal to another Gnutella client. That client then tells eight other clients that it has established contact with the new client. Each of those eight then tells seven others, who tell six others, and so on. This way, each client tells many other clients it is online and what content it has available.

P2P utilities, such as Gnutella, that employ this decentralized approach provide another unique set of legal challenges. Because there is no central server maintaining an index of users, there is no easy way to target and stop the use of the network and its software. Many content developers in music, video, and similar creative industries are beginning to realize that fundamental changes are on the horizon. Shutting down Napster might stop the first wave of digital distribution, but will it have much effect on the tidal wave of digital distribution issues that are yet to come?

▼ INTERACTIVE QUESTIONS

○ Yes   ○ No   ○ Not sure   **1.** Do you think that most people realize that copyright law gives musicians and record companies the exclusive right to distribute their music?

○ Yes   ○ No   ○ Not sure   **2.** Do you believe that music-sharing networks should not allow their members to swap copyrighted music without the permission of the copyright holder?

○ Yes   ○ No   ○ Not sure   **3.** Can you envision any way to monitor Gnutella networks to make sure that they don't contribute to illegal activities?

▼ EXPAND THE IDEAS

1. Do you believe that it is not a breach of the law to take music off the Web and create CDs or to copy purchased music for personal use? Why or why not? Write a short paper supporting your position.

2. Research three current music-sharing networks. Are their policies stated on their Web sites? What restrictions, if any, do they impose on music taken from their sites? Find a site that charges for downloading music. Create a table to compile your findings. Write a brief summary comparing and contrasting the trends that you found.

3. Can you envision any way to monitor Gnutella networks to make sure that they don't contribute to illegal activities? What monitoring strategies are currently in place or in development? Write a short paper discussing your findings. Be sure to include your sources.

End of Unit Exercises

▼ KEY TERMS

24-bit bitmap
32-bit bitmap
Analog video camera
ASF
Audio Interchange Format
AVI
Bitmap graphics
Bitmap image
BMP
Card reader
Codec
Color depth
Color palette
Compression algorithm
Compression ratio
Cropping
Data compression
Density
Desktop video
Dictionary-based compression
Digital camera
Digital signal processor
Digital video camera
Digitizing tablet

Dithering
Drawing software
External video
File compression utility
FireWire port
Flash graphics
Flash memory
Floppy disk adapter
Frame rate
GIF
Gradient
Grayscale palette
Infrared port
Internal video
JPEG
Key frame
Linear editing
Lossless compression
Lossy compression
Megapixels
Memory card reader
Metafile
MIDI
MIDI sequence

Monochrome bitmap
MP3
MP3 encoder
MPEG
Non-linear editing
Paint software
Phonemes
Pixel interpolation
PNG
QuickTime
Rasterization
Ray tracing
RealAudio
RealMedia
Rendering
Resolution
Resolution dependent
Run-length encoding
Sampling rate
Scanner
Sound card
Spatial compression
Speech recognition
Speech recognition software

Speech synthesis
Statistical compression
Streaming video
SVG
Synthesized sound
System palette
Temporal compression
Text-to-speech software
TIFF
Tracing software
True Color bitmap
Unzipping
USB port
Vector graphic
Video
Video capture device
Video capture software
Video editing software
Wave
Waveform audio
Wavetable
Web palette
Wireframe
Zipping

▼ UNIT REVIEW

1. Use your own words to define bold terms that appear throughout the unit. List 10 of the terms that are least familiar to you and write a sentence for each of them.

2. Make a list of the file extensions that were mentioned in this unit and group them according to digital media type: bitmap graphic, vector graphic, digital video, waveform audio, and MIDI. Circle any formats that are used on the Web.

3. Make a list of the software mentioned in this unit, indicating the type of task that it helps you accomplish.

4. Describe the devices that transfer photos from a digital camera to a computer. Explain the different procedures required to transfer analog or digital video from camera to computer.

5. Describe how resolution and color depth contribute to the size of a graphic file.

6. Explain how a computer monitor displays color, and how a color palette can be used to reduce file size.

7. Explain how the concept of layering relates to your ability to modify a vector graphic.

8. Make a list of the advantages and disadvantages of bitmaps and vector graphics.

9. Explain how streaming audio and video work and contrast them to non-streaming technology.

10. Explain sampling rate. Be sure to discuss how it affects sound quality and file size.

▼ FILL IN THE BEST ANSWER

1. While a(n) _____ digitizes printed images, a digital _____ digitizes images of real objects.

2. JPEG, _____, and PNG are bitmap graphics formats and are supported by most browsers.

3. The dimensions of the grid that forms a bitmap graphic are referred to as its _____.

4. Bitmap graphics are resolution _____, which means that the quality of an image relies on its resolution.

5. Color _____ refers to the number of colors available for use in a bitmap graphic.

6. A color _____ holds the selection of colors and allows you to select a group of colors to use for a bitmap graphic.

7. A(n) _____ graphic contains the instructions that a computer needs to create the shape, size, position, and color for each graphic.

8. _____ graphics tend to have a cartoon-like rather than a realistic appearance.

9. Graphics that contain both bitmap and vector data are called _____.

10. The process of applying color and texture to a 3-D graphic wireframe is called _____.

11. Ray _____ is the process of adjusting the colors in a rendered image to coincide with the highlights and shadows that would be produced by a light source.

12. _____ editing moves footage from one video-tape to another, whereas _____ editing uses a random-access device, such as a hard disk, to hold both the original footage and finished video.

13. The _____ of a video file can be reduced using three techniques: reducing the frame rate, decreasing the size of the video window, and compressing the video data.

14. AVI, QuickTime, MPEG, and RealMedia are examples of _____ video formats.

15. When you transfer footage from an analog or digital camera to your computer, you must use either a(n) _____ port or a(n) _____ port.

16. You use video _____ software to start and stop the transfer and select the display size, frame rate, filename, and file format for your video footage.

17. A(n) _____, such as MPEG or Indeo video, is the software that compresses a video.

18. The number of times per second that a sound wave is measured is referred to as the _____ rate.

19. The popular waveform audio format that is based on MPEG is called _____.

20. Speech _____ is the process by which machines, such as computers, produce sound that resembles spoken words.

▼ PRACTICE TESTS

CD
EXERCISE

When you use the Interactive CD, you can take Practice Tests that consist of 10 multiple-choice, true/false, and fill-in-the-blank questions. The questions are selected at random from a large test bank, so each time you take a test, you'll receive a different set of questions. Your tests are scored immediately, and you can print study guides to determine which questions you answered incorrectly. If you are using a Tracking Disk, insert it in the floppy disk drive to save your test scores.

▼ INDEPENDENT CHALLENGE 1

Do you own a digital camera? Do you know someone who does? If you look at the advertisements that come with the local papers, you will see that most electronic retailers are selling digital cameras. How can you know which is best for you?

1. Research the latest offerings in digital cameras. Find three leading manufacturers of digital cameras.

2. List and compare the features and prices for the cameras that are being sold in your area.

3. What is the range of prices? How is price related to megapixels?

4. Select three models, one in each price range (inexpensive, moderate, and expensive) that you might consider purchasing.

5. List any accessories that you would have to purchase with the camera.

6. Create a table comparing features and prices. Determine what is the best value. Write a summary of your findings and which camera you might purchase.

▼ INDEPENDENT CHALLENGE 2

Do you own a digital video camera? Do you know someone who does? If you look at the advertisements that come with the local papers, you will see that most electronic retailers are selling digital video cameras as well as the Hi8 and VHS format video cameras.

1. Research the latest offerings in digital video cameras. Find three leading manufacturers of digital video cameras.

2. List and compare the features and prices for the cameras that are being sold in your area.

3. What is the range of prices? How is price related to features?

4. Select three digital models, one in each price range (inexpensive, moderate, and expensive) that you might consider purchasing. Also select one HI8 or VHS video camera.

5. List any accessories that you would have to purchase with the camera.

6. Create a table comparing features and prices. Determine which is the best value. Write a summary of your findings and which camera you might purchase.

▼ INDEPENDENT CHALLENGE 3

 The Web has a wide variety of music, video, and sound files available for download. You can sample new artists and, if you like what you hear, you can purchase the CD.

1. Log onto the Internet and search for music by your favorite artist.

2. Download and listen to the audio file. Was it the entire song? What was the format of the file? Write a brief summary of how you found the music, the source of the file, what software you used to download and then listen to the music.

3. Locate, download, and view a video file from the Internet.

4. What was the content of the video? Was it an inline or external video? Did the video play all at once or did it stream? What was the format of the file? Write a brief summary of how you found the video, and what software you used to download and then view the video.

▼ INDEPENDENT CHALLENGE 4

The GIF format is very popular for Web graphics. Its use is controversial because the GIF format uses the LZW compression technology, which is owned by UniSys. Currently, UniSys allows individuals to use GIF graphics on Web sites freely, as long as these graphics were created by software approved and licensed by UniSys. Although the GIF format is popular, some Web developers express concern about further restrictions or fees that UniSys might require in the future.

1. Research the GIF controversy. Write a short paper that includes information answering the following questions.

    a. Who invented LZW compression and when was the information first published?

    b. When was the LZW compression technique incorporated into the GIF format?

    c. Why did GIF become so popular?

    d. What are the alternative non-proprietary graphics formats that can replace GIF?

    e. What information about GIF usage restrictions has been provided by UniSys?

    f. What is the current status of the GIF controversy?

2. Make sure you incorporate specific bibliographic information to indicate the sources of your answers in your report.

▼ LAB: WORKING WITH BITMAP GRAPHICS

1. Start the interactive part of the lab. Insert your Tracking Disk if you want to save your QuickCheck results. Perform each of the lab steps as directed and answer all of the lab QuickCheck questions. When you exit the lab, your answers are automatically graded and your results are displayed.

2. Use the Start button to access the Programs menu for the computer that you typically use. Make a list of the available bitmap graphics software.

3. Capture a photographic image from a digital camera, scanner, or Web page. Save it as "MyGraphic." Open the image using any available graphics software. Use this software to discover the properties of the graphic. Indicate the source of the graphic, then describe its file format, file size, resolution, and color depth.

4. Prepare this graphic file to send to a friend as an e-mail attachment that is less than 200 KB. Describe the steps that were required.

5. Suppose that you want to post this image on a Web page. Make the necessary adjustments to file size and bit depth. Describe the resulting graphic in terms of its resolution, bit depth, palette, and dithering.

▼ LAB: VIDEO EDITING

1. Start the interactive part of the lab. Insert your Tracking Disk if you want to save your QuickCheck results. Perform each of the lab steps as directed and answer all of the lab QuickCheck questions. When you exit the lab, your answers are automatically graded and your results are displayed.

2. Use the Control Panel's Add/Remove Programs icon to view and make a list of the video players that are available on your computer.

3. Locate a video clip on the Web and indicate the URL of the Web page on which it can be found. Describe the video's properties, including file size and format.

4. Play the video that you located for Lab Assignment #3. Describe the visual and sound qualities of the video and discuss how they relate to your Internet connection speed. Also describe the length and content of the video, the use of transitions or special effects (if any), and the use of sound tracks. If you could edit this video yourself, what changes would you make to make it more effective?

▼ VISUAL WORKSHOP

Speech-enabled technology is being incorporated into software packages, specifically productivity packages. Microsoft and IBM (ViaVoice technology) along with many other companies are making tremendous inroads in research and development. Apple Computer Company uses Apple's Speech Recognition and Speech Synthesis Technologies. See Figure H-30.

FIGURE H-30

1. Log onto the Internet and use your favorite search engine to research speech technology for productivity software. What features of Office XP and Lotus SmartSuite for the PC incorporate speech technology? How does the current version of MAC OS incorporate speech? Click the applications link on the Apple Web site and find two Mac applications that use speech. What are the similarities and differences between these applications and those for PCs?

2. Can you picture yourself sitting at a desk talking to your computer? What about a busy office of people sitting in close proximity speaking to their computers? Would this work? Why or why not?

3. Speech technology is a very hot topic. Research developments in speech technology and write a brief paper on the types of software that would benefit from a speech component. What are the drawbacks and benefits to a speech-enabled software package?

TRENDS

Trends in Technology

OBJECTIVES

Exploring evolving trends in ...

Computer I/O components

Processors and memory components

Storage

Networking

Wireless connectivity

The Internet

Productivity software

Leisure technology

Technologies once the domain of science fiction writers and filmmakers are now integral to people's daily lives. Today, you can pick up a device small enough to fit comfortably in your pocket, press a few keys, and then communicate by speaking or exchanging images instantly with anyone anywhere in the world. Now, you can have the breadth of the world's knowledge through the World Wide Web instantly at your fingertips. Learning about and understanding the technology that makes this all possible is fascinating and overwhelming—fascinating because of the way technology impacts our daily lives, overwhelming because the science behind the technologies continually changes and evolves at rapid rates. For the average consumer it is not important to fully understand or keep up with every aspect of technology. However, it is important to have a general idea of market trends. This unit highlights a sampling of emerging trends in computer technology.

Exploring evolving trends in ...
Computer I/O components

The trend in PC development (desktop, notebook, and handheld computers) is to produce systems that are more powerful, smaller, faster, cheaper, and lighter than their previous counterparts. This lesson explores recent developments and trends in computers and in the external input and output components that are part of a computer system.

DETAILS

● **Supercomputers:** Although supercomputers don't usually sit on the desk of the average person, technology for supercomputers is advancing. For example, the Macintosh G4 has the capability of creating computer clusters capable of **high–performance computing (HPC)**. Processing speeds of HPC systems are measured in **FLOPS (floating point operations per second)** or **MIPS (millions of instructions per second)**. As explained on the Apple Web site, "What makes a supercomputer 'super' is its ability to execute at least one billion floating-point operations per second, a staggering measure of speed known as a 'gigaflop'." An HPC computer called ASCI Q at the US Department of Energy works at 30 teraflops (30 trillion calculations per second). One hour at 30 teraflops can do the work that a typical PC running at 2.2 GHz might take 60 years to complete.

● **Internet appliances:** Internet appliances are designed for the sole purpose of accessing the Internet. All of the software, the browser, the operating system, any programs, and utilities, come on a CD-ROM disk. An Internet appliance boots from a CD and has no storage capacity. Because you cannot write files to an Internet appliance, there are no file management issues, disk organization concerns, or security and virus concerns. Internet appliances can be used for a variety of tasks, including sending and receiving e-mail via the Web, subscribing to newsgroups, and accessing the Web. Internet appliances are being embraced by consumers who want easy Internet access at home, and by businesses that need domain name and dial-up services but that don't want to devote a PC to that service.

● **Display Technologies:** Imagine being able to fold a monitor into your pocket and then simply to roll it out when you need it. **Organic light emitting diode (OLED)** is a technology that creates display devices that are thinner, have higher resolutions, and are more power efficient than the dominant technologies used in monitor displays today: Cathode Ray Tube (CRT) displays or Liquid Crystal Displays (LCD). Two British companies— Cambridge Display Technology (CDT) and Opsys—estimate that the first roll-up computer screens and TVs will be available by

2005. Another company, Universal Display, envisions a flexible flat panel display, like the one prototype shown in Figure T-1.

Liquid Crystal Display (LCD) technology is the primary technology used in **flat panel displays (FPD)**. Although still more expensive than CRTs, FPD monitors are becoming the monitor of choice because they have less glare and images have a more realistic appearance. A new technology called **Field Emission Display (FED)** is being developed for use in FPDs. FED technology makes possible the thin panel of today's LCDs, offers a wide field of view, provides a high image quality, and requires less power than today's CRT displays. Some believe FPD monitors using FED technology are more environmentally friendly both when in use (because they emit less radiation and are more energy efficient) and when they are disposed (because they are not made with mercury, lead, and glass like CRT monitors).

● **Input Devices:** Recent developments in pointing devices include mice that use **force feedback technology**, optical technology, or wireless connections. Force feedback means you can feel motion coming back to you though the pointing device. This is particularly useful when pointing devices are used in medical applications and training situations. **Optical mice** use optical technology rather than a roller ball to transmit information. No roller ball means that the mouse will not behave erratically when the ball gets dirty or worn. **Wireless mice** use infrared or radio frequency rather than cables to communicate with the computer so you aren't restricted or tangled by the wires. Today's wireless mice are power conscious. They run on batteries. Some mice have power-saver options where a tap on the mouse puts it to "sleep" to save power. Many manufactures have added customizable buttons, such as the Forward and Back buttons, which can be used to facilitate Internet browsing. The design of the mouse has also changed over time to be more ergonomic to help avoid repetitive stress injuries to the hand and wrist of users.

Research into interface technology includes devices that transport motion into commands without the use of keys. University of Delaware researchers have developed a device called iGesture, see Figure T-2, which uses a touch pad as the input device.

FIGURE T-1: Prototype of FOLED

▶ Rollout or flexible display panels use a more efficient production method, which effectively prints a special type of OLED on a surface. Hopes for the technology are high because such displays do not require a back light. This makes rollout displays energy efficient and thin—so thin they can be folded.

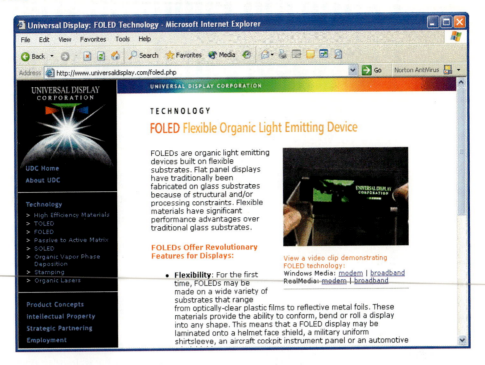

FIGURE T-2: iGesture

▶ The touch pad works much like a video camera, but records the finger movements of a user. The processor inside the pad then turns the finger movements into commands.

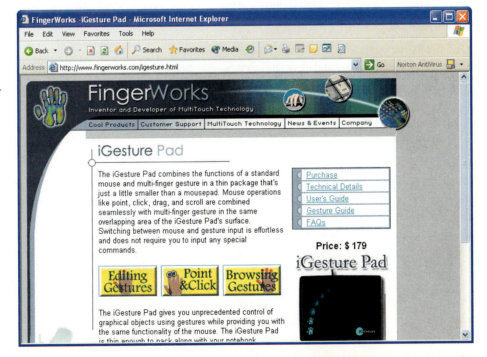

Keyboards

Keyboard technology has continued to evolve. There are researchers working on **membrane keyboards**, which cost less than keyboards with mechanical switches and, because they can be sealed, are designed to work in a variety of environmental conditions. Some new keyboards are very flexible and can be rolled up for portability. Advances have been made in **wireless keyboards** that work with IR (infrared) devices to transmit input to the computer and that can be used up to 50 feet away from a computer or printer. There are new keyboard designs that offer viable alternatives to the typical layout, such as keyboards designed to allow you to place your hands, wrists, and forearms in a natural position for greater comfort while typing or keyboards designed to be used by just one hand.

Exploring evolving trends in ... Processors and memory components

The microprocessor is the heart of the personal computer. Advances in microprocessor technology drive the personal computing market. Before purchasing a computer with a new processor, it is a good idea to research the processor. Benchmark tests on processors provide current information about a chip—the manufacturer's claims and the reality. The terms "memory" and "storage" used to be clearly distinct, but the line for differentiating these concepts as they relate to computers is blurring. This lesson explores processors and memory.

DETAILS

● **Processors:** The leading manufacturers of processors are IBM, Intel, Advanced Micro Devices (AMD), and Transmeta. Generally, a company manufactures several lines of processors; each one in a series builds on and improves the features and the functionality of the processor that came before it.

● **Intel:** The trend in personal computing today is toward more media applications, which require faster and more efficient processing than word processing applications. Intel supports that trend with its **Pentium® 4** processor, which is its premier desktop processor. The chip delivers higher clock speeds with lower thermal output. The Pentium 4 uses Intel's **Hyper-Threading Technology**, which lets one chip act almost like two.

● **Advanced Micro Devices (AMD):** AMD processors include the **Athlon** and **Duron** family of processors. These processor families are designed for desktop, mobile, server, and workstation computers. See Figure T-3. In addition to processors for the PC, AMD offers solutions for wireless connectivity. New technology advances in the **Alchemy** processor for Wireless LAN include low power consumption, compact design, and increased battery life. AMD's **Opteron** is a new family of enterprise-class processors for servers and workstations. Sandia National Laboratories is installing a $90 million supercomputer from Cray that will run on Opteron processors. The supercomputer, code-named Red Storm, will contain approximately 10,000 Opteron chips and will be capable of churning 40 trillion calculations per second (40 teraflops) when it becomes operational in 2004.

● **Transmeta:** Transmeta's premier product is the **Crusoe** processor. With Crusoe, Transmeta pioneered a revolutionary new approach to microprocessor design. It uses an innovative software layer called **Code Morphing** software that dynamically "morphs" (that is, translates) x86 instructions into the hardware engine's native instruction set. See Figure T-4. The Crusoe chip is a low-power chip. This makes it ideal for Internet devices and the ultra-light mobile PC category because it has low power consumption and has an extended battery life.

● **Other processors:** In addition to the processors in desktop and laptop computers, other devices such as handhelds and cell phones use processors. Advances in processors for these other devices are driving their markets as well. Currently, processors for cell phones and other wireless devices are somewhat limited because different chips generally are needed to handle the devices' memory, processing, and communications tasks.

● **Memory: Flash memory, memory sticks**, and **smart media** are referred to as memory, but these components don't lose their contents when the power goes off, making them more like storage. This is a new and evolving class of storage. Digital cameras and portable devices such as PDAs, portable computers, and cell phones make use of these memory technologies.

RAM technology has gotten cheaper, faster, and smaller, as with most technology. Desktop computers now come standard with 256-512 MB RAM. Those that come with less can be easily upgraded. Advances are being made in research and development for alternative RAM technology. One alternative is **magnetic RAM (MRAM)**, which is being developed by IBM in cooperation with Infineon Corporation. The potential benefits of magnetic RAM are instant-on capability and longer life batteries.

FIGURE T-3: AMD chips

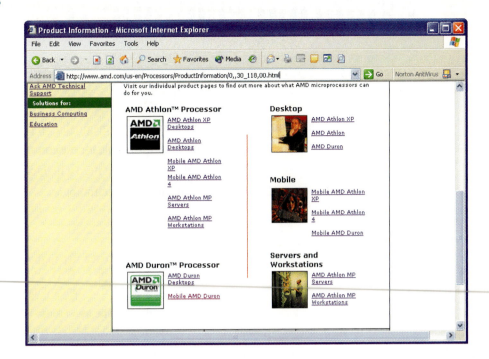

FIGURE T-4: Transmeta's Crusoe chip

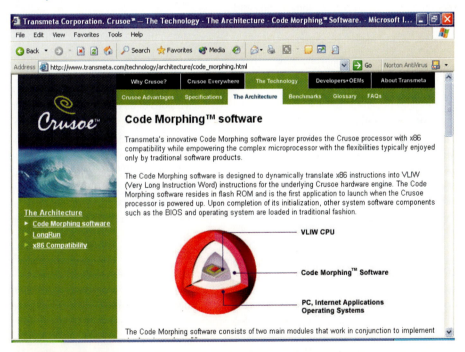

Chip technology research

Millions of dollars are spent on chip technology research and development. Research at Intel has resulted in many new breakthroughs in chip engineering. According to Intel, the latest new chip technology will use "strained silicon." A strained silicon chip can function with less energy, which means devices consume less power and work faster. In addition to this research, Intel is exploring low power circuit technology, high performance/low power data path circuits, and high speed signaling.

IBM researchers have been working on molecular computing for chips. They have built and operated a computer circuit using **qubits**, which have the potential of representing not just a 1 or a 0, but of representing both a 1 and a 0 at the same time. This definitely means faster and more powerful computing.

These advances in processors are still in the research and development stage, but they represent trends in microprocessor development—smaller, faster, and more energy efficient than what is currently available.

Exploring evolving trends in ... Storage

There was a time when a one gigabyte hard drive was unimaginable. Today, hard disk drives with capacities ranging from 50 GB to 133 GB are readily available for the consumer market. If you're into editing and storing digital photos or home movies, you need a high-capacity hard drive. This lesson explores the recent trends in storage devices and technologies.

DETAILS

● **Hard disks:** Hard disk trends include hard disk drives that have gotten smaller in physical size. One example is the IBM **Microdrive**. See Figure T-5.

Another development in storage technology is **MEMS-based storage**. MEMS-based storage is based on MEMS (MicroElectroMechanical Systems) technology that combines storage and processing on one chip. It is expected to have access times much faster than current conventional disks. Being able to integrate the processor and the storage device will improve power consumption and cost. MEMS-based storage is not currently available commercially; however, MEMS-based storage is laying the foundation for advances in systems and storage devices.

● **Removable storage: Removable storage devices** allow you to store your data in a safe place. Another benefit to removable storage is the ability to work on a computer, remove the storage device, then plug it into another computer in another location and continue to work. These removable storage devices plug into USB ports and many are platform independent. One drawback, however, is that removable storage devices tend to have slower transfer rates and lesser capacities than high-capacity hard drives that are installed in a computer. A discussion of some options regarding removable storage devices follows:

• **Flash memory** is a solid-state storage device. **Solid state** means that there are no moving parts—everything is electronic instead of mechanical. Flash memory devices include CompactFlash, SmartMedia cards, and PCMCIA Type I and Type II memory cards. These devices are small and sturdy—for example, they can be dropped without losing data and they are not affected by extreme heat or cold. The next generation of flash memory is based on 0.13 micron technology and is aimed at use in wireless devices.

• **CD-ROM and DVD technology:** Some researchers indicate that DVD (Digital Video/Versatile Disk) technology is the next step beyond the CD-ROM. The trend is for DVD drives to be included as standard hardware in desktop systems.

Taking that concept a step further, Philips Electronics has developed a design for DVD-rewritable drives that soon could be included as standard hardware in PCs.

● **Network drives:** The trend today is to network computers—in the workplace and at home when more than one computer is being used. **Network drives** are drives that are directly connected to a network and are accessible from all computers on the network. One advantage to a network drive is shared space without having the overhead of sharing a folder on a PC. There are some security risks in having access to shared folders on a network. To address that concern in a business environment, a new storage technology known as self-securing storage is becoming available. **Self-securing storage** devices keep all versions of all data for a specified period of time and continually monitor requests. This allows system administrators to review requests and determine if data has been compromised.

Another trend today is to facilitate the business practice of remote backup by providing access to online drives. **Online drives** allow businesses and individuals to store files on a "virtual hard drive" via an Internet connection. Figure T-6 shows the home page for one online company, My Docs Online. At present, there are some concerns with online drives. For example, the storage space available in the online drives is determined by the online drive vendor and so the user might find only limited space available. Access to online drives is typically slower than access to system hard drives because the access is dependent on the Internet connection. Finally, vendors can go out of business with little or no notice, which leaves the user without access to data.

● **Pixie dust:** A technology that IBM is using, informally called **pixie dust**, is pushing the limits of current drive technology by increasing capacity levels. The multilayer coating technology is expected to permit hard disk drives to increase current area density limits. IBM's Travelstar laptop hard disk drive is the industry's first using this new magnetic data storage media. Travelstar notebook hard disk drive products have data densities up to 25.7 gigabits per square inch.

FIGURE T-5: IBM Microdrive

▶ The Microdrive family of products holds from 340 MB to 1 GB of data storage capacity on a disk that is the size of an American quarter! Microdrive is compatible with devices from many manufacturers, including laptops, digital cameras, handhelds, and card readers.

FIGURE T-6: Online storage service

▶ As broadband access to the Internet becomes the norm, online storage services allow businesses and individuals to back up data to remote locations.

Tape is not gone

Tape storage, an early system before hard disks, is still very much used for backup and storage. While CDs are an inexpensive way to quickly back-up data for a personal system, CDs may not hold the quantity of data that a business user needs. Tape technology has advanced to the point where storing terabytes of data are possible. IBM was the first to record 1 terabyte (TB) of data to a linear digital tape cartridge, storing nearly 10 times more data than any linear tape cartridge previously available. One terabyte is equal to 16 days of continuously running DVD movies, or 8,000 times more data than a human brain retains in a lifetime.

Exploring evolving trends in ... Networking

Networks drive connectivity. Whether by cable, satellite, radio, or telephone, networks define our interconnected world. There is the Internet, intranets, LANs, and WANS. Even handheld devices are now more likely than not to be working interactively with other computers. New technologies being developed allow for greater amounts of data to move at faster rates and in a secure environment. This lesson explores advances in networking technologies and standards.

DETAILS

● **Virtual Local Area Network (VLAN):** Businesses today are implementing VLANs. A VLAN is a group of personal computers, servers, and other network resources that are on physically different segments of a network, but communicate as though they were on the same segment. A VLAN is a logical grouping rather than a physical grouping. It is a network created by software that combines stations and network devices into a single unit, regardless of the physical LAN segment they are actually attached to. Because these networks are software based, there are many advantages. For example, changes do not have to be hard wired. Users and resources that are likely to work together can be grouped in common VLANs to optimize the network. VLANs free up bandwidth to boost traffic through the network and allow more control in securing the network.

● **Virtual Private Network (VPN):** A VPN is a private network that is configured within a public network, typically the Internet, to regulate the users who can access it. VPNs are built on common carriers so, in effect, they appear as private networks; but, in fact, they are in a shared network with many other users. VPNs have the appearance of a private network but take advantage of the built-in facilities of large public networks. Typically, businesses have used VPNs for outsourcing remote access, connecting sites over the Internet, and connecting outside users over an extranet. VPN security poses unique challenges. Encryption has been a primary defense.

● **Clustering: Cluster computing** allows computers to work together to maximize performance. Researchers frequently use clustering to maximize processing power. A **cluster** is a group of devices that share a server or group of servers. They can share processing tasks or provide backup in case of failure of any of the connected servers. Clustering technology was used by both the International Human Genome Sequencing Consortium and Celera Incorporated to sequence the human genome. Clustering technology is essential to e-business, and it is used to balance traffic on high-traffic Web sites. *Red Herring*

magazine identifies clustering technology as one of the top 10 trends in computing.

● **Home networks:** If you have more than one computer, you don't need more than one scanner or printer if you are able to network your computers to those peripheral devices. Towards this end, home networking has become a requirement for many people who own computers. Basic options for home networks include powerline networking (such as HomePLC), phone-line networking (such as HomePNA), and wireless networking (such as HomeRF). Apple's AirPort is a home networking wireless solution. See Figure T-7.

● **Free Space Optics (FSO):** Consumers are currently connected to the Internet using a variety of connections, such as dial-up modems over existing phone lines, broadband connections through local cable service, broadband through existing phone lines (DSL), or wireless connections through satellite connections. But an up-and-coming technology being used to bridge the connection between businesses and the Internet's fiber optic backbone is **Free Space Optics (FSO) technology**. FSO uses line of sight technology and can be used with various protocols including ATM, IP, and Ethernet networks. The transceiver is about the size of a security video camera.

● **Enterprise computing network:** A recent trend in business networks is enterprise computing networks, which are information systems that share data and typically provide information to very large groups of users. FedEx or UPS use enterprise computing networks to track customers, billing, shippers, and packages by combining computers across several systems in a very large scale network. These networks handle data in several formats across many communication systems. Enterprise hardware integration and software integration link together for enterprise system integration to allow systems to share data and link diverse types of processing, input, and output.

FIGURE T-7: AirPort

IEEE standards

All networks are built on standards, which are constantly being updated and revised. LAN and MAN standards are available through the Institute of Electrical and Electronics Engineers, Inc. (IEEE). The IEEE (pronounced Eye-triple-E) is a non-profit, technical professional association of more than 377,000 individual members in 150 countries. The standards set by this association are what keep past, present, and future networks communicating. You can visit sites, like the one shown in Figure T-8, to keep up with current trends in industry standards.

FIGURE T-8: IEEE

Exploring evolving trends in ... Wireless connectivity

Freedom, the ability to get what you want when you want it, is a driving force behind wireless computing. Advances in chip technology and battery life made portable computing a reality. Now, remote and wireless connectivity has freed the user from the physical limits of cables. Devices are being developed that combine the features of wireless connectivity and essential productivity tools—such as cell phones, portable computers, and personal data assistants (PDAs)—into a single device. This lesson focuses on the technologies and products that enable you to connect to your company, your friends, and the world from wireless devices.

DETAILS

802.11 standards: The IEEE Standard **802.11b** establishes wireless network speed, which can reach up to 11Mbps. The 802.11b standard lets you hook up an appropriately configured portable device to your Ethernet network wirelessly. The **802.11a** standard, which succeeds the 802.11b standard, supports high-speed wireless LANs and delivers data rates up to 54Mbps. As consumer demand for improved wireless connections increases, subsequent versions of the 802.11a standard are expected to result in future speed improvements. Wireless LAN products that are IEEE 802.11 compliant and available today include routers, network adapters, PCI or PCMCIA cards, and printer servers.

Wi-Fi (Wireless Fidelity) is the commercial term for any 802.11 network. Wi-Fi technology is the wireless equivalent of Ethernet, providing seamless network connection. See Figure T-9. Many laptops are equipped with Wi-Fi technology which allows for wireless Internet access over 802.11 networks. In fact, Wi-Fi is being used in public places such as restaurants, airports, hotels, and conference centers—any place where users might want access to information while on the go. Some cellular companies are planning to expand markets into Wi-Fi networks.

Bluetooth: Another technology used for wireless networking is Bluetooth technology. Bluetooth technology uses a globally available frequency range. While Bluetooth is well suited for mobile and cellular products, it has had some problems, such as limited range, that are keeping it from becoming the leader in wireless connectivity.

As these trends in wireless communication become more prevalent, one of the issues they will have to deal with is potential interference with each other. They both use the same RF (radio frequency) band. One solution to the problem is to allow channel selection so that devices can switch channels and not be in conflict with one another.

2.5G and 3G networks: While most people use their cell phones for voice communication, some are using their cell phones for data. The new 2.5G packet-oriented data transfer technologies and the emerging high-speed access 3G systems are designed to combine voice, data, and Internet into portable wireless appliances. 3G, which stands for "third-generation," combines wideband radio communications and IP-based services. Several major companies deliver mobile IP (Internet Protocol) standards based on 2.5G and 3G high-speed wireless networks. For example, Cingular Wireless has GPRS (General Packet Radio Service) 3G wireless data service. "GPRS provides consumers, as well as business users, with an improved wireless Internet experience with 'always on' access to information," said Stephen Carter, CEO of Cingular. "It gives consumers the flexibility to toggle between an Internet session (say wireless access to e-mail) and a phone call or text message without having to abandon their connection."

Wireless Application Protocol (WAP): Open Mobile Alliance (OMA) is a group of companies and organizations that have come together to drive the growth of the mobile industry. Their mission is "to grow the market for the entire mobile industry by removing the barriers to global user adoption and by ensuring seamless application interoperability while allowing businesses to compete through innovation and differentiation." OMA supports the development of products and services that are based on WAP—a global open standard that gives mobile users access to the Internet.

FIGURE T-9: Wi-Fi

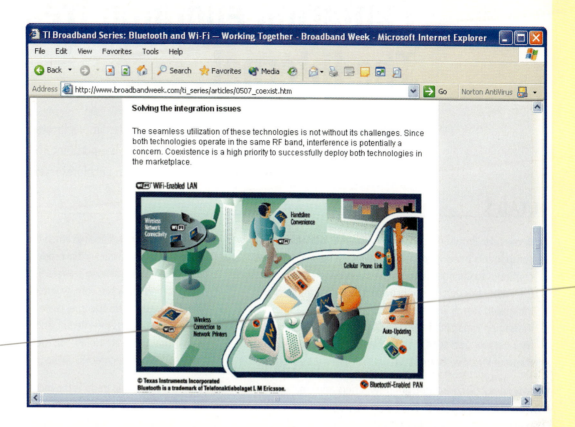

Impact on consumers

So what does all of this promise of seamless, wireless connectivity mean for consumers? One benefit is the deployment of **E911 (Enhanced 911)** technology by 2005 in all mobile phones. See Figure T-10. E911 technology seeks to provide 911 dispatchers with better information from wireless calls, such as location. One area for growth is **m-Commerce (mobile commerce)**, which gives consumers the ability to communicate and conduct business transactions through mobile devices (such as cell phones and PDAs) and wireless networks.

One area of concern involves security and privacy issues. Consumers will need to be assured their wireless transmissions are secure.

Another area of concern is health issues that might arise because of increased and prolonged exposure to potentially dangerous radio waves associated with wireless connectivity. While studies in this area are being conducted, some companies are proactively seeking to calm concerns. For example, Levi Strauss has introduced a line of jeans in Germany that has a pocket to hold a cell phone, claiming that this pocket has a special lining that might protect the wearer from cell phone radiation. Another company has introduced a specially lined hat with earflaps to protect from cell phone radiation. As wireless connectivity continues to evolve, benefits and concerns will be explored.

FIGURE T-10: E911

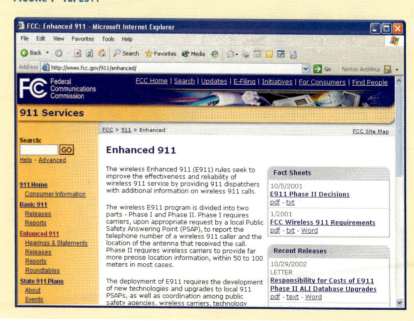

Exploring evolving trends in ...
The Internet

Internet-related technologies are developing quickly. For example, browsers, which are the window to the Web, have become more sophisticated, user-friendly, and ubiquitous as they are now being built into PDAs, cars, cell phones, and watches. This lesson explores recent trends in the Internet.

DETAILS

● **Browsers:** Browser technology is not new, but advances in components integrated into browsers are new. As the Web continues to change, so too must the browsers used to navigate the Web. New versions of browsers include enhanced and integrated search and explorer bars, media bars, and instant messaging capabilities. **AIM (AOL Instant Messaging), MSN Messenger,** and **ICQ (I Seek You)** are instant messaging communities. See Figure T-11.

● **Internet2:** A consortium of researchers and universities are working together with high-tech corporations and some government agencies to build the next generation of the Internet—Internet2. Internet2 is not a separate physical network and will not replace the Internet. Internet2 researchers are performing experiments using new and existing resources, including **middleware**. Middleware is intelligent software that prioritizes packets on the Internet. It is the "glue" that binds together major applications and negotiates communications between them. Middleware is used to help applications work more effectively over advanced networks through standardization and interoperability.

● **Future of HTML:** HTML, originally the building block of Web page development, can now look toward XML (Extensible Markup Language), which is the future of Web page development. XML is a meta-language. It describes the structure of data.

● **New top-level domains: ICANN (Internet Corporation for Assigned Names and Numbers)** is the nonprofit corporation that was assigned the responsibility for IP addresses and domain name system management. Just as use of the Internet and the Web has grown over the years, so too has the need for domain names. In November 2000, ICANN selected seven new top-level domains (TLD). See Table T-1.

● **File sharing:** Napster was the pioneer in providing music MP3 files through peer-to-peer networking. Even though Napster

encountered legal difficulties when the courts determined they were infringing on intellectual property, other Web sites continued to offer similar file-sharing services. The music industry has started sites, such as MusicNet.com, where users can buy music. As broadband Internet access becomes more prevalent, movies are also being shared across the Internet. Following the example set by the music industry, major Hollywood movie studios are delivering movies over the Internet via online movie-rental services.

● **Advertising:** One trend is the inclusion of advertising windows in software. Some software developers are opting to include advertising to help offset the cost of development.

● **Services on the Net:** The trend is for brick-and-mortar stores to offer their services online. Today, you can bank, plan vacations and purchase airline tickets, purchase concert tickets, and more—all over the Internet. You can share photos through online photo services. Mortgage brokers can take and process your applications online. Ebay and other online auction services let you buy, sell, and swap goods right from your computer. All you need is a digital image and a credit card. Payment services handle the financial transactions to protect both buyers and sellers.

Some day you may even be able to close a business deal over the Internet with a handshake. Research scientists have developed a device that let them "shake hands" over the Web. They accomplished this handshake by moving a computer-generated cube between them, each responding to the force the other exerted on it. Devices called **phantoms** recreated the sense of touch by sending small impulses at very high frequencies via the Internet. Not only can scientists feel the force being exerted by colleagues across the Atlantic Ocean, they can also feel the texture of the object their colleagues are feeling. This has implication for training across the Internet where sensory feedback is required to teach skills.

FIGURE T-11: ICQ home page

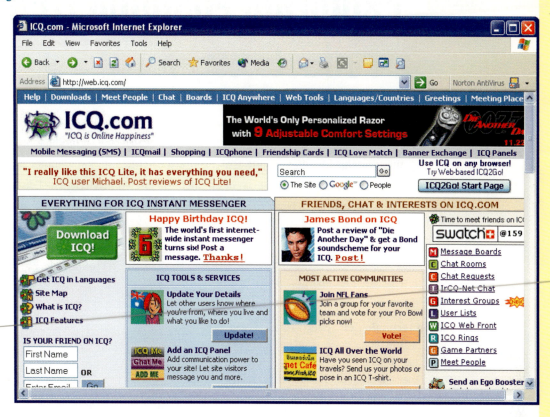

TABLE T-1: New top-level domains

DOMAIN	DESCRIPTION	DOMAIN	DESCRIPTION
.biz	Unsponsored; but intended for businesses	.aero	Sponsored; for air transport industry
.info	Unsponsored; but intended for information Web sites	.coop	Sponsored; for corporations
.name	Unsponsored; but intended for individuals	.museum	Sponsored; for museums
.pro	Unsponsored; but intended for accountants, lawyers, physicians, and other professionals		

An "unsponsored" TLD operates under policies established by the global Internet community directly through the ICANN process, while a "sponsored" TLD is a specialized TLD that has a sponsor representing the narrower community that is most affected by the TLD. The sponsor carries out delegated policy-formulation responsibilities over many matters concerning the TLD. *Source: http://www.icann.org/tlds*

Modems and dialup

Since dial-up modems will remain a popular way to access the Internet for several years, standards are being developed to improve user experience. Two standards include **V.92** and **V.44**. The V.92 standard provides faster upstream transport than that currently available using a V.90 modem. V.44 standard is a compression standard that compacts the data before it is sent. The V.44 compression standard will be incorporated in many modems designed to comply with the V.92 standard. Three new features that will be included in some modems built to the V.92 standard include Quick Connect, Modem-on-Hold™ (MOH), and PCM Upstream.

Exploring evolving trends in ... Productivity software

Productivity software is software designed to help individuals increase their ability to perform tasks associated with most jobs. The basic categories of productivity software include document production, graphics, database, spreadsheet, presentation graphics, and Web development. As electronic communication becomes more prevalent, connectivity (such as e-mail and instant messaging) may need to be added to the categories. This lesson looks towards the future of productivity software—not only exciting new applications and new features being added to existing products, but also to the ways productivity software is delivered.

DETAILS

- **Speech recognition technologies: Speech-to-text (STT)** technology lets you speak to digital devices and have your words translated into digital code that is "understood" by your computer. Leaders in the field of speech recognition technology include Dragon Systems' Dragon Naturally Speaking (NatSpeak), IBM ViaVoice, Microsoft, and Apple's Speech Recognition and Speech Synthesis Technologies. Using STT to "train" your computer to understand your voice and customize the application dictionary, you can dictate words into documents, numbers into spreadsheets, and data into databases. Microsoft Office XP already has this capability. Advances are being made in the area of STT and handheld recording devices, which will be used by medical and legal professions.

- **Productivity software for the office:** Software is available that automates just about every corporate administrative function. The trend has been to use improved B2B communications software as well as integrated software tools to improve production and hold down costs. Recent advances in database, word processing, presentation graphics, e-mail client, scheduling, and spreadsheet technologies include greater integration with the Web and greater potential for collaboration. New features include: adding compressed MP3 files into slide shows, compatibility with open standards including HTML with cascading style sheets, and support for XML for document files. Software such as those that Macromedia publishes allows you to publish high impact slide shows for the Web. Clients download the player, such as Macromedia's Flash program (see Figure T-12), for free.

In this way, a business can disseminate high definition graphics presentations for their products or courses directly to a client's desktop though the Web. Another trend is the increased use of networks to share resources.

- **Graphics and imaging software:** Digital cameras are changing the way many businesses capture and process their images. Real estate professionals, artists, law enforcement officials, medical professionals, and educators, are using digital cameras for digital imaging and video editing.

- **Web-based Application Service Providers (ASPs):** The traditional model for purchasing software in a box off a shelf in an office business center (whether it be an online retailer or a physical store) is changing. Many software publishers are turning to the Web as a delivery system. Clients no longer have their software on servers in their companies; instead, ASPs charge customers via a contract for access to Web-hosted applications. Advantages to using ASPs include automatically having the most recent version of software and having fixes to known bugs already installed in the software. However, hosted applications have some disadvantages. They work only when you're connected to the Internet. If you lose the connection, you are no longer able to access the application. Performance depends on the speed of the connection; therefore, high-speed connections are required. If the ASP has problems, you may find you cannot use the application at a critical moment, even if your computer is working perfectly.

FIGURE T-12: Flash home page

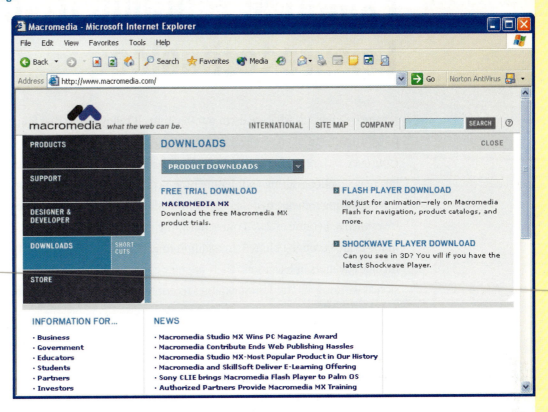

Future trends

Advances in productivity software are making technology transparent and pervasive. Categories of productivity software will need to be expanded to include such areas as robotics and artificial intelligence. For example, doctors are using cutting-edge productivity software to perform robot-assisted surgery. They are using communications productivity software to practice telemedicine, which is the transmission of healthcare data—such as a consultative diagnosis. See Figure T-13.

Businesses are exploring wearable PCs so technicians and specialists can have access to their productivity software at all times. Some wearable PCs are projected to be voice-controlled so they can be used hands-free. No matter what advances in productivity software are made, the basic premise—that productivity software increases user ability to perform tasks—will never change.

FIGURE T-13: An example of telemedicine

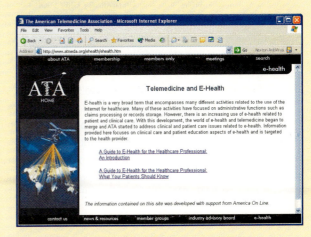

Exploring evolving trends in ... Leisure technology

Leisure is defined as what we do in our free time. It follows then that leisure technology is the technology that helps us accomplish what we want to do in our free time. Often, business technologies cross over and are used as leisure technologies. For example, you might use software often used in business situations during your leisure time—communications software to do personal e-mail, desktop publishing software to design party invitations, or finance software to track your personal investments. Because of 24/7 connectivity, the lines between business technologies and leisure technologies are becoming blurred. In addition to technologies associated with PCs, leisure technologies include advances in television. There are new computer-based technologies that will change television as we know it. This lesson explores recent trends in gaming and other leisure technologies. As you explore these trends, think about how these systems change the way we live and play.

DETAILS

● **PCs as TVs:** Watching TV is a favorite leisure time activity that crosses cultures and age groups. New technologies make it possible to watch TV on your PC. Many new PCs include a DVD drive and TV tuner along with built-in recording technology. The Sony Vaio Digital Studio PC features a Giga Pocket Personal Video Recorder, which allows consumers to watch TV programs streamed from digital TV, satellite, cable, or other sources. HP MediaCenter and Windows XP MediaCenter (see Figure T-14) are two software packages that can enable your PC to record and play TV programs, play almost any removable media such as CDs and DVDs, play games, and connect to the Internet.

● **Digital video recorder (DVR):** Not only do people like to spend their leisure time watching TV, they like to watch it when it is convenient for them to do so. Up until recently, video recorders provided the main technology to record TV programs and play movies. However, this technology may soon be replaced by DVRs, which allow viewers to record TV and video digitally. There are four primary parts to a DVR: a hard drive, a TV tuner card, a channel guide, and a modem. Currently, these are standalone boxes; the future is to build DVRs into television sets. Personal TV services, such as TiVo and SONICblue's ReplayTV, are computer-based systems that allow you to control how and when you watch television. TiVo powers a DVR and works with every TV system. It is a subscription-based service that automatically records programs that you specify. Because TiVo is computer-based, you can pause, rewind, and instantly replay live TV. ReplayTV includes software that allows viewers to

skip over commercials. This has lead to court battles, whose outcomes may help to redefine how television generates revenue.

● **Set-top box controllers:** Many set-top box devices, those devices that sit on top of your television to access services that display through the television, have begun to use IBM's STBP (Set-Top Box Peripheral) chip technology. These are designed for use in a wide range of digital television products including **integrated digital television (IDTV)** sets, **personal video recorders (PVRs)**, and satellite, cable, and digital terrestrial receivers. IBM's new set-top box processors also support the emerging **multimedia home platform (MHP)**, considered to be an integral component to the future success and expansion of digital interactive television—an emerging leisure technology.

● **eBooks:** In addition to watching TV, reading is another favorite leisure pastime, making **eBooks** and online magazine readers two new leisure technologies. eBooks and online magazines are similar to their print versions but with several electronic features linked directly to your computer. Advances in type technology, such as Adobe Cooltype and Microsoft ClearType, improve text resolution. The software makes it easier to read the content on a computer display because of the improved text display. Adobe Acrobat eBook Reader and Microsoft Reader are provided free from the Internet and enable you to read eBooks directly on your notebook or desktop computer. Online magazine readers are also available for free. Zinio Reader for Windows is an example of a digital magazine reader. See Figure T-15.

FIGURE T-14: Windows XP MediaCenter

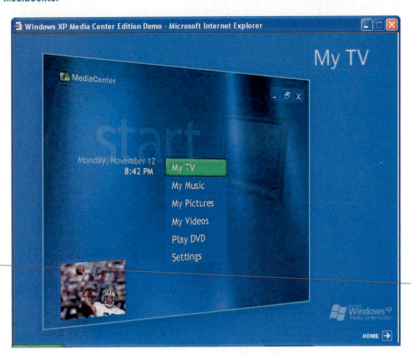

FIGURE T-15: Zinio Magazine Reader

Gaming systems

Where does the PC end and the gaming system begin? Can the same PC be used for both or should a gaming system be used for playing games? You can buy software games that play quite adequately on your PC, but you will probably find that the games play better on a video game system, which is a highly specialized computer. A video game system differs from a computer in that there are no compatibility issues, and the gaming system is designed to connect to an entertainment system (stereo and TV). The newest gaming systems include DVD players and Internet connectivity. Internet connections and online hard drives with large storage capacities allow publishers to provide "episodic content," that is, content that can be continually changed and updated and allow you to play other people online.

Should the Internet be regulated?

Originally thought to be the truest venue for unregulated free expression, it seems that the Internet may fall under restrictions and regulations once thought impossible. With the advent of new technologies and some recent laws (both national and international), it seems that online regulation of content and expression may not only be possible but probable.

Those who favor Internet restrictions and monitoring do so for a variety of reasons. In its communication "Illegal and harmful content on the Internet," the Commission of European Communities summarized the reasons governments feel pressure to regulate the Internet:

- national security (fear of terrorist activities, bomb-making instructions)
- protection of minors (from violence, pornography)
- protection of human dignity (from racial hatred or racial discrimination)
- economic security (protection against fraud)
- information security (malicious hacking)
- protection of privacy (unauthorized distribution of personal data such as medical records)
- protection of reputation (libel)
- intellectual property (unauthorized distribution of copyrighted works)

Those groups and governments who favor regulating the Internet will soon have sophisticated tracking programs to do just that. Such programs will be capable not only of stopping the transfer of selected content on the Web, but also of locating those users who work outside the regulations. In addition to regulating content, there are a variety of issues related to business conducted over the Internet that some groups feel need to be regulated.

Software programs currently exist that provide for Internet regulation by individuals, parents, or organizations. Programs such as CyberSitter can filter content to protect against unwanted content. Some parents, schools, and libraries find these programs a first step in regulating the Internet. However, the bigger issue—should there be global regulation of the Internet—remains.

There are many questions that must be answered before regulating the Internet fairly can become a reality. First, what would be the purpose of regulating the Internet? Presumably, the purpose would be to address the concerns listed previously. Next, who would make up the regulations?

One challenge that faces those who believe the Internet should be regulated is the global aspect of the Internet. Each country and its government bring a different set of rules and a different cultural perspective to the Internet. These must all be understood and respected if regulation of the Internet is to succeed. Finally, who would monitor the Internet and enforce the regulations? Once again, the global nature of the Internet makes this a difficult question to answer.

Even if the "right" answers to the above questions can be found, there are those who do not believe the Internet should be regulated and who believe in the original premise of the Internet–free and open communication. Groups such as the Electronic Frontier Foundation (EFF) and the American National Standards Institute (ANSI) are working with policy-makers to ensure the Internet remains a venue for free and open communication. The EFF, for example, has as one of its goals to "develop among policy-makers a better understanding of the issues underlying free and open telecommunications." [Source: http://www.eff.org/abouteff.html#mission.]

Some movement has already been made to regulate the Internet. For example, with the Internet quickly becoming the global marketplace, the Federal Trade Commission (FTC) in the United States has been implementing various regulations regarding protection of consumer privacy information. Internationally, governments are proposing legislation to regulate business dealings on the Internet by providing basic rules to ensure that transactions and contracts completed online have the same protections and guidelines as those done face-to-face or on paper. In addition, new laws are being considered regarding ways to collect taxes on the sales of goods that fall outside the jurisdiction of a state's ability to collect taxes. There has also been talk of charging and taxing Internet use. The Federal Communications Commission (FCC), which has been in favor of lifting some of the existing telecommunications restrictions in order to bring high-speed Internet access into homes, also, has been debating what, if any, restrictions they should place on the content that is delivered.

All these ideas are contrary to the original premise of the Internet, which was developed to provide an open, unregulated, and free forum for the exchange of ideas. With the Internet moving into areas of commerce and education, however, are laws to regulate the Internet necessary?

▼ EXPAND THE IDEAS

1. Log onto the Internet, then use your favorite search engine and the key phrase "regulate the Internet." Create an outline of the key ideas related to regulating the Internet discovered in your research. Write a brief summary indicating your answer to the question: Should the Internet be regulated? Be sure to provide support through your research for your conclusion.

2. Is regulating the Internet a good idea? Consider such laws as the following that were passed by the U.S. Congress: The U.S. Communications Decency Act (1996) and the Child Online Privacy Protection Act (2000). Research these laws. Are they still in effect today or have they been overturned? If still in effect, summarize how they regulate the Internet, who is protected, and who monitors the regulations. If overturned, summarize on what grounds.

3. Will the new laws as described above hamper trade and e-commerce, or will they provide a secure and stable environment to promote and expand Internet trade and commerce? Research recent proposals and developments regarding e-commerce both in the US and around the world. Write a short paper on your findings. In your conclusion, state how the proposals regulate the Internet. Do you think the proposals will work? Why or why not?

4. In the United States, the FCC regulates cable and broadcast television. If the Internet is provided via cable through television, does regulation fall within the FCC's jurisdiction? What are the issues and recent regulations? Write a short paper discussing your findings.

End of Unit Exercises

▼ KEY TERMS

2.5G and 3G networks
802.11a
802.11b
Advanced Micro Devices (AMD)
AIM (AOL Instant Messaging)
Alchemy
Athlon
Cluster computing
Code Morphing
Crusoe
Digital video recorder (DVR)
Duron
E911 (Enhanced 911)
eBooks
Enterprise computing network
Field Emission Display (FED)
Flash memory
Flat panel display (FPD)

FLOPS (floating point operations per second)
Force feedback technology
Free Space Optics (FSO)
High-performance computing (HPC)
Home network
Hyper-Threading technology
ICANN (Internet Corporation for Assigned Names and Numbers)
ICQ (I Seek You)
IEEE
Integrated digital television (IDTV)
Internet2
Internet appliance
Liquid Crystal Display (LCD) technology
Magnetic RAM (MRAM)

m-Commerce (mobile commerce)
Membrane keyboard
Memory stick
MEMS-based storage
Microdrive
Middleware
MIPS (Millions of instructions per second)
MSN Messenger
Multimedia home platform (MHP)
Network drive
Online drive
Open Mobile Alliance (OMA)
Opteron
Optical mouse
Organic light emitting diode (OLED)

Pentium® 4
Personal video recorder (PVR)
Phantom
Pixie dust
Qubit
Self-securing storage
Smart media storage
Solid state
Speech-to-Text (STT)
V.44
V.92
VLAN
VPN
Wi-Fi (Wireless Fidelity)
Wireless Application Protocol (WAP)
Wireless keyboard
Wireless mouse

▼ UNIT REVIEW

1. Review all of the bold-face terms in this unit to gain a better understanding of current terminology. In your own words define each term. Use online resources to explore the terms in more detail.

2. Look at the objectives list in the unit opener. Without referring to the lesson itself, write about one trend discussed for that lesson. Write additional questions you have about that trend and list resources where you might find information.

3. Create a three-column table for each lesson. List the trends mentioned in each lesson in column 1. In column 2 record the status of the trend—e.g., is it having an impact in that technology sector, is it no longer a player in that technology sector, it has had its day but is now replaced by [name trend that has supplanted the one named in column 1]. In column 3 write your reaction to the status of the trend—e.g., to be expected, disappointing, it never caught the imagination of the consumer, and so on.

4. By definition, some "trends" become integrated into society (like VHS for videotaping and CDs for data and music storage) and others disappear, never to be heard of again (like Beta, the competitor to VHS in the early days of videotaping and 8-track tapes for music). In the lesson on wireless connectivity, you read about two trends—Wi-Fi and Bluetooth—related to wireless communication. Describe each. What are the possible conflicts between these technologies? Will those conflicts be enough to cause one to "win" over the other? Do you think both technologies will become integral to the way we communicate wirelessly? Why or why not? To answer these questions, you may choose to use additional resources to expand your understanding of these technologies.

5. The lessons discussed various ways (both current and future trends) to access the Internet, as well as ways browsers and Web services have evolved. Use that information to answer these questions: How do you access and use the Internet? What devices do you use to log on and access Web sites? What other features of the Internet (discussion groups, forums, e-mail, e-commerce) do you use? Make lists in answer to the questions. Then put an asterisk next to each item that uses a technology or trend discussed in these lessons.

6. Review the lesson on productivity software. List the various categories named in the lesson and some enhancements that have been made in those areas. Then consider other software you have read about in this unit, such as browsers, eBooks, and online magazine readers. State at least three types of software, then discuss whether or not this software could be considered productivity software. Use the information to write a concluding paragraph identifying trends you see in productivity software.

7. The lesson on wireless connectivity discussed various standards associated with wireless devices. Make a four-column table and list the standards discussed, who or what devices should comply with each standard, the oversight committee associated with the standard, and questions you have about the standard. If you would like to enhance the information in your table, you might log onto the Internet and use your favorite search engine to search for links to standards for wireless computing. Review the site for any new standards and advances in wireless technology. Add your findings to the table.

▼ FILL IN THE BEST ANSWER

1. Field emission display (FED) technology is being developed for use in _____ displays.

2. Optical mice use optical technology rather than _____ to transmit data.

3. The Pentium® 4 uses _____ technology which lets one chip act as two.

4. Researches have built a computer circuit using _____, which have the potential of representing not just 1 or 0, but of representing both 1 and 0 at the same time.

5. The Crusoe chip is known for its innovative _____ software.

6. MEMS-based storage combines _____ and _____ on one chip.

7. One or more information systems that share data and typically provide information to very large groups of users is _____ computing.

8. CompactFlash and SmartMedia cards are _____ state storage devices.

9. A _____ is a group of personal computers, servers, and other network resources that are connected logically but are on physically different segments of a network.

10. A _____ is a private network that is configured within a public network.

11. _____ is a commercial term for any 802.11 network.

12. A _____ is a group of devices that share a server of group of servers that share processing tasks and can provide backup in case of failure of any of the connected servers.

13. The wireless home networking solution offered by Apple Computer, Inc. is called _____.

14. The _____ standard established by IEEE establishes wireless network speeds to deliver data at rates up to 54 Mbps.

15. AIM, ICQ, and MSN are _____ messaging communities.

16. The intelligent software that prioritizes packets on the Internet and binds major applications together is called _____.

17. The technology that lets you speak to digital devices and have your words translated to text on the screen is known by the acronym _____.

18. The trend towards using the Web as a delivery system for services and products is called Web-based _____ service provider.

19. Windows XP _____ is a software package that can enable your PC to record and play television programs.

20. The four primary parts of a digital video recorder are a hard drive, a TV tuner, a channel guide and a _____.

▼ INDEPENDENT CHALLENGE 1

How have PC components changed over time? Did the first computer look similar to the current offering by computer companies? As with automobiles, the basic appearance of a desktop computer has not changed. You still have the keyboard, the system unit, and the monitor or display device. Accessories have improved and expanded. The general consumer first used the mouse in 1983 on the Apple Lisa computer. What have been some other developments and major changes to the computer?

1. Research the history of the desktop computer for major developments and historic moments in personal computers.

2. Include photos from the Web, if you can find them, of the TRS-80, early external modems, early mice, and dot-matrix printers.

3. What technological development do you think is the most significant? Why? What new technologies do you think will be major driving forces in the way PCs look, feel, and work?

4. Based on your research, what have been the trends in PC development? Do you expect future trends to continue along the same path? Explain.

▼ INDEPENDENT CHALLENGE 2

It is your job as an office manager in a new startup company to select the computers and office productivity software package that will be used by your employees. Your offices are in a new four-story office building in a commercial office park off a major highway. The building is wired with network cable and you are renting 1,000 square feet on one floor. Your advertising is mostly local, although you have a new Web site and are planning to expand your client base.

1. What computers will you purchase? Components? Will they be standalone or networked? If networked, explain any special considerations.

2. The three leading office suites are Corel WordPerfect, Microsoft Office, and Lotus SmartSuite. Which package is best for you? Create a chart of features for each, and list which ones are most important and why.

3. What e-mail client will you select and why? Research available software packages.

4. What current trends discussed in this unit, such as voice recognition software or optical mice, will you include in your plan? Discuss why you would include each. Is knowing whether or not the trend is fully functional and supported an important consideration? Explain.

5. Write a report detailing your plan.

▼ INDEPENDENT CHALLENGE 3

Electronic game consoles are a large sector in the consumer market. You have to create a marketing campaign for a new console that your company MyCoolGAMZ is creating.

1. Research the current markets and trends in electronic gaming and prepare a statement that compares the top sellers.

2. List the top-selling games, and if they are marketed across platforms.

3. Draw a set of plans that lists the features that you would include in your gaming console. Name the device and list the price and ways consumers can buy and access games designed for your system.

4. Which strategies are in use to market the new console you are creating?

5. What trends or technologies discussed in this unit would you include as part of your gaming console? Explain why you would include them.

6. Create a poster that sells your new product. Emphasize the new trends or technologies that make your product the one that will take consumers into the future of gaming.

▼ INDEPENDENT CHALLENGE 4

 Medical science is often at the frontline of computer advances. People are benefiting greatly from new technologies that help in all fields of medicine. There are new techniques to assist those with disabilities; there are new tools to deliver insulin to diabetics; there are systems in place in hospitals that help nurses track tests and medications that have been dispensed to patients. As mentioned in the unit, new technology and software are providing opportunities for robot-assisted surgery and telemedicine. The field is wide open and fascinating in its trend-setting efforts.

1. Log onto the Internet and use your favorite search engine to research new applications for computers in the medical field.

2. Create a list of five new computer-based products that have been introduced in the field of medicine.

3. Print out any Web pages that show images of a device or application.

4. Write a summary report detailing your findings. Write a concluding paragraph summarizing any trends you see emerging or opportunities for cross-applications, that is, technologies developed for the medical field that might have uses in another area.

▼ INDEPENDENT CHALLENGE 5

 The Internet was visualized and made a reality by pioneers. People such as Vannevar Bush, J.C.R. Licklider, Larry Roberts, and Tim Berners-Lee have all had instrumental roles in shaping the Internet. Who are the Internet pioneers? What contributions did they make?

1. Log onto the Internet. Use your favorite search engine and the key phrase "Internet Pioneers." Follow links to several pioneers and read briefly about them.

2. Select one pioneer to research in more depth. Prepare a short paper on your findings. Be sure to include information about the individual's contribution to the Internet.

3. Discuss whether the contribution was viewed as a trend, a passing fancy, or an innovation when it was originally conceived.

4. Discuss what pieces had to be in place to make the innovation a reality.

5. Conclude your report with a brief statement about what surprised you the most as you researched Internet pioneers.

6. If class reports are to be given, organize the reports to be presented in sequential order, based on Internet contributions. After all the presentations have been made, discuss which contributions were dependent on other Internet pioneer contributions and why. Discuss why the Internet is such an integral part of our lives today and not a passing trend.

UCITA (Uniform Computer Information Transactions Act) was drafted by the Chicago-based National Conference of Commissioners on Uniform State Laws (NCCUSL) and sent to all 50 states for their consideration as part of an effort to develop uniform commercial laws easing interstate commerce. See Figure T-16. This law is intended to govern all contracts involving computer software and information that you get electronically. It would apply to software, multimedia products, computer data and databases, online information, and any software product. This includes software from CDs, Web sites, and file transfers. The proposed law would cover software that is in most consumer electronics products today, including televisions, cars, and cell phones.

The rules set forth in UCITA have significant opposition from consumer groups and many corporate users. The opponents, who set up a group called Americans for Fair Electronic Commerce Transactions, claim that UCITA is too favorable to software vendors. For example, UCITA grants new rights to software and information publishers. Essentially, it says that, by default, the software developer or distributor is liable for flaws in the program, but allows a shrink-wrap license to override the default. UCITA backers argue that the measure has been misunderstood and erroneously maligned. In order for UCITA to become law, it must be ratified by each state through the state's legislature. Several states have adopted the law including Maryland and Virginia.

FIGURE T-16: UCITA Online

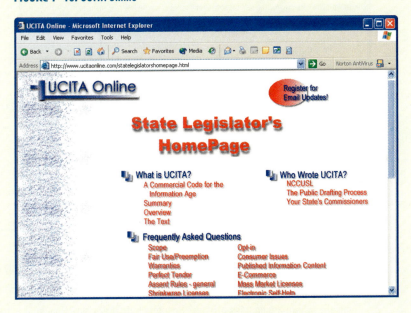

1.   Research the UCITA. What is it all about? What is the current status of the UCITA? What is the status in your state? Based on your findings, do you support the act? If so, explain why. If not, explain why not.

2.   If UCITA is not the answer, what is? Research other proposals that address software contracts and electronic information today. Identify one to study in more detail. Write a brief summary of your research. Include responses to these questions: What is the purpose of the proposal? Who supports it? Why? Who opposes it? Why? Summarize your opinion of the proposal based on your research.

3.   There are many organizations that are interested in policy-making as it relates to technology today and tomorrow. Research several of these organizations. A good starting point is the Electronic Frontier Foundation (EFF), the IEEE (I triple E), and the W3C. Review the mission statement and goals of each organization you research. Make a chart to help compare the organizations. Summarize your findings. Are these organizations working toward similar goals or are they at cross-purposes? Do these organizations support or oppose UCITA?

You finish school with a degree in computer science and want to go out into the world to get a job in the computer information systems area at a major company. Are your qualifications enough? You read through the classified want ads in the local paper only to find that many companies are requiring certifications, such as the ones illustrated in Figure T-17, that you did not take as part of your undergraduate training. You also look back and find that want ads from two years ago had certification requirements that don't seem to exist now. Certification and training classes are costly and time consuming. How can you know which certificate you should pursue?

FIGURE T-17: List of available certifications

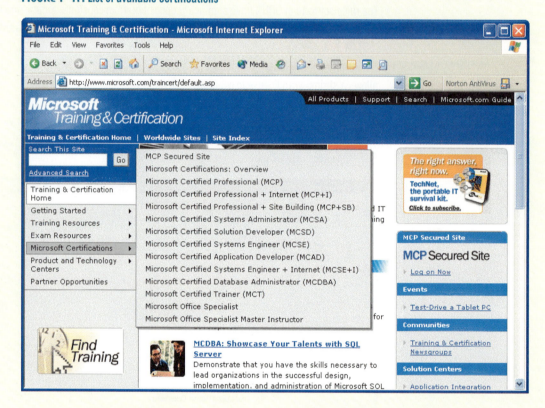

1. Log on to the Internet and research current certifications that are available for computer specialists. Look on the Microsoft, Oracle, Sun, Novell, and Cisco sites. What types of certifications are offered?

2. Typically, where are courses offered? How much do they cost? How long is the training for each certification? What types of jobs require the certification? Which companies require employees to be certified? Make a chart for three certifications and answer the questions just stated to complete the chart. Add a final column to your chart to include other information you found interesting or helpful but that is not covered by the questions.

3. Look in the local want ads or research online job sites such as monster.com, job-hunt.org, and flipdog.com. Do a keyword search on the certifications you found in Step 1. What did you find? Do these jobs require certification? Summarize your findings.

Bonus Issues and Up-To-Dates

Unit	Issue	Up-To-Date
A	What are the effects of ubiquitous computing?	Buying computers
B	How do new storage technologies impact piracy and privacy?	Advances in computer intelligence
C	What's all the fuss about open source development?	Speech recognition software
D	New chip technologies—what's next?	New processors
E	Free Wi-Fi? Why or why not?	Internet2
F	Spyware—a virus or a legal business practice?	Controlling security breaches in software
G	How does the Information Age impact business ethics?	Controlling pop-up ads, pop-under ads, and spam
H	Digital file sharing—is there a compromise?	What's new in digital photography?

Computer technology is constantly evolving. Before buying a computer you should ask yourself: How important is it for me to have the latest technology? There is no one right answer to this question. Since computers affect almost all aspects of daily life, you should know about basic computer concepts and about recent advances in computer technology. It is nearly impossible, however, to keep up with advances in all areas. What you should know are general trends and significant developments. But what defines significant? Sometimes an innovation that seems significant one year has minor impact on society or business and is gone within months, and sometimes a development that is barely noticed at first turns out to lead the way for technological advances for years to come. The issues and up-to-dates in this unit cover topics that signal current technology trends.

What are the effects of ubiquitous computing?

You wake up, put in your contact lenses, and rush over to the computer to check your e-mail. After reading and responding to the messages that came in overnight, you write a few new messages to get the day going, check out world events on several of your favorite news sites, play a quick game of solitaire, and then an hour or two later, remember you haven't yet dressed or had breakfast. Then fast forward to the end of the day…you get home from the job—which may or may not require you to sit at a computer, say a quick hello to your family, and then sit down for a few hours of "leisure" time at the computer.

As computers are becoming more ubiquitous, people are spending more and more time at the keyboard. What are the implications for personal health (physical, emotional, and mental), language usage, and society? How does all this time people are spending at the computer affect society in general? Are we spending too much time online? The Internet is available 24 hours a day, 7 days a week…and as a result people can check their e-mail, stay in touch with work (even when they should be on vacation), research their stocks, and so on any time of the day or night. Is all this time at the computer necessary, or are we computer addicted?

Computer users who spend excessive amounts of time at the keyboard are prone to a variety of computer-related health issues. Physical health issues include repetitive stress injuries, such as carpal tunnel syndrome. Repetitive stress injuries are caused by repetitive motions, such as using the same arm or wrist motion to enter data, and are not solely computer-related. Other physical health issues include eye strain and fatigue, as well as headaches, which can be the result of sitting for long periods of time looking at a monitor without proper eyewear or at inappropriate distances.

A comprehensive research study on the effects of prolonged daily use of computers, particularly the effects of sitting in front of a monitor, was conducted by researchers at Chiba University in Japan. The study, published in the American Journal of Industrial Medicine (Volume 42, Issue 5, 2002), investigated more than 25,000 workers three times over a 3-year period (1995-1997) using a self-administered questionnaire. The researchers looked at three primary factors: mental, physical, and sleep-related symptoms. Even after adjusting for mitigating factors, they found that there was a significant relationship between the amount of time people sit at a computer and look at a monitor and physical and mental ailments. People working at a computer longer than five hours per day seemed to exhibit the most symptoms. Physical ailments included headache, eyestrain, and joint pain. Mental ailments for people working more than five hours at a computer included increased lethargy, insomnia, anxiety, and fatigue.

The science of ergonomics, which is the study of people and their work environments to improve work conditions and to enhance productivity, has tried to address physical issues related to ubiquitous computing by creating ergonomically-designed workspaces. These workspaces include proper furniture, such as desks that can be adjusted to the needs of the user, special keyboard layouts, and adjustable chairs. Ergonomics also addresses the issue of proper lighting to help reduce eyestrain and headache. The science also provides information on proper posture—a key element in helping to reduce physical injuries.

In addition to physical injuries, healthcare workers are concerned about the emotional and mental issues stemming from excessive computer use. One such problem is that of computer addiction disorder (CAD), sometimes referred to as Internet addiction disorder (IAD). As of this writing, CAD/IAD has not been recognized officially as a psychological or psychiatric diagnosis, but the addiction to computers and computer use is being studied seriously by healthcare professionals.

Apparently, computer usage is affecting not only our physical health but also our language skills. Several major news organizations have reported on the effect of computers in the way students write. Teachers report that essays and school assignments are being submitted with some words written in the language of text messaging (short abbreviations used for communicating over the Internet) rather than full words and correct English. Many teens are incorporating text messaging, which they use when sending instant messages through services such as ICQ and AOL Instant Messaging or when sending text messages on their cell phones, into their school work. For example, "gr8 2 b ur friend cuz u r kewl, c u l8r @ home" may seem like an odd collection of symbols and letters but for a teen it's a simple message: "Great to be your friend because you are cool, see you later at home."

Text messaging is also called Short Message Service. Webopedia defines Short Message Service (SMS) as "the transmission of short text messages to and from a mobile phone, fax machine and/or IP address. Messages must be no longer than 160 alpha-numeric characters and contain no images or graphics." If you only have 160 characters, you tend to get creative, such as using "gr8" for great! Recently, the Oxford University Press added an appendix that includes a glossary of abbreviations used in electronic text messaging to its Concise Oxford Dictionary. These shorthand terms were developed and defined by e-mail users. Some worry that including this glossary of abbreviations in the Concise Oxford Dictionary is a step toward acceptance of these abbreviations as Standard English.

It is a well-known fact that language is always evolving. Each new generation contributes words to its language, words that then become part of the accepted language. However, the Internet generation is pushing the boundaries of written language by suggesting that simply typing "lol" (laughing out loud), "brb" (be right back), and "ttyl" (talk to you later) should be universally accepted as Standard English. Regardless of whether or not these abbreviations are accepted as Standard English, they are clearly impacting language usage by their pervasive intrusion into our written language.

What is the impact on society of ubiquitous computing? Is the computer changing the way we interact with our family and friends? How do you tell your neighbors good news? Bad news? There was a time when you would walk next door or down the block and tell a friend face-to-face about a promotion, a success, or a sad event. With our circles widening in large geographic areas, it's a good thing to be able to stay in touch with people who no longer live down the block. However, are we losing the ability to face people and tell them things personally?

Computer usage will continue to expand. The 24/7 accessibility to computers is changing society—for example, the way businesses do business, the way the economy runs, and the way people work. As it does, we would be wise to consider its impact on our lives.

▼ EXPAND THE IDEAS

1. What are the pertinent health issues for computer users who spend more than 5 hours each day at a keyboard? Research two topics on this issue. Write a short paper summarizing two studies or articles.

2. How well do you know the shorthand used in text messaging? Could you understand an Instant message if it came to you? Have you ever used abbreviations (such as b/c for "because" or w/in for "within") in a formal communication such as a school paper or business letter? Write a message on any topic that is no longer than 160 characters and that uses text messaging. In a group, exchange papers and see if the messages can be interpreted. As a group, create a two-column chart that discusses the advantages and disadvantages of using these abbreviations.

3. Research the impact of being available 24/7 to marketers and clients. What are the benefits and drawbacks to such extended accessibility? Who is most affected by this accessibility? Comment on how the 24/7 availability of computers affects our society and what we as a society should do about it, if anything.

If you don't have a computer, it is only a matter of time before you will find that you need to have one. Whether for school, a job, or household chores, computers have become essential home appliances. If you already have a computer, it is often the need to upgrade your software that drives the need to upgrade your existing computer or to buy a new one because new software and newer operating systems often require more hardware resources. It seems that as soon as you purchase a computer and as soon as you get your computer home and out of the box, a more powerful one supercedes the model you bought. It is indeed difficult to keep up with this fast-paced industry. At some point, however, you need to buy a computer, upgrade an existing one, or build your own. No matter which path you take, you need to know that the computer you end up with is capable of doing the work you need to do. Figure 1 shows the Web site for the Buyer's Guide available online for this book.

FIGURE 1: The online Buyer's Guide

1. Log onto the Internet, and then go to http://www.course.com/downloads/illustrated/concepts4/guide.html.

2. Click the link for Basic Computer Systems and read through the links on that page.

3. Click the Hardware link, then click and read through each of the links for architecture considerations.

4. Use your favorite search engine to locate at least one online retailer for computer systems. Consider the features you read about in Step 3, and then locate three different computer systems that fall into distinct pricing categories: inexpensive, moderate, and expensive. Create a chart that compares the price, features, and retailers for the three computers.

5. Write a short summary answering the following questions:

    • Were you able to find computers for sale in a large price range?

    • What feature, if any in particular, created the largest price gap?

    • What features do newer models offer?

    • Write a short paragraph summarizing the important decisions you need to make when specifying a computer system for yourself.

How do new storage technologies impact piracy and privacy?

Bytes, kilobytes, megabytes, gigabytes, terabytes … New storage technologies are creating ways to store more data reliably and efficiently. But what does this mean to the consumer? On the personal computing front, new technologies allow users to save large amounts of data easily. Removable hard drives make it possible for you to work on a computer, remove the drive, take it across the country, and then place it in a bay in a different computer and continue working as if you never left the original computer system. From a personal computing viewpoint, the increase in storage capabilities often means increases in efficiency—no more digging through lots of disks to find a file since files are all able to be stored in one place.

In addition to computer use, consumers are seeing the benefits of new storage technologies in consumer products. For example, the TiVo and Replay TV units come with hard drives that can store hours of recorded television. Hard-drive manufacturers are using hard disks as portable storage devices for set-top boxes, game consoles, and digital stereo receivers. Consumers can slide drives containing music, digital photos, or recorded TV programs into an empty bay, similar to the bay on PCs that holds CD drives. Great for the consumer, but some movie and record companies are objecting to these devices. They are concerned that the increase in storage capability will mean more people will be storing their own movies and music, which will result in a decrease in revenues. They are also concerned that consumers will fast forward through the commercials and advertisers will find other avenues for product exposure. These piracy fears are similar to the ones that the movie industry expressed when VCRs were first introduced.

The consumer is also affected by the way these advances in storage technologies are being used by businesses and the government. The US government digitally stores and retrieves a variety of data about all its citizens, including tax forms and other legal documents. Volumes of data about consumers are stored by insurance companies, manufacturers, telephone companies, and advertisers. Large databases are everywhere and getting larger.

Smart cards are an example of a new storage technology that is being embraced by businesses and organizations. This technology is raising concerns among individuals. A smart card is similar to a credit card, but it contains a computer chip that stores information and can transfer data to and from a central database. For example, some universities are using smart cards as ID cards. These smart ID cards serve multiple purposes: students can use their smart cards as an ID card to retrieve their student records, as a library card to keep track of books borrowed and returned, as an e-wallet to keep track of purchases and a prepaid balance on the card, and as a health card to provide access to medical records. Some consumers are concerned about the amount of data and type of data being stored on smart cards. They claim privacy issues are at stake.

The amount of stored data is growing exponentially. The concern is not so much that data is being stored, but rather what is being done with that data. Advocates of new storage technologies point out that these advances mean a wealth of information is available and that with proper search techniques it is easily accessible. Those opposed to excessive storage raise piracy, privacy, and security concerns.

▼ EXPAND THE IDEAS

1. Research smart cards. How are they being used? How are they being received by the general public? Write a brief paper listing the benefits and drawbacks. Discuss ways that security and privacy concerns are being addressed.

2. Personal information (such as birth, banking, loans, health, and marriage) was stored in different locations and with differing levels of accuracy, so it was often difficult to gather lots of information about one individual. Today, the Internet provides access to a wide range of personal data. Use your favorite search engine and search to find out what type of personal information is available over the Internet. Make a list of your findings. Write a short paragraph stating your opinion of whether or not accessibility to such information should raise privacy or security concerns.

Ever since the first computer performed simple mathematical computations many scientists have asked the question, "Will a computer ever be able to outsmart a human?" Computer chess games were among the earliest programs to pit man against machine. In 1958, the IBM 704 was the first computer to play chess. It could consider 200 positions a second. By 1987, the IBM computer Deep Thought was the first to use parallel processors and could consider 750,000 moves per second. In 1996, IBM's Deep Blue won the opening game against Garry Kasparov in the ACM Chess Challenge in Philadelphia; however, Kasparov ultimately won the match 4-2. In 1997, Kasparov, by now the undisputed World Chess Champion for 15 years, challenged Deep Blue in New York. Deep Blue defeated Kasparov 3.5 to 2.5.

With continued advances in processing power, a German group decided to once again pose the challenge with their computer Deep Fritz 7, which can evaluate 16 million moves per second. It was a tough challenge watched by the world at large. The eight-game match ended in a draw of 4 to 4 as shown in Figure 2.

FIGURE 2: Computer v. human chess matches

1. Log onto the Internet and use your favorite search engine to research Deep Blue and Deep Fritz. Use your research to answer the questions: Will a computer ever be able to outsmart a human? Did Deep Blue or Deep Fritz outsmart its opponents? Why or why not?

2. Proponents of artificial intelligence (AI) view the Deep Blue match as a turning point in AI. Research the history of AI. List pivotal historic events in AI. Summarize your findings about AI and why advances in storage technologies are beneficial to AI. Discuss how advances in this technology are benefiting society.

3. Do you think the computer's processing ability will ever surpass the human ability to think and reason? Why or why not? Provide a report to support your opinion.

What's all the fuss about open source development?

To understand the fuss, you need to understand what open source development is: the development and use of free software. Open source development means that the source code for a software package or operating system is freely available. Developers who use the source code for other projects often suggest changes to the original source code to fix bugs or provide improvements. These "fixes" are then incorporated into the code so that all users have access to them. As the saying goes, "Many hands make light work," but in the case of open source development projects some would say, "Many programmers make for a stronger source code."

The non-profit corporation Open Source Initiative (OSI) is dedicated to promoting an understanding of open source as a software development model. The OSI Web site lists examples of open source software that is being used for commercial purposes and that can be found readily on the Internet. For example:

- Apache—the storage that runs over 50% of the world's Web servers

- Perl—the engine behind most of the "live content" on the Web

- BIND (Berkeley Internet Domain Name)—the software that provides the DNS (domain name service) for the entire Internet

- sendmail™—a widely used e-mail transport software on the Internet

So what's all the fuss about? The word "free" in the definition should give a clue to part of the controversy. Commercial companies spend a tremendous amount of money on research and development of software. Commercial companies are generally not open to the idea of the development and use of free software since their goal is to make money. But the Internet has opened the door for open source development and there are some companies that are embracing it—and still making money. Examples of open source development projects include Netscape Navigator, Linux, and Apache.

Netscape is a leading proponent of open source development. It pioneered the distribution of software online when it offered Netscape Navigator for no fee over the Internet. A few years later, Netscape became the first commercial company to make its source code for Netscape Communicator free for modifications. Netscape has been both praised and criticized for its role in the open source development strategy.

Linux, developed under the GNU General Public License, is a free Unix-type operating system that was originally developed by Linus Torvalds. The source code for Linux is distributed freely and is available to anyone who wants it. Even though the source code is free, the applications that are developed under Linux are not. Linux is available in several formats called distributions. These are distributed for no charge by developers either by File Transfer Protocol (FTP) or for a nominal fee for shipping and handling by CD. The Linux tools and utilities that are available include Linux applications for Administration, Multimedia, Graphics, system development, scientific applications, communications, and graphics.

Apple Computer Company is also using open source projects to allow developers to enhance and customize Apple software for its computers. MAC OS X is based on the Darwin open source project. Darwin is the core of the MAC OS X. The Darwin project combined the efforts of Apple engineers and programmers in the open source community to create the source code for MAC OS X. Apple continues to make open source development a key component of its software development strategy and invites users to participate in the Darwin open source project.

Versions of the Microsoft operating system have gone from MS-DOS in 1980 to Windows XP in 2001. Since the beginning of the PC revolution, Microsoft's operating systems have dominated the market. Microsoft, to date, has not made source code available to developers. Recently, Microsoft has come under increasing pressure to "open up." The company has been trying to overcome negative public images and, after settling the antitrust suit with the US government, has determined that it is time to address this problem. One solution might be for Microsoft to provide access to its source code.

Overwhelming world-wide public opinion is that open source operating systems, such as Linux, are viable and cost effective alternatives to proprietary operating systems, such as Windows. With Linux or other open source software, products can be customized and upgraded on the user's schedule, and upgrades don't necessarily erase customized code.

Linux has been making inroads into the personal digital assistant markets (PDAs). In addition, several large corporations that have traditionally used Windows NT servers to handle various computing tasks—such as Corel, Oracle, and SAP—are moving their tasks onto IBM mainframe computers running Linux. In fact, IBM has been boosting its support for Linux by launching new Unix servers that make bringing Linux into large corporate systems easy. Major software developers have created alliances with Linux and are developing their applications to run under the Linux system. As a result of the successes of these alliances, Linux has created an interesting dilemma for the Microsoft developers who have always resisted and been able to avoid the release of the source code for their operating systems. The operating system code is the intellectual property that is so highly coveted by Microsoft and is what the company bases its success on. It is what Microsoft sells.

The unexpected early success of Linux has led some experts to rethink the software development model—moving from a closed model to the open source model. Is it possible that more and more companies will share their source code in the hope of developing better software products? Will the consumer benefit from such a change in software development?

▼ EXPAND THE IDEAS

1. What is the GNU General Public License? The General Public License differs from other software licenses in that it provides for the sharing, understanding, and modification of free software. Research the various software licenses that are available and create a comparison chart. In the chart explain, for each type of distribution license, who owns the software, and what provisions for distribution and change exist for each type of software license.

2. Is the open source approach to software distribution the way to go? What is Microsoft doing to meet the demands of the open source movement? You can find out more about open source principles by going to www.opensource.org and www.fsf.org. Research existing arguments for and against the GNU. Write a brief paper on how you think it will affect the software development market in the future.

3. Some software programs developed using the open source software model were listed in this Issue. Research other products developed using the open source software model. Create a list of these software programs. Do these programs have competitive programs that were developed using the closed development model? Which product is more widely used? Why do you think that is?

Currently, the keyboard is the main input device for computer systems. Some believe that computers in the not too distant future will use speech recognition software as the main input device. Can you picture yourself sitting at a desk talking to your computer? What about a busy office of people sitting in close proximity speaking to their computers? Would this work?

Two speech recognition technologies are speech-to-text (STT) and text-to-speech (TTS), where typed text is converted to spoken words (see Figure 3). TTS lets you hear e-books, Web pages, e-mail, and any text on your PC or portable MP3 player. STT lets you convert spoken words with an incredible accuracy that can account for nuances in speech as well as dialect to interpret the spoken word into data. Speak, and your words appear on screen and in letters, spreadsheets, and forms. A third trend in speech recognition technology is Speech Application Language Tags (SALT), which is being developed by Intel. SALT, which is platform independent, enables people to use speech to navigate and interact with the Web using devices such as PCs, notebooks, tablets, cell phones, and wireless PDAs.

FIGURE 3: Speech recognition technology

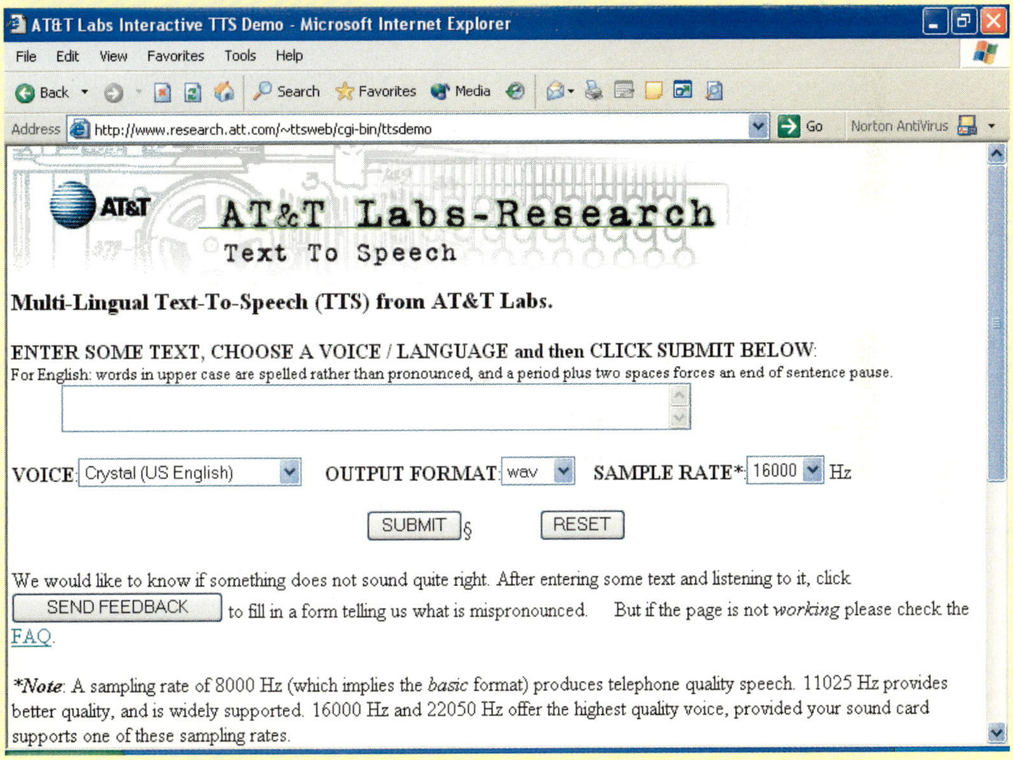

1. Log onto the Internet, then use your favorite search engine to research speech recognition technology. Explain how speech technology is being used today. Research speech recognition technologies that are part of personal computer operating systems, such as Windows XP. Discuss advantages and disadvantages of speech recognition software, as well as groups who benefit from it.

2. Go to a site that offers TTS demos. If your computer is capable of sound, try to run a demo. Write a brief paragraph on your experience at that site.

3. SALT is speech recognition technology designed for use over the Web. Use your favorite search engine to research SALT. Where has SALT been implemented? What are the drawbacks and benefits to using SALT? Summarize your findings in a brief paper.

New chip technologies—what's next?

The need for more and more storage and faster and faster processors has teams of scientists in all the major labs around the world working on ways to create new chips. Ever since Robert Noyce and Jack Kilby constructed the first integrated circuits with components connected by aluminum lines on a silicon-oxide surface layer on a plane of silicon in 1959, scientists have been working to create ways of storing and processing data on smaller devices with greater reliability and speed.

In 1965, Gordon Moore, head of research and development for Fairchild Semiconductor and co-founder of Intel, predicted that transistor density on integrated circuits would double every 12 months for the next ten years. This prediction, known as Moore's Law, was revised in 1975 to state that the density would double every 18 months. To everyone's amazement, including Moore himself, Moore's Law holds true even today as scientists have continued to create faster and denser chips using silicon. If Moore's Law is to continue to hold true, then chip features must shrink or the technologies must greatly improve to keep increasing functionality and performance.

The limitations of silicon have been known for years, and the challenge has been to find new materials to take chip development to the next level. Current manufacturing processes use lithography to imprint circuits on semiconductor materials. While lithography has improved dramatically over the last two decades, it is widely believed that lithography is quickly approaching its physical limits.

So where do chip developers go next? Some scientists are researching nanotechnology, which is the "field of science whose goal is to control individual atoms and molecules to create computer chips and other devices that are thousands of times smaller than current technologies permit" (Webopedia), as a means of creating smaller, more powerful chips. What are the benefits of smaller and more powerful chips? One benefit is energy consumption. Smaller chips should consume less energy and should produce less heat. Both of these factors will make these smaller chips more environmentally friendly. But what is the best way to make these smaller chips?

For more than a decade, Intel has been driving the pace of Moore's Law. Recent developments at Intel include a 90-nanometer microprocessor. To create this microprocessor, Intel developed a new type of technology in the production of its microprocessors that stretches atoms across the transistor to increase speed and efficiency. According to Intel, the technology uses "strained silicon," in which atoms in the 90-nanometer chips are spaced farther apart than normal. According to scientists at Intel, a strained silicon chip can function with less energy, which means devices consume less power and work faster.

The technique of using strained silicon has been proven on larger transistors, but until the announcement of the 90-nanometer microprocessor, it has remained a question as to whether or not it could work in significantly smaller scales. Intel's new production method is expected to be implemented concurrently with the company's follow-up to the Pentium 4 chip. The first 90-nanometer chip is slated for release in the fall of 2003. Intel officials have said that the company will be able to use nearly one-fourth of its existing manufacturing equipment with the new technology.

Are there alternatives to silicon-based chips? Yes, in fact, some of the most promising research involves carbon nanotubes, first discovered by Japanese scientist Sumio Iijima in 1991. A carbon nanotube is a single cylinder-shaped molecule about 10,000 times thinner than a human hair. The electrical properties of carbon nanotubes are similar to the semiconductors used in today's microprocessors. Because carbon nanotubes are so small, they could be used for microprocessors and memory. IBM researchers were able to construct a prototype carbon-nanotube transistor in 2001.

IBM has been working on molecular computing for years as it tries to find an alternative to silicon-based semiconductors. IBM scientists have built the tiniest computer circuit yet using individual molecules, a move they say advances their push toward smaller, faster electronics. IBM researchers at its Almaden Research Center in San

Jose, California, have built and operated a computer circuit in which individual molecules of carbon monoxide move like top-pling dominoes across a flat copper surface. This computer circuit involves nanotechnology and quantum computing.

Quantum computing is the application of quantum mechanics to computer systems. It has been described as a "bizarre, subatomic world in which two electrons can be two places at the same time." This description is fairly accurate. The sub-atomic bits used in quantum computing are called qubits. The good news for chip development is that qubits have the potential of representing not just a 1 or a 0, but of representing both a 1 and a 0 at the same time. This definitely means faster and more powerful computing. As research in these areas continues, the goal for chip developers is to translate the work in research labs into chips based on nanotechnology and quantum computing that can be manufactured and then used in products like cell phones and personal computers.

As scientists look at alternative methods for developing chips, some researchers are thinking beyond the physical restrictions of a chip and thinking instead about the computing process. These scientists are finding tremendous potential in a cheap, non-toxic, renewable material found in all living creatures—DNA. DNA (deoxyribonucleic acid) molecules are the material of which our genes are made. In fact, DNA is very similar to a computer hard drive in how it stores permanent information about your genes. DNA computing is the science of using DNA to code mathematical systems.

In 1994, Leonard Adleman, a computer scientist at the University of Southern California, introduced the idea of using DNA to solve complex mathematical problems. Adleman is often called the inventor of DNA computers. DNA molecules have the potential to perform calculations very quickly. DNA molecules have already been harnessed to perform complex mathematical problems. DNA might one day be integrated into a computer chip that will push computers even faster.

What is the future of computer chips? Will Moore's Law continue to hold with advances in computer chip technology? Current research suggests that Moore's Law might not be applicable to new mediums being considered for chips. But current research does suggest new chips will be faster, more energy efficient, and more environmentally friendly.

▼ EXPAND THE IDEAS

1. We may be reaching the limit of Moore's Law as it applies to silicon-based chips. Research Moore's Law. Discover what scientists believe is the upper limit to Moore's Law and when they think we might reach that limit. Write a concluding paragraph indicating what will happen to computing if we reach the limit of Moore's Law and no alternative means for computing has been developed.

2. Advances in microprocessor technology are announced frequently. Log onto the Internet and locate two news stories on recent advances. You can research developments at Intel by going to www.intel.com. What are the new barriers that are being broken? Is Moore's Law still being upheld? Write a short paragraph discussing your findings.

3. The new chips are becoming faster, more energy efficient, and more environmentally friendly. All of this is a move toward "green" computing. Use your favorite search engine to research the concept of "green" computing. Summarize your findings. Discuss how energy efficient chips contribute to "green" computing.

While we are waiting for the quantum computers of the future and the chips that will drive them, there continue to be advances that use the existing tried and true technologies. We need to be aware of new processors for today's technology. Competition among chip makers such as Transmeta, Intel, and AMD is as strong as ever. Figure 4 shows the chip offerings from Intel. It's quite an impressive list.

PC makers are manufacturing systems containing Intel's Pentium 4, which contain **Hyper-Threading Technology**. As described on the Intel Web site, "Hyper-Threading Technology is a groundbreaking innovation from Intel® Corporation that enables multi-threaded software applications to execute threads in parallel within each processor." This is a leap in parallel processing which lets one chip act almost like two for increased speed and efficiency in computing.

What impact do these new chips have on consumers? Will new software be needed to maximize the capabilities of the chip? Will new hardware be needed to house the chips?

FIGURE 4: Intel chips

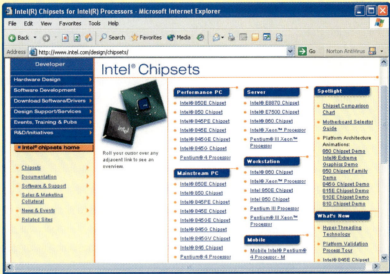

1. Log onto the Internet and use your favorite search engine to search for recent advances in chip technology. What are the current claims for the newest chips for desktop computers from the three leading chip manufacturers: Intel, AMD, and Transmeta? What is the market distinction between the three leading chip manufacturers? Create a table or other visual aid to help readers distinguish among the chips made by these manufacturers.

2. Use your favorite search engine to read more about Hyper-Threading Technology. Do any other manufacturers use Hyper-Threading Technology or is it proprietary to Intel? Why have or why haven't other manufacturers begun to develop their chips using Hyper-Threading Technology? Write a short paper regarding your findings. Include a summary paragraph indicating whether or not Hyper-Threading Technology will soon be a feature of all chips.

3. Who else makes chips? What chips are included in computers manufactured by Apple? How are their chips similar to and different from the three leading PC chip manufacturers? Does it really make a difference to the consumer which chip is in the computer he or she uses? Make a list of guidelines a consumer might consider when trying to decide which chip to look for in a personal computer.

Free Wi-Fi? Why or why not?

How would you like a high-speed Internet connection that requires no cables, no modem, and best of all—no subscription fees? Free community wireless access in cities as diverse as San Francisco, Miami, New York, Prague, and Amsterdam is made possible by free WLANs (wireless LANs). Dubbed "renegade WLANs" by some members of the press, these free networks were pioneered by public-spirited individuals who like to tinker with technology and who want to provide a useful community service. Free WLAN operators typically subscribe to a DSL or cable provider for high-speed Internet access. They pay their monthly fees, but instead of curtailing access to their own personal use, they make their connections available to friends, neighbors, and just about anyone who passes within about 300 feet with the right computer equipment.

Schlotzsky's Deli, a chain of franchised sandwich shops, is offering no-cost wireless access at some of its eateries. The company offers Schlotzsky's Deli Cool Cloud network, which allows people with Wi-Fi wireless setups on their computers or handhelds to get online for free. They believe that if you stick around to access the Internet, you will buy more from their establishments. The free access will also draw in new patrons. "Free Internet access just makes sense to us," said John Wooley, Schlotzsky's CEO. "Now that we have the signal in our restaurants, we'd like to share it with the neighborhood and communities where we operate." Starbucks is jumping on the Wi-Fi bandwidth wagon and offering free access in its shops as well. Without a doubt, many other establishments will follow suit.

Free WLANs are based on Wi-Fi technology, which uses the 802.11b networking standard to create wireless Ethernet-compatible local area networks. Wi-Fi is a technology that allows devices located within a 300-foot radius to communicate without wires. The technology itself is not inherently a renegade one. It is used for many mainstream applications. In fact, Wi-Fi networks are popular in corporations and universities where users are mobile and the flow of information typically requires broadband capacity.

The 802.11b standard uses an unlicensed telecommunications spectrum, so it is perfectly legal to set up an antenna to transmit and receive Wi-Fi signals without obtaining a broadcast license or paying fees to the Federal Communications Commission. Not only is it legal, setting up a Wi-Fi antenna is simple and inexpensive. Using a Wi-Fi network is even cheaper and easier than setting one up. The latest laptop computers have Wi-Fi antennas built into the lids. If a transceiver is not built into your computer, one can be added for less than $100. With a Wi-Fi ready computer you can literally walk down the street, and your computer will look for and connect to any available Wi-Fi network.

Some free WLAN advocates envision a nationwide Web or interconnected Wi-Fi network that will form a seamless broadband network built by the people and for the people. In this vision of a world connected by free WLANs, Internet access is less restricted: libraries can offer Internet access to people in low income neighborhoods; local schools can provide Internet access in all classrooms; parents, kids, and grandparents, as well as corporate executives, can exchange e-mail and instant messages from locations that include the kitchen table, the corner coffee shop, and the little league field—all can be done without exorbitant cabling expenses. With Wi-Fi technology, people can move freely knowing they can connect to the Internet at any time and from any place.

But some broadband providers, such as Comcast and Time Warner Cable, fear that every user of a free wireless network is one less paying customer. According to one industrial analyst, "The telecom industries are addicted to the one-wire, one customer philosophy." Sharing an Internet connection that is intended for single-user access does not coexist with this philosophy. Most subscriber agreements contain wording that limit the use of a broadband connection to one user, and perhaps immediate family members. Although wording varies from one provider to another, most agreements expressly prohibit subscribers from using their connections for commercial purposes. Some free WLAN operators, however, don't believe that sharing their subscription is the same as using their subscription for commercial use.

Whether or not free WLANs are legal, their benefits are tempered by several potentially negative repercussions. For example, tightening up subscriber agreements to eliminate the sharing loophole could affect many broadband subscribers who currently operate private wired or wireless networks that link several computers to a single Internet connection. Broadband providers could force private network operators to purchase more expensive multiuser licenses—an option that might be too expensive for many home networks.

Most free WLANs are operated as a hobby. Some operators are very conscientious, but others have a laid-back attitude toward Quality of Service: If one is not charged for a service, then one cannot complain when the network doesn't work. Consequently, free WLAN access can be unreliable. If broadband providers threaten to pull out of areas where free WLANs are popular, community members may have to use more reliable, but more costly, services supplied by for-profit providers.

The wisdom of unregulated network availability is called into question by the proliferation of free WLANs. A publicly accessible LAN that requires no passwords or accounts can be used anonymously for a variety of illegal and dangerous activities. Like drug dealers who use public telephones to avoid taps and traces, terrorists and other criminals can simply walk into a free WLAN zone, tap into the Internet, and walk away without leaving a trace.

Widespread distribution of free WLANs can reduce the bandwidth available to paying customers. If your neighbor sets up a free WLAN that becomes popular with customers in a nearby coffee house, your previously sedate network neighborhood might suddenly become an overcrowded metropolis with major Internet access traffic jams.

Despite possible repercussions, the free WLAN movement appears to be growing and becoming more controversial. Some industry analysts expect a battle similar to the one that ensued when Napster's peer-to-peer music-sharing network was attacked by the music industry. The free WLAN controversy could pit a group of telecommunications giants against a rag-tag alliance of free WLAN advocates. The outcome has the potential to affect broadband subscribers everywhere.

▼ EXPAND THE IDEAS

1. Research Wi-Fi technology. Write a brief description of what it is and how it works. Then consider: Is it ethical to set up a Wi-Fi? Is it ethical to use one? Will restaurants have to provide free Wi-Fi access just to stay competitive? Research two articles that present both viewpoints, for and against the unregulated use of free WLANs. Compare the viewpoints and then summarize the findings. Draw your own conclusion at the end of a short paper.

2. Do you believe that pirate WLANS can provide service alongside for-profit broadband ISPs? Consider how it might be possible for both services to coexist. Who might use each service? Why might one group prefer to use one service over the other? Might a for-profit broadband ISP consider offering Wi-Fi service? How could that be beneficial for the consumer? Write a short description of your ideas.

3. Are broadband ISPs justified in limiting the terms of their service agreements to "one subscription, one customer"? Relate broadband ISP services to other services such as telephone, cable TV, software licenses, radio, and print media. How are the services similar? How are they different? Does the difference justify the "one subscription, one customer" service agreements? Should exceptions be made for the following: same family users, same dwelling users, or home network users? Explain your position in a media presentation.

More than 180 universities in the United States and industry leaders and government agencies are developing Internet2 to create the next generation Internet. Just as the original Internet was a collaborative effort, so too is Internet2. Developers want a leading edge network that can provide connectivity for a wide variety of applications. Tele-immersion, virtual laboratories, digital libraries, and distributed instruction are just a few examples of Internet2 applications areas. Internet2 allows users to collaborate and access information in ways that the current Internet cannot handle.

Internet2 developers have plans for advanced digital laboratories where people can interact with high-definition images in real time. Exciting showcases are being conducted using this technology. For example, in the fall of 2002, Internet2 and the University of Southern California (USC), with support from the Manhattan School of Music in New York City, presented a music and dance performance event in conjunction with the Fall 2002 Internet2 Member Meeting, titled "Cultivating Communities: Dance in the Digital Age." It was a live net-cast of a dance performance taking place on the USC campus. The program featured live performances by musicians and dancers both onstage at USC and remotely from the Manhattan School of Music. See Figure 5.

FIGURE 5: Internet2

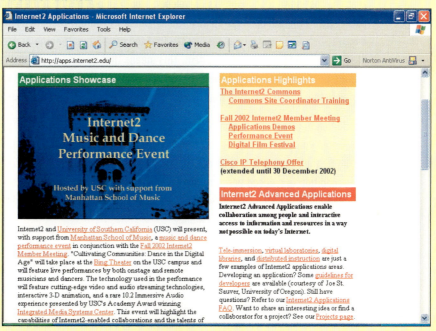

1. Log onto the Internet, then use your favorite search engine to find out more about Internet2. You might start at www.internet2.edu. Write a short paper on the goals of Internet2. Include information as to who is currently involved in the development of Internet2. Be sure to list at least 5 partners in the project.

2. The Internet was originally developed to enhance communication. But over time, the Internet has become "clogged" by commercial interests. Even though access speeds are improving, some still describe their Internet experiences as the World Wide Wait. Perhaps this is because the Internet is not regulated. What will Internet2 have to do to ensure that it does not get clogged with commercial interests and that the bandwidth for the applications being developed for Internet2 is available? Research to find out if Internet2 will be regulated. Write a short paper explaining the issues involved in regulating the Internet and Internet2. Provide a concluding paragraph stating your opinion regarding whether or not either should be regulated.

3. Browse through the Internet2 Web site to answer: Why is middleware important for Internet2?

Spyware—a virus or a legal business practice?

Spyware: just the name sounds ominous. Loosely defined, spyware is a software program that is installed on your computer without your knowledge. To be functional, spyware requires an Internet connection. Spyware is used for various purposes, such as advertising, collecting marketing data, or CPU sharing—also known as distributed processing. These activities can be accomplished without asking for permission each time—or ever. Bottom line: spyware is used to gather data about a person without the person knowing it, and then to send that information to advertisers or other interested parties, usually for commercial use.

One source of spyware is via a computer virus. Another source is via software that you download, which guarantees that the user of these programs has an Internet connection. For example, shareware and free-ware programs are often downloaded over the Internet and can include spyware. When you install the down-loaded program, the spyware program is also installed. Once installed, spyware works behind the scene, making it difficult for the end user to detect. In fact, spyware works even when you are not using the applica-tion that installed the spyware.

Adware is a type of program that displays ads, usually in banners, whenever a program is running. It is simi-lar to spyware in that it is included in a software package to help offset the cost of development and to help keep the cost down for consumers. Developers, for example, might agree to include an adware program as part of their program because an advertising company will pay them to do so. It is different from spyware, however, because the user can readily see that the program is running and, perhaps most importantly, it does not include a tracking component. This means that no data about the user is being collected when the adware program is running. Adware crosses the line and becomes spyware when a tracking component is added to the adware program that allows the program to track user data stealthily.

In addition to privacy and security concerns, spyware and adware can cost you time and money. Both can cause your computer to run significantly slower or make your system crash. If your CPU is being used by others for their purposes, you do not know what you are contributing your resources to—you are not asked. So, in addition to reduced performance and the risk of browser crashes or system crashes, you are blindly volunteering your CPU. If you pay for time online, dialup services running advertisements and hidden com-munications with servers cost you money.

Spyware and adware should not be confused with common e-business practices such as banner ads and cookies. Banner ads that appear on your computer as you work on the Internet are different from both spy-ware and adware because, unlike spyware and adware, banner ads are not installed on your computer. Banner ads, though annoying, can ultimately be removed by you despite the fact that some banner ad developers have tried to find their way around "easy removal." For example, they have tried to hide the close button or continue to play the sound in closed windows. Banner ads differ significantly from spyware because they do not track data about the person viewing them. Although banner ads may be annoying, they do not pose privacy or security threats.

Another e-business practice is the use of cookies, which are commonly used by Web site developers to store information on a user's computer. Cookies are often used to track the contents of an online shopping cart or to remember the geographic location of requested weather information. While it is true that cookies are stored on a user's computer, there are several major differences between cookies and spyware: users can set their preferences to know when cookies are being saved to their computers, users can delete cookies, and, perhaps most importantly, no tracking component is included with cookies.

When you install shareware, you are often asked to agree to license requirements. Sometimes you are asked to register and even pay a fee. Disclaimers are sometimes hard to find. If you are not sure whether or not a program includes spyware, you should pay particular attention to the licensing agreement and registration information requested at the time of the program's installation. Most people simply click the Agree button on these installation screens just to get through the installation; however, you may be granting unlimited access to your computer and your data by doing so. Take, for example, the shareware program KaZaA. When you accept the KaZaA fair use agreement, you grant the right to the folks at KaZaA to farm out CPU time on your computer to others. In addition, the spyware program installed when you install KaZaA can collect information from you and send it back to the advertisers who pay for the right to be installed with the KaZaA shareware.

Download sites, such as ZDNet Downloads, and CNET have begun posting notices on applications that use ad-sponsored spyware. In many cases, a non-ad sponsored version of the application is also available, usually for a fee. Several of these sites have compiled lists of known installation offenders. You can find out which programs to watch for, how to opt out of some installation traps, and what your safest bets are for uninstalling unwanted software.

When you decide that you no longer want to use the free application on your PC, you can usually remove it via Windows Add/Remove Programs Wizard. Unfortunately, the spyware that was installed with the free application will remain on your computer, often buried within the Windows System Registry. Generally, you need a program such as Ad-aware from www.lavasoftusa.com to remove the spyware. Ad-aware is a free multi-spyware removal utility that scans your memory, registry, and hard drives for known spyware components and lets you remove them safely. Similar to virus protection programs such as Norton AntiVirus, it is updated frequently so you can always have the latest definitions.

Why should you worry about spyware? Why would you agree to use a program that installs spyware? According to companies that promote spyware, while it is true that data is collected, none of the data is sensitive and all of it is anonymous. The companies that incorporate spyware into their shareware say they are very clear about the fact that the spyware is part of the shareware program. Despite the public's awareness of the inclusion of spyware, it seems that some download programs remain quite popular even though they include spyware that secretly transmits user information via the Internet to advertisers in exchange for free use of the downloaded software.

▼ EXPAND THE IDEAS

1. Log onto the Internet and then use your favorite search engine to research spyware. Has there been any movement towards regulating spyware? Find two articles that discuss the current situation. Do you think spyware should be illegal? Write a short paper on your findings and support your position with your research.

2. What are the current trends in spyware removal? Go to a site such as www.spychecker.com and see how spyware has spawned a whole new type of software for spyware removal. Find three types of software that claim to rid your computer of spyware. Create a comparison chart of your findings. Select the one that you think is most effective, and then support your claim in a short paragraph explaining why you think it's the best.

3. As discussed in this Issue, some very popular programs available for download include spyware. Make a list of popular downloads that include spyware. Research each of the download programs. Are there any commercially available programs that could be used for the same purposes? Why do people put up with the spyware? Write a short paper discussing your findings.

Controlling security breaches in software

People trying to do harm using computers often take advantage of security breaches in commercial software. These breaches are flaws in the program that permit unauthorized access to the computer on which the software is installed. The software might allow malicious programmers to hide a virus within a file that is commonly used in the software program. Hackers might gain access to computers through back doors—a program function that provides administrative access to a program usually during program development—or other security breaches in software. Computer viruses, the most common form of destructive activity, often take advantage of security breaches in commercial software.

Microsoft devotes several pages on its Web site to security updates and privacy concerns. See Figure 6. These security updates, which often include security patches, are not the same as virus protection; however, they do help protect against viruses and other malicious attacks by patching potential security holes that hackers have been known to exploit. These breaches in security raise genuine concerns for the safety of your data and your computer. When using commercial software, it is critical that you stay informed about security breaches and ways to fix them. You can never be too safe or too careful in protecting your network or your computer.

FIGURE 6: Safeguarding against security and privacy breaches

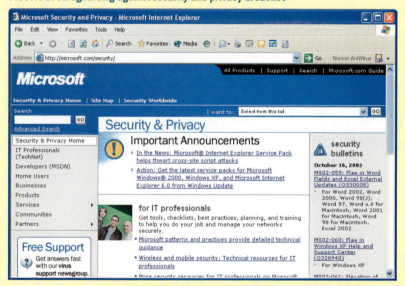

1. Microsoft regularly provides updates to eliminate security breaches in its software. Visit the Microsoft Web site at www.microsoft.com. Click the Security link under resources, then click through some of the links for home users. Find one article that you find relevant and interesting. Write a brief paper summarizing why users might or might not follow the advice given in the Web page.

2. Security patches can be used to protect against security breaches. What is a security patch? How does it help to protect against security breaches in commercial software? Are they all the same or is each unique to a particular software package? Write a brief paper describing how security patches can work to guard your safety and secure your computer. Include a plan describing how you protect your computer.

3. What types of software are most susceptible to security breaches? Use your favorite search engine and the keywords "software security breach." Make a two-column chart. In column one, list software that has experienced security breaches; in column two, describe how the developer of the software recommends protecting against the security breach. Add a concluding paragraph indicating what type of software seems to be most vulnerable and why.

How does the Information Age impact business ethics?

What are ethics? According to the Cambridge Unabridged Dictionary, ethics are "a system of accepted beliefs which control behavior, especially such a system based on morals." Personal ethics help to guide one's personal behavior and business ethics help to guide one's business behavior.

Ethics often impact business decisions—such as the products a business sells or does not sell and the way it treats its employees. The debate about ethics is not new, but the issues employees are facing as a result of the Information Age are new. In today's fast paced business world, the technology may outpace current ethical guidelines, which leaves business leaders with ambiguous situations about which they must make ethical decisions. Sometimes, the technology may provide tempting avenues for unethical behavior.

What types of ethical questions does the Information Age pose? One that is prevalent centers on privacy issues related to databases. The Information Age has made it possible to create large, detailed databases that store incredible amounts of data about consumers. These databases might be generated by marketing firms which gather information submitted by consumers when they fill out registration information for a new product, by healthcare companies or insurance companies which keep detailed records of patients, by political groups which track membership through surveys, and so on.

Businesses are constantly struggling with the issue of selling their databases. Why would a business want to sell its database? Sometimes the company needs to make a quick profit or needs to show quick monetary gain, and selling its database is one way to do that. Other times, the database is sold as part of bankruptcy proceedings. Some e-commerce businesses have no assets besides their databases, so these are sold to help pay off debtors. Interested parties, often marketing firms, purchase the information in the database to target segments of the population. Most business leaders agree that losing consumer confidence by selling consumer information may result in short-term gain, but it is bad for long-term growth.

The impact of selling a business' databases must be considered not only from a financial viewpoint but also from an ethical viewpoint. Did the consumer whose data is stored in the database know that the information could be used for financial gain? Does the company have the right to use an individual's data for financial gain? Did the consumer willingly agree to have the information sold? Will sharing the information cause harm to individuals listed in the database—for example, does a health-related database contain sensitive data that could keep an individual from acquiring health insurance? These are ethical questions that a company must consider when deciding whether or not to sell its database.

The Information Age poses other ethical questions for businesses as well, especially for e-businesses. A business must always decide what type of merchandise it will sell. For example, the nationwide drugstore chain Walgreens sold alcoholic beverages for years, but when it reorganized a few years ago, the Walgreens leadership decided to discontinue the sale of alcoholic beverages in its stores (in most cases). This decision could have been made for financial reasons (removing alcoholic beverages from its footprint might leave more space for other merchandise) or for ethical reasons (removing alcoholic beverages, which are generally not considered healthy, might be more in keeping with the company's main merchandise health-related products).

Brick-and-mortar stores that sell products such as alcoholic beverages and cigarettes have systems in place for checking the age of consumers. But what about e-businesses that sell these same products? For example, studies have shown that underage smokers can bypass state and federal regulations prohibiting sales of tobacco products to minors by purchasing cigarettes through Web sites. How do e-businesses ensure that they are meeting the requirements of the law by not selling to minors? Is it enough to say that they will not sell to anyone who does not have a credit card (which assumes the holder is 18 years of age or older)? Is it enough to have the Web visitor click a disclaimer stating that he or she is over 18 years of age and therefore legally able to purchase the merchandise? Should the e-business be held responsible if indeed the merchandise is being sold and shipped to minors? Should the shipping companies be responsible for checking whether these products are being sold and delivered to minors? These are some of the ethical questions e-businesses face regarding the merchandise they sell. The technology of the Information Age makes it much easier for minors to obtain merchandise that they cannot readily obtain at brick-and-mortar stores.

Today, electronic transmission of data raises other ethical questions. Take, for example, the high-ranking financial official at Lockheed Martin who received a bid template with a competitor's information, including financial data, in the bid where blank lines should have been. Having this information gave Lockheed Martin a financial, as well as an unethical, advantage because Lockheed Martin would know exactly how to underbid its competitor. The problem could not be easily solved simply by deleting the file or erasing the information. To protect Lockheed Martin, its lawyers needed to be involved. The company releasing the bid template had to be notified that the template contained sensitive data. The Lockheed Martin IT staff needed to be consulted, and they had to adjust how they normally back up the files. The template needed to be backed up to a secure site and then removed from the mainstream correspondence so that no one else would have access to it. The original file needed to be returned to the sender. A company with less sophisticated knowledge of business ethics may not have known how to handle this situation.

Another point of discussion involving business ethics is the use of electronic monitoring to track employee activities or to log customer activities. Still other ethical issues related to the Information Age involve the use of business resources for personal activities such as sending personal e-mail via the company ISP, visiting online auctions via the company Internet connection, playing games online during business hours, checking stock prices for one's personal portfolio, and downloading inappropriate files to one's company computer.

The Information Age has spawned many new technologies and with it ethical questions regarding their use. What is being done to help business leaders sort through the ethical dilemmas they face? Many business schools recognize the need to offer courses in business ethics that relate specifically to e-business issues. Some companies, like Lockheed Martin, require employees to take an ethics course offered by the company once a year, thereby bringing all employees up to speed on ethical issues facing the company and how the company is responding to those issues. Still other companies, like Lands' End, test their IT administrators on ethical issues. As explained by Linda Severson, director of business systems at Lands' End, "We test to make sure they make data available only to those who should see it….You have to have tests that continually challenge your security and privacy processes. Ethics has to become more of a way of life, not a one-time policy posting."

▼ EXPAND THE IDEAS

1. Log onto the Internet and use your favorite search engine to research ethics in e-commerce. Read three articles. Do the articles agree on how to approach ethical questions, or do they contradict one another? Why might that be? Write a short summary of each article, and be sure to cite your sources.

2. Research course offerings at major universities or colleges on ethics and e-business. What are the types of courses offered? Do you believe that ethical issues in e-business are that much different from ethical issues in brick-and-mortar business? Write a short paper supporting your views and citing your findings.

3. Universities and businesses often have a code of ethics that must be followed. Research to find out whether or not your school or business has a code of ethics. If it does, read the code. If it does not, visit the Web sites of major corporations and look for links to their code of ethics, or use your favorite search engine using the keywords "code of ethics" to find a code of ethics. Read the code. Write a short paper summarizing the code of ethics. Indicate if the code applies to business in general or if it applies specifically to e-business activities.

Controlling pop-up ads, pop-under ads, and spam

It seems each time you sign onto the Internet you are bombarded with pop-up ads, pop-under ads, and endless spam. If you dislike these ads, it turns out you are not alone. So much so, that the largest ISPs are promoting services that block pop-up ads and spam as part of their promotions to get you to sign on. In fact, in the last quarter of 2002 the two largest software media conglomerates set out to capture the largest market share with their new ISP services. Microsoft, in promoting MSN8, spent over $300M on their MSN media blitz. See Figure 7. Will these ISPs really help control unwanted ads and spam? What will the cost to the consumer be?

FIGURE 7: Selecting your ISP to control spam

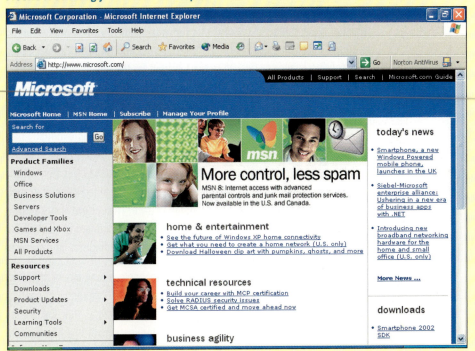

1. Log onto the Internet and go to www.aol.com. Create a list of features that they are using as promotion for their newest service. Go to www.msn.com. Create a list of features that they are using to promote their newest service. What are the differences? Is controlling spam a big factor in the services offered by either or both of these major ISPs?

2. What other ways are available for controlling pop-up ads, pop-under ads, and spam? Are there products commercially available that can be used to block these marketing activities? Why might some people not want to block the ads? Use your favorite search engine to research software products available for blocking pop-up and pop-under ads. Review three products and make a comparison table. Summarize by saying why you would or would not use one of these products.

3. Spam is electronic junk mail. Spammers are using new ways to get through filters by eliminating the known keywords in the subject text box. They also use common names in the sender field to bypass the blocker lists at ISPs and e-mail clients. Use your favorite search engine to find Web sites devoted to stopping spam. List three sites that you found and their strategies for controlling spam on the Internet.

Digital file sharing—is there a compromise?

Since the early days of computing, piracy has been on the table as an issue for software publishers. With today's wide range of digital equipment, digital files such as data files, music files, and video files can be easily copied and distributed. People can copy software and share it without paying a royalty fee to the original developer. People can copy music files and enjoy them without ever buying the original CD. People can copy movie files and see the movie without ever stepping foot in a theater or renting a video or DVD. While it may seem like the consumer is getting something for nothing, when all is said and done, everyone loses— the artists, the manufactures, the distributors, and the consumers.

The impact of software piracy on the software industry and file sharing on the music and movie industries has been studied, debated, and litigated. At first, software and music companies worried when CD burners could be added to PCs as standard equipment because this certainly made it easier for consumers to copy CDs. But quite another issue arose for the music industry when millions of potential customers were able to swap and access music files through the Internet and through Napster. Indeed, the magnitude of the software copying issue was pushed to the forefront for the music industry by Napster. With advances in Internet technology, acceptance and proliferation of broadband, improvement of file compression techniques, and low cost hardware, file sharing became all the rage.

In fact, Napster sent the music industry into a frenzy. The music industry has long blamed Internet song-sharing for a fall in music sales. It has spent time and money trying to shut down file sharing sites and threatening to prosecute users. The music industry squashed Napster, which was unable to recover after fighting all the legal action. Though the music industry killed Napster, it fueled the fires of file sharing. Napster was not the only file sharing game in town. The culture of file sharing has created a generation of music buyers who believe that content should be free. Competing sites such as KaZaA, Gnutella, BearShare, AudioGalaxy, along with others, have come along. Some flourish, and some have gone.

In addition to file sharing via Web sites, new technology broadcasts digital music directly to radio receivers via satellite radio. For example, XM radio broadcasts 101 channels of continuous digital programming from its two satellites (named Rock and Roll), usually commercial-free. XM revenue comes from listener subscriptions and some advertising. So, what are the implications of this new technology as it relates to file sharing? It means that listeners can quickly and easily make copies of their favorite songs as they are played, without ever buying the original. XM has radios for the car or home. Digital satellite broadcast has no static or distortion, so copies of music made from a digital broadcast are clear and CD-quality perfect.

Digital TV broadcasts are similar to digital radio broadcasts in that they send clear, perfect images of films directly to TVs across the country. With the new hard drive TV systems, such as TiVo and ReplayTV, you can watch your favorite shows or films on your schedule. An even larger issue is that these systems have software that allows you to easily skip the commercials. This directly impacts the way media giants generate revenue. In addition, people receiving television directly to hard drive systems can store, copy, and then redistribute these image-perfect video files. It seems that file sharing has come of age for digital TV as well.

The new revolution in digital media is MPEG-4. This next-generation, global multimedia standard delivers professional-quality audio and video streams over a wide range of bandwidths, from cell phone to broadband and beyond. MPEG-4 is designed to deliver DVD (MPEG-2) quality video at lower data rates and smaller file sizes.

Copying original works has always been an issue for businesses. Long before digital file sharing, there was the "threat" from the invention of the photocopy machine. Businesses expressed concern that a machine that allowed you to photocopy a page would start a trend toward the copying of books. Soon businesses had to be concerned about the audio cassette, the VHS-tape, and the CD. But, in each case, these technologies became widespread and accepted and the media giants did not fail as a result of these technologies. Now, with the proliferation of file sharing, the music and film industries are faced with a generation that believes content is free. They must develop new business models for acquiring revenue or they will lose much of their copyright and royalty revenue.

Some in the music and film industries are fighting file sharing by creating programs to block copying. This method is proving to be unsatisfactory because, while the average user cannot easily bypass these blocks, those who are determined to copy the content usually can. Also, consumers are crying foul because they say these restrictions impede their right to copy a CD for personal use. Meanwhile, others in the music and film industry, including some big names, are living by the old saying, "if you can't beat them, join them!" They are realizing that they need to get themselves in the download market. Official subscription downloads have emerged, but they are not expected to make money any time soon. EMI, AOL Time Warner, and Bertlesmann have licensed their content to a new subscription-based streaming and downloading service called MusicNet, which is available to consumers through RealNetworks and America Online.

Meanwhile, the battle to prevent music piracy continues. Why? Because piracy results in price hikes by distributors, which means higher prices for consumers. Because piracy results in more restrictions on consumers, possibly impeding their right to fair use. Because piracy results in more advertisements and other revenue-generating activities to help offset lost revenue. So who loses? The music and record companies lose revenue, and consumers lose when products are more expensive and not as easy to manipulate for fair use purposes. What is the answer to all this file sharing? Perhaps, the answer lies somewhere between new business models and education on the value of content.

▼ EXPAND THE IDEAS

1. Do you think you should be able to download music for free and burn your own CDs? Research recent legal rulings for and against the music industry. Find two articles on the issue. Write a summary paper that explains the issue, stating the reasons for and against file sharing.

2. Imagine you are a budding filmmaker and want to get your film out there. Could you use the power of the Internet? How would you generate revenue for your work if all people who view your film got it for free? Write a brief plan to explain your ideas.

3. What is the latest on MPEG-4? Research MPEG-4. Use your favorite search engine and the key phrase MPEG-4. Visit several sites. Write a description of MPEG-4. Be sure to include your sources.

What's new in digital photography?

Digital photography and digital cameras have changed the way we view images. Without having to incur the cost of film or the cost and time for developing to see your images, you can enjoy the freedom of taking as many pictures as your digital camera memory card will permit. You can send and share pictures instantly with friends and family in your home or across the world. Online photo sites such as Ofoto and Snapfish make it possible to instantly upload the images and then send e-mail notification to anyone you want. Viewing the photos online is free, and then you or whoever views your online photo album can order the prints.

The International Imaging Industry Association (I3A)—a nonprofit trade group supported by Eastman Kodak, Hewlett-Packard, Fujifilm, and others—announced plans for the Common Picture eXchange environment (CPXe). The CPXe is a ground-breaking initiative by the digital photography industry to advance growth in the consumer digital photo services category. The Kodak Photoquilt is an international project to share images from around the world. See Figure 8. This can only be done with digital images.

Digital image manipulation is readily available at the consumer level with affordable software packages that put professional tools right on the desktop. Adobe Photoshop and ULead PhotoImpact are two of many commercial packages that are available. This software includes professional digital editing tools for your photos. Most digital cameras come with some kind of proprietary software to not only download and save files but also to erase lines and reduce redeye through airbrush and other tools.

FIGURE 8: The Photoquilt project

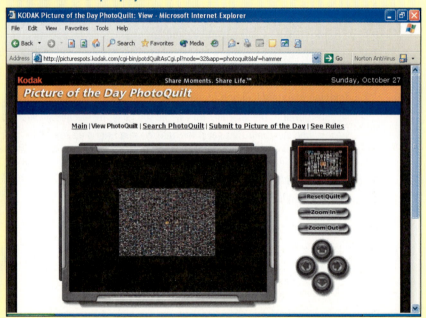

1. Log onto the Internet and search for information on CPXe. You can go to the Web site www.I3A.org. List three advantages of CPXe for photo companies, for consumers, for retailers, and for camera and software manufacturers.

2. Use your favorite search engine to find three online photo sites. Two suggested sites are Ofoto.com and Snapfish.com. Create a comparison chart for the three sites. List and compare features such as services offered, pricing, and various options.

3. Review digital image manipulation software packages that are available today. Make a comparison chart for at least three software packages. Write a summary paragraph indicating how the packages are alike, how they are different, and why a consumer might purchase one over the other.

Glossary

2.5G and 3G network ▶ A packet-oriented data transfer technology and high-speed access system designed to combine voice, data, and Internet into portable wireless appliances. 3G, which stands for "third-generation," combines wide-band radio communications and IP-based services.

3-D graphic ▶ A type of digital graphics format that represents a three-dimensional image in a two-dimensional space.

3-D graphics software ▶ The software used to create three-dimensional wireframe objects and render them into images.

10BaseT network ▶ An Ethernet network that uses twisted-pair cables with a maximum length of 100 meters and supports data transmission rates of 10 Mbps.

100BaseT network ▶ An Ethernet network that uses 100BaseT cables and supports data transmission rates of 100 Mbps.

24-bit bitmap ▶ A True Color graphic that requires 24 bits for each pixel, used for photographic-quality images that can include any of 16.7 million colors.

32-bit bitmap ▶ A True Color graphic that requires 32 bits for each pixel, used for photographic-quality images that can include any of 16.7 million colors.

802.11a ▶ A standard that succeeds the 802.11b standard, supports high-speed wireless LANs and delivers data rates up to 54 Mbps.

802.11b ▶ A popular wireless network standard that operates between 200 and 400 Kbps, with a range of up to 300 feet. Establishes wireless network speed, which can reach up to 11 Mbps. The 802.11b standard lets you hook up an appropriately configured portable device to your Ethernet network wirelessly.

Absolute reference ▶ In a worksheet formula, cell references (usually preceded by a $ symbol) that cannot change as a result of a move or copy operation.

Access time ▶ The estimated time for a storage device to locate data on a disk, usually measured in milliseconds.

Active matrix screen ▶ A type of LCD technology that produces a clear, sharp image because each pixel is controlled by its own transistor.

Advanced Micro Devices (AMD) ▶ The company that produces AMD processors, which include the Athlon and Duron family of processors.

AGP (accelerated graphics port) ▶ An AGP is a type of interface, or slot that provides a high-speed pathway for advanced graphics.

AIF ▶ See Audio Interchange Format.

AIM (AOL Instant Messaging) ▶ Instant messaging service through America Online; software that allows for chatting through the Internet by using screen names to identify users.

Alchemy ▶ AMD processor for Wireless LAN, includes low power consumption, compact design and increased battery life.

ALU (arithmetic logic unit) ▶ The part of the CPU that performs arithmetic and logical operations on the numbers stored in its registers.

Always-on connection ▶ A permanent connection, as opposed to a connection that is established and dropped as needed.

Amplitude ▶ The height of a sound wave.

Analog device ▶ A device that operates on continuously varying data, such as a dimmer switch or a watch with a sweep second hand.

Analog video camera ▶ A device used to collect, store, and process video in an analog format on a magnetic tape.

Animated GIF ▶ A type of GIF image that displays a sequence of frames to create the appearance of continuous motion.

Antivirus software ▶ A computer program used to scan a computer's memory and disks to identify, isolate, and eliminate viruses.

Application software ▶ Computer programs that help you perform a specific task such as word processing. Also called application programs, applications, or programs.

Archiving ▶ The process of moving infrequently used data from a primary storage device to a storage medium such as a CD-R.

ASCII (American Standard Code for Information Interchange) ▶ A code that represents characters as a series of 1s and 0s. Most computers use ASCII code to represent text, making it possible to transfer data between computers.

ASF (Advanced Streaming Format) ▶ Microsoft's video format for streaming video on the Web.

Asynchronous protocol ▶ A data transmission method in which the sender and receiver are not synchronized by a clock signal, and which uses start and stop bits to control the beginning and ending of transmissions.

Athlon ▶ A family of processors produced by AMD.

ATM (asynchronous transfer mode) ▶ A network technology that transmits all packets in a message over the same channel.

Audio Interchange Format (.aif) ▶ A popular cross-platform audio format developed by Apple.

Automatic recalculation ▶ A feature found in spreadsheet software that automatically recalculates every formula after a user makes a change to any cell.

AVI (Audio Video Interleave) ▶ A video file format developed by Microsoft that is the most common format for desktop video on the PC.

B2B (business-to-business) ▶ An e-commerce exchange of products, services, or information between businesses.

B2C (business-to-consumer) ▶ An e-commerce transaction involving products, services, or information between businesses and consumers.

B2G (business-to-government) ▶ An e-commerce transaction involving products, services, or information between businesses and governments.

Backup ▶ A duplicate copy of a file, disk, or tape. Also refers to a Windows utility that allows you to create and restore backups.

Bandwidth ▶ The data transmission capacity of a communications channel.

Baud rate ▶ The transmission speed of a modem measured as the number of times per second that a signal in a communications channel varies; a 300-baud modem's signal changes state 300 times each second; however, each baud doesn't necessarily carry one bit, so a 300-baud modem might be able to transmit more than 300 bits per second.

Beep code ▶ A series of audible beeps used to announce diagnostic test results during the boot process.

Benchmark ▶ A test used to measure computer hardware or software performance.

Binary digits ▶ Series of 1s and 0s representing data.

Binary number system ▶ A method for representing numbers using only two digits, 0 and 1; contrast this system to the decimal system, which uses ten digits: 0, 1, 2, 3, 4, 5, 6, 7, 8, and 9.

Biometrics ▶ A method of personal identification based on some unique physical trait, such as a fingerprint or the pattern of blood vessels in the retina of the eye.

Bit ▶ A bit is the smallest unit of information handled by a computer. A bit can hold one of two values, either a 0 or a 1. Eight bits comprise a byte, which can represent a letter or number.

Bit depth ▶ The number of bits that determines the range of possible colors that can be assigned to each pixel. For example, an 8-bit color depth can create 256 colors. Also called color depth.

Bitmap graphic ▶ An image, such as a digital photo, that is stored as a gridwork of colored dots.

Bitmap image ▶ See Bitmap graphic.

Bluetooth technology ▶ A wireless technology used in conjunction with standard Ethernet networks that allows data transfer rates between 200 and 400 Kbps, up to a maximum range of 35 feet.

BMP ▶ The native bitmap graphic file format of the Microsoft Windows OS.

Body section ▶ A part of a Web page that begins with the <BODY> HTML tag and contains the text, graphics, and links.

Boot disk ▶ A floppy disk or CD that contains the essential instructions needed for the boot process.

Boot process ▶ The sequence of events that occurs within a computer system between the time the user starts the computer and the time it is ready to process commands.

Boot sector virus ▶ A computer virus that infects the sectors on a disk containing the data a computer uses during the boot process.

Bootstrap program ▶ A program stored in ROM that loads and initializes the operating system on a computer.

Broadband ▶ A term used to refer to communications channels that have high bandwidth.

Broken link ▶ A non-functioning hyperlink on a Web page.

Browser ▶ A program that communicates with a Web server and displays Web pages.

Brute force method ▶ A method of breaking encryption code by trying all possible encryption keys, usually employing supercomputers.

Byte ▶ An 8-bit unit of information that represents a single character.

C2C (consumer-to-consumer) ▶ An e-commerce exchange of products, services, or information between consumers.

Cable ▶ Used to connect a peripheral device to a computer through a port.

Cable modem ▶ A communications device that can be used to connect a computer to the Internet via the cable TV infrastructure.

Cache ▶ Special high-speed memory that gives the CPU rapid access to data that would otherwise be accessed from disk. Also called RAM cache or cache memory.

Capacitor ▶ An electronic circuit component that stores an electrical charge; in RAM, a charged capacitor represents an "on" bit, and a discharged one represents an "off" bit.

Card reader ▶ A small device connected to your computer's USB or serial port to read the data that's contained in a flash memory card; acts just like an external disk drive by treating your flash memory card like a floppy disk.

Cascading style sheet (CSS) ▶ A template that can be set to control the layout and design of Web pages.

CD-R ▶ An acronym for compact disc-recordable. CD-R is a type of optical disk technology that allows the user to create CD-ROMs and audio CDs.

CD-ROM drive ▶ A storage device that uses laser technology to read data from a CD-ROM.

CD-RW ▶ An acronym for compact disc-rewritable. CD-RW is a type of optical disk technology that allows the user to write data onto a CD, then change that data.

CD-writer ▶ A general term for recordable CD technologies such as CD-R and CD-RW.

Cell ▶ In spreadsheet terminology, the intersection of a column and a row. In cellular communications, a limited geographical area surrounding a cellular phone tower.

Cell reference ▶ The column letter and row number that designates the location of a worksheet cell. For example, the cell reference C5 refers to a cell in column C, row 5.

CEPT (Conference of European Postal and Telecommunications) ▶ High-speed (1.544 Mbps) digital network service available in Europe; it is similar to the T1 line.

Character data ▶ Letters, symbols, or numerals that will not be used in arithmetic operations (such as name, social security number, or phone number).

Chat group ▶ A discussion in which a group of people communicates online simultaneously.

Checksum ▶ A value calculated by combining all the bytes in a file that is used by virus detection programs to determine whether any bytes have been altered.

Ciphertext ▶ An encrypted message.

Circuit switching ▶ The method used by the telephone network to temporarily connect one telephone with another for the duration of a call.

CISC (complex instruction set computer) ▶ A general-purpose microprocessor chip designed to handle a wider array of instructions than a RISC chip.

Client ▶ A computer or software that requests information from another computer or server.

Client/server network ▶ A network where processing is split between workstations (clients) and the server.

Client-side script ▶ Scripting statement, embedded in an HTML document, that is executed by a client's browser.

Clip art ▶ Graphics designed to be inserted into documents, Web pages, and worksheets, usually available in CD-ROM or Web-based collections.

Cluster ▶ Sectors on a storage medium that, when accessed as a group, speeds up data access.

Cluster computing ▶ A group of computing devices that share a server or group of servers.

CMOS (complementary metal oxide semiconductor) memory ▶ A type of battery-powered integrated circuit that holds semi-permanent configuration data.

Coaxial cable ▶ A type of cable with BNC connectors made of a center wire surrounded by a grounded shield of braided wire and used to connect nodes on a network. Also called coax cable.

Code Morphing ▶ Software that dynamically "morphs" (that is, translates) x86 instructions into the hardware engine's native instruction set.

Codec (COmpressor/ DECompressor) ▶ A hardware or software routine that compresses and decompresses digital graphics, sound, and video files.

Color depth ▶ The number of bits that determines the range of possible colors that can be assigned to each pixel. For example, an 8-bit color depth can create 256 colors. Also called bit depth.

Color palette ▶ The selection of colors used in graphics software.

Commercial software ▶ Copyrighted computer applications sold to consumers for profit.

Communications channel ▶ Any pathway between the sender and receiver; channel may refer to a physical medium or a frequency.

Communications network ▶ A combination of hardware, software, and connecting links that transports data.

Communications protocol ▶ A set of rules for ensuring orderly and accurate transmission and reception of data.

Communications satellite ▶ Satellite used to send to and receive data from ground stations.

Compact Privacy Policy ▶ The HTTP header defined in a standard set of security tags that becomes part of the header for every cookie, that describes how cookie data is used by a Web site.

Compiler ▶ Software that translates a program written in a high-level language into low-level instructions before the program is executed.

Compression algorithm ▶ The steps required to shrink data in a file and restore it to its original state.

Compression ratio ▶ A measurement of the amount of shrinkage when data is compressed.

Compression software ▶ Software, such as WinZip, that effectively reduces the size of files. See file compression utility.

Computer ▶ A device that accepts input, processes data, stores data, and produces output.

Computer file ▶ A single collection of data stored on a storage medium.

Computer language ▶ A set of tools that allows a programmer to write instructions that a computer can execute.

Computer network ▶ A collection of computers and related devices, connected in a way that allows them to share data, hardware, and software.

Computer program ▶ A set of detailed, step-by-step instructions that tells a computer how to solve a problem or carry out a task.

Computer programmer ▶ A person who codes or writes computer programs.

Computer system ▶ The hardware, peripheral devices, and software working together to input data, process data, store data, and produce output.

Computer virus ▶ A program designed to attach itself to a file, reproduce, and spread from one file to another, destroying data, displaying an irritating message, or otherwise disrupting computer operations.

Concurrent-user license ▶ Legal permission for an organization to use a certain number of copies of a software program at the same time.

Control unit ▶ The part of the ALU that directs and coordinates processing.

Controller ▶ A circuit board in a hard drive that positions the disk and read-write heads to locate data.

Cookie ▶ A message sent from a Web server to a browser and stored on a user's hard disk, usually containing information about the user.

Copy Disk utility ▶ A utility program that duplicates the contents of an entire floppy disk.

Copyright ▶ A form of legal protection that grants certain exclusive rights to the author of a program or the owner of the copyright.

Copyright notice ▶ A line such as "Copyright 2005 ACME Co." that identifies a copyright holder.

CPU (central processing unit) ▶ The main processing unit in a computer, consisting of circuitry that executes instructions to process data.

Cropping ▶ The process of selecting and removing part of an image.

CRT (cathode ray tube) ▶ A display technology that uses a large vacuum tube similar to that used in television sets.

Crusoe ▶ A low-power processor chip from Transmeta—ideal for Internet devices and the ultra-light mobile PC category because it has low power consumption and it has an extended battery life.

Cryptographic algorithm ▶ A specific procedure for encrypting and decrypting data.

Cryptographic key ▶ A specific word, number, or phrase that must be used to encrypt or decrypt data.

CSMA/CD (Carrier Sense Multiple Access with Collision Detection) ▶ A method of responding to an attempt by two devices to use a data channel simultaneously; used by Ethernet networks.

Cursor ▶ A symbol that marks the user's place on the screen and shows where typing will appear.

Cylinder ▶ A vertical stack of tracks that is the basic storage bin for a hard disk drive.

Data ▶ In the context of computing and data management, the symbols that a computer uses to represent facts and ideas.

Data bus ▶ An electronic pathway or circuit that connects the electronic components (such as the processor and RAM) on a computer's motherboard.

Data compression ▶ The process of condensing data so that it requires fewer bytes of storage space.

Data file ▶ A file containing words, numbers, or pictures that the user can view, edit, save, send, or print.

Data management software ▶ Software designed for tasks associated with maintaining and accessing data stored in data files.

Data module ▶ A file linked to a program and provides data necessary for certain functions of the program.

Data representation ▶ The use of electrical signals, marks, or binary digits to represent character, numeric, visual, or audio data.

Data security ▶ Techniques that provide protection for data.

Data transfer rate ▶ The amount of data that a storage device can move from a storage medium to computer memory in one second.

Database ▶ A collection of information that may be stored in more than one file.

Database management software ▶ Software developed for the task of manipulating data in the form of a database.

Decryption ▶ The process of converting ciphertext into plaintext.

Defragmentation utility ▶ A software tool used to rearrange the files on a disk so that they are stored in contiguous clusters.

Demodulation ▶ The process of restoring a received signal to its original state. For example, when a modem changes an audio signal back to a digital pulse.

Denial of Service attack ▶ The result of hackers sending malicious software that is designed to overwhelm a network's processing capabilities, shutting it down.

Density ▶ A measure of an image, expressed as dots per inch (dpi) for a printer or scanner, or as pixels per inch (ppi) on a monitor. The denser the grid, the smaller the image will appear.

Desktop computer ▶ A computer small enough to fit on a desk and built around a single microprocessor chip.

Desktop operating system ▶ An operating system such as Windows Me or Mac OS X that is specifically designed for personal computers.

Desktop publishing software ▶ Software used to create high-quality output suitable for commercial printing. DTP software provides precise control over layout.

Desktop video ▶ Video stored in digital format on a PC's hard disk or CD.

Device driver ▶ The software that provides the computer with the means to control a peripheral device.

DHTML (dynamic HTML) ▶ A variation of the HTML format that allows elements of Web pages to be changed while they are being viewed.

Dial-up connection ▶ A connection that uses a phone line to establish a temporary Internet connection.

Dictionary-based compression ▶ A data compression scheme that uses a codeword to represent common sequences of characters.

Differential backup ▶ A copy of all the files that changed since the last full backup of a disk.

Digital ▶ Any system that works with discrete data, such as 0s and 1s, in contrast to analog.

Digital camera ▶ An input device that records an image in digital format.

Digital certificate ▶ A security method that identifies the author of an ActiveX control.

Digital device ▶ A device that works with discrete (distinct or separate) numbers or digits.

Digital electronics ▶ Circuitry that's designed to work with digital signals.

Digital signal processor ▶ Circuitry that is used to process, record, and playback audio files.

Digital video camera ▶ A device used to collect, store, and process video in a digital format.

Digital video recorder (DVR) ▶ A device that allows viewers to record TV and video digitally.

Digitize ▶ The conversion of non-digital information or media to a digital format through the use of a scanner, sampler, or other input device.

Digitizing tablet ▶ A device that provides a flat surface for a paper-based drawing, and a "pen" used to create hand-drawn vector drawings.

DIMM (dual in-line memory module) ▶ A small circuit board that holds RAM chips. A DIMM has a 64-bit path to the memory chips.

DIP (dual in-line package) ▶ A chip configuration characterized by a rectangular body with numerous plugs along its edge.

Direct satellite service (DSS) ▶ A service that uses a geosynchronous or low earth orbit satellite to send television, voice, or computer data directly to satellite dishes owned by individuals.

Direct source input device ▶ An input device, such as a bar code reader, that collects data directly from a document or object; used to reduce the incidence of operator error.

Directory ▶ A list of files contained on a computer storage device.

Disk density ▶ The closeness of the particles on a disk surface. As density increases, the particles are packed more tightly together and are usually smaller.

Distribution disks ▶ One or more floppy disks or CDs that contain programs and data, which can be installed to a hard disk.

Dithering ▶ A means of reducing the size of a graphics file by reducing the number of colors. Dithering uses patterns composed of two or more colors to produce the illusion of additional colors and shading.

DOCSIS (Data Over Cable Services Interface Specification) ▶ A security technology used for filtering packets to certain ports.

Document production software ▶ Computer programs that assist the user in composing, editing, designing, and printing documents.

Domain name ▶ An identifying name by which host computers on the Internet are familiarly known; for example, cocacola.com. Also referred to as fully qualified domain name.

Domain name server ▶ A computer that hosts the domain name system database.

Domain name system ▶ A large database of unique IP addresses that correspond with domain names.

DOS (disk operating system) ▶ The operating system software shipped with the first IBM PCs and used on millions of computers until the introduction of Microsoft Windows.

Dot matrix printer ▶ A printer that creates characters and graphics by striking an inked ribbon with small wires called "pins," generating a fine pattern of dots.

Dot pitch ▶ The diagonal distance between colored dots on a display screen. Measured in millimeters, dot pitch helps to determine the quality of an image displayed on a monitor.

Downloading ▶ The process of transferring a copy of a file from a remote computer to a local computer's disk drive.

DPI (dots per inch) ▶ Printer resolution as measured by the number of dots it can print per linear inch.

Drawing software ▶ Programs that are used to create images with lines, shapes, and colors, such as logos or diagrams.

Drive bay ▶ An area within a computer system unit that can accommodate an additional storage device.

Drive mapping ▶ In network terminology, assigning a drive letter to a network server disk drive.

DSL (Digital Subscriber Line) ▶ A high-speed Internet connection that uses existing telephone lines, requiring close proximity to a switching station.

DSL modem ▶ A device that sends to and receives digital data from computers over telephone lines.

DSLAM (DSL Access Multiplexor) ▶ Special equipment used to interpret, separate, and route digital data in telephone lines for DSL providers.

DSS (Digital Satellite System) ▶ A type of Internet connection that uses a network of satellites to transmit data.

Duron ▶ A family of processors produced by AMD.

DVD (digital video disc or digital versatile disc) ▶ An optical storage medium similar in appearance and technology to a CD-ROM but with higher storage capacity.

DVD drive ▶ An optical storage device that reads data from CD-ROM and DVD disks.

DVD-ROM ▶ A DVD disk that contains data that has been permanently stamped on the disk surface.

Dye sublimation printer ▶ An expensive, color-precise printer that heats ribbons containing color to produce consistent, photograph-quality images.

Dynamic IP address ▶ A temporarily assigned IP address usually provided by an ISP.

E911 (Enhanced 911) ▶ Technology that seeks to provide 911 dispatchers with better information from wireless calls, such as location.

EBCDIC (Extended Binary-Coded Decimal Interchange Code) ▶ A method by which digital computers, usually mainframes, represent character data.

eBooks ▶ Digital versions of books that read similar to print versions of books but with several electronic features.

E-commerce (electronic commerce) ▶ Business connected over the Internet, including online shopping, linking businesses to businesses (sometimes called e-business or B2B), online stock trading, and electronic auctions.

EIDE (enhanced integrated drive electronics) ▶ A type of drive that features high storage capacity and fast data transfer.

Electronic wallet ▶ Software that stores and processes customer information needed for an e-commerce transaction.

E-mail (electronic mail) ▶ A single electronic message or the entire system of computers and software that handles electronic messages transmitted between computers over a communications network.

E-mail account ▶ A service that provides an e-mail address and mailbox.

E-mail address ▶ The unique address for each mailbox on the Internet, which typically consists of a user ID, an @ symbol, and the name of the computer that maintains the mailbox.

E-mail attachment ▶ A separate file that is transmitted along with an e-mail message.

E-mail client software ▶ Software that is installed on a client computer and has access to e-mail servers on a network. This software is used to compose, send, and read e-mail messages.

E-mail message ▶ A computer file containing a letter or memo that is transmitted electronically via a communications network.

E-mail server ▶ A computer that uses special software to store and send e-mail messages over the Internet.

E-mail system ▶ The collection of computers and software that works together to provide e-mail services.

Encryption ▶ The process of scrambling or hiding information so that it cannot be understood without the key necessary to change it back into its original form.

Enterprise computing network ▶ A recent trend in business networks—information systems that share data and typically provide information to very large groups of users.

EPROM (erasable programmable read-only memory) ▶ ROM chips that can be erased and reused.

Ethernet ▶ A type of network on which network nodes are connected by coaxial cable or twisted-pair wire; the most popular network architecture, it typically transmits data at 10 or 100 megabits per second.

Even parity ▶ In a parity bit error-checking system, the requirement that there be an even number of bits in a data block.

Exa- ▶ Prefix for a quintillion.

Executable file ▶ A file, usually with an .exe extension, containing instructions that tell a computer how to perform a specific task.

Expansion bus ▶ The segment of the data bus that transports data between RAM and peripheral devices.

Expansion card ▶ A circuit board that is plugged into a slot on a PC motherboard to add extra functions, devices, or ports.

Expansion port ▶ A socket into which the user plugs a cable from a peripheral device, allowing data to pass between the computer and the peripheral device.

Expansion slot ▶ A socket or slot on a PC motherboard designed to hold a circuit board called an expansion card.

Extended ASCII ▶ Similar to ASCII but with 8-bit character representation instead of 7-bit, allowing for an additional 128 characters.

External link ▶ A hyperlink to a location outside the Web site.

External style sheet ▶ A template that contains formatting specifications for a group of Web pages.

External video ▶ A video on the Web that downloads and opens in a media player window when its link is clicked.

Extranet ▶ A network similar to a private internet that also allows outside users access.

Favorites ▶ A list of URLs for Web sites that you can create for your browser to store so that you can revisit those sites easily.

FDDI (Fiber Distributed Data Interconnect) ▶ A high-speed network that uses fiber-optic cables to link workstations.

Fiber-optic cable ▶ A bundle of thin tubes of glass used to transmit data as pulses of light.

Field ▶ The smallest meaningful unit of information contained in a data file.

Field Emission Display (FED) ▶ Technology that makes possible the thin panel of today's liquid crystal displays (LCD), offers a wide field of view, provides a high image quality, and requires less power than today's CRT displays; is being developed for use in flat panel displays.

File ▶ A named collection of data (such as a computer program, document, or graphic) that exists on a storage medium, such as a hard disk, floppy disk, or CD-ROM.

File allocation table (FAT) ▶ A special file that is used by the operating system to store the physical location of all the files on a storage medium, such as a hard disk or floppy disk.

File compression utility ▶ A type of data compression software that shrinks one or more files into a single file that occupies less storage space than the separate files.

File format ▶ The method of organization used to encode and store data in a computer. Text formats include DOC and TXT. Graphics formats include BMP, TIFF, GIF, and PCX.

File management software ▶ Computer programs that help the user organize records, find records that match specific criteria, and print lists based on the information contained in records.

File management utility ▶ Software, such as Windows Explorer, that helps users locate, rename, move, copy, and delete files.

File size ▶ The physical size of a file on a storage medium, usually measured in kilobytes (KB).

File specification ▶ A combination of the drive letter, subdirectory, filename, and extension that identifies a file (for example, A:\word\ filename.doc). Also called a path.

File structure ▶ A description of the way in which data is stored in a file.

File system ▶ A system that is used by an operating system to keep files organized.

File virus ▶ A computer virus that infects executable files, such as programs with .exe filename extensions.

File-naming conventions ▶ A set of rules established by the operating system that must be followed to create a valid filename.

Filename ▶ A set of letters or numbers that identifies a file.

Filename extension ▶ A set of letters and/or numbers added to the end of a filename that helps to identify the file contents or file type.

FireWire port ▶ A port on a digital camera or computer used to transfer photo data. Also called IEEE-1394 port.

Flash graphics ▶ A popular vector graphics format developed by Macromedia that can be used for still images or animations.

Flash memory ▶ A type of EPROM memory module that can store data without power consumption. It can be reused, making it popular for portable devices, such as digital cameras, PDAs, portable computers, and cell phones. Flash memory devices include CompactFlash, SmartMedia cards, PCMCIA Type I and Type II memory cards.

Flat file ▶ The electronic version of a box of index cards, each of which stores information about one entity, such as a person.

Flat panel display (FPD) ▶ Display technology that is flat, has less glare, and images have a more realistic appearance than CRTs. Although still more expensive than CRTs, FPD monitors are becoming the monitor of choice.

Floppy disk ▶ A removable magnetic storage medium, typically 3.5" in size, with a capacity of 1.44 MB.

Floppy disk adapter ▶ A device that contains a slot for a flash memory module that, when inserted into a floppy disk drive, enables users to transfer data to their PCs.

Floppy disk drive ▶ A storage device that writes data on, and reads data from, floppy disks.

FLOPS (floating point operations per second) ▶ A measure of processing speed for high performance computers.

Folder ▶ The subdirectory, or subdivision, of a directory that can contain files or other folders.

Font ▶ A typeface or style of lettering, such as Arial, Times New Roman, and Gothic.

Force feedback technology ▶ Technology that allows the user to feel motion coming back though a pointing device.

Formatting tags ▶ HTML code that is used to change the appearance of text.

Formula ▶ In spreadsheet terminology, a combination of numbers and symbols that tells the computer how to use the contents of cells in calculations.

Fragmented file ▶ A file stored in scattered, noncontiguous clusters on a disk.

Frame ▶ An outline or boundary frequently defining a box. For document production software, a pre-defined area into which text or graphics may be placed.

Frame rate ▶ Refers to the number of frames displayed per second in a video or film.

Free Space Optics (FSO) ▶ Technology being used to bridge the connection between businesses and the Internet's fiber optic backbone that uses line of sight technology and can be used with various protocols including ATM, IP, and Ethernet networks. The transceiver is about the size of a security video camera.

Freeware ▶ Copyrighted software that is given away by the author or owner.

Frequency ▶ The number of times that a wave oscillates (moves back and forth between two points) per second. Short wave lengths have high frequencies.

Full backup ▶ A copy of all the files for a specified backup job.

Full duplex ▶ A system that allows messages to be sent and received simultaneously.

Fully justified ▶ The horizontal alignment of text in which the text terminates exactly at both margins of the document.

Function ▶ In worksheets, a built-in formula for making a calculation. In programming, a section of code that manipulates data but is not included in the main sequential execution path of a program.

Function key ▶ One of the keys numbered F1 through F12 located at the top of the computer keyboard that activates program specific commands.

Gateway ▶ An electronic link that connects one computer system to another.

GIF (Graphics Interchange Format) ▶ A bitmap graphics file format popularized by CompuServe for use on the Web.

Giga- ▶ Prefix for a billion.

Gigahertz (GHz) ▶ A measure of frequency equivalent to one billion cycles per second, usually used to measure speed.

Gradient ▶ A smooth blending of shades of different colors from light to dark.

Graphical user interface (GUI) ▶ A type of user interface that features on-screen objects, such as menus and icons, manipulated by a mouse. Abbreviation is pronounced "gooey."

Graphics ▶ Any pictures, photographs, or images that can be manipulated or viewed on a computer.

Graphics card ▶ A circuit board inserted into a computer to handle the display of text, graphics, animation, and videos. Also called a video card.

Graphics software ▶ Computer programs for creating, editing, and manipulating images.

Graphics tablet ▶ A device that accepts input from a pressure-sensitive stylus and converts strokes into images on the screen.

Grayscale palette ▶ Digital images that are displayed in shades of gray, black, and white.

Half duplex ▶ A communications technique that allows the user to alternately send and receive transmissions.

Handheld computer ▶ A small, pocket-sized computer designed to run on its own power supply and provide users with basic applications.

Handshaking ▶ A process where a protocol helps two network devices communicate.

Hard disk ▶ See hard disk drive.

Hard disk drive ▶ A computer storage device that contains a large-capacity hard disk sealed inside the drive case. A hard disk is not the same as a 3.5" floppy disk that has a rigid plastic case.

Hard disk platter ▶ The component of a hard disk drive on which data is stored. It is a flat, rigid disk made of aluminum or glass and coated with a magnetic oxide.

Hardware ▶ The electronic and mechanical devices in a computer system.

Head crash ▶ A collision between the read-write head and the surface of the hard disk platter, resulting in damage to some of the data on the disk.

Head section ▶ A part of a Web page that begins with the <HEAD> HTML tag and contains information about global properties of the document.

Helper application ▶ A program that understands how to work with a specific file format.

High-level language ▶ A computer language that allows a programmer to write instructions using human-like language.

High–performance computing (HPC) ▶ Computers that have processing speeds that are measured in FLOPS (floating point operations per second) or MIPS (millions of instructions per second).

History list ▶ A list that is created by your browser of the sites you visited so that you can display and track your sessions or revisit the site by clicking the URL in the list.

Home network ▶ A requirement for many people who own computers. Basic options for home networks include Powerline networking (such as HomePLC), phone-line networking (such as HomePNA), and wireless networking (such as HomeRF). Apple's Airport is a home networking wireless solution for Macintosh users.

Home page ▶ In a Web site, the document that is the starting, or entry, page. On an individual computer, the Web page that a browser displays each time it is started.

HomePLC ▶ A network that uses a building's existing power line cables to connect nodes.

HomePNA ▶ A network that uses a building's existing phone lines to connect nodes.

HomeRF ▶ A low-power, wireless network designed for home use.

Horizontal market software ▶ Any computer program that can be used by many different kinds of businesses (for example, an accounting program).

Host computer ▶ A computer system that stores and processes data accessed by multiple terminals from remote locations. In Internet terminology, any computer connected to the Internet.

Hot spot ▶ An area on a Web page that is designated as a hyperlink.

HTML (Hypertext Markup Language) ▶ A standardized format used to specify the format for Web page documents.

HTML document ▶ A plain text or ASCII document with embedded HTML tags that dictate formatting and are interpreted by a browser.

HTML form ▶ An HTML document containing blank boxes prompting users to enter information that can be sent to a Web server. Commonly used for e-commerce transactions.

HTML frame ▶ Part of a Web page that scrolls independently of other parts of the Web page.

HTML tag ▶ An instruction, such as <B>...</B>, inserted into an HTML document to provide formatting and display information to a Web browser.

HTTP (Hypertext Transfer Protocol) ▶ The communications protocol used to transmit Web pages. HTTP:// is an identifier that appears at the beginning of most Web page URLs (for example, http://www.course.com).

HTTP status code ▶ A code used by Web servers to report the status of a browser's request.

Hub ▶ A network device that connects several nodes of a local area network.

Hyper-Threading Technology ▶ Technology used by Intel's Pentium 4 that lets one chip act almost like two.

Hypertext ▶ A way of organizing an information database by linking information through the use of text and multimedia.

Hypertext link ▶ An underlined word or phrase that, when clicked, takes you to its designated URL; also called link.

ICANN (Internet Corporation for Assigned Names and Numbers) ▶ A global organization that coordinates the management of the Internet's domain name system, IP addresses, and protocol parameters.

ICQ (I Seek You) ▶ An instant messaging community; the software needed to be part of the community that allows for chatting through the Internet by using screen names to identify users.

IEEE (Institute of Electrical and Electronics Engineers, Inc.) ▶ A non-profit, technical professional association of more than 377,000 individual members in 150 countries. Pronounced (Eye-triple-E). The standards set by this association are what keep past, present, and future networks communicating.

Image map ▶ An area on a Web page consisting of a single graphic image containing multiple hot spots.

IMAP (Internet Messaging Access Protocol) ▶ A protocol similar to POP that is used to retrieve e-mail messages from an e-mail server, but offers additional features, such as choosing which e-mails to download from the server.

Incremental backup ▶ A copy of the files that changed since the last backup.

Information ▶ The words, numbers, and graphics used as the basis for human actions and decisions.

Infrared light ▶ A wireless transmission technology that uses a frequency range just below the visible light spectrum to transport data signals for short distances with a clear line of sight. Its most practical uses seem to be transmission of data between a notebook computer and a printer, between a PDA and a desktop computer, and in remote controls to change television channels.

Infrared port ▶ Device that accepts infrared light containing photo data that was beamed by a camera to a computer. This method, though slow, eliminates the need for a cable.

Ink jet printer ▶ A non-impact printer that creates characters or graphics by spraying liquid ink onto paper or other media.

Input ▶ As a noun, "input" means the information that is conveyed to a computer. As a verb, "input" means to enter data into a computer.

Input device ▶ A device, such as a keyboard or mouse, that gathers input and transforms it into a series of electronic signals for the computer.

Install ▶ The process by which programs and data are copied to the hard disk of a computer system and otherwise prepared for access and use.

Installation agreement ▶ A version of the license agreement that appears on the computer screen when software is being installed and prompts the user to accept or decline.

Instant messaging ▶ A private chat in which users can communicate with each other.

Instruction cycle ▶ The steps followed by a computer to process a single instruction; fetch, interpret, execute, then increment the instruction pointer.

Instruction set ▶ The collection of instructions that a CPU is designed to process.

Integrated circuit (IC) ▶ A thin slice of silicon crystal containing microscopic circuit elements, such as transistors, wires, capacitors, and resistors; also called chips and microchips.

Integrated digital television (IDTV) ▶ A digital television product that incorporates television, recording, and computing.

Internal link ▶ A hyperlink to a location within the same Web site.

Internal video ▶ A video on the Web that plays within a frame inside the Web page when its link is clicked.

Internet ▶ The worldwide communication infrastructure that links computer networks using TCP/IP protocol.

Internet2 ▶ A consortium of researchers and universities working together with high-tech corporations and some government agencies to build the next generation of the Internet.

Internet appliance ▶ A device designed for the sole purpose of accessing the Internet.

Internet backbone ▶ The major communications links that form the core of the Internet.

Internet Service Provider ▶ See ISP.

Internet telephony ▶ A set of hardware and software that allows users to make phone-style calls over the Internet, usually without a long-distance charge.

Internetwork (internet) ▶ A network composed of many smaller networks.

Interpage link ▶ A hyperlink that links to a different location on the same Web page.

Interpreter ▶ A program that converts high-level instructions in a computer program into machine language instructions, one instruction at a time.

Intranet ▶ A LAN that uses TCP/IP communications protocols, typically for communications services within a business or organization.

IP (Transmission Control Protocol) ▶ One of the main protocols of TCP/IP that is responsible for addressing packets so they can be routed to their destination.

IP address ▶ A unique identifying number assigned to each computer connected to the Internet.

ISA (Industry Standard Architecture) ▶ A standard for moving data on the expansion bus. Can refer to a type of slot, a bus, or a peripheral device. An older technology, it is rapidly being replaced by PCI architecture.

ISDN (Integrated Services Digital Network) ▶ A telephone company service that transports data digitally over dial-up or dedicated lines.

ISDN terminal adapter ▶ A device that connects a computer to a telephone jack and translates the data into a signal that can travel over an ISDN connection.

ISP (Internet Service Provider) ▶ A company that provides Internet access to businesses, organizations, and individuals.

Joystick ▶ A pointing input device used as an alternative to a mouse.

JPEG (Joint Photographic Experts Group) ▶ A format that uses lossy compression to store bitmap images. JPEG files have a .jpg extension.

Kernel ▶ The core module of an operating system that typically manages memory, processes, tasks, and disks.

Key frame ▶ A frame that contains all data for that frame. Key frames are set at equal intervals. The rest of the frames in the video contain only the information that is different from the last key frame.

Keyboard ▶ An arrangement of letter, number, and special function keys that acts as the primary input device to the computer.

Keyboard shortcut ▶ The use of the [Alt] or the [Ctrl] key in combination with another key on the keyboard to execute a command, such as copy, paste, or cut.

Keyword ▶ A word or term used as the basis for a database or Web-page search.

Kilobit (Kbit or **Kb)** ▶ 1,024 bits.

Kilobyte (KB) ▶ Approximately 1,000 bytes; exactly 1,024 bytes.

LAN (local area network) ▶ An interconnected group of computers and peripherals located within a relatively limited area, such as a building or campus.

Land ▶ A non-pitted surface area on a CD that represents digital data.

Laser light ▶ A focused beam of light that, with a clear line of sight, can transmit data over long distances.

Laser printer ▶ A printer that uses laser-based technology, similar to that used by photocopiers, to produce text and graphics.

LCD (liquid crystal display) technology ▶ The primary technology used in flat panel displays (FPD).

LCD screen ▶ See LCD.

Linear editing ▶ A video editing technique that records segments of video from one tape to another.

Link ▶ Underlined text that allows users to jump between Web pages.

Link bar ▶ A navigation tool that contains links to other pages in a Web site based on the hierarchy—the relationship—of the pages. Themes often include link bars, which appear as the same graphic links and in the same location on each page.

Link tag ▶ HTML code that is used to designate text as a hyperlink in a document.

Linux ▶ A server operating system that is a derivative of UNIX and available as freeware.

Logical address ▶ A network address that is assigned to a network device when the physical address is in an incorrect format.

Logical port ▶ A non-physical connection point between network nodes.

Logical storage model ▶ Any visual aid or metaphor that helps a computer user visualize a file system.

Logical topology ▶ Network topology that corresponds with the way messages flow across the network, not necessarily identical to the network's physical topology.

Lossless compression ▶ A compression technique that provides the means to restore all of the data in the original file.

Lossy compression ▶ Any data compression technique in which some of the data is sacrificed to obtain more compression.

Mac (Macintosh computer) ▶ A personal computer platform designed and manufactured by Apple Computer.

MAC address (Media Access Control address) ▶ A unique address given to a NIC.

Mac OS ▶ The operating system software designed for use on Apple Macintosh and iMac computers.

Machine code ▶ Program instructions written in binary code that the computer can execute directly.

Machine language ▶ A low-level language written in binary code that the computer can execute directly.

Macro ▶ A small set of instructions that automates a task. Typically, a macro is created by performing the task once and recording the steps. Whenever the macro is played back, the steps are repeated.

Macro virus ▶ A computer virus that infects the macros that are attached to documents and spreadsheets.

Magnetic RAM (MRAM) ▶ Memory technology with the potential for instant-on capability and longer life batteries.

Magnetic storage ▶ The recording of data onto disks or tape by magnetizing particles of an oxide-based surface coating.

Mailing list server Any computer and software that maintains a list of people who are interested in a topic and that facilitates message exchanges among all members of the list.

Mailto link ▶ A link on a Web page that automatically opens a pre-addressed e-mail form.

Main executable file ▶ A program that is used to start and run software, usually with an .exe file extension.

Mainframe computer ▶ A large, fast, and expensive computer generally used by businesses or government agencies to provide centralized storage processing and management for large amounts of data.

MAN (metropolitan area network) ▶ A public, high-speed network that can transmit voice and data within a range of 50 miles.

Markup language ▶ A language that provides text and graphics formatting through the use of tags. Examples include HTML, XML, and SGML.

m-Commerce (mobile commerce) ▶ The ability to communicate and conduct business transactions through mobile devices (such as cell phones and PDAs) and wireless networks.

Media tags ▶ HTML code that specifies how to display media elements in a document.

Megabit (Mb or Mbit) ▶ Approximately 1 million bits; exactly 1,048,576 bits.

Megabyte (MB) ▶ Approximately 1 million bytes; exactly 1,048,576 bytes.

Megahertz (MHz) ▶ A measure of frequency equivalent to 1 million cycles per second.

Megapixel ▶ A million pixels; used to express the resolution and quality of an image.

Membrane keyboard ▶ A keyboard that is sealed and is designed to work in a variety of environmental conditions.

Memory ▶ The computer circuitry that holds data waiting to be processed.

Memory card reader ▶ A device that connects to a PC via a USB or Serial cable that reads data from a flash memory module.

Memory stick ▶ A class of storage. Digital cameras and portable devices, such as PDAs, portable computers, and cell phones, make use of this memory technology.

MEMS-based storage (MicroElectroMechanical Systems) ▶ Technology that combines storage and processing on one chip. It is expected to have access times much faster than current conventional disks.

Metafile ▶ Graphics file that contains both vector and bitmap data.

Microcomputer ▶ A category of computer that is built around a single microprocessor chip.

Microdrive ▶ Family of very small removable storage device products that hold from 340MB to 1GB of data storage capacity on a disk and that are compatible with devices from many manufacturers.

Microprocessor ▶ An integrated circuit that contains the circuitry for processing data. It is a single-chip version of the central processing unit (CPU) found in all computers.

Microprocessor clock ▶ A device on the motherboard of a computer responsible for setting the pace of executing instructions.

Microsoft Windows ▶ An operating system developed by Microsoft Corporation that provides a graphical interface. Versions include Windows 3.1, Windows 95, Windows 98, Windows Me, Windows XP, Windows NT, and Windows 2000.

Microwaves ▶ Electromagnetic waves with a frequency of at least 1 gigahertz.

Middleware ▶ Intelligent software that prioritizes packets on the Internet and is used to help applications work more effectively over advanced networks through standardization and interoperability; it binds together major applications and negotiates communications between them.

MIDI (Musical Instrument Digital Interface) ▶ A standardized way in which sound and music are encoded and transmitted between devices that play music.

MIDI sequence ▶ Digitally encoded music stored on a computer. Usually a file with a .mid, .cmf, or .rol file extension.

Millisecond (ms) ▶ A thousandth of a second.

MIME (Multipurpose Internet Mail Extension) ▶ A conversion process used for formatting non-ASCII messages so that they can be sent over the Internet.

MIPS (millions of instructions per second) ▶ A measure of processing speed for high performance computers.

Modem ▶ A device that sends and receives data to and from computers over telephone lines.

Modem card ▶ A device that provides a way to transmit data over phone lines or cable television lines.

Modifier key ▶ The [Ctrl], [Alt], or [Shift] key, used in conjunction with another key to expand the repertoire of available commands.

Modulation ▶ The process of changing the characteristics of a signal. For example, when a modem changes a digital pulse into an analog signal.

Monitor ▶ A display device that forms an image by converting electrical signals from the computer into points of colored light on the screen.

Monochrome bitmap ▶ Displayed by manipulating the pattern of off and on pixels on the screen. Each pixel is set to display either a black dot or a white dot. Monochrome bitmaps require very little storage space.

Motherboard ▶ The main circuit board in a computer that houses chips and other electronic components.

Mouse ▶ An input device that allows the user to manipulate objects on the screen by moving the mouse on the surface of a desk.

MP3 ▶ A file format that provides highly compressed audio files with very little loss of sound quality.

MP3 encoder ▶ Software that compresses a WAV audio file into an MP3 audio file.

MP3 player ▶ Software that plays MP3 audio files.

MPEG (Moving Pictures Expert Group) ▶ A highly compressed file format for digital videos. Files in this format have a .mpg extension.

MPEG-2 ▶ A special type of data coding for movie files that are much too large to fit on a disk unless they are compressed.

MSN Messenger ▶ Microsoft's instant messaging service; software that allows for chatting through the Internet by using screen names to identify users.

MTBF (mean time between failures) ▶ The reliability of computer components as calculated by observing test equipment in a laboratory, then dividing the number of failures by the total number of hours of observation. This statistic is an estimate based on laboratory tests of a few sample components.

Multimedia home platform (MHP) ▶ Combines several media for home use; an integral component to the future success and expansion of digital interactive television.

Multi-partite virus ▶ A computer virus that is able to infect many types of targets by hiding itself in numerous locations on a computer.

Multiple-user license ▶ Legal permission for more than one person to use a particular software package.

Multitasking operating system ▶ An operating system that runs two or more programs at the same time.

Multiuser operating system ▶ An operating system that allows two or more users to run programs at the same time and use their own input/output devices.

Nanosecond ▶ A unit of time representing 1 billionth of a second.

Narrowband ▶ A term that refers to communications channels that have low bandwidth.

Native file format ▶ A file format that is unique to a program or group of programs and has a unique file extension.

Natural language query ▶ A query using language spoken by human beings, as opposed to an artificially constructed language such as machine language.

Netiquette ▶ Internet etiquette or a set of guidelines for posting messages and e-mails in a civil, concise way.

Network address translation (NAT) ▶ An Internet standard that allows a LAN to use one type of IP address for LAN data and another type of address for data to and from the Internet.

Network card ▶ An expansion board mounted inside a computer to allow access to a local area network.

Network drive ▶ A drive that is directly connected to a network and is accessible from all computers on the network. One advantage to a network drive is shared space.

Network interface card (NIC) ▶ A small circuit board that sends data from and collects incoming data for a workstation over a network.

Network operating system ▶ Programs designed to control the flow of data, maintain security, and keep track of accounts on a network.

Network service provider (NSP) ▶ A company that maintains a series of nationwide Internet links.

Newsgroup ▶ An online discussion group that centers around a specific topic.

Node ▶ Each device on a network, including workstations, servers, and printers; in a hierarchical database, a segment or record type.

Non-linear editing ▶ A digital video editing technique that requires a PC and video editing software.

Notation software ▶ Software used to help musicians compose, edit, and print musical scores.

Notebook computer ▶ Small, lightweight, portable computer that usually runs on batteries. Sometimes called laptop.

Novell network ▶ A local area network that uses Novell NetWare as its operating system.

Numeric data ▶ Numbers that represent quantities and can be used in arithmetic operations.

Numeric keypad ▶ Calculator-style input devices for numbers located towards the right side of a keyboard.

Object code ▶ The low-level instructions that result from compiling source code.

Object-oriented database ▶ A database model that organizes data into classes of objects that can be manipulated by programmer-defined methods.

Online ▶ Refers to being connected to the Internet.

Online drive ▶ Allows businesses and individuals to store files on a "virtual hard drive" via an Internet connection.

Online shopping cart ▶ An e-commerce cookie that stores information about items selected and collected for purchase.

Op code (operation code) ▶ An assembly language command word that designates an operation, such as add (ADD), compare (CMP), or jump (JMP).

Open Mobile Alliance (OMA) ▶ A group of companies and organizations including WAP that have come together to drive the growth of the mobile industry.

Open source software ▶ Software, such as Linux, that includes its uncompiled source code, which can be modified and distributed by programmers.

Operand ▶ The part of an instruction that specifies the data, or the address of the data, on which the operation is to be performed.

Operating system (OS) ▶ Software that controls the computer's use of its hardware resources, such as memory and disk storage space.

Operational tag ▶ HTML code used to specify the basic setup and database integration for Web pages.

Operator error ▶ The most common cause of lost and/or inaccurate data; mistakes made by a computer user such as entering the wrong data or deleting a needed file.

Opteron ▶ A family of enterprise-class processors from AMD for servers and workstations.

Optical mouse ▶ A device that uses optical technology rather than a roller ball to transmit information to a computer.

Optical storage ▶ A means of recording data as light and dark spots on a CD, DVD, or other optical media.

Organic light emitting diode (OLED) ▶ A technology that creates display devices that are thinner, have higher resolutions, and are more power-efficient than Cathode Ray Tube (CRT) displays or Active Matrix Liquid Crystal displays (LCD).

Output ▶ The results produced by a computer (for example, reports, graphs, and music).

Output device ▶ A device, such as a monitor or printer, that displays, prints, or transmits the results of processing from the computer memory.

P3P (Platform for Privacy Preferences Project) ▶ A specification that allows Web browsers to detect a Web site's privacy policies automatically.

Packet ▶ A small unit of data transmitted over a network or the Internet.

Packet switching ▶ A technology used by data communications networks, such as the Internet, in which a message is divided into smaller units called "packets" for transmission.

Page layout ▶ The physical positions of elements on a document page, such as headers, footers, page numbers, and graphics.

Paint software ▶ The software required to create and manipulate bitmap graphics.

Parallel port ▶ Commonly used to connect most printers to a computer; however some printers are designed to connect to a USB port or a serial port.

Parallel processing ▶ A technique by which two or more processors in a computer perform processing tasks simultaneously.

Parity bit ▶ A bit added to the end of a data block to allow for error checking during data transmission.

Passive matrix screen ▶ A display found on older notebook computers that relies on timing to ensure that the liquid crystal cells are illuminated.

Password ▶ A special set of symbols used to restrict access to a computer or network.

Path ▶ A file's location in a file structure. See File specification.

PC ▶ A microcomputer that uses Windows software and contains an Intel-compatible microprocessor.

PC card ▶ A credit card-sized circuit board used to connect a modem, memory, network card, or storage device to a notebook computer.

PCI (Peripheral Component Interconnect) ▶ A method for transporting data on the expansion bus. Can refer to type of data bus, expansion slot, or transport method used by a peripheral device.

PCMCIA (Personal Computer Memory Card International Association) slot ▶ An external expansion slot typically found on notebook computers.

PDA (Personal Digital Assistant) ▶ A computer that is smaller and more portable than a notebook computer. Also called a palm-top computer.

Peer-to-peer network ▶ The arrangement in which one workstation/server shares resources with another workstation/server; each computer on such a network must act as both a file server and workstation.

Pentium® 4 ▶ Premier Intel Processor for desktop computers. The chip is built on Intel's NetBurst technology, which allows it to deliver higher clock speeds with lower thermal output, and Intel's Hyper-Threading Technology, which lets one chip act almost like two.

Peripheral device ▶ A component or equipment, such as a printer or scanner, that expands a computer's input, output, or storage capabilities.

Personal computer ▶ A microcomputer designed for use by an individual user for applications such as Internet browsing and word processing.

Personal firewall ▶ Software designed to analyze and control incoming and outgoing packets.

Personal video recorder (PVR) ▶ A device that allows you to record digital video based on personal preferences.

Person-to-person payment ▶ An e-commerce method of payment that bypasses credit cards and instead uses an automatic electronic payment service.

PGA (pin-grid array) ▶ A common chip design used for microprocessors.

PGP (Pretty Good Privacy) ▶ A popular program used to encrypt and decrypt e-mail messages.

Phantom ▶ A device that recreates the sense of touch by sending small impulses at very high frequencies via the Internet.

Phonemes ▶ Units of sound that are basic components of words and are produced by speech synthesizers.

Physical address ▶ An address built into the circuitry of a network device at the time of its manufacture.

Physical storage model ▶ The way data is stored on a storage media.

Physical topology ▶ The actual layout of network devices, wires, and cables.

Ping (Packet Internet Groper) ▶ A command on a TCP/IP network that sends a test packet to a specified IP address and waits for a reply.

Pipelining ▶ A technology that allows a processor to begin executing an instruction before completing the previous instruction.

Pit ▶ A dark spot that is burned onto the surface of a CD to represent digital data.

Pixel (picture element) ▶ The smallest unit in a graphic image. Computer display devices use a matrix of pixels to display text and graphics.

Pixel interpolation ▶ A process used by graphics software to average the color of adjacent pixels in an image.

Pixie dust ▶ A technology developed by IBM that uses multilayer coating technology and permits hard disk drives to increase current area density limits.

Plaintext ▶ An original, un-encrypted message.

Platform ▶ A family or category of computers based on the same underlying software and hardware.

Plug and Play ▶ The ability of a computer to recognize and adjust the system configuration for a newly added device automatically.

Plug-in ▶ A software module that adds a specific feature to a system. For example, in the context of the Web, a plug-in adds a feature to the user's browser, such as the ability to play RealVideo files.

PNG (Portable Network Graphics) ▶ A type of graphics file format similar to, but newer than, GIF or JPEG.

Polymorphic viruses ▶ Viruses that can escape detection by antivirus software through changing their signatures.

POP (Post Office Protocol) ▶ A protocol that is used to retrieve e-mail messages from an e-mail server.

POP server ▶ A computer that receives and stores e-mail data until retrieved by the e-mail account holder.

PostScript ▶ A printer language developed by Adobe Systems that uses a special set of commands to control page layout, fonts, and graphics.

POTS ▶ An acronym for plain old telephone service.

Power failure ▶ A complete loss of power to the computer system, usually caused by something over which you have no control.

Power spike ▶ An increase in power that lasts only a short time—less than one millionth of a second. Spikes can be caused by malfunctions in the local generating plant or the power distribution network, and they are potentially more damaging to your computer system and data than a power failure.

Power strip ▶ A device that provides additional outlets for power but provides no protection against power spikes, surges, or failures.

Power surge ▶ A fluctuation in power that lasts a little longer than a power spike—a few millionths of a second. Surges can be caused by malfunctions in the local generating plant or the power distribution network, and they are potentially more damaging to your computer system and data than a power failure.

Power-on self-test (POST) ▶ A diagnostic process that runs during startup to check components of the computer, such as the graphics card, RAM, keyboard, and disk drives.

Presentation software ▶ Software that provides tools to combine text, graphics, graphs, animation, and sound into a series of electronic slides that can be output on a projector, or as overhead transparencies, paper copies, or 35-millimeter slides.

Printer ▶ A peripheral device used to create hard copy output.

Printer Control Language (PCL) ▶ A standard language used to send page formatting instructions from a computer to a laser or ink jet printer.

Private IP address ▶ IP address that cannot be routed over the Internet.

Processing ▶ The manipulation of data using a systematic series of actions.

Project management software ▶ Software specifically designed as a tool for planning, scheduling, and tracking projects and their costs.

PROM (programmable read-only memory) ▶ Memory that can be created using a special machine through a process called burning.

Protocols ▶ Rules that ensure the orderly and accurate transmission and reception of data. Protocols start and end transmission, recognize errors, send data at the appropriate speed, and identify the correct senders and recipients.

Public domain software ▶ Software that is available for use by the public without restriction, except that it cannot be copyrighted.

Public key encryption (PKE) ▶ An encryption method that uses a pair of keys—a public key (known to everyone) that encrypts the message, and a private key (known only to the recipient) that decrypts it.

Qubit ▶ Storage that has the potential of representing not just 1 or 0, but of representing both 1 and 0 at the same time leading to faster and more powerful computing.

Query ▶ A search specification that prompts the computer to look for particular records in a file.

Query by example (QBE) ▶ A type of database interface in which users fill in a field with an example of the type of information that they are seeking.

Query language ▶ A set of command words that can be used to direct the computer to create databases, locate information, sort records, and change the data in those records.

QuickTime ▶ A video and animation file format developed by Apple Computer that can also be run on PCs. QuickTime files have a .mov extension.

RAID (redundant array of independent disks) ▶ Disks used by mainframes and microcomputers in which many disk platters provide data redundancy for faster data access and increased protection from media failure.

RAM (random access memory) ▶ A type of computer memory circuit that holds data, program instructions, and the operating system while the computer is on.

Random access ▶ The ability of a storage device (such as a disk drive) to go directly to a specific storage location without having to search sequentially from a beginning location.

Rasterization ▶ The process of superimposing a grid over a vector image and determining the color depth for each pixel.

Ray tracing ▶ A technique by which light and shadow are added to a 3-D image.

RDRAM (Rambus dynamic RAM) ▶ A fast (up to 600 MHz) type of memory used in newer personal computers.

Read-write head ▶ The mechanism in a disk drive that magnetizes particles on the storage disk surface to write data, or senses the bits that are present to read data.

RealAudio (.ra) ▶ An audio file format developed by Real Networks especially for streaming audio data over the Web.

RealMedia ▶ A video file format developed by Real Networks that is popular for streaming Web videos.

Record ▶ In the context of database management, a record is the set of fields of data that pertain to a single entity in a database.

Recovery CD ▶ A CD that contains all the operating system files and application software files necessary to restore a computer to its original state.

Register ▶ A "scratch pad" area of the ALU and control unit where data or instructions are moved so that they can be processed.

Relational database ▶ A database structure incorporating the use of tables that can establish relationships with other similar tables.

Relative reference ▶ In a worksheet, cell references that can change if cells change position as a result of a move or copy operation.

Rendering ▶ In graphics software, the process of creating a 3-D solid image by covering a wireframe drawing and applying computer-generated highlights and shadows.

Repeater ▶ A network device that receives and retransmits amplified signals so that they can retain the necessary strength to reach their destinations.

Rescue disk ▶ A boot disk that contains operating system files plus antivirus software.

Reserved word ▶ A word used as a command in some operating systems that may not be used in a filename.

Resolution ▶ The density of the grid used to display or print text and graphics; the greater the horizontal and vertical density, the higher the resolution.

Resolution dependent ▶ Graphics, such as bitmaps, for which the quality of the image is dependent on the number of pixels comprising the image.

Restore ▶ The act of moving data from a backup storage medium to a hard disk in the event original data has been lost.

Retro virus ▶ Virus designed to corrupt antivirus software.

RF signals (radio frequency signals) ▶ Data that is broadcast and received via radio waves with a transceiver.

RIMM (Rambus in-line memory module) ▶ A memory module using RDRAM.

RISC (reduced instruction set computer) ▶ A microprocessor chip designed for rapid and efficient processing of a small set of simple instructions.

Risk Management ▶ The process of weighing threats to computer data against the amount of expendable data and the cost of protecting crucial data.

ROM (read-only memory) ▶ One or more integrated circuits that contain permanent instructions that the computer uses during the boot process.

ROM BIOS (basic input/output system) ▶ A small set of basic input/output system instructions stored in ROM that causes the computer system to load critical operating files when the user turns on the computer.

Root directory ▶ The main directory of a disk.

Router ▶ A device found at each intersection on the Internet backbone that examines the IP address of incoming data and forwards the data towards its destination. Also used by LANs.

Run-length encoding ▶ A graphics file compression technique that looks for patterns of bytes and replaces them with messages that describe the patterns.

Safe Mode ▶ A menu option that appears when Windows is unable to complete the boot sequence. By entering Safe Mode, a user can gracefully shut down the computer then try to reboot it.

Sampling rate ▶ The number of times per second a sound is measured during the recording process; a higher sampling rate means higher-quality sound.

Scanner ▶ An input device that converts a printed page of text or images into a digital format.

Script ▶ Program that contains a list of commands that are automatically executed as needed.

Scripting error ▶ An error that occurs when a browser or server cannot execute a statement in a script.

SCSI (small computer system interface) ▶ An interface standard used for attaching peripheral devices, such as disk drives. Pronounced "scuzzy."

SDRAM (synchronous dynamic RAM) ▶ A type of RAM that synchronizes itself with the CPU, thus enabling it to run at much higher clock speeds than conventional RAM.

Search engine ▶ Program that uses keywords to find information on the Internet and return a list of relevant documents.

Search operator ▶ A word or symbol that has a specific function within a search, such as "AND."

SEC (single edge contact) cartridge ▶ A common, cassette-like chip design for microprocessors.

Sectors ▶ Subdivision of the tracks on a storage medium that provide a storage area for data.

Self-securing storage ▶ Devices that keep all versions of all data for a specified period of time and continually monitor requests.

Sequential access ▶ A form of data storage, usually on computer tape, that requires a device to read or write data one record after another, starting at the beginning of the medium.

Serial processing ▶ Processing of data that completes one instruction before beginning another.

Server ▶ A computer or software on a network that supplies the network with data and storage.

Server farm ▶ A group of multiple Web servers used to handle large volumes of requests.

Server-side script ▶ A scripting statement that is executed by a Web server in response to client data.

Server software ▶ Software used by servers to locate and distribute data requested by Internet users.

SET (Secure Electronic Transaction) ▶ A system that ensures the security of financial transactions on the Web.

Setup program ▶ A program module supplied with a software package for the purpose of installing the software.

Shareware ▶ Copyrighted software marketed under a license that allows users to use the software for a trial period and then send in a registration fee if they wish to continue to use it.

Shrink-wrap license ▶ A legal agreement printed on computer software packaging that goes into effect when the package is opened.

S-HTTP (Secure HTTP) ▶ A method of encrypting data transmitted between a computer and a Web server by encrypting individual packets of data as they are transmitted.

Simplex ▶ A communications technique that allows communication in only one direction.

Single-user license ▶ A legal agreement that typically allows only one copy of the software to be in use at a time.

Single-user operating system ▶ A type of operating system that is designed for one user at a time with one set of input and output devices.

Site license ▶ A legal agreement that generally allows software to be used on any and all computers at a specific location, such as within a corporate office or on a university campus.

Smart media ▶ A class of storage technology used by portable devices such as digital cameras, PDAs, portable computers, and cell phones.

SMTP (Simple Mail Transfer Protocol) server ▶ A computer used to send e-mail across a network or the Internet.

Socket ▶ A communication path between two remote programs.

Software ▶ The instructions that prepare a computer to do a task, indicate how to interact with a user, and specify how to process data.

Software license ▶ A legal contract that defines how a user may use a computer program.

Solid state ▶ No moving parts; everything is electronic instead of mechanical.

SO-RIMM (small outline Rambus inline memory) module ▶ A small memory module that contains RDRAM, used primarily in notebook computers.

Sound card ▶ A circuit board that gives the computer the ability to accept audio input from a microphone, play sound files stored on disks and CD-ROMs, and produce audio output through speakers or headphones.

Source code ▶ Computer instructions written in a high-level language.

Spatial compression ▶ A data compression scheme that replaces patterns of bytes with code that describes the patterns.

Speakers ▶ Output devices that receive signals for the computer's sound card to play music, narration, or sound effects.

Speech recognition ▶ The process by which computers recognize voice patterns and words and convert them to digital data.

Speech recognition software ▶ Software that analyzes voice sounds and converts them into phonemes.

Speech synthesis ▶ The process by which computers produce sound that resembles spoken words.

Speech-to-Text (STT) ▶ Translates spoken words into text; lets you speak to digital devices and have your words translated into digital code that is "understood" by your computer.

Spreadsheet ▶ A numerical model or representation of a real situation, presented in the form of a table.

Spreadsheet software ▶ Software for creating electronic worksheets that hold data in cells and perform calculations based on that data.

SQL (Structured Query Language) ▶ A popular query language used by mainframes and microcomputers.

SSL (secure sockets layer) ▶ A security protocol that uses encryption to establish a secure connection between a computer and a Web server.

Stateless protocol ▶ A protocol that allows one request and response per session, such as HTTP.

Static IP address ▶ A permanently assigned and unique IP address, used by hosts or servers.

Statistical compression ▶ A data compression scheme that uses an algorithm that recodes frequently used data as short bit patterns.

Stealth virus ▶ Virus that can escape detection from antivirus software by removing its own signature and hiding in memory.

Storage ▶ The area in a computer where data is retained on a permanent basis.

Storage device ▶ A mechanical apparatus that records data to and retrieves data from a storage medium.

Storage medium ▶ The physical material used to store computer data, such as a floppy disk, a hard disk, or a CD-ROM.

Store-and-forward technology ▶ A technology used by communications networks in which an e-mail message is temporarily held in storage on a server until it is requested by a client computer.

Stored program ▶ A set of instructions that resides on a storage device, such as a hard drive, and can be loaded into memory and executed.

STP (shielded twisted pair) ▶ A type of cable consisting of two wires that are twisted together and encased in a protective layer to reduce signal noise.

Streaming video ▶ An Internet video technology that sends a small segment of a video file to a user's computer and begins to play it while the next segment is sent.

Strong encryption ▶ Encryption that is difficult to decrypt without the encryption key.

Structured file ▶ A file that consists of a collection of records, each with the same set of fields.

Style ▶ A combination of attributes—colors, sizes, and fonts—that specify the way text is displayed.

Style sheet ▶ Acts as a template to control the layout and design of Web pages. Style sheets work in conjunction with HTML tags to make it easy to change the format of elements in a Web page globally and consistently. Also called cascading style sheet (CSS).

Subdirectory ▶ A directory found under the root directory.

Supercomputer ▶ The fastest and most expensive type of computer, capable of processing more than 1 trillion instructions per second.

SuperDisk ▶ A storage technology manufactured by Imation. Disks have a capacity of 120 MB and require special disk drives; a standard floppy disk drive will not read them. However, they are backward-compatible with standard floppy disk technology, which means you can use a SuperDisk drive to read and write to standard floppy disks.

Support module ▶ A file that can be called by the main executable program to provide auxiliary instructions or routines.

Surge strip ▶ A low-cost device used to protect computer systems from power spikes and surges. Also called surge protector or surge suppressor.

SVG (Scalable Vector Graphics) ▶ A graphics format designed specifically for Web display that automatically resizes when displayed on different screens.

Symmetric key encryption ▶ An encryption key that is used for both encryption and decryption of messages.

Synchronous protocol ▶ Sender's signals and receiver's signals are synchronized by a signal called a clock; the transmitting computer sends data at a fixed clock rate, and the receiving computer expects the incoming data at the same fixed rate.

Synthesized sound ▶ Artificially created sound, usually found in MIDI music or synthesized speech.

System palette ▶ A selection of colors that are used by an operating system to display graphic elements.

System requirements ▶ Specifications for the operating system and hardware configuration necessary for a software product to work correctly. The criteria that must be met for a new computer system or software product to be a success.

System software ▶ Computer programs that help the computer carry out essential operating tasks.

System unit ▶ The case or box that contains the computer's power supply, storage devices, main circuit board, processor, and memory.

T1 ▶ A high-bandwidth telephone line that can also transmit text and images. T1 service is often used by organizations to connect to the Internet.

T3 ▶ A type of ISDN service that uses fiber-optic cable to provide dedicated service with a capacity of 45 megabits per second.

Table ▶ An arrangement of data in a grid of rows and columns. In a relational database, a collection of record types with their data.

Tape backup ▶ A copy of data from a computer's hard disk, stored on magnetic tape and used to restore lost data.

Tape cartridge ▶ A removable magnetic tape module similar to a cassette tape.

TCP (Transmission Control Protocol) ▶ One of the main protocols of TCP/IP that is responsible for establishing a data connection between two hosts and breaking data into packets.

TCP/IP (Transmission Control Protocol/Internet Protocol) ▶ A standard set of communication rules used by every computer that connects to the Internet.

Telnet ▶ A common way to remotely control another computer or server on a network or the Internet.

Temporal compression ▶ A data compression scheme that, when applied to video or audio data, eliminates unnecessary data between video frames or audio samples.

Tera- ▶ Prefix for a trillion.

Text editor ▶ A program similar to a word processor that is used to create plain, unformatted ASCII text.

Text-to-speech software ▶ Software that generates speech based on written text, that is played back through a computer's sound card.

TFT (thin film transistor) ▶ An active matrix screen that updates rapidly and is essential for crisp display of animations and video.

Theme ▶ A collection of coordinated graphics, colors, and fonts applied to individual pages or all pages in a Web site. Themes are generally available as part of Web authoring software.

Thermal transfer printer ▶ An expensive, color-precise printer that uses wax containing color to produce numerous dots of color on plain paper.

Thumbnail ▶ A graphical link that expands in size when clicked.

TIFF (Tag Image File Format) ▶ A file format (.tif extension) for bitmap images that automatically compresses the file data.

Toggle key ▶ A key that switches back and forth between two modes, such as Caps Lock on or Caps Lock off.

Token Ring network ▶ A type of network on which the nodes are sequentially connected in the form of a ring; the second most popular network architecture.

Top-level domain ▶ The major domain categories into which groups of computers on the Internet are divided: com, edu, gov, int, mil, net, and org.

Topology ▶ The configuration of a network.

Touchpad ▶ An alternative input device often found on notebook computers.

Traceroute ▶ A network utility that records a packet's path, number of hops, and the time it takes for the packet to make each hop.

Tracing software ▶ Software that locates the edges of objects in a bitmap graphic and converts the resulting shape into a vector graphic.

Track point ▶ An alternative input device often found on notebook computers.

Trackball ▶ Pointing input device used as an alternative to a mouse.

Tracks ▶ A series of concentric or spiral storage areas created on a storage medium during the formatting process.

Transceiver ▶ A combined transmitter/receiver used to send and receive data in the form of radio frequencies.

Transponder ▶ A device on a telecommunications satellite that receives a signal on one frequency, amplifies the signal, and then retransmits the signal on a different frequency.

Trigger event ▶ An event that activates a task often associated with a computer virus.

Trojan horse ▶ A computer program that appears to perform one function while actually doing something else, such as inserting a virus into a computer system, or stealing a password.

True Color bitmap ▶ A color image with a color depth of 24 bits or 32 bits. Each pixel in a True Color image can be displayed using any of 16.7 million different colors.

Twisted-pair cable ▶ A type of cable used to connect nodes on a network; has RJ-45 connectors on both ends and two separate strands of wire twisted together.

UDMA (Ultra DMA) ▶ A faster version of DMA technology.

Ultra ATA ▶ A disk drive technology that is an enhanced version of EIDE. Also referred to as Ultra DMA or Ultra IDE.

Unicode ▶ A 16-bit character representation code that can represent more than 65,000 characters.

Uninstall routine ▶ A program that removes software files, references, and Windows Registry entries from a computer's hard disk.

UNIX ▶ A multi-user, multitasking server operating system developed by AT&T's Bell Laboratories in 1969.

Unzipped ▶ Refers to files that have been uncompressed.

Unzipping ▶ Restoring files that have been compressed to their original size.

Uplink port ▶ A connection port on a router to which additional hubs can be attached.

Uploading ▶ The process of sending a copy of a file from a local computer to a remote computer.

UPS (uninterruptible power supply) ▶ A device containing a battery that provides a continuous supply of power and other circuitry to prevent spikes and surges from reaching your computer. It represents the best protection against power problems because it is designed to provide enough power to keep your computer working through momentary power interruptions.

URL (Uniform Resource Locator) ▶ The address of a Web page.

USB port (Universal Serial Bus) ▶ An interface between a computer and peripheral device; used to transfer photo data between a camera and a computer.

Usenet ▶ A worldwide Internet bulletin board system of newsgroups that share common topics.

User ID ▶ A combination of letters and numbers that serves as a user's identification. Also referred to as user name.

User interface ▶ The software and hardware that enable people to interact with computers.

User rights ▶ Rules that limit the directories and files that each user can access; they can restrict the ability to erase, create, write, read, and find files.

Utility ▶ A subcategory of system software designed to augment the operating system by providing ways for a computer user to control the allocation and use of hardware resources.

UTP (unshielded twisted pair) ▶ A type of cable consisting of two unshielded wires twisted together. It is less expensive but has more signal noise than a shielded twisted pair.

V.44 ▶ A compression standard that compacts the data before it is sent. The V.44 compression standard will be incorporated in many modems designed to comply with the V.92 standard.

V.92 ▶ Standard that provides faster upstream transport than currently available using a V.90 modem.

Value ▶ A number used in a calculation.

Vector graphic ▶ Image generated from descriptions that determine the position, length, and direction in which lines and shapes are drawn.

Vertical market software ▶ Computer programs designed to meet the needs of a specific market segment or industry, such as medical record-keeping software.

Video ▶ A recorded series of images that displays motion with sound.

Video capture device ▶ A device that is used to convert analog video signals into digital data stored on a hard drive.

Video capture software ▶ Software used to control the capture process of digital and analog video data.

Video editing software ▶ Software that provides tools for capturing and editing video from a camcorder.

Videogame console ▶ A computer specifically designed for playing games using a television screen and game controllers.

Viewable image size (vis) ▶ A measurement of the maximum image size that can be displayed on a monitor screen.

Virtual memory ▶ A computer's use of hard disk storage to simulate RAM.

Virus hoax ▶ A message, usually e-mail, that makes claims about a virus problem that doesn't actually exist.

Virus signature ▶ The unique computer code contained in a virus that helps with its identification. Antivirus software searches for known virus signatures.

VLAN (virtual local area network) ▶ A group of personal computers, servers and other network resources that are on physically different segments of a network, but communicate as though they were on the same segment. A VLAN is a logical grouping rather than a physical grouping.

Voice band modem ▶ The type of modem that would typically be used to connect a computer to a telephone line. See Modem.

Voice over IP (VoIP) ▶ A technology that allows computer users with Internet access to send and receive both data and voice simultaneously.

Volatile ▶ Data that can exist only with a constant power supply.

VPN (virtual private network) ▶ A private network that is configured within a public network, typically the Internet, to regulate the users who can access it.

WAN (wide area network) ▶ An interconnected group of computers and peripherals that covers a large geographical area, such as multiple branches of a corporation.

Wave (.wav) ▶ An audio file format created as Windows "native" sound format.

Waveform audio ▶ A digital representation of sound in which a sound wave is represented by a series of samples taken of the wave height.

Wavelength ▶ The distance between the peaks of a wave.

Wavetable ▶ A set of pre-recorded musical instrument sounds in MIDI format.

Weak encryption ▶ Encryption that is relatively simple to decrypt without the encryption key.

Web (World Wide Web) ▶ An Internet service that links documents and information from computers distributed all over the world using the HTTP protocol.

Web authoring software ▶ Computer programs for designing and developing customized Web pages that can be published electronically on the Internet.

Web browser ▶ A software program that runs on your computer and helps you access Web pages. Also called a browser.

Web page ▶ A document on the World Wide Web that consists of a specially coded HTML file with associated text, audio, video, and graphics files. A Web page often contains links to other Web pages.

Web page header ▶ A subtitle that appears at the beginning of a Web page, also called "header."

Web page table ▶ A grid of cells that is used as a layout tool for elements such as text and graphics placement on a Web page.

Web palette ▶ A standard selection of colors that all Internet browsers can display.

Web resource ▶ Any data file that has a URL, such as an HTML document, a graphic, or a sound file.

Web server ▶ A computer that uses special software to transmit Web pages over the Internet.

Web site ▶ A location on the World Wide Web that contains information relating to specific topics.

Web-based e-mail ▶ An e-mail account that stores, sends, and receives e-mail on a Web site rather than a user's computer.

Wi-Fi (wireless fidelity) ▶ Commercial term for any network built on 802.11 standards. Wi-Fi technology is the wireless equivalent of Ethernet, providing seamless network connection.

Windows Explorer ▶ A file management utility included with most Windows operating systems that helps users manage their files.

Windows Registry ▶ A crucial data file maintained by the Windows operating system that contains the settings needed by a computer to correctly use any hardware and software that has been installed on the system. Also called the Registry.

Windows Startup Disk ▶ A disk that is created by the user to load the operating system and the CD-ROM drivers, allowing for system restoration.

Wireframe ▶ A representation of a 3-D object using separate lines, which resemble wire, to create a model.

Wireless Application Protocol (WAP) ▶ A group of companies and organizations including Open Mobile Alliance (OMA) who have come together to drive the growth of the mobile industry.

Wireless keyboard ▶ A device that works with IR (infrared) devices to transmit input to the computer and which can be used up to 50 feet away from a computer or printer.

Wireless mouse ▶ A device that uses infrared or radio frequency rather than cables to transmit data to the computer so you aren't restricted or tangled in the wires.

Wireless network ▶ Network that uses radio or infrared signals (instead of cables) to transmit data from one network device to another.

Word processing software ▶ Computer programs that assist the user in producing documents, such as reports, letters, papers, and manuscripts.

Word size ▶ The number of bits a CPU can manipulate at one time, which is dependent on the size of the registers in the CPU and the number of data lines in the bus.

Worksheet ▶ A computerized, or electronic, spreadsheet.

Workstation ▶ (1) A computer connected to a local area network. (2) A powerful desktop computer designed for specific tasks.

World Wide Web Consortium (W3C) ▶ An international consortium of companies involved with the Internet and developing open standards.

Worm ▶ A software program designed to enter a computer system, usually a network, through security "holes" and then replicate itself.

Write-protect window ▶ A small hole and sliding cover on a floppy disk that restricts writing to the disk.

Zip disk ▶ Floppy disk technology manufactured by Iomega available in 100 MB and 250 MB versions.

Zipped ▶ Refers to files that have been compressed.

Zipping ▶ The process of compressing files.

Index

X

Y

Z